WYM

BLITZKRIEG

By the same author

Kursk: The Greatest Battle
Arnhem: Jumping the Rhine 1944 and 1945
Anzio: The Friction of War

BLITZKRIEG

Myth, Reality and Hitler's Lightning War –

France, 1940

LLOYD CLARK

Atlantic Books
London

First published in hardback in Great Britain in 2016 by Atlantic Books, an imprint of Atlantic Books Ltd.

1 2 3 4 5 6 7 8 9

A CIP catalogue record for this book is available from the British Library.

Hardback ISBN: 978-0-85789-732-9
E-book ISBN: 978-1-78239-742-7
Paperback ISBN: 978-1-78239-136-4

Printed by CPI Group (UK) Ltd, Croydon, CR0 4YY

Atlantic Books
An Imprint of Atlantic Books Ltd.
Ormond House
26–27 Boswell Street
London
WC1N 3JZ

www.atlantic-books.co.uk

For my parents – John and Pauline Clark – and Jasper Clark

Contents

Illustrations

French fighter patrol (© *IWM, GSA Album 17 850, Image 76*)

Joachim Meissner, Rudolf Witzig and Walter Koch listen to Hitler (*Bundesarchiv, Bild 146-1993-033-26*)

A Bren Carrier passes across the Belgian border (© *IWM, F4348*)

Section two

Two light German tanks in the Ardennes (*Bundesarchiv, Bild 101I-382-0248-33A*)

The pontoon bridge over the Meuse at Gaulier (*Bundesarchiv, Bild 146-1978-062-24*)

A French army signals post (© *IWM, GSA Album 15 848, Image 219*)

Sergeant Walther Rubarth (*Bundesarchiv, Bild 183-L05202*)

Hermann Balck (*Bundesarchiv, Bild 183-L05202*)

German tanks advance across Belgian terrain (*Bundesarchiv, RH 82 Bild-00058*)

Heinz Guderian in his command and communications halftrack (*Bundesarchiv, 101I-769-0229-11A*)

Rommel with General Hermann Hoth (© *IWM, RML182*)

French tank crews run to their Renault D2 tanks (© *IWM, HU75654*)

Rommel and a group of officers from 7th Panzer Division (*Bundesarchiv, 146-1972-045-02*)

Heinz Guderian receives the remains of a captured French Army standard (© *IWM, MH10935*)

British troops march through Dunkirk (© *IWM, MH24141*)

Major General Victor Fortune glowers at Rommel (© *IWM, RML342*)

Surrendered Belgian troops being goaded by Wehrmacht troops (© *IWM, HU75891*)

French refugees heading south (© *IWM, GSA Album 16 849, Image 270*)

Two Schutzpolizisten visit a damaged bunker (*Bundesarchiv, 121-0486*)

An RAF Fairey Battle attacks a German transport column (© *IWM, C1737*)

German infantry march through Paris (*Bundesarchiv, 183-L11769*)

German infantry and armour pushing deeper into France (*Bundesarchiv, 101I-769-0228-22*)

Marshal Philippe Pétain greets Hitler (© *IWM, HU76027*)

Maps

The Invasions of Poland, Denmark and Norway, 1939–40

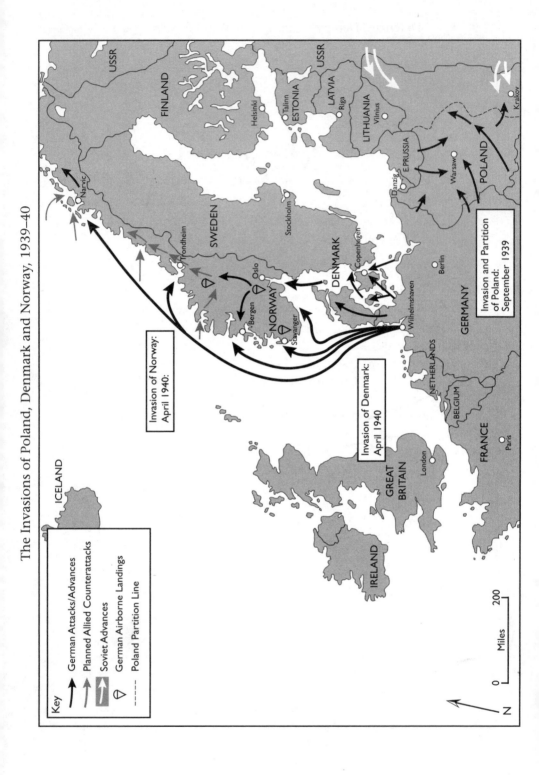

Defences, Deployments and Plans, May 1940

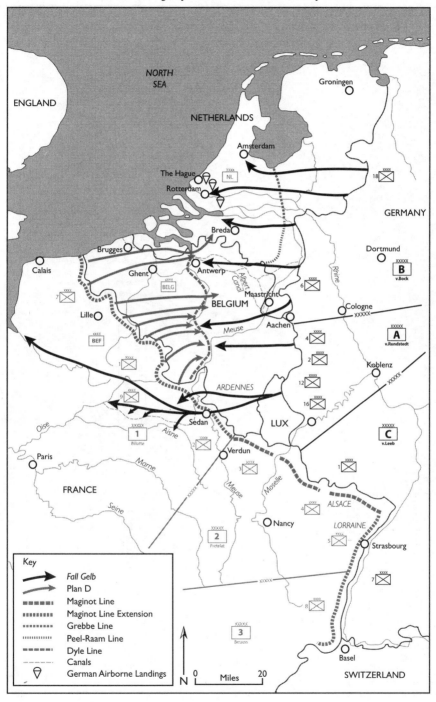

Key

→ Fall Gelb
→ Plan D
▪▪▪▪▪▪ Maginot Line
▪▪▪▪▪▪▪▪ Maginot Line Extension
············ Grebbe Line
············ Peel-Raam Line
▬ ▬ ▬ Dyle Line
‒ ‒ ‒ Canals
☝ German Airborne Landings

10–11 May 1940

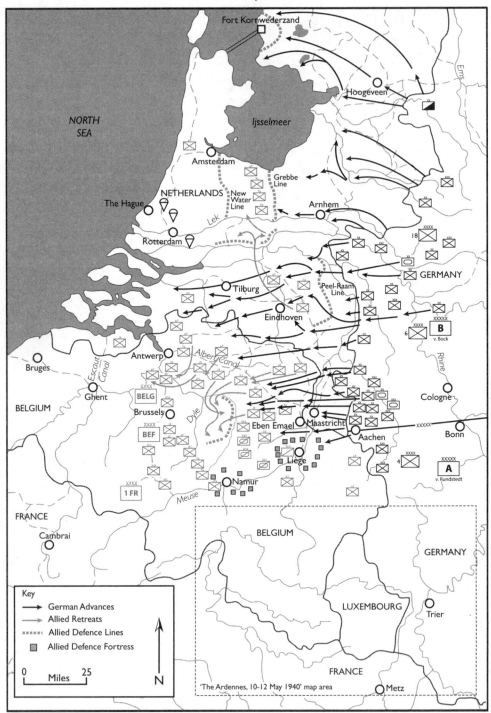

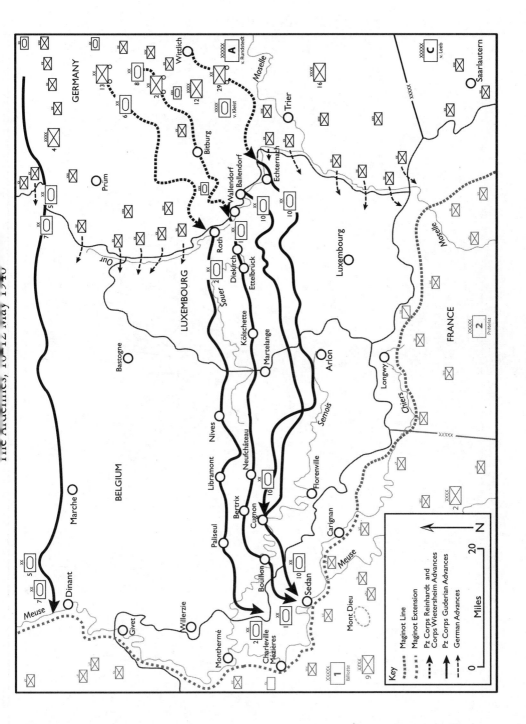

Approach and Crossing of Meuse by Panzer Corps Guderian, 13 May 1940

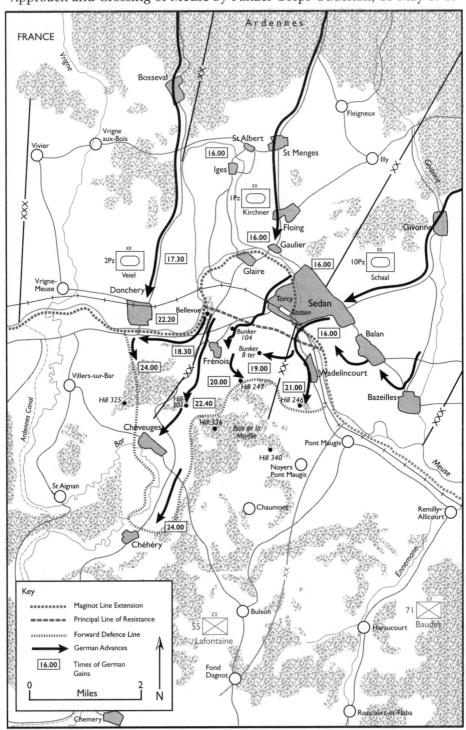

FRANCE

Ardennes

Bosseval

Vrigne

Fleigneux

Vrigne
aux-Bois

St Albert

St Menges

Illy

Vivier

16.00

Iges

1Pz XX
Kirchner

Floing

Givonne

2Pz XX
Veiel

17.30

16.00

Gaulier

10Pz XX
Schaal

Vrigne-
Meuse

Donchery

Glaire

16.00

Torcy
Station

Sedan

Balan

Bellevue

22.20

Bunker
104

16.00

Bunker
8 ter

Madelincourt

Villers-sur-Bar

18.30

24.00

Frénois

19.00

20.00

Hill 247

21.00

Bazeilles

Hill 325

Hill
301

22.40

Hill 246

Chéveuges

Bar

Hill 336

Bois de la
Marfée

Pont Maugis

St Aignan

Hill 340

Noyers
Pont Maugis

Remilly-
Allicourt

Chaumont

24.00

Meuse

Ennemane

Chéhéry

71 XX
Baudet

Key

- ▪▪▪▪▪▪▪▪ Maginot Line Extension
- ▬ ▬ ▬ ▬ Principal Line of Resistance
- ▪▪▪▪▪▪▪▪ Forward Defence Line
- ➤ German Advances
- 16.00 Times of German Gains

55 XX
Lafontaine

Bulson

Haraucourt

Fond
Dagnot

Roncourt-et-Flaba

Chemery

0   Miles   2   N

xvi

German Advances and French Counter Attack, 14 May 1940

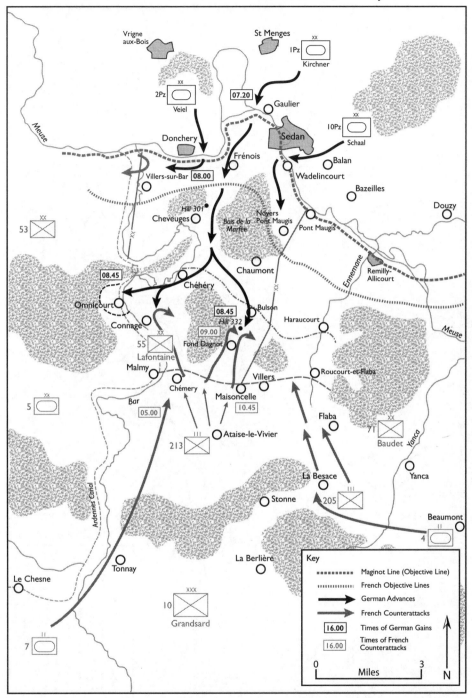

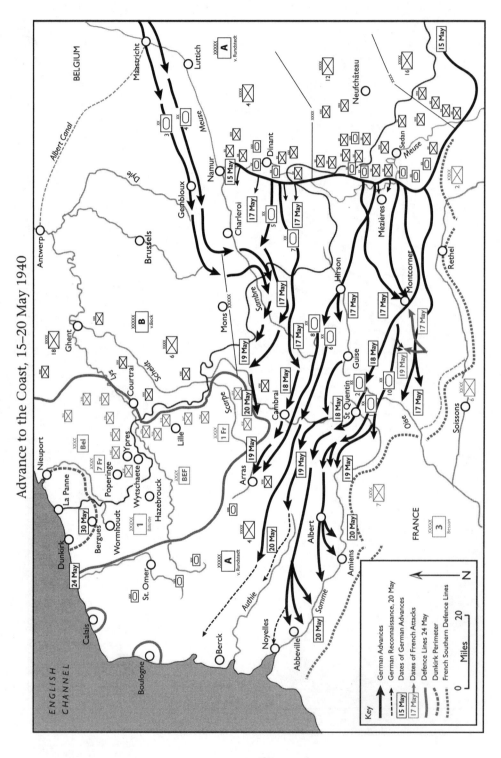

Advance to the Coast, 15–20 May 1940

GERMANY

C v. Leeb

A v. Rundstedt

B v. Bock

BELGIUM

LUX.

SWITZERLAND

ITALY

FRANCE

ENGLISH CHANNEL

Cotentin Peninsula

Cherbourg

Rennes

Alençon

Le Havre

Fécamp

Dieppe

Abbeville

Péronne

Amiens

Rouen

Seine

Oise

Marne

Aisne

Paris

Chartres

Orléans

Tours

Loire

Sens

Briare

Rethel

Sedan

Rheims

Troyes

Chaumon

Meuse

Verdun

Metz

Toul

Moselle

Strasbourg

Epinal

Colmar

Besançon

Dijon

Beaune

Le Creusat

Vichy

Lyon

Rhône

Soâne

Isère

Armée des Alpes

2 Pretelat

Armée de Paris

Bresson

4 (Remnants)

3

5 Jun

9 Jun

9 Jun

14 Jun

16 Jun

14 Jun

14 Jun

14 Jun

18 Jun

18 Jun

18 Jun

18 Jun

18 Jun

0   50
Miles

N

Key

Allied Front Lines

German Panzer Advances

Panzer Movements

German/Allied Dates

Allied Troop Concentration

18 Jun   18 Jun

Inset map (lower right):

FRANCE

ENGLISH CHANNEL

N

0   20
Miles

Amiens

Poix

Abbeville

Le Quesnoy

Somme

Bresle

Incheville

Le Treport

Dieppe

Arques-la-Bataille

Ouville-la-Rivière

Eaulne

Bethune

Varenne

Andelle

Argueil

Rouen

Totes

Yvetot

St Valéry

Fécamp

Seine

18 Jun

The Advance to the Armistice, 25 June 1940

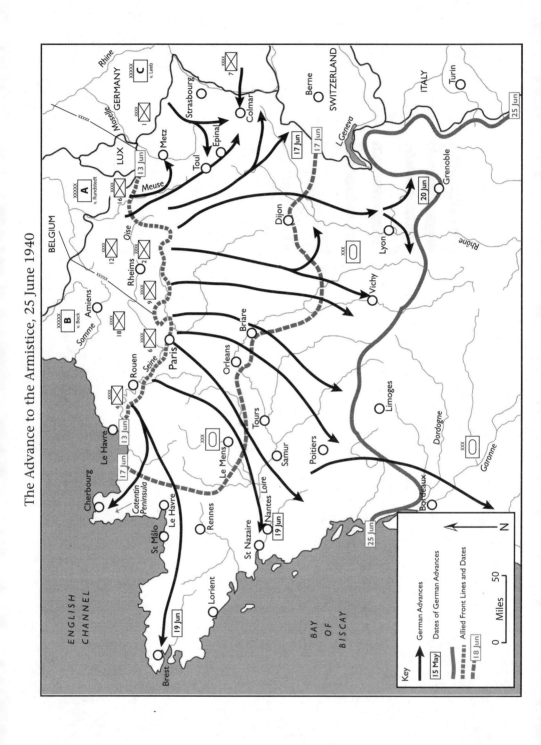

BLITZKRIEG

Prologue

HORDES OF PARISIANS choked the streets on their journey to the Gare de l'Est. A mother used the time to tell her thirty-seven-year-old son André how proud she was of him and, looking into his tired eyes, told him that his decision to fight was the correct one. The son felt no fear, no excitement, just a desire to get to the front now that he had made his decision. On arriving at the station, he was keen to be on his way. He scythed through the masses which blocked his route to the platform from where his train was due to depart. He made slow progress through fretful soldiers who embraced ashen-faced women. Both were on the cusp of an entirely new and shocking reality of war.

What would André's fate be? His mother could not help but recall a similar farewell to her brother, who had left her to fight the Prussians in 1870 and returned with a mortal illness. André had enlisted as a private soldier – just another *poilu* with a wife and young children – ignoring the opportunity to take a comfortable staff job in a headquarters away from the fighting. In fact, the only influence he had used as under-secretary of state for war was to ensure that he was assigned to a unit defending his beloved Lorraine. Consequently, on 1 August 1914, André Maginot slipped off to war without public fanfare or farewell.

André's destination was Verdun, a city which lay in a vulnerable salient created by the German thrust through the heavily wooded Ardennes. The French had fallen back towards Sedan, Stenay and

1

Verdun, but only Verdun held, protected by enhancements to Vauban's original seventeenth-century fortifications. The totemic city remained in French hands that autumn, an achievement assisted in a small way by André's reconnaissance patrols. At six foot three inches tall, he was not an inconspicuous figure on the battlefield clad in his horizon-blue jacket and red pantaloons but, unlike many others, he remained unharmed after fifty patrols. On 9 November 1914, however, the newly promoted sergeant's good fortune came to an end. The day after he had been awarded the Médaille Militaire for his personal courage and leadership, André was leading a patrol when he was struck by a great blow to his left leg and then another to his knee. Lying in a pool of blood and in agony, he expected to die.

Six years later, on 10 November 1920, walking with the assistance of canes, his left leg useless, André Maginot, who was now minister of pensions, found himself in Verdun's cold, damp underground citadel. In exquisite pain, he watched as Auguste Thien, a young soldier of the 123rd Regiment of Infantry who had been invited to make a choice, pointed to the sixth of eight caskets containing the remains of an unknown soldier. Three years later, on 11 November 1923, the casket was interred below the Arc de Triomphe in Paris in a ceremony during which Maginot, now minister of war, ignited an eternal flame on the tomb.

It was five years since the armistice that had ended the First World War. France was still in mourning, traumatized by the hideous destructiveness of protracted industrial warfare and fractured, just like the bodies and minds of so many of its surviving veterans. It was an experience that Maginot was determined to spare the next generation and he supported Marshal Philippe Pétain, France's senior soldier and the Victor of Verdun, in his desire to fortify the common border with Germany. Completed after his death, the defences took André's name – the Maginot Line – and so it was that a brave and principled man became forever associated with his nation's defeat.[1]

Introduction

They were conquerors, and for that you want only brute force – nothing to boast of when you have it, since your strength is just an accident arising from the weakness of others.

Joseph Conrad, Heart of Darkness

THE FALL OF FRANCE and the Low Countries in May and June 1940 was one of the most remarkable military campaigns in Western history and, arguably, one of the most distinguished victories ever won. The fighting in those weeks shocked the world, not for its protracted horror but for the lack of it. The Germans managed to conjure up a decisive victory over a first-class military power that was predicted by very few and which proved to be a significant step towards an increasingly global and destructive conflict. As such, it is an event that has retained a great vibrancy to all of those who have recognized its military and historical importance. There are few other campaigns that have raised more questions about its origins, conduct and outcome, and offered so many contrasting answers in response. Part of its fascination – and complexity – stems from the fact that its main participants had been fighting each other over much of the same terrain a little over two decades before. It is, of course, almost impossible not to contrast images of the Stuka dive-bomber and dust-coated panzer in a war of great movement with others of the heavy artillery and mud-encrusted rifles of that war of position fought earlier in the century. Whether either pair of images is an accurate representation of either conflict is a matter of debate, but the fact that they have seeped into Western consciousness is irrefutable and challenges us to remember that the two conflicts were separated by just a single generation and, moreover, that the 1940 campaign took place within living memory of the seminal French defeat by Prussia in 1870.

The First World War was but the latest episode in a long history of Franco-German enmity. It was an antagonism that – together with Germany's chronic anxieties about the East – was central to the history and development of Europe. It was an hereditary enmity nourished by territorial rivalry, the aspiration to dominate continental Europe, national pride and shame, and a desire for revenge. It was marked by centuries of threats, invasion, aggressive diplomacy and, on occasion, simmering antipathy which helped forge national identities. It led to bloodshed, and to twenty-three Franco-German wars from the mid-fourteenth century to the early sixteenth century alone. As one commentator has written: 'For centuries, the history of France and Germany has been a continual effort of the two nations to get closer, to understand, to unite, to merge. Indifference was never possible for them; they had to hate or love one another, fraternize or go to war. France's and Germany's destiny will never be established nor assured individually.'[1] The Treaty of Versailles – signed in late June 1919 in the same building where in 1871 a conceited Prussian king had proclaimed himself Kaiser – was an attempt by France to put a full stop to its old rival's ambitions. But the Germans only perceived the terms of the treaty as a humiliation and determined to take their revenge.

Franco-German enmity provides some useful context for an understanding of Hitler's campaign against France, but that task is made much more difficult not only by the pain, humiliation and division caused by the French defeat in 1940, but also by the eventual German defeat in 1945. As a result, despite voluminous publications by academics and authors, attempts to hit the bullseye of Leopold von Ranke's insistence that historians establish 'what really happened' have, in this instance, largely failed. Such attempts have been further hampered by the fact that any campaign is a fast-moving target, for with each passing decade events are reinterpreted to reflect changing times, themes and attitudes, writing styles and methods of research. Consequently, the 1940 campaign is no longer the province of the military historian alone for, in the words of Sir Michael Howard:

> The roots of victory and defeat often have to be sought far from the battlefield, in political, social, and economic factors which explain why armies are constituted as they are, and why their leaders conduct them in the way they do … Without some knowledge of the broader background to military operations one is likely to reach totally erroneous conclusions about their nature and the reasons for their failure and success.

This book provides some new ideas about why events happened as they did in May and June 1940 from the perspective of a military historian who has been studying the subject for over a quarter of a century and has walked the battlefield many times. It offers new interpretations and challenges some enduring myths – of which this campaign has more than its fair share – about how Germany was able to achieve in six and a half weeks in 1940 what it could not achieve in over four years of fighting between 1914 and 1918. It will do so by asking three key questions: what preparations did the belligerents make for war and why? What were the belligerents' fighting capabilities in 1940? And how well did the belligerents conduct operations during the campaign? In doing so, it seeks to establish how well those nations involved managed to blend their ability to conduct operations with their strategic ambitions, whether the Allies ever had a chance of defeating the Germans and, likewise, whether the Germans could have failed. It rejects the erroneous, lazy and dangerous argument that Hitler's victory was somehow inevitable due to qualitatively and quantitatively superior forces using new, carefully honed and mechanized fighting methods that combined air and ground operations within a unifying plan. Yet it also hopes to cut through the complexity to see whether the campaign is an illustration of General James Mattis's argument that 'Ultimately a real understanding of history means that we face *nothing* new under the sun.'[3]

It is, of course, for readers to draw whatever lessons they think pertinent from what follows, although as they do so it should be remembered that an historian's conclusions are made with the benefit of hindsight – and often with the luxury of source material which was not available at the time. Yet while an historian making criticisms from the comfort of an armchair and a commander making decisions in the heat of battle might not seem to have too much in common, both share the responsibility to make sense when there seems to be none and to create some degree of order out of chaos. And there was chaos aplenty on and over the battlefields of the Netherlands, Belgium and France in 1940.[4]

CHAPTER ONE

Ingredients

There are always antecedent causes. A beginning is an
artifice, and what recommends one over another is how
much sense it makes of what follows.

Ian McEwan, *Enduring Love*

You live in interesting times. Interesting times are always
enigmatic times that promise no rest, no prosperity or
continuity or security. [In our age] there coexist a number
of incompatible forces, none of which can either win or lose
… Never has humanity joined so much power and so much
disarray, so much anxiety and so many playthings, so much
knowledge and so much uncertainty.

Paul Valéry, poet and philosopher, in a
prize-giving speech at a Paris lycée in 1932[1]

IT WAS THE END FOR WARSAW and Poland. After days and nights
of pounding by the Germans, the nation's leadership reviewed
the situation. The city's brave civilians could, and would, continue
their resistance if necessary, but to what ends? Not for the first time
in Polish history, the enemy was grinding Warsaw's buildings into
dust, its barely recognizable streets filled with thousands of dead.

Further fighting was deemed to be futile and there seemed to be no hope of salvation. On 28 September 1939, a spokesman of the High Command announced in a clear, cold voice that 'After twenty days of heroic defence … [and] practically the destruction of half the city' an armistice had been agreed and conditions for capitulation were being discussed.[2] It was a remarkable military achievement for Germany, which was now reaping the benefits of Hitler's investment in the nation's military machine. Swift and effective, the campaign filled the excited German chancellor with a confidence that was evident to senior officers at a Führer Conference on 27 September at which he announced his intentions to invade the West. A long-held ambition was to be realized: France was to be invaded and the humiliation of 1918 and 1919 avenged. Yet Hitler's audience, still digesting events in Poland, was stunned by the news. Neither the army (Heer) nor the air force (Luftwaffe) believed that they could possibly be ready in time: disengagement and post-surrender duties would vie with the need to relocate, rearm and reorganize, to learn lessons and train and plan accordingly – the list was endless. Hitler had anticipated their concerns – in his view this was the apprehension of the feeble – but his attempt to remind the military professionals of victories over the old enemy in 1815 and 1870 was not relevant in the circumstances. Further attempts to reassure them with ideological mumbo-jumbo about the German soldier's 'natural superiority' which, when combined with 'experience and aggressiveness', made a German division 'worth more than a French division' also failed to hit their mark.[3] General Franz Halder, Chief of Staff to the Army High Command (OKH), could not hide his misgivings and expressed his belief that any invasion plans for the West would have to be delayed by months or even years if the necessary preparations were to be made. Hitler dismissed the opinion. 'The relative strength will not improve in our best interests,' he said testily. 'The enemy strength will gradually improve….'[4] The meeting was left under no illusion that Hitler, as Supreme Commander of the German Armed Forces, sought invasion before the year was out.

Hitler's Führer Directive No. 6, dated 9 October 1939, provided a little more detail about his ambitions towards France and spoke of a 'swift and shattering blow in the West' in an attack through Luxembourg, Belgium and Holland. The aim was to:

> [D]efeat as much as possible of the French Army and of the forces of the allies fighting on their side, and at the same time to win as much territory as possible in Holland, Belgium, and Northern France to serve as a base for the successful prosecution of the air and sea war against England and as a wide protective area for the economically vital Ruhr. [6]

Keen to instil a sense of urgency into proceedings and to guide OKH's planning of the invasion, Hitler followed the directive with a Führer Conference the very next day. Here he asserted that an attack against France would prove 'no more difficult than Poland' although, he conceded, a decision might only be achieved after Germany had been 'forced into positional' warfare.[7] Such a situation was deemed a distinct possibility because it was accepted that, despite significant improvements to the German military over recent years, any invasion would still need to outflank the Maginot Line to the north and so run into a waiting enemy in central Belgium. Altogether, it was an undertaking that horrified the generals as they considered the damage which was likely to be done to their still-developing military machine, and one they thought could well end in defeat.

General Wilhelm Keitel, the chain-smoking head of Hitler's strategic decision-making body Oberkommando der Wehrmacht (OKW) who was 'temperamentally unequipped to deal with Hitler'[8] and trusted his brilliance unreservedly, offered his resignation over the issue, but it was refused. General Walther von Brauchitsch, the commander-in-chief of the army who was becoming increasingly deferential to the Supreme Commander, nonetheless shared his field army commanders' concerns that the operational challenges involved in the scheme were too great. One of their number was the dour General Wilhelm von Leeb, of whom a fellow officer said if he 'ever tried to smile, it would crack his face'.[9] He had recently been called out of retirement to command Army Group C, had lost a son in the Polish campaign and was one of several senior officers who used the word 'insane' to describe Hitler's proposal.[10] In the wake of the new directive, private conversations were had between old professional colleagues, but although they agreed that an invasion was ill-advised, it did not take them long to recognize the futility of encouraging an argument with a man whose mind was already made up.

Disagreement and friction between Hitler and his senior generals was not a new phenomenon and gained an edge as the Führer's demands became more exacting and risky. Hitler felt threatened by the traditional and aristocratic Prussian officer class, with their influence, easy confidence, sense of entitlement and conservatism – didn't these men want to fight? In return, the generals despised his lack of self-control, his political fanaticism, his cult of personality and the power he had accumulated, even if they did share his vision of a Germany returning to greatness. Most found their Führer and his associates boorish, stained by the politics of the gutter, and believed him ill-suited to be their country's leader, let alone their Supreme Commander. Hitler had assumed this position in 1938 and exploited the officer corps' abiding sense of honour by having them all swear a personal oath of loyalty and obedience to him: he needed to control these leaders of men and to harness their professionalism in order to achieve his political aims in Europe. To which end, he used OKW as his central military staff; it had been formed in 1935 to replace the War Ministry and direct the service commands and was comprised of both loyal and competent men. These officers took Hitler's strategic ideas and translated them into orders that were passed on to the subordinate service commands, whose latitude of action was increasingly confined solely to operational issues.

Further undermining their influence, Hitler rarely invited service chiefs to the same Führer Conferences and ruled by creating division. Disunited, the services posed less of a threat to OKW's strategic plans.

Hitler was particularly keen to neuter OKH since Germany was a great land power and the army had always directed strategy and acted as the politicians' principal adviser on war policy. By succeeding in this, he made the General Staff less a focal point for military creativity and more an organization which turned his strategic whim into operational reality. Nevertheless, as the autumn of 1939 set in and winter loomed, Hitler believed that OKH was deliberately and unnecessarily vacillating over the production of its own plans. Frustrated and sensing treachery, he decided that it was time to reassert his authority and on 23 November held a command conference at the imposing new Reich Chancellery on Berlin's Vossstrasse at which he reaffirmed: 'My decision is unalterable. I will attack France and England at the best and soonest moment … I will stop at nothing and I will annihilate anybody who is against me.'[11] OKH's reaction was immediate, the tipping point had been reached, and staff officers – led by Halder – did their utmost to produce a plan that would satisfy the Supreme Commander.

OKH's concerns about Germany's ability to emerge victorious in a campaign in the West remained undiminished, despite the successful outcome of the Poland campaign. The recent strengthening of the armed forces had been welcomed by the service chiefs, but it had been a long and arduous road to recover from the strict military provisions of the Treaty of Versailles. During the 1920s, a number of talented officers had seen the armed forces through intensive care, waiting patiently until strength could be regained. Nurturing both the physical and intellectual abilities of the new Reichswehr, a quasi-military organization, early in this period was General Hans von Seeckt. Intelligent and shrewd, as head of the 'defence force' from 1920 to 1926 he laid the foundations for a new, modern German military ready to contest industrialized warfare.[12] It was von Seeckt who put the German military on a course that his successors duly followed, and Hitler took full advantage of this gift and, in full defiance of Versailles, openly rearmed.

Just weeks after coming to power in January 1933, Hitler announced to his ministerial colleagues that 'billions of marks are necessary for German rearmament ... the future of Germany depends exclusively and alone on the rebuilding of the armed forces. Every other task must take second place to rearmament....'[13] This, together with the reintroduction of conscription in 1935, was part of a process of mass mobilization for war. The German people, keen to right the wrongs of 1919, were carefully conditioned for war and came to believe their destiny was closely tied to the military and personal sacrifice. Meanwhile, the armed forces prospered in the knowledge that they were an essential part of Hitler's vision. A glimpse of the future was provided in March 1936 with the reoccupation of the Rhineland by German troops. Although this risky operation involved just three battalions of infantry and two squadrons of aircraft, Hitler believed it essential if Germany was to confront the status quo successfully. As it was, France blinked first, and Germany stepped back into the international sunlight. The confidence that the episode gave Hitler further fuelled the nation's preparations for war. Within a year, almost every area of economic life had been brought under the control of the Nazi state and the speed of rearmament was increased. By 1938, Germany was spending 17 per cent of its GNP on the military (it had been 3 per cent in 1914). This was twice the figure for both Britain and France, and in 1939 it rose to 23 per cent.[14] Yet the tempo of rearmament was sometimes impossible to maintain. In 1936, for example, there was a plan to increase the army's forty divisions to over 100 and to have them ready for action three years later. Within twelve months, however, the schedule was thrown into disarray as half of the 1937 target was missed. Hitler, though, displayed a stubborn unwillingness to accept reality, and he refused to acknowledge the army's advice that they would not be ready for a general war until 1943. Such, in fact, was the senior officers' pessimism that they argued that the *Westwall* – nearly 400 miles of defences on the border with France which sought to deter an attack in the West, and particularly one undertaken to aid France's allies in the East – would not be completed until 1953.

The military consistently challenged the demanding schedule required by Hitler's unfurling foreign policy. In the wake of the *Anschluss* with Austria during May 1938, for example, while the army had concerns about aspects of their performance which demanded attention, Hitler looked to use force in Czechoslovakia. Major General Alfred Jodl, Chief of the Operations Staff of OKW, noted in his diary at the time: 'Sharp controversy between Hitler and army leaders. Hitler says: we must go ahead this year, the army says we cannot.'[15] The invasion of Czechoslovakia was eventually replaced by a negotiated settlement, but Hitler was furious that his clenched fist had been prised open into a handshake. As he eschewed anything that smacked of German weakness, the military had to fight a constant battle to make Hitler recognize the practicalities involved in the application of force. Yet while the military wanted to develop its strength and capability, Hitler was keen to strike as early as possible in order not to give his enemies more time to prepare. He could not help being vexed by the military's persistent hand-wringing, even if he also knew that the Germans were still not ready for another war. His response was characteristic: the service chiefs would be brought into line and the population's mental conditioning would be completed through a renewed propaganda effort. The armed forces were given another year to develop muscle – and, in Hitler's eyes, a spine – and the populace to become hardened to the idea of war. Both would be tested at the end of the summer of 1939 by the invasion of Poland. But while the German people were relatively keen to see territory lost at Versailles regained, the generals recognized that the invasion would very likely lead to war with France and Britain.

As it was, by August 1939 the armed forces were on stand-by once again and a sense of anticipation gripped the nation. Uniforms were to be seen everywhere while barracks, training areas and new airfields sprang up across the country. By this time, Germany's armed forces had grown to over 4,564,000 personnel – 3,737,104 in the army, 677,000 in the Luftwaffe and 150,000 in the navy – out of a population of 80 million. Yet such figures hint more at potential capability, and the generals were very aware that only 1.31 million troops were in active units, 647,000 were fully trained in reserve, around 1.8 million were partly trained and 808,000 had received no training at all.[16] This meant that the field army of 103 divisions that had been raised in four waves was of widely varying quality. The first wave consisted of fifty-two active divisions – fifteen of which were armoured and motorized – with 78 per cent regulars and the remainder being reservists recently released from active duty. These divisions were fully trained and equipped. In contrast, the third wave was comprised of fourteen divisions containing men up to the age of forty-five who had not been trained since 1918, and a supply train that contained more horses than trucks.[17] Indeed, equipment and weapons were in such short supply that the field army had thirty-four divisions that were only half-equipped.[18] To this end, von Leeb informed Halder that the third-wave divisions were only fit for static defence and the fourth wave needed more training to be capable of anything.

But while past German military success had been firmly rooted in its army, air power was now a factor too, which meant that the Luftwaffe also had to be carefully developed. Central to this was the identification of whether it would be most effective at the strategic, operational or tactical level, or a mix of all three. Reichsminister of aviation and former fighter pilot Hermann Göring was keen on the strategic potential of heavy bombers to bring about a rapid and decisive victory. Even so, by 1935 Germany had proved unable to produce the 450 aircraft required and changed tack towards a more flexible air fleet. Evidence of this can be seen in August 1939, for by this date the Luftwaffe's operational strength included 788 fighters, 431 long-range fighters, 361 dive-bombers, 1,542 medium bombers, 630 reconnaissance aircraft and 488 transport aircraft.[19] It was an impressive force and certainly offered more potential than the navy, which became relatively neglected because, other than its U-boats, it was deemed to offer few strategic advantages. Indeed, as Admiral Erich Raeder, its commander-in-chief, noted: 'The navy is not ready for the great fight with England. The only thing the fleet can do is to prove that it can sink honourably.'[20]

Yet although both the army and air force had mass by August 1939, their potential for offensive success depended on the application of the relevant fighting methods and how well those methods could be integrated into a suitable operational plan. Throughout the rapid development of air and ground forces under the Nazis, staff officers had to remain keenly aware of what Hitler might ask the military to achieve, against whom and where. It was these considerations, therefore, that shaped German doctrine and thence, procurement, organization and training.[21] That doctrine was built on the foundations laid by von Seeckt and his successors which sought not only to provide the basis for a large army but also, through the hard work of a general staff – the brain of the army – an intelligent one. It demanded excellence in every facet of the Reichswehr in order to make it the best small force anywhere. Its officers, from whom the general staff were chosen, were rigorously and competitively selected, trained and educated. It was a system that produced a doctrine that was to remain influential throughout the opening years of the war, but also a general staff that was instinctively deferential to history and tradition, and therefore uncomfortable with the unorthodox and radical.[22]

— □ —

German fighting methods were therefore developed in a conservative context, even if directed by von Seeckt's belief that 'The goal of modern strategy will be to achieve a decision with highly mobile, highly capable forces, before the masses have even begun to move.'[23] As a result, by 1939 the German army had a doctrine emphasizing speed, aggression, combined arms and initiative. Yet while modern, it looked back in as many ways as it looked forward as that same doctrine incorporated traditional German concepts – for example, striking first, hard and deep – which were given a modern edge through the embrace of new technology and organizations. Even so, von Seeckt also advised that such methods were 'useless if they are not guided by a grand idea and if they are not combined toward and aimed at the purpose of the campaign, yes, the entire war.'[24] To him, local tactical advances were for nothing if not linked to wider operational success which would have a decisive strategic impact. Indeed, Prussian and later German military leaders had historically sought decisive battles of annihilation using swift and skilful troops – Frederick the Great in the eighteenth century, Helmut von Moltke in 1870, and Alfred von Schlieffen in his 1905 plan to outflank Paris, to name but three. Thus, during the inter-war years the operational concept that dominated was a war of movement (*Bewegungskrieg*) followed by a battle of annihilation at the operational level (*Vernichtungsschlacht*) which might include the battle of encirclement (*Kesselschlacht*). Doctrine facilitated this concept, and so it is worth exploring it in a little more detail.

Army Regulation 487, *Leadership and Battle with Combined Arms*, was published in the early 1920s and, despite the restrictions of Versailles, referred to infantry assault battalions, artillery preparation and support, combined arms and the use of tanks (*panzers*) in an offensive setting. It emphasized surprise, initiative and infiltration tactics to penetrate weak points in the enemy's defences as well as the requirement to find the point where a decisive action could be achieved (*Schwerpunkt*). It discussed the importance of the continuous battle, by-passing centres of resistance, maintaining the initiative and creating a psychological blow to create panic as breaches were widened by follow-up forces which then reduced the centres of resistance. It was a method that demanded rapid, 'on the spot' decision-making with subordinate commanders using their initiative to achieve their superiors' intent. It was founded on the German tradition of *Auftragstaktik* (mission-orientated tactics) and sought to take advantage of fleeting opportunities. As a consequence, doctrine emphasized the requirement for excellent communications forwards, rearwards and laterally. Although *Leadership and Battle with Combined Arms* was duly revised to incorporate lessons learned and new technology, it was the foundation of German inter-war doctrine.[25] Its heavy influence, therefore, can be found in Army Regulation 300, *Troop Leadership* (*Truppenführung*), which was published in 1933 and remained in use until 1945. The major difference between the two regulations lay in the weight given to motorized (wheeled transport without protection) and mechanized (armoured and armed transport – armoured fighting vehicles) commands, and armoured formations, which included motorized and mechanized units along with other elements. The 1933 doctrine recognized that all vehicles were now more reliable and possessed greater speed and range. This meant that, when married with the improved communications offered by high-powered and portable radios, armoured warfare demanded serious consideration. As one Wehrmacht general later observed: 'The decisive breakthrough into modern military thinking consisted not of a breakthrough in armour weapons, but a breakthrough in the communications weapons.'[26] Suddenly there was the possibility of restoring the operational opportunities for Germany that had proved so difficult to achieve in 1914.

The potential for motorization and mechanization to have a tactical *and* operational impact in a war of movement that could achieve decision was vigorously debated. Several schools of thought emerged among its advocates. Oswald Lutz, Walter Spannenkrebs and Heinz Guderian, for example, argued for tanks to be massed in all-tank armies with independent missions to intensify and fully utilize their firepower and mobility. Ernst Volckheim and Ludwig von Eimannsberger, however, believed that tanks should form part of larger combined arms formations with – in most cases – an emphasis on their tactical utility, particularly for infantry support.[27] The massed tank school was far too radical for the senior generals to embrace comfortably. This was partly because they saw the inherent risks and difficulties in operations which aimed to strike at the enemy in depth, but also because of the threat this approach posed to the traditional arms, with tanks playing the lead and the rest of the field army in a supporting role. As a result, it was the combined arms school – a concept at the heart of German doctrine – that emerged victorious and led to a powerful yet flexible formation being developed. Following successful experimental manoeuvres with a full combined arms armoured division in 1934, the first three panzer divisions came into existence in October of the following year. It was a remarkable development.

A German panzer division was comprised of a tank brigade of two regiments and, commonly by the end of 1939, two motorized infantry regiments. Supporting arms included a regiment of artillery and motorcycle, reconnaissance, anti-tank, pioneer and signals battalions. Thus, despite their title, panzer divisions were not tank divisions but all-arms divisions which were also developed to co-operate with air power. It was a division, its supporters contended, that was stronger than the sum of its individual parts and, rather than operating independently, would work with the rest of the army to improve mobility. The massed tank school, however, saw the potential of the panzer divisions to enjoy independent operations if given the responsibility, for they had the ability to manoeuvre, and to assault and pursue a defeated enemy to his destruction. This was because the striking power of the formation was comprised of tanks – each division had a notional establishment of 561 – and these were generally swift and mobile.[28]

The *PanzerKampfwagen* (PzKpfw) I was the most common tank and had a top speed of 22 mph, but was only lightly armoured and had but two machine guns. The similarly numerous PzKpfw II was also lightly armoured, although it was armed with a 2cm gun as well as a machine gun and had a top speed of 35 mph. The PzKpfw III and IV were far less common but more heavily armed and armoured. The Mk III boasted a 3.7mm gun and two machine guns and a top speed of 20 mph and armour up to 30mm thick. The Mk IV was similarly armoured, had the same top speed, a 7.5cm gun and two or three machine guns. The preponderance of PzKpfw Is and IIs made the panzer divisions far more inclined towards high mobility and far less so towards heavy contact and slugging it out against powerful enemy positions, especially if these included anti-tank guns. Such considerations were not immaterial to the debate about how these divisions might be used in an operational context. Indeed, having been given command of one of the new panzer divisions in October 1935, Guderian remained a passionate advocate of independent operations and, as more of these formations became available, argued for them to be massed together in panzer corps. To him, the panzer division, if correctly used, was a campaign-winning asset.

One of the reasons that men like Guderian were convinced that panzer divisions were so useful was because they could fight at a distance from the main body, and particularly if supported by air power. Although it would seem reasonable that the Germans' move away from strategic bombing, coinciding as it did with the birth of the panzer division, would see the Luftwaffe naturally gravitate towards the support of ground units, this was not the reality. Far from being a mere adjunct of the army, the Luftwaffe had evolved a doctrine that focused on the broader role of defeating the enemy's armed forces through the breaking of his will and of supporting ground forces where required.[29] *The Conduct of the Air War*, a regulation published in 1935, advocated gaining air superiority and air supremacy at the decisive point. This would allow for bombing strikes against enemy assets in depth, but also provide close air support when the circumstances of its impact might be decisive. The air power-panzer division combination therefore offered considerable potential and was brought to a relatively high degree of tactical effectiveness through trials in 1937 which included the largest manoeuvres undertaken since Versailles. During one exercise held in northern Germany during September, 3rd Panzer Division scored a stunning success. Moving rapidly, its armour, supported by air power, broke through the enemy, drove into his rear, cut his supply lines and created an encirclement while reinforcements were kept at bay by air power. By the fourth day of a seven-day exercise, the attackers had secured victory. Hitler made a personal visit with Mussolini to watch proceedings, moving from site to site by car and cheered by troops. A new era was dawning.

By the end of 1937, the panzer division had made its mark in German military thinking and became the face of the army to the people. It was a period marked by Hitler's support of the Nationalists in the Spanish Civil War with both air and armoured units, but not panzer divisions. It allowed the Germans to blood a small number of troops and test some concepts which saw, for example, the Luftwaffe increasingly called on to perform close air support missions. It was here that practical solutions to challenges were tested and some lessons learned – including the vital importance of air-to-ground communications and vice versa. Even so, the experience did not lead to a major Luftwaffe reorganization and although close air support was hardly neglected, in general terms the war was deemed to be of limited value in preparation for a war against first-class opponents. But Spain did offer valuable experience as regards planning and staff work, fighting experience with important weapons systems, and minor tactics; in other words those involving formations of company size and below. The same was also true of the March 1938 annexation of Austria – the *Anschluss*. The success of Guderian's 2nd Panzer Division in racing 420 miles in just two days was remarkable, although not achieved without a third of its tanks breaking down, logistic frailty and horrendous traffic jams. The mistakes, however, demanded a solution and so subsequently mobile workshops were integrated into the panzer divisions for repair and recovery, lead elements of the divisions carried up to five days' worth of vital supplies with them, and traffic control became better organized.

The German military machine had come a great distance in a short time by the summer of 1938, but it remained untested in the sort of conflict and against the sort of enemy that Hitler was hurtling towards. This is not, of course, an uncommon position for the military to be in but senior officers remained concerned by the risks inherent in such rapid evolution without the requisite time for reflection, adjustment and training. What the Germans had in fact developed was a two-speed army since they were unable to put such a large number of divisions on wheels. Even the flagship panzer divisions were under-strength, while the rest of the field army remained very largely unmotorized and unmechanized, instead relying on boot leather and beasts of burden. This proved a great challenge to those with responsibility for developing plans that were to incorporate both the motorized and mechanized elements of the army – there were six panzer divisions by the summer of 1939 – and the standard infantry divisions. Should operations be limited to the speed and ability of the traditional majority, or should the potential of the minority be unleashed in a vanguard of risky independent operations by massed panzer divisions in panzer corps? Put another way, should the Germans fight conservatively and with little hope of a decisive outcome, or radically by utilizing their costly mobile divisions in search of a decisive result?

The fact that no decision had been made about massing panzer divisions to seek such a decisive operational impact was partly due to a lack of relevant formations, but more to the conservative approach to fulfilling Hitler's strategic ambitions. There was no *Blitzkrieg* (lightning war) concept in existence to shape a campaign and it certainly was not formalized in doctrine. Although the German army had used the word *Blitzkrieg* in military articles since 1935 to describe a swift and decisive operation or strategy, there was no unifying definition of the term at this time.[30] Indeed, far from preparing for a *Blitzkrieg*, Germany was in the midst of preparing for a protracted, attritional war and it was the failure to properly prepare for such a war that was seen by the High Command as a reason why any attack on a first-class military opponent should be delayed. It was in this context that the debate between the traditionalists and radicals about how Germany should conduct operations developed. Might not, argued some, German military assets be used in such a way as to allow Germany to swiftly defeat the likes of France? It was a question that had not been answered when, in the summer of 1939, Germany planned her invasion of Poland and remained only partially answered eight months later when Hitler launched his attack in the West.

Hitler's confidence in eventually overcoming France was based partly on his belief in 'natural' German superiority, but also because he considered his enemy to be 'decadent', 'tired' and 'divided' after a prolonged period of political and social division.[31] France was, he believed, broken – its inter-war governments lasting, on average, a mere seven months – and thus ripe for the picking. There was more than a kernel of truth in this appraisal as the country's leaders had failed to ensure its armed forces were sufficiently strong and possessed a robust strategy: France lacked a vital self-awareness and was consequently vulnerable to Germany's arrogant aggressiveness. French historian and reserve officer Marc Bloch argued in his memoir *Strange Defeat: A Statement of Evidence Written in 1940* that the armed forces reflected the weaknesses of France:

In no nation is any professional group ever entirely responsible for its own actions. The solidarity of society as a whole
is too strong to permit the existence of the sort of moral
autonomy, existing in isolation, which any such total
responsibility would seem to imply. The staffs worked with
tools that were put into their hands by the nation at large.
The psychological conditions in which they lived were
not altogether of their own making, and they themselves,
through their members, were as their origins had moulded
them. They could only be what their totality of the social
fact, as it existed in France, permitted them to be.[32]

The situation was not helped by the poor relationship between
France's politicians and the military. This meant that the executive's
ideas regarding defence could not always be critically or properly
evaluated by those who would put them into action and it led to
mutual suspicion and mistrust. Such friction was not new as the
French officer corps had feared the revolutionary ambitions of the
political left for 150 years, while the left feared a large standing
army's potential as an instrument of repression. As a consequence,
ever since Versailles a series of leftist governments had attempted
to emasculate the army and reaffirm political mastery over those
in uniform. The Superior War Council (SWC or Conseil Supérieur
de la Guerre), the supreme body controlling military affairs in both
peacetime and wartime, was consequently placed under civilian
control. It consisted of senior army generals and members of the
executive and was headed by the minister of war. The designated
wartime army commander, the chief of staff, was its vice-president.
The SWC became, de facto, a general staff under close civilian
control and it lacked autonomy and dynamism and was slow
to react. Even so, it played an important role as an advisory and
consultative body across nearly all military matters but left a great
deal of discussion about defence and military matters to councils,
committees and the labyrinthine routines of bureaucracy.

— ⌑ —

The French military decision-making system wanted for both efficiency and effectiveness, but it reflected a national inclination to hold the armed forces in check. The population was weary of war, guns and uniforms. Losses of 1.4 million men in the First World War (one in ten of the country's population of military age) were greater – and proportionally higher – than those of any other western European belligerent.[33] Furthermore, over half of the 6.5 million that served and survived the war had sustained injuries. The most visible were the 1.1 million *mutilés* – those that were maimed, disfigured or invalided – but there were millions of others who suffered from deafness or nightmares or were psychologically damaged. The First World War was an experience that had a fundamental impact on France during the inter-war years. As Omer Bartov has written: '[I]t is impossible to understand any of the major political, cultural, military or popular trends and attitudes without realizing that visions of war, memories of past massacres and fears of their recurrence dominated the minds of the French.'[34] The result was that, when there were competing claims on dwindling national resources during exacting economic times, it was only the political right that stood against swingeing cuts to the military budget. This led directly to the cutting of the length of military service from three years to two in 1921, then to eighteen months in 1923 and finally to just twelve months in 1928. In line with this, the peacetime army was reduced from forty-one to thirty-one and then just twenty infantry divisions. It was a situation that was partially justified by the argument that, with a declining population, France just could not countenance a large standing army. In 1919, its population had been 39 million, with the prospect of 184,000 men being of military age by the mid-1930s. Germany, however, had a population of 59 million and 464,000 men of military age in 1933. It was only in 1935, when this disparity became dangerously obvious, that two-year military service was reintroduced in France.[35]

The latent German threat, although hardly a popular concern, remained a worry for the country's leaders during the 1920s. As a consequence, despite appalling economic difficulties and a diminishing army, plans were put in place to ensure that France was prepared for renewed aggression from its angry and frustrated neighbour to the east. Thus in 1926 the country began to develop a national defence policy based on 'total war'. In the whirlpool of short-term French decision-making, this was instead an attempt to take a long-term view in order to defend the population. The problem with the policy, though, was its lack of flexibility. An all-or-nothing strategy, one which demanded that the nation mobilize totally before committing the army, meant that France became unable to use military force in a more restrained manner.[36] Yet while the policy at least offered some sort of plan, the military continued to express their concern that upon mobilization any mass national army needed to be a large, modern and flexible force capable of offence as well as defence. There was little to be gained, it was argued, from neglecting the armed forces and then dramatically expanding them only when absolutely necessary.

The difficulty was, of course, that maintaining a highly capable army meant considerable investment as this force would require the latest weaponry and equipment, a carefully constructed doctrine and relevant training and education, not to mention high morale. This, it seems, was far too much to ask and instead the army atrophied. It was simply directed to use the surplus weapons of the First World War, while the quality of its regular troops was diminished by poor opportunities for promotion in a shrinking force, increasingly uncompetitive rates of pay, unenticing living conditions and unedifying social standing. It was an army that looked hopefully to tomorrow while, unlike its German equivalent, it did little to prepare for it. Indeed, many decisions thoroughly undermined its future capability, such as that which directed that each active division be divided in three upon mobilization, with each part acting as the 'hub' for a new division which would be two thirds reservist. Thus it would become the job of the active personnel to train the reservists and act as a cadre for some of the mobilized units, although there was not the opportunity for reserve units to train with their wartime brother units or parent division. 'Having accepted the concept of total warfare,' argues Allan Doughty, 'the French – including the High Command – thus viewed the military as a relatively rough and blunt instrument, not as a highly tuned, highly flexible force.'[37]

The choice of a defensive strategic stance with armed forces of a limited capability saw the French naturally gravitate towards the building of defensive positions. The High Command had been ruminating over the development of defensive works since Versailles and in May 1920 the SWC examined future German threats to France. The Council decided that it was essential to defend the heavily industrialized territory in the north-east of the country which contained the majority of French natural resources and the workforce critical to the fighting of an industrialized war.[38] This area had been overrun by the Kaiser's troops in 1914, but there was a desire not to fight on French soil again and an equally fervent wish to keep the Germans out of artillery range of the border. There was, however, also the threat of a surprise attack (*attaque brusquée*) across the historically sensitive and relatively long common border of Alsace-Lorraine. As the defence of this area would require more men to defend it than the frontier with Belgium, the recommendation from the SWC was to fortify the Alsace-Lorraine border. Although the industrial north-east was vital territory, the strategic depth offered by Belgium would give time for France to mobilize and race to meet the invaders, fighting them on another nation's soil with its own forces in pre-prepared positions. This would be possible because since September 1920 there had been a Franco-Belgian military agreement which not only diluted French isolation, but added a prop to her strategy and morale. It was also a consideration, of course, that building fortifications on the French border *behind* the Belgians would not have been diplomatically astute.[39] France needed all the friends it could get, and it was also hoped that German violation of Belgian territory would bring the otherwise isolationist Britain back into the great alliance as this would threaten that country's own interests. It was then anticipated that after a period of attritional warfare, the Allies, their troops now seasoned by combat, could then – just as in 1918 – exploit the enemy's weakness before attacking to victory.

The form that the defences of Alsace-Lorraine were to take was not quickly decided. In the early 1920s, a special commission under the SWC was established to look into the issue. The generals feared that strong, expensive, permanent defences were the thin end of a defensive wedge which would further fracture the military budget, severely compromise French strategic and operational flexibility, undermine capability and limit the potential for creative military thinking.[40] Yet while the generals cogently argued for temporary and inexpensive defences which did not make offence impossible, their words made little impression on one of the best-known and most respected soldiers in the country, the victor of Verdun, Marshal Henri Philippe Pétain. In 1922, while minister of war, André Maginot inserted Pétain as Inspector General between himself and the High Command with the power to review all military decisions. It was an appointment which sought to ensure that the Marshal's belief in a strong defence would be influential. And so it proved, for in October 1927, after protracted discussion, a decision was taken to construct deep underground fortifications in key areas of the Alsace-Lorraine front, and smaller block-houses connected by other obstacles along the other parts of the common frontier with Germany. It took two years for the figures and plans to be drawn up and so it was not until January 1930, at the start of a new period of financial instability in Europe, that a very strong majority of the National Assembly voted in favour of the scheme. It was a massive capital investment at the start of what was to prove a desperate decade economically, but was seen as an efficient use of public finances considering the alternative of massive rearmament. The work was to be spread over four years and construction was to start immediately. The first phase would cover the frontier with fortifications along the joint front and continue along the border with Luxembourg to a point just beyond the Belgian frontier, stopping where the Ardennes began. This densely forested region consisted of hills and winding roads, rivers, streams and narrow bridges, forming a front facing the French border of around seventy-five miles in length. The nature of the terrain, together with the fact that here the River Meuse offered a considerable obstacle just within French territory, led to a decision not to fortify the region. It was argued that the Ardennes was too difficult for a motorized and mechanized force to negotiate successfully. Indeed, Pétain appeared before the Senate Army Commission in March 1934 to say that the sector was 'not dangerous'.[41]

The initial Maginot Line construction phase was completed by 1935. It cost far in excess of the estimate and led to further defence cuts. Just as the generals had foreseen, when married with a national defence policy of total war, the 'Great Wall' marked a further shift away from a large, flexible and capable force and towards a defensively minded one which could not be used for a pre-emptive strike, or even limited offensive action across the German border. It was a stance defended by Pétain's disciple, General Louis Maurin, who, when minister of war, said to loud applause in the Chamber of Deputies on 3 March 1935: 'How could it be that we are still thinking of the offensive when we have spent billions to establish a defensive barrier? Would we be mad enough to advance beyond this barrier upon goodness knows what adventure?'[42] The impact of the defensive total war strategy was starkly illustrated by France's inaction in response to the German reoccupation of the Rhineland in 1936. The French had decided to dig in physically and mentally, leading to an oppressive 'Maginot mentality', eschewing the offensive, rejecting the initiative and reflecting a sense of vulnerability, fear, defensiveness, conservatism, feebleness and self-delusion. This mindset was 'designed to guarantee France the greatest chance of surviving an unwanted war from which it had nothing to gain. Not a formula for decisive victory, it was meant to be proof against catastrophic failure.'[43] However, events moved fast and soon after the completion of the Maginot Line and the reoccupation of the Rhineland, Belgium lost its confidence and, fearing that it might get drawn into a war with Germany due to its alliance with France, declared its neutrality. No longer could the French expect to be allowed easy access into Belgium; they would have to be invited, and any limited staff planning between the two states' militaries would have to be secret. With Belgium taking a path away from France, Britain playing hard to get and the rise in German military expenditure threatening to catch Europe wrong-footed, French rearmament made its way back up the political agenda in 1936.

The remarkable aspect of the French undertaking rearmament at the end of the 1930s was that it was done in the teeth of continued popular anti-war feeling. Yet Edouard Daladier, who from December 1932 to May 1940 held the position of minister of war for all but twenty-eight months, provided vital stability and continuity of decision-making. Although a former pacifist, Daladier had come to recognize that fascism in Europe could not be removed without resorting to war. He therefore backed rearmament as part of a left-of-centre Popular Front government elected in May 1936 under Léon Blum – the first socialist prime minister of France – although it had ostensibly been elected to deliver social reform. Daladier managed to achieve increased defence spending and in September 1936 a programme of 14 billion francs was announced, to be divided evenly between the three services.[44] With this new funding the Maginot Line could now be extended with defences running up to the North Sea coast – an insurance policy now that the Belgians had abandoned the French.[45] Even so, the new defences that were to be built were lightest in the area where the French hoped to advance to contact with the Germans in central Belgium, and heavier – but not as heavy as the Maginot Line – across the Ardennes front. Here they merely consisted of 'special dispositions' – roadblocks, earthworks, demolitions and the like. This Maginot Line extension was barely completed by the end of 1939. Nevertheless, it seems that the French had forgotten the old military maxim: he who decides to defend everything, defends nothing. After visiting the Line in 1939, British corps commander Alan Brooke, who had been brought up and educated in France, wrote that the defences were 'a masterpiece in its way and there is no doubt that the whole concept of the Maginot Line is a stroke of genius. And yet! It gave me but little feeling of security, and I consider that the French would have done better to invest the money in the shape of mobile defences such as more and better aircraft and more heavily armoured divisions than to sink all this money into the ground.'[46] It was a point of view with which many of Brooke's French colleagues agreed.[47]

Rearmament could not come soon enough for the army and air force, even if the navy had soaked up a larger proportion of the defence budget, for it was a strategic force, vital for the maintenance of communications with the country's colonies and the supply of raw materials and manpower from them. Yet renewed investment in ground and air assets did not mean that France immediately became transformed into a nation ready for war. Daladier recognized this during the 1938 Czechoslovakian Crisis. Prime minister for the third time from April 1938 to March 1940, he saw that time was needed for the military to bulk up, and for the population to share his belief in the need for war. Indeed, explaining the government's pursuit of appeasement in 1938, French foreign minister Georges Bonnet later said:

[The] Czechoslovak army would have been quickly overrun. England could do nothing, France hardly more. France did not have an air force, and General Gamelin [France's Commander-in-Chief] admitted the impossibility of a strong ground offensive 'within at least two years'.[48]

Recognizing that time was not on France's side and that it did not hold the initiative, Daladier, supported by finance minister Paul Reynaud, provided the armed forces with what he expected to be a final financial boost at the end of 1938. Funding had averaged a little over 13 billion francs between 1931 and 1935, but by 1938 had risen to 29.1 billion francs and was increased to 93.6 billion francs in 1939.[49] Yet finance was not the only issue; there was a difficulty turning francs into firepower after so many years of economic hardship in which there had been little investment in modern industrial technology, while there was also a lack of raw resources and skilled labour. The system groaned and creaked into action, however, and industry eventually started producing new weapons – weapons which the armed forces would require time to familiarize themselves and train with. Nevertheless, when in the wake of the capitulation of the Czech army and of Prague in March 1939 the French government offered guarantees to Poland, a turning point was reached and the population recognized not only that war was necessary, but that in all likelihood it would start soon over Poland.[50] From this point on, the government would stand up to Germany and there was evidence that the people, albeit reluctantly, would stand shoulder to shoulder with it in using war as a political tool.Hitler managed to do what a generation of politicians in France had failed to do: unite the country in a common cause. As Richard Overy has written: 'The ordinary Frenchman did not welcome war, but he welcomed Hitler less.'[51]

This left the French army and air force in a position where they were likely to face the Germans in a general war, relying on a defensive strategy and a doctrine based on lessons drawn from the First World War.[52] Indeed, convinced as they were that Germany was the once and future enemy, largely reliant on those stockpiles of First World War weaponry and heavily influenced by Pétain, the French were more likely than not to adopt a conservative approach to operations. As it was, they sought mobility, but only inasmuch as it allowed for the wearing down of the enemy in a protracted attritional struggle which placed strength against strength. This was reflected in doctrine which was first formulated in the *Provisional Instructions for the Tactical Employment of Larger Units* in 1921 and continued in various forms through to 1939. Its supporting pillars were the Methodical Battle (*Bataille Conduite*) and supremacy of firepower ('*Le feu tue*', literally 'Firepower kills') in defence and attack. From the outset, regulations focused on the centralized use of massive artillery fire to dominate the battlefield, either fragmenting and destroying enemy attacks, or supporting the infantry in the offensive. As in the First World War, there was a central strand to this thinking: the artillery destroys and the infantry conquers. Thus in the attack, the infantry were limited to the effective range of the artillery and would advance in successive bounds of around three miles so as not to over-stretch logistics and communications. The aim was not the prompt exploitation of an enemy's disintegration but instead the physical destruction of his troops and equipment. Moreover, any rapidity of movement was stifled by a highly centralized organization of the battle itself in which movement of all units and fire from all weapon systems were fully synchronized and strictly executed in accordance with prepared timetables and written orders. Such a system of control aimed to minimize casualties, marshal resources carefully, guide decision-making and ensure that officers played their part in a carefully choreographed battle. It all made for a very unresponsive chain of command, and it discouraged commanders from using their own initiative or seizing fleeting opportunities on the battlefield.

The Methodical Battle was, in essence, an offensive doctrine until the early 1930s. Armour was to be used to support the infantry in small groups. Yet despite technological developments in the 1920s, tanks remained tied to the speed and requirements of the infantry and were certainly not massed into formations for an operational impact. The 1921 *Instructions* had reflected this by clearly stating, 'Tanks are not able to conquer or occupy terrain by themselves alone.'[53] Aircraft, meanwhile, retained their First World War roles for reconnaissance, acting as the eyes of the artillery and harassing enemy positions. More radical ideas for the employment of tanks, in particular, gained little traction. General Jean-Baptiste Estienne's 1919 *Study of the Mission of Tanks in the Field* argued for the massing of motorized and mechanized vehicles supported by aircraft. Despite Estienne having established the French tank force and its fighting methods in co-operation with other arms during the First World War, his theory was derided as impractical, not least because he advocated a 100,000-man army with 4,000 tanks and 8,000 other vehicles, and was quashed by the traditionally minded High Command. Thus, by 1929, the manner in which the French used tanks, as outlined in *Instructions on the Employment of Combat Tanks*, remained essentially backward-looking: they were to be nothing more than penny-packeted assets in support of the infantry.

Although the French did not embrace new operational roles for armour, the 1930s saw tanks acquire a better blend of firepower, protection and mobility that enabled them to undertake different tactical tasks, even within the limitations of infantry support. The heaviest was the Char B1 – for infantry breakthrough – with a 47mm gun in the turret and a 75mm howitzer in the hull which could kill any other tank, and armour which could not be penetrated by enemy tank guns or most towed anti-tank guns. It was also the only French tank routinely equipped with radio. The Char B1 possessed only limited range and there were significant weaknesses in its design: like other French tanks, it had a single-man turret, an arrangement which required the commander both to load and aim the gun mounted there. Its complicated design and high cost, moreover, meant that few Char B1s were produced. The SOMUA S35, meanwhile, was a medium tank which specialized in exploitation and was, perhaps, the best tank of its type in Europe. It also had the 47mm gun and, for reasons of economy, the same turret as the B1, a fair turn of speed and armour that was impervious to German shells in most areas. The French also had a number of light tanks which, being less expensive and easier to manufacture, were most numerous. The Renault R35 was designed for reinforcing the infantry in breakthrough battles, but although it was heavily armoured, its 37mm gun lacked killing power. The cavalry also used armour for its role at the head of the main body and deployed the Hotchkiss H35/39, a tank very similar to the R35, while reconnaissance units used lightly armoured and armed armoured vehicles such as the AMR 35 ZT and the admirable Panhard 178 armoured car.

The French therefore had a variety of tanks and other armoured vehicles but, although they were undertaking gradual mechanization, their conservative outlook ensured that they lagged behind the Germans in terms of the development of a balanced all-arms division. Nevertheless, by the mid-1930s, the French were planning on a move into Belgium which required mobility and thus at first five and ultimately seven infantry divisions became motorized, while one brigade in each of four light cavalry divisions was equipped with half-tracks and armoured cars. In 1934 France's first Light Mechanized Division (Division Légère Mécanique or DLM) was introduced. A combination of reconnaissance units together with 220 light and medium tanks, truck-mounted infantry and towed artillery, it was a move towards a more combined arms formation. Four DLMs were eventually formed and were assigned the cavalry missions of reconnaissance and security which would lead the French forces into Belgium when the Germans attacked. Even so, the majority of French armour continued to be diluted through its dispersal – the numbers varied between forty-five and sixty tanks – in battalions for infantry support. The ideas of Estienne and his follower, Lieutenant Colonel Charles de Gaulle, whose 1934 book

Towards the Professional Army called for a huge armoured army in all-arms divisions with a manoeuvre capability, were simply too expensive and radical for the taste of politicians and the High Command. As a result, the 1936 Regulations – summarized in *Instructions on the Tactical Employment of Large Units*, the doctrine with which the French army went to war – introduced some new concepts yet continued to acknowledge the dominance of the previous maxims. The Methodical Battle remained the model, firepower was 'the preponderant factor of combat' and where static positions were involved, defence was preferred over offence.[54]

Meanwhile, the French relied on radios only when there was no other means of communication available. The Methodical Battle did not require flexible communications as battles with a slow tempo meant that commanders could rely on field telephones and couriers. These would connect the various elements of the defensive system. First, an Outpost Line would alert the main position and endeavour to delay the enemy. The Principal Position of Resistance, the strongest and most important line, would then corral the enemy between natural and staggered, man-made obstacles to force him onto routes that were pre-surveyed artillery killing zones and covered by fire from mutually supporting positions. These positions, which included machine guns and anti-tank weapon systems, were to slow the enemy's momentum and sap his strength. If the attacker was not destroyed in the principal line, he would then have to make his way past a number of strongpoints before being engaged at a Stopping Line, where he would be halted and counter-attacked. If the Stopping Line was broken, the French would then endeavour to *colmater* or plug a gap as a mobile reserve was moved smartly into the threatened area.

In theory, this was a sensible and well-judged defensive system, but it relied on completed and well-sited positions as well as well-trained and prepared troops who knew those positions well. The first phase of the Maginot Line was certainly more in keeping with these requirements than the second phase extension, which had yet to be completed. Moreover, upon mobilization the majority of divisions would be partially trained non-regulars with limited – if any – acquaintance with the area they were to defend and particularly so if it was deemed low-risk. In addition, it was a system that anticipated slow-moving German infantry with perhaps fifty supporting tanks concentrated in just over half a mile of front. However, since French anti-tank weapons were in theory to be deployed one every 110 yards and with only fifty-eight guns available per division, commanders had to consider carefully where to concentrate them. There were also too few anti-tank and anti-personnel mines and so the artillery – the old 75mm guns still packed a punch – had a crucial role in targeting, fragmenting and destroying enemy penetrations.

Of course, the great unanswered question – unanswered because it was not asked loudly, if at all – was how the system would cope if the German attack did not fit in with preconceived French ideas about its location, focus and strength. The French were just not organized and trained to react to the unexpected and to regain the initiative quickly. In such circumstances, the flexibility and mobility of the French air force would prove critical. Although in the 1920s the air force had been an appendage of the army, by the early 1930s it had been tempted by the independence offered by becoming a heavy bomber fleet and the politicians were keen on such a force's ability to deter. In these circumstances, the air force gradually lost the ability to support the army although by 1937, four years after it had gained independence, it was still not entirely committed to strategic bombing.

As the air force drifted, caught between strategic and tactical pressures on its resources, air minister Pierre Cot had sought to add clarity in 1936 by favouring a massive enlargement of the bomber force. In keeping with the fast-moving times and constant political change in France, two years later the new air minister, Guy La Chambre, recognized that it would take too long to build

Cot's vision and, acknowledging the ever-increasing German threat to French airspace, changed tack to a plan that would see the air force fight for air superiority and provide support to ground forces. This too, however, ran into problems for, as with tank production, despite some good designs and technology, there was insufficient industrial capacity, too little skilled labour and too much poor organization to meet targets. Modern aircraft were only slowly built and, along with trained ground and air crews, drip-fed into the system. By the outbreak of war, along with 250 bombers, the French had 826 fighters. Inevitably, some of these were obsolete, although modern types like the Bloch MB 151 and precious Morane-Saulnier MS 406 could challenge the German Bf 109. The upshot of all this was that by the end of 1939 the air force, commanded by an elderly former bomber pilot, General Joseph Vuillemin, was, despite its size, the least effective and most confused military service. Its valuable aircraft were – like the tanks – to be parcelled out to units in small quantities to provide localized air cover across the front and were caught in a command and control maze.[55]

It was therefore the case that by the end of the 1930s, whether on the ground or in the air, the French had undermined their own ability to be in the right place at the right time and with the required numbers, weaponry and skills. To make matters worse, senior officers, although aware of flaws and foibles in the system, believed that they had a winning formula. Focused on their own defence, lacking contrary military experience and rejecting lessons from Spain, Austria and Czechoslovakia as not pertinent to their situation, the French took a tack and stuck to it no matter in what direction the wind blew. A generation of officers held on to the hard-won knowns – the lessons of the First World War – for dear life and would not be swayed from them as they settled into a velvet-lined rut. This was partly due to the unexceptional quality of the officer corps during this period, but also to the education of those officers, which emphasized an understanding of doctrine and procedures rather than the development of critical faculties and the application of initiative.[56] It was a dangerous culture, claustrophobic and unquestioning, one in which officers sought reassurance and avoided creative thinking. Obedience was a virtue that was extolled and nowhere was this more clearly seen than in the Methodical Battle. It fostered a lack of imagination that was dangerous not only because French methods were not challenged by new ideas but also because the enemy's options and how he might use his own initiative were not usefully explored. Thus, in short, the French failed to develop a capacity which allowed its military to anticipate the enemy and make adequate preparations to apply their will to the battlefield.[57]

In a system that so heavily leant on the past, that was chary of the radical, denuded battles of boldness and personality, and favoured procedure over flexibility and dynamism, it was hardly surprising that competent but uninspiring officers with good staff skills – men such as Gamelin and Vuillemin – rose to the top rather than charismatic leaders.[58] They were not the sort of men to shake their services out of an unhealthy complacency because, as products of the French system and promoted for certain organizational abilities, they could not identify that complacency. There was a belief that, as in 1914, the outcome of a war would eventually favour France. General Weygand, for example, said in July 1939, the month before he was called out of retirement: 'The French army is stronger than ever before in its history; its equipment is the best, its fortifications are first-rate; its morale excellent, and it has an outstanding High Command. Nobody wants war but if we are forced to win a new victory then we will win it.'[59] Foreign observers tended not to demur from this view, clearly seeing impressive adult plumage from a distance, rather than the less impressive specimen close up. Indeed, *Time* magazine commented in August 1939, '[Gamelin] is head of what, by almost unanimous acclaim, is today the world's finest military machine.'[60]

The British also proclaimed French military strength. Winston Churchill, seeking to give reassurance to the British people at a time of rearmament efforts in 1937, remarked that the French had an 'incomparable military machine'[61] and in the following year that the French army was 'the most perfectly trained and faithful mobile force in Europe'.[62] The plaudits became commonplace after London drew closer to Paris in the wake of Munich and continued even when staff talks and joint military planning began in early 1939 and the British general staff began to furrow its collective brow about French preparations. Nevertheless, Britain wanted to believe in French military strength as much as France did and so the nation bought into the popular French slogan 'We shall win because we are stronger'. All the time, however, France adopted a swagger that was based on little more than a 'mixture of faith, hope [and] resignation'.[63]

As was to be expected, it was the Germans that took the most objective view of French military capability. Berlin had identified weaknesses through agents and intelligence work by the late 1930s: the limitations imposed by France's lack of manpower, the plethora of poor equipment, and the military's lack of flexibility and grasp of modern mobile warfare. Indeed, Halder and his team had studied Germany's latest enemy in detail and in August 1939 he wrote that the French army:

> [R]esembles a weak man trying to carry machine guns, guns etc., on his back. Age classes of conscripts are small, and service for a long time has been only one year. Armament, too, is not in the best condition. Potential of army on the whole limited.[64]

Yet even such an assessment did not lead the Germans to feel that France was anything other than a first-class power. The First World War had taught them to respect defensive preparations and not to underestimate their enemy. The German ambassador to Paris from 1936 to 1939, German Count Johannes von Welczeck, was aware that agents in France were sending optimistic reports back to Berlin, '[telling] their masters what they wish to hear and not what they ought to know'. Von Welczeck, however, urged caution.[65] It remained to be seen whether or not he was right.

CHAPTER TWO

Plans

O N THE AFTERNOON OF 26 AUGUST 1939, Albert Winkler
was in a Bavarian wood engaged in a tactical leadership
exercise. It was the last phase of his officer training which, apart
from an NCO's mistake during a live-firing exercise which had
killed one of his comrades and a gash on his forearm caused
by a grenade malfunction that required twenty stitches, had all
gone well. He returned to his barracks that evening, a wooden
hut infested with mosquitoes and lacking hot water, to be told
that the commanding officer would be holding a briefing in ten
minutes. Having stored his kit, Winkler immediately headed for an
old gymnasium, which, unusually, was being patrolled by guards,
and he noted that traffic had been held at the entry gate. Winkler's
heart began to beat just a little faster, his instincts telling him that
something was afoot. The young men, some 150 in total, stood to
attention as the lieutenant colonel limped onto a stage. He was in
his early fifties, grey at the temples, his right upper lip curled into
a permanent smile by a deep scar. Russia 1915. His stories had held
the potential officers entranced, but each one of them had a point,
lessons to learn. Their respect for him was undoubted and many
said that they would gladly be led by him 'into the mouth of hell'.
Once he had been stood easy, Winkler retrieved a notebook and

pencil from his breast pocket to take notes, as he always did when the colonel spoke:

> Gentleman, although your training has another two days to run, I can inform you that from midnight tonight, by order of General Brauchitsch, you will become commissioned officers with the rank of leutnant. My congratulations. You may well be wondering why this is the case. The reason for this is simple: the army needs officers and at 0400 hours tomorrow morning you will parade outside this building before being transported to the railway station. From there you will take a train to München and thence make your way to your units. War is about to break out in Europe. You will be heading east into Poland. It will, I am sure, be the first in a series of campaigns which the Führer has deemed necessary and I have little doubt that the war will be long. Remember your training. Trust your instincts. Rely on your comrades. Do your duty.[1] *

The Polish campaign gave the German High Command an occasion to test their capability against a stronger enemy than previously, and it was still deemed to be winnable inexpensively and quickly. It was a stepping-stone to a war with the West, but it was not one that Hitler thought would lead to confrontation in the very near future as he believed France and Britain were too militarily weak and their populations too unsupportive to risk a war over Poland. Emphasizing the point to his senior generals, Hitler told them in August 1939: 'Our enemies are little worms. I saw them at Munich.'[2] With the West seemingly impotent and a non-aggression pact signed with Stalin by the end of August to ensure the passivity of the Soviet Union, Germany had created the chance to strike at

---

* In Poland, Winkler lost his left foot during a Polish artillery barrage. Lucky to survive, he was taken by train back to Germany where he spent three months in hospital. He married his nurse.

Poland unfettered by fighting on another front. Hitler had, however, significantly underestimated the rapidly growing sense of outrage and fear generated latterly in Paris and London by the Munich Crisis and the later German occupation of the rest of Czechoslovakia. Although there was a desire in both capitals to win more time to strengthen their armed forces, both Édouard Daladier, the French prime minister, and Neville Chamberlain, his British counterpart, believed that the time had come to make a stand and had agreed in the spring that they would declare war on Germany if Hitler invaded Poland. Partial French mobilization took place in the last week of August as tensions began to rise, and full mobilization followed on 1 September when Germany attacked eastwards. The next day France and Britain issued an ultimatum demanding that Germany withdraw from Poland, or there would be war. Hitler, described by Halder at this time as 'Worn, haggard, creaking voice, preoccupied',[3] had the ultimatum read to him by interpreter Paul Schmidt in the Reich Chancellery. 'When I finished,' recalled Schmidt, 'there was complete silence. Hitler sat immobile, gazing before him … after an interval which seemed an age he turned to [Foreign Minister] Ribbentrop, who had remained standing at the window. "What now?" asked Hitler with a savage look.'[4]

The Allied stance had taken Hitler by surprise. They had torpedoed his loose schedule for an invasion of the West – he would now have to act sooner than planned because he did not want France and Britain to benefit from any delay to gain strength. Thus, from these declarations of war on Germany, which were announced on 3 September, the clock was ticking for both sides. Yet while Hitler believed that Germany was ready enough for general war, the High Command was extremely concerned that the combined strengths of France and Britain were better placed to win an attritional conflict. It was a belief articulated by Franz von Papen, a former general staff officer who had been briefly chancellor in 1933: 'Germany can never win this War. Nothing will be left but ruins.'[5] It was the 'ruins' of war that were still so fresh in the minds of the German people, who did not greet the onset of hostilities with Poland enthusiastically. There were no cheering masses in Berlin as there had been in 1914, only anxious, silent men and women looking mournful.

The French and British also failed to greet Hitler's refusal to respond to the Allied ultimatum with unbridled joy. Sending the sons of the soldiers of 1914–18 off to war was a trauma that they had desperately hoped to avoid, and yet Hitler's prediction that such a state of affairs would lead to mobs bringing down their governments proved wide of the mark. Indeed, some in France felt that for the first time in a generation the country appeared united against a common foe and were confident of success, even if there was likely to be a cost. Reserve Captain Daniel Barlone, a man in his forties, was called up on 23 August and wrote in his diary that his colleagues in Paris 'fully believe that I shall be back in the office by next week' and opined: 'We do not doubt our victory, but wonder what price we shall have to pay.'[6]

While Hitler may have misunderstood the strength of feeling in France and Britain against his recent actions, OKH had nonetheless correctly advised him that the French were incapable of launching a major offensive against Germany while its forces were engaged in Poland. On 14 August Halder had noted: '[I]n view of what we know about French operational doctrine and the political difficulties which would first have to be overcome, such a thrust would be unlikely'.[7] His forecast was accurate, for Gamelin's nine-division-strong show of force against the Saar which began on 7 September, was half-hearted, ponderous and retreated not long after running into the defences of the *Westwall*. The British, meanwhile, did nothing of note and their planned bombing campaign of the Ruhr was reduced to a lame propaganda leaflet-dropping exercise because the French feared that the Luftwaffe would retaliate by raiding their cities. What might have followed had the British struck with bombs and the French been bolder can only be guessed at, but Halder was relieved that Allied reaction had been so timid as the German presence in the Saar was a scratch force of second-line divisions with no tanks or supporting aircraft.[8]

For their part, the Germans needed operations in Poland – *Fall Weiss* (Case White) – to be completed as quickly as possible in order not to expend valuable resources and to ensure the invasion of the West could now be launched without delay. With German or German-occupied territory on three of Poland's four sides, Army Group North's Third and Fourth Armies under Generaloberst Fedor von Bock formed one pincer while Army Group South's Eighth, Tenth and Fourteenth Armies under Generaloberst Gerd von Rundstedt, who had recently been called out of retirement, formed the other. Between them, the aim was to catch the Polish army in a great *Kesselschlacht* – a task in which they would be assisted by the Soviet invasion of eastern Poland, which had been agreed as part of the non-aggression pact and began on 17 September. All the German armies involved were a mix of infantry, panzer and motorized divisions. Von Bock and von Rundstedt commanded three and four panzer divisions respectively, with one army in each Army Group containing a corps strike force consisting of a panzer division and two motorized divisions. In von Bock's Fourth Army, for example, XIX Corps was the strike force. Commanded by Heinz Guderian, it consisted of 3rd Panzer Division, 2nd and 20th Motorized Divisions with the attached Panzer Lehr (Panzer) Battalion and a Reconnaissance Battalion. All thirty-four of Germany's tank units – divisions, independent brigades and regiments – went to war in Poland: 2,820 tanks with 1,051 PzKpfw Is and IIs, 361 PzKpfw IIIs and IVs, and 301 35(t) and 38(t) tanks commandeered from the Czechs.[9]

It was a campaign designed around the tenets of strike first, hard and deep, and operations were conducted in line with the doctrinal emphasis on speed, aggression, combined arms and initiative with air power. Although panzer divisions did not have independent missions, violent assaults by massed panzer columns made successful penetrations by driving reserves of tanks and motorized infantry deep into the rear of the Polish positions, preventing the defenders from re-forming their line or bringing up their reserves. The Luftwaffe, meanwhile, won air superiority and then supported ground forces through tactical missions by Ju 87 Stuka dive-bombers and operational missions by Heinkel He 111s and Dornier Do 17s. The Poles could not cope with the mobility, tempo and intensity of German operations; their defences were unhinged within four days, and Warsaw fell on the twenty-seventh day of the campaign. It was little wonder Daniel Barlone was so shaken by the news that he felt compelled to write in his diary, 'We refuse to believe in the smashing advance announced by the Germans. Besides, things will change.'[10] The Poles lost 65,000 killed in action, 144,000 wounded and 587,000 prisoners of war while the Germans lost less than 16,500 killed, 30,000 wounded and 3,500 missing.[11]

The sheer speed and scale of German operations were such that strategic victory, albeit with the assistance of the Soviets, was assured. It had achieved OKW's aims without a protracted fight and provided Hitler with a solid platform from which to launch an offensive in the West before the end of the year. OKW did, however, want time to relocate its troops and to identify and then apply the lessons learned in Poland: the French and British would pose a sterner challenge. While von Brauchitsch and Halder did what they could to forestall an early offensive in the West, the general staff and field commands collaborated closely and their conclusion was that yet more work was needed to improve logistics and to create the necessary tactical and operational momentum before any invasion of France could be attempted. Panzer divisions were big, hungry, thirsty organizations which occupied seventy miles of road space or eighty trains of fifty-five wagons on rail, and if they were moving fast, their supply was of the essence. The result of study and discussion about how this could be best facilitated led to the sharing of best practice as well as some innovation. Older ideas such as the attachment of mobile field workshops to panzer divisions became standard, as did the *Rucksack-Prinzip* (backpack principle), which saw each formation carry as many supplies as was practical to make them as self-sustaining as possible. Such developments were further enhanced by using the Luftwaffe to deliver fuel and ammunition to forward airfields and the panzer divisions then using trucks, which were increased in number, to retrieve the supplies and deliver them direct to the spearhead units. Highly mobile Luftwaffe units were also to keep in close contact with the leading elements of the divisions in order that they might open their own temporary airfields close to the front, which would allow short-range German aircraft to fly timely close air-support and interdiction missions. 'This,' Robert M. Citino argues, 'was the true birth of the *Air-Land battle*.' [12]

Wherever the army and air force could better their performance in both old and new roles, they were willing to do so. Improving what was already in place was critical as time was short. There was a plethora of initiatives to achieve this. The infantry, for example, having been taken to task for being too slow to achieve objectives, found its leadership coming under intense scrutiny. The result was the establishment of a two-week 'fundamentals of practical leadership' course for junior officers and NCOs and something similar for battalion and regimental commanders but pitched at a higher level. OKH was keen to increase the army's striking power, and so changes were instigated. With no resources to establish new armoured divisions from scratch, a practical alternative was found by adding a panzer regiment to light divisions in order to create four more panzer divisions. More motorized formations were also formed by each established division of this type losing a motorized infantry regiment, which then became the basis for a new motorized formation. Meanwhile, concerns over the vulnerability of light tanks in combat after the loss of 217 tanks in Poland[13] were dealt with in two ways: first, by the ordering of more PzKpfw IIIs and IVs and second, by panzer commanders, who were aware of Germany's own difficulties in tank production, developing new tactics that would protect their assets. Yet while a welter of influential adjustments were made over the autumn of 1939, one important organizational issue of potentially great importance was not grasped: the massing of panzer divisions for independent operations. It was an issue that went to the heart of German campaign-fighting methods, but it also challenged tradition and therefore the conservative nature of many in senior command. As the planning for the invasion of the West took shape, this was a confrontation that became increasingly inevitable and one which the Wehrmacht would ignore at its peril.

Franz Halder was well aware of the various debates swirling around the army about how tanks might best be used in future operations, but they were just one influence on his planning for Hitler's offensive in the West. It was his job as chief of the general staff to draft plans that would fulfil OKW's ambitions and so he had to have a firm grasp of what the army was capable if it was to be effective. His initial attempts revealed much about what he and von Brauchitsch believed the capability of the field armies to be in the immediate wake of Poland – mediocre. During the period termed the Phoney War or *Sitzkrieg* before the invasion of France, Halder did all that he could to ensure that his plans did not ask too much of the armed forces and were produced quickly enough, but not so quickly as to give Hitler the opportunity to launch a snap offensive. The first task of his staff officers was to give shape to Hitler's broad scheme as outlined on 9 October in Führer Directive No. 6, which required an attack through Luxembourg, Belgium and Holland and into France in order to destroy the French army. Halder's first draft plan, known as the First Deployment Directive, was produced ten days later. Army Group B would carry out two separate but related thrusts: the main force was to advance through central Belgium in two armies, including six panzer divisions, to converge on Brussels before arcing towards the River Somme, while a subsidiary attack would also be launched into the Netherlands with two more armies. Army Group A, meanwhile, would strike out to protect the left or southern flank of the advance into central Belgium. One of its armies would traverse the Ardennes with a single panzer division while, just to the south, the second would make a minor push through Luxembourg to the northern end of the Maginot Line. Army Group C's part in the plan was to develop pressure on the Maginot Line in order to pin and fix French divisions in Alsace-Lorraine. The bear-like Keitel was underwhelmed by Halder's offering, saying that it was 'just the old Schlieffen Plan, with the strong right along the Atlantic coast' and adding caustically, 'You won't get away with an operation like that twice running.'[14] This was not entirely true, because the First Deployment Directive lacked the strategic ambition of Schlieffen's projected encirclement of Paris as carried out in 1914 (the 1914 version of the plan was, of course, a bastardised version of the original) and merely advanced German forces to make contact with the enemy in Belgium. Indeed, this was exactly the sort of plan envisioned by the French themselves, and even Halder considered the plan a rushed 'tangle'[15] without a *Schwerpunkt* because the whole concept lacked emphasis on achieving a decisive result.

Hitler, who dismissed OKW's early plans as being akin to the 'ideas of a military cadet', sent the first draft back, demanding something that produced more 'breakthroughs'.[16] To focus the generals' attention, Hitler announced that he wanted the invasion to commence on 12 November.[17] Halder felt that his options were severely limited, and not only by the time constraint imposed by his Supreme Commander. At heart a conservative staff officer but with a good sense of what was and was not achievable, he struggled with the restrictions on his creativity imposed by the Maginot Line, the Ardennes and an army still in development. Nevertheless, the Second Deployment Directive was delivered on 29 October 1939, just ten days after his first attempt. In it, all three Army Groups kept their previous roles, but Army Group B was enhanced to give it the extra power to make a breakthrough at the expense of Army Group A's Ardennes advance. Hitler received it with a coolness that made his dissatisfaction only too clear. He ordered Halder to produce a third version of the plan. Frustrated by Hitler's lack of practical understanding of what could be achieved with the resources available and in the area selected, the general lamented in his journal: 'None of the higher Hq. thinks that the offensive ordered by OKW has any prospect of success. No decisive success can be expected on ground operations.'[18] Fedor von Bock, the serious and single-minded commander of Army Group B, agreed and confided to his diary: 'The Führer knows that the bulk of the generals do not believe that attacking now will produce a decisive success.'[19]

It was in early November, just after the rejection of the Second Deployment Directive, that Hitler began to show a heightened interest in the wooded Ardennes region of Belgium and Luxembourg, a sector which abutted the German border and was assumed to be impossibly difficult ground to cross quickly. Halder was directed to enhance the push through the Ardennes in order to protect the southern flank of the main effort and, in so doing, take Sedan, where Napoleon III had been captured in 1870. Halder, however, saw Sedan as militarily unimportant and a stronger push through the region as an unwarranted dilution of resources. OKW was well aware, however, that vital supplies remained scarce and on 5 November von Brauchitsch met with Hitler and not only pointed out the army's lack of readiness and the challenges imposed by the weather, but also invented mutinies, widespread ill-discipline and a lack of fighting spirit at the front. Hitler's rage at such allegations led to him accusing von Brauchitsch of a lack of loyalty towards his own army and branding the general a liar as he spat, 'Not one frontline commander mentioned any lack of attacking spirit to me!' Von Brauchitsch had committed professional suicide, while his falsehoods had only diverted attention from what were very real resource difficulties.[20]

Von Bock's diary is full of references on the resources theme: on 30 October he wrote, '[R]eplacement of materiel is far from adequate';[21] on 3 November, 'Today the 4th Army reported that its divisions are nowhere near up to strength and ready for operations!'[22] and on 12 November, '[Army Group B is] capable of a brief offensive; major operations only when timely replacement of everything, especially motor vehicles, is assured. Additional training time desirable in any event.'[23] Added to these concerns was von Bock's continuing unease about the plan's lack of a clear focus. Thus, on hearing about the new emphasis that Hitler was seeking to put on the Army Group A area of operations, the humourless, arrogant and ambitious officer was moved to write: 'Originally the point of main effort was supposed to lie with me, now there are three attack spearheads! I was right about my concern over the blurring of the point of main effort.'[24] It seemed, as Halder had been complaining in recent weeks, that Hitler wanted a 'breakthrough everywhere'.[25] But although Hitler's interference in the operational realm was not welcomed by OKH, the Ardennes sector was heavily laden with potential – a potential that had not been missed by Generalleutnant Erich von Manstein, the chief of staff to Army Group A.

Von Manstein was a fifty-two-year-old Prussian aristocrat who had been beaten to the coveted appointment of chief of the general staff by Halder but not through any lack of self-confidence. He had dismissed his rivals' early plans as 'intellectually bankrupt'[26] and, encouraged by Gerd von Rundstedt, the Prussian commander of Army Group A who had been an important figure in the reorganization of the Wehrmacht in the mid-1930s, immediately set about producing an alternative. Having had previous contact with his fellow officers and armoured warfare proponents Oswald Lutz and Heinz Guderian, von Manstein believed that Germany should seek a bold operational plan that offered the possibility for a decisive strategic result through the daring use of armoured forces and yet was in keeping with German military tradition. His ideas were given time to develop when in mid-November, with no agreed plan, deteriorating weather and concerns over resources, Hitler reluctantly postponed the launch of the offensive until 'conditions improved'. The start date was subsequently postponed on a further twenty-eight occasions – well into 1940. It was early during this period, on 23 November, that Hitler held a command conference at the Reich Chancellery, the attendees of which included his three Army Group commanders: von Rundstedt, von Bock and Generaloberst Wilhelm Ritter von Leeb, the commander of Army Group C. Here he asserted his military authority, re-emphasized his aims and further detailed the deficiencies he found in Halder's Second Deployment Directive. In doing so, he further undermined the authority of OKH, a point not missed by von Brauchitsch, who offered his resignation to Hitler that day over the issue, although it was not accepted and the army's subservience only grew thereafter. This was the Führer's final warning to stop dithering, cease whingeing and instead to act decisively to fulfil his will. It was an admonition that, despite Hitler's clear ambition to subvert the traditional relationship between OKH and the head of state, and despite their own mutinous feelings, von Brauchitsch, Halder and the field commanders felt poorly placed to ignore.

While the Germans struggled through their preparations, the Allies embarked on their own. The central figure in this was General Maurice Gamelin, who upon mobilization had been made both commander-in-chief of land forces and Supreme Commander of the Allied forces. The diminutive sixty-six-year-old had been born into a Parisian family that had produced many generals over the centuries and from an early age had absorbed some of the skills required for high command. One of them was a calm assuredness that had been noted when he stood as a staff officer beside Joffre when the Germans were denied Paris in 1914, and in his appointments before being promoted to chief of the general staff in 1931. Since then his knowledge, confidence and tact had made him well-respected across the military, in political circles and by the populace at large. *L'Époque* opined in July 1939 that in war Gamelin would 'more than fulfil the high expectations the nation has of him'[27] and that same year *Time* described him as being exactly what the French like their generals to be – 'mute and professional … the good grey little General leads a good grey little life'.[28] Yet there were men of influence, including Paul Reynaud, the finance minister who was to become prime minister in March 1940, with a much lower opinion of the general's abilities and who believed him to be devoid of bold ideas, fusty and too set in his ways. There was, though, little doubt that Gamelin was the personification of just the sort of officer that the French army sought to produce: professional, orthodox and systematic.[29]

On the day that Germany invaded Poland, Gamelin had established his war headquarters at Château de Vincennes in eastern Paris with a staff directed by Colonel Jean Petibon. It was from here that he sought to oversee the final developments of a trap that had been set for the Germans across central Belgium into which, he believed, France's mortal enemy could not fail to fall. His army would then, with the assistance of Britain, destroy the German armies in an attritional – but thoroughly methodical – manner. It was a confrontation for which the French had been preparing themselves for the last twenty years but which Britain had studiously sought to avoid. There was no desire on the part of the latter's politicians or people to go to war or to finance a hungry military machine, and as a result Britain was psychologically and materially late in readying itself for war.[30] It had consistently reduced defence spending in the wake of the First World War, and it was not until Hitler's Germany began to threaten Britain's vital interests in 1934 that there was a reassessment of such expenditure. Initially, the Royal Air Force was the main beneficiary of this increase in funding, but Hitler's increasing menace meant that spending was more broadly spread across all three services. It was a period during which Britain relied heavily on France to provide a 'great army' on the continent, the RAF to protect her islands and the Royal Navy to protect her empire. London also depended on a policy of appeasement towards Germany to provide the time in which to rearm, but by the *Anschluss* in March 1938 defence spending accounted for 38 per cent of all government expenditure.[31] It was only after Munich, however, that the financial brakes on defence spending were finally and fully released.[32]

British rearmament was a compromised, extemporized and rushed process. Preparation for war was poorly co-ordinated as the services still scrapped for funding, took self-serving decisions and eschewed co-operation in what amounted to a strategic vacuum.[33] By the outbreak of war, the RAF boasted a total of 832 fighters and 2,520 bombers.[34] Bomber Command would undertake strategic bombing and attack targets of significance in any ground campaign, while Fighter Command would defend British airspace. Support for the army was not considered to be important; indeed, the Air Staff stated in Regulations that it would only happen 'in exceptional circumstances'.[35] There was also little emphasis on the need to win air superiority over the battlefield and Fighter Command was determined not to see its capability diluted by attempts to draw off its aircraft to fight over the continent.[36] In the end, just fifteen squadrons were sent across the English Channel for dedicated army support, along with the light and medium bombers of the Advanced Air Striking Force (AASF) which would bomb targets in Germany from airfields across the English Channel while preparations were made to facilitate operations direct from British soil by aircraft with greater range. It was a decision that was to lead Lieutenant General Alan Brooke, the commander of the British Expeditionary Force's (BEF) II Corps, to make a typically insightful entry in his diary:

> The feeling the [War Office] give me is that whilst concentrating on ensuring that they are going to win the war in 3 years from now they neglect to realize the danger of losing it this year! ... [W]e are courting disaster against an enemy who adheres to the doctrine of concentrating of effort at the vital

point at the right time. To contemplate bombing the Ruhr
at a time when the Germans are using their combined army
and air force effort in one mighty uniform attempt to crush
the French and British forces to clear their way into France,
is in my mind sheer folly.[37]

The BEF of which Brooke was a part had been formed after
the start of joint staff talks with the French in mid-February 1939.
Initially consisting of a general headquarters and two corps, each
of two regular divisions together with its small RAF air component,
by May 1940 it comprised ten infantry divisions, half of which
were regular, and an armoured brigade, with the whole organized
into three corps. Its fighting methods were an evolution of those
used in the later stages of the First World War, but there had been
some experimentation with mechanization and motorization since
then. The result was a doctrine which bore all the hallmarks of a
compromise between the old, limited, closely controlled battles
and new experimental thinking.[38]

Such thinking could be seen in the establishment of the
Experimental Mechanical Force – later called the Armoured
Force – on Salisbury Plain in 1927. It was a small, prototype
mechanized division consisting primarily of armoured fighting
vehicles designed to co-operate with RAF bomber and fighter
squadrons, but without infantry. During exercises over the next
couple of years, this formation provided a number of important
lessons, chief among them that it could achieve little without
strong infantry support. Within the confines of what financial
resources and deference to tradition would allow, the British army
endeavoured to modernize in an attempt to avoid the stalemate of
the First World War and, in the words of Field Marshal Sir George
Milne, Chief of the Imperial General Staff and an advocate of
mechanization, to aim for 'mobility, activity and quickness from
the beginning ...'.[39] Its doctrine in the late 1930s thus touched on
armoured units attacking enemy centres of gravity and emphasized

combined arms but this was not reflected in the development of balanced formations cut loose from the artillery. Instead, Britain motorized all of its infantry and offered support with quite separate tank brigades while the ability to exploit any opportunities or gains made on the battlefield lay with mobile divisions – little more than cavalry in light tanks – which, by the spring of 1940, took the shape of 1st Armoured Division. It was therefore an army that, due to its massive recent expansion, entered the war bursting with untrained and poorly equipped personnel. The BEF was its most capable component: brave, tenacious and well organized, but lacking relevant fighting experience and a rooted doctrine. Here was a force in transition which, although mobile, was probably better suited to defence than to high-tempo manoeuvre warfare.[40]

Neither the BEF nor the French army had any great concern about what they were likely to be asked to do as part of a co-ordinated Allied action to meet the German offensive. Both had the ability, if required, to move towards the enemy, settle into defensive positions and then fight a series of battles designed to grind the opposing forces down. This facility suited Gamelin's nascent planning for countering a German invasion. The plan was founded on the 450-mile-long line of defences from the Swiss border to the North Sea incorporating seventy-two divisions. Second Army Group was in the Maginot Line, with First Army Group occupying the line north to the coast. With Allied intelligence indicating that the Germans were massing 116 divisions along their western border, Gamelin assumed that their main offensive effort would be north of the Ardennes and so decided to deploy the most mobile Allied troops to advance towards them. Although Belgium's neutrality would preclude Allied troops from preparing defensive positions on its soil, Gamelin hoped that its own troops would make the necessary preparations so that, in the event of an invasion, the Allied troops could advance to occupy them. The entire plan hung on the ability of the Belgians to hold forward defensive positions long enough to give the French and British troops the time they needed to set themselves. Second-rate troops were deemed good enough to man both the Maginot Line and the Ardennes sector. Any attack through the difficult wooded Ardennes was, the High Command concurred, likely to be minor but, even if it happened to be more significant, they believed that it would take nine days for the enemy to penetrate the area and amass sufficient troops to launch an attempt to cross the Meuse. In such circumstances, reinforcements would immediately be moved into position in time to foil German plans. Map exercises conducted in May and June 1938 by General André-Gaston Prételat, at that time the commander of Second Army with responsibility for the Sedan-Montmédy region,[41] concluded that the Germans could reach the Meuse with three corps in just sixty hours, but these findings were dismissed as unduly pessimistic. Indeed, there was a growing feeling that the High Command wished for war games to be used only to refine existing plans and not challenge decisions that had already been made. This stance was in keeping with the uncritical ethos that had permeated the French army, but it meant that no alternatives to a mechanized version of the 1914 Schlieffen Plan were considered as viable German invasion options.[42]

With French minds made up about where the enemy would place his main effort in an invasion, the question remained as to how far forward the Allies should push into Belgium before establishing a defensive line. Too far to the east and the Allies would struggle to reach it before the Germans arrived, but too close to the French frontier and the Belgian 'buffer zone' would have been unnecessarily surrendered to the enemy. During the autumn of 1939, while defences were prepared along the Franco-Belgian border by General Gaston Billotte's First Army Group, a decision was made to advance to a line from the French border at Givet, up to Namur, across the Gembloux Gap – an ancient invasion route due to its lack of natural obstacles – and the Dyle River to Antwerp. This scheme, known as Plan D, demanded a challenging yet achievable advance for Billotte's formations – which included the mobile BEF, the First Army with its attached Cavalry Corps and Seventh Army in reserve – while the Belgians fought on the Albert Canal, and it allowed key battles to be fought on Belgian soil away from the French border. By the first days of January, as the details of Plan D were being worked out and the necessary preparations made, OKW was still waiting for what it considered a suitable offensive plan by OKH. The hours of daylight were short, but for Halder's discouraged staff officers the hours of work were long as they sought to produce an offensive that met Hitler's requirements. It was while they were looking into how Hitler's requirement for an enhanced push through the Ardennes might be incorporated into a wider operational plan, that events took a turn which resulted in Halder developing a plan that made the Ardennes thrust the main effort.

On the freezing morning of 10 January, Hitler received news for which he had been waiting since the late autumn: two weeks of clear weather would start in five days' time. It took him just moments to decide that the invasion would be launched on 12 January. Time was of the essence and even though the Second Deployment Directive lacked finesse, it would catch the enemy cold and considerably weaker than if the attack was launched in the spring. However, when a light aircraft on an unauthorized flight from Münster to Cologne made an emergency landing at Vucht, just north of Maastricht on neutral Belgian territory by the Meuse, the Germans needed to think again. The aircraft contained fifty-year-old Major Helmuth Reinberger, a general staff officer in the airborne force who was carrying secret documents which provided enough detail for the enemy to deduce the context of the overall campaign. The capture of Reinberger, his pilot, the incompetent fifty-two-year-old reserve officer Major Erich Hoenmanns, and the documents by Belgian frontier guards on 10 January, was a potential disaster for the campaign.[43] The Belgians inevitably asked themselves whether the event was an elaborately staged ruse to widely mislead and provoke the government into calling on British and French support, thereby giving the Germans a pretext to invade Belgium. After secretly recording conversations between the two officers and German air and army attachés, however, the Belgians had no reason to believe the documents to be fakes. The Germans, meanwhile, had to assume that the enemy now had the basic outline of their current offensive plans. Jodl's diary for 12 January has a brief entry: 'If the enemy is in possession of all the files, situation catastrophic!'[44] Hitler, it was said, was simply furious. The offensive was postponed once more, and the opening offered by the fine weather was wasted by the idiocy of two junior officers.

Yet while the inadvertent death of the Second Deployment Directive might have caused a lesser general staff to panic, OKH did not and became more receptive to radical ideas. This coincided with Hitler's own interest in developing the advance through the Ardennes even further than he had demanded in late November. His new focus had been stimulated by war games on 27 December and 7 January which, using intelligence that the French were developing a strong mobile reserve in the Verdun area, suggested that this posed a significant threat to the southern flank of the proposed German offensive. Thus, the Third Deployment Directive of 30 January, although not radically different from the previous plan, included two panzer divisions in Twelfth Army's advance through the Ardennes to fall on Sedan and so protect the vulnerable flank. This left six panzer divisions for Army Group B's main effort and one in reserve. Even so, the third iteration of OKH's plan remained predictable and conservative and was still unlikely to achieve a decisive victory. It was in this barren landscape that von Manstein's fertile imagination began to find a receptive audience.

The advancement of von Manstein's ideas came about very largely due to fortunate happenstance. Army Group A's headquarters was at the fashionable Hotel Riesen-Fürstenhof overlooking the Rhine in Koblenz, and for its day-to-day work its staff took over the headquarters building of 34th Division close to Deutsches Eck six miles to the north. It was here that von Manstein was to write seven memorandums – the first on 31 October 1939 and the last on 12 January 1940 – which provided alternatives to OKH's plans. He had a good working relationship with his commander, the tough sixty-five-year-old von Rundstedt who, despite his rank, had the odd habit of dressing in his uniform as honorary colonel of the 18th Infantry Regiment and relaxed during the day with paperback detective novels. Von Rundstedt rated his chief of staff's skills highly, liked to encourage his ideas and was content to leave details to him. Although essentially an old-school, traditional officer, von Rundstedt at least agreed with von Manstein that OKW's plans 'contained no clear-cut intention of fighting the campaign to a victorious conclusion'.[45] Furthermore, Halder's plan ran contrary to German military history, tradition and understanding of war while von Manstein's scheme ran with them as he advocated Army Group A becoming the campaign's armoured main effort to achieve a decisive result. Army Group B was to advance as the Allies expected in order to pin and fix Gamelin's best formations in central Belgium while von Rundstedt's panzer divisions sped to the Channel coast to effect an encirclement. Other formations would plunge simultaneously south having crossed the Meuse in order to thwart a Verdun counter-attack, pierce any developing defensive protecting Paris on the Aisne, and unhinge the Maginot Line position. It was a plan, von Manstein argued, that avoided protracted attritional warfare and offered the prospect of strategic victory in the next phase of operations because the Allies would already have lost the decisive battle.

Von Manstein was an arrogant officer who did not suffer fools gladly, but he was not so self-confident as to offer his scheme up without having ensured that it was a practical proposal. Accordingly, by early 1940 he had discussed his idea with several other officers, but none were as enthusiastic or as important as Heinz Guderian. The most experienced armoured commander in the Wehrmacht and commander of XIX Panzer Corps was accommodated in a hotel adjacent to Army Group A's headquarters. The two men knew each other from the War Academy in 1907,[46] had met periodically since then and now discussed the feasibility of large tank forces passing through the Ardennes, where both men had served during the First World War. By the end of their detailed discussions, both Manstein and Guderian could see no reason why, with careful preparation, panzer divisions could not reach the Meuse within four days. Both men subsequently sensed a great opportunity: von Manstein to trump OKW's plan and Guderian to command the spearhead formation in a campaign that could alter the course of history. Halder, however, had continually rejected his rival's increasingly detailed memorandums not just because they contained proposals that were too radical for his taste, but because he believed them to be a form of insubordination. Indeed, by the new year Halder had become so piqued by von Manstein's persistence that he convinced von Rundstedt that his chief of staff – whose ideas the commander of Army Group A now considered to be flights of fancy – should be 'moved on' to make better use of his talents and, on 27 January, von Manstein learned that he had been given command of a paper corps in a military backwater. His ideas, however, were not lost, for by the time he was preparing to move to a small town 120 miles north-east of Berlin, Hitler had already expressed his dissatisfaction with Halder's Third Deployment Directive.

Despite his innate conservatism and his distaste for von Manstein's methods, Halder nonetheless found himself increasingly enthusiastic about the main effort forging its way through the Ardennes and across the Meuse. It was a position confirmed by the outcome of an Army Group A war game held on 7 February. Organized by von Manstein to take place two days before he left for his new post, it convinced him that Halder was now coming round. As a consequence, OKH began to feed OKW the outline of the spurned staff officer's plan. This process can be followed in Jodl's diary entry for 13 February, which states:

I hand over to the Führer a summarized report, from which the great possibility for formation of a centre of gravity south of the line Lüttich [Liège]-Namur becomes obvious (at least five times the strength of the forces committed north of that line). I bring to his attention that the thrust against Sedan is a tactical secret path, where one can be surprised by the God of War. If the French attack from the south flank, we must veer to the south.[47]

In fact, Hitler was already aware of the existence of von Manstein's scheme after Rudolf Schmundt, his adjutant, had come across it while visiting the headquarters of Army Group A at the end of January. Schmundt subsequently arranged for the plan's author to discuss his proposals with Hitler at the Reich Chancellery on 17 February. At the meeting the Führer revealed his enthusiasm for Army Group A's strengthened attack. There was an important difference of focus, however, between the two men: while von Manstein looked for von Rundstedt's spearheads to push west all the way to the coast as well as south behind the Maginot Line, Hitler was fixated on Sedan. The differences led the banished officer to write one final detailed memorandum on the subject which he sent to Army Group A:

The *aim of the offensive in the West* must be to *bring about a decision on land* [emphasis in the original]. For the limited objectives given in the present deployment order, the defeat of [the] largest possible enemy grouping in Belgium and the seizure of parts of the Channel coastline, the political and military stakes are too high. The goal must be the final victory on land. Operations must therefore be directed [immediately] towards achieving a final decision in France, and the destruction of French resistance.[48]

Hitler, meanwhile, spoke to Jodl and asked him to order Halder to develop a new directive based on von Manstein's concept. In fact,

Halder was already working out the practical details of just such a plan and, having met with Hitler and von Brauchitsch on 18 February, produced the Fourth – and last – Deployment Directive six days later. It was this document that was to be enacted as Germany's offensive against France and the Low Countries as *Fall Gelb* (Case Yellow).

Fall Gelb was a remarkably bold blend of 'experience, intuition and understanding'. [49] Army Group B with three panzer divisions would attack into the Netherlands using Eighteenth Army and central Belgium using Sixth Army. Everything about von Bock's advance was designed to make Gamelin believe that this was the main effort, and so the Luftwaffe was to initially focus on supporting Sixth Army while airborne forces would be deployed against the position known as Fortress Holland and the key bridges over the Albert Canal to aid the ground advance. The attack on the Netherlands had been questioned due to the country's challenging terrain and the resources that would be required to force its capitulation. Göring, however, demanded the country as a base from which to launch future Luftwaffe operations against Britain while also noting that its occupation would deny the Allies a base from which they could bomb Germany. It was also believed that Fortress Holland might be reinforced by the Allies in the midst of their offensive and then used to threaten the Wehrmacht's northern flank. The invasion of the Netherlands therefore became a subsidiary offensive for von Brauchitsch's troops, but one of considerable import to *Fall Gelb* and German strategy. Meanwhile, as Army Group C demonstrated against the Maginot Line in order to contain its defenders, Army Group A was to move across Luxembourg and Belgian territory to reach the Meuse centred on Sedan. On the right, Fourth Army would be led by a panzer corps of two panzer divisions to cross the Meuse around Dinant while on the left, Twelfth Army would fall on Sedan using five panzer divisions and the motorized corps.

Advancing through Luxembourg, the non-armoured Sixteenth Army was to seal off the left flank of the penetration south of Sedan and, by engaging the northern end of the Maginot Line, feign a turning movement to its rear in order to tie up French resources in the area.[50]

At this stage, it had not been decided whether the crossing of the Meuse was to be accomplished by the panzer divisions before the arrival of the infantry, or a pause to be taken for the infantry to arrive and assume the lead. Moreover, mindful of the old military dictum that 'no plan survives first contact', the Germans only formalized theirs as far as the Meuse for Army Group A in order to retain a degree of flexibility: much would depend on how the enemy reacted to the offensive. For now, the plan only speculated about what might happen after the Meuse had been crossed, but highlighted the possibility for 'an operational probing attack by armoured and motorized elements and of pushing toward the mouth of the Somme river'.[51] There was no mention of a simultaneous thrust south behind the Maginot Line. Halder had embraced a high degree of boldness, but he was not willing to put the entire operation in jeopardy for what he considered to be a non-essential manoeuvre when resources were tight and the co-ordination of the attacking formations was challenging enough already.

The plan was divisive. While von Manstein and Guderian lamented the fact that the Fourth Deployment Directive had clipped the radical wings of the original scheme and in so doing had preferred operational success to strategic victory, many seem to have regarded the plan as far too risky. Similarly, while some advocates of armoured warfare dubbed Halder the 'gravedigger of the Panzer force', some infantry generals who were uneasy at the potential of mechanization and motorization deemed the plan 'crazy and foolhardy'.[52] Having had command of the main effort taken away from him, von Bock wrote despairingly in his diary: 'I can't warm to this operation, because it has to bog down if the French haven't taken leave of their senses ... [and] Army Group B will be too weak to carry out the missions left to it.'[53] There were also concerns expressed by a number of senior officers – particularly those from the traditional arms – that OKH was placing the relatively untried panzer divisions centre-stage while the tried and tested infantry languished behind as a support player. All of the old arguments about the vulnerability and weaknesses of armoured forces were brushed down and now given a specific operational context: Were armoured forces capable of penetrating the Ardennes quickly? Was it possible for panzer divisions to establish themselves across the Meuse without close infantry support? If armoured and motorized elements did exploit the river crossing, wouldn't they risk dangerous exposure if they advanced far ahead of the infantry? The sceptical von Bock seemed to sum up the concerns of many when he wrote to OKH:

> You will be creeping ten miles from the Maginot Line with the flank of your breakthrough and hope the French will watch inertly! You are cramming the mass of the tank units together into the sparse roads of the Ardennes mountain country, as if there were no such thing as air power! And, you then hope to be able to lead an operation as far as the coast with an open southern flank 200 miles long, where stands the mass of the French Army![54]

By this stage, von Rundstedt had completed his transformation from a supporter of von Manstein's original idea to a doubter of the Halder plan. Recognising that his success depended on the achieving of operational surprise followed by speed and momentum, he had understandable concerns considering he needed to cross the Ardennes, the Meuse and then, most likely, conduct an extended dash to the coast. It was at this point that von Rundstedt's traditional leaning came to the fore because he could not help but think that the operation's risk could be significantly mitigated by the panzer divisions and infantry working together as they had in Poland. It was not for nothing that Halder noted in his diary that the commander of his main effort was 'sceptical about the effectiveness of the armoured wedge. Is afraid that the second and third echelons would not be able to catch up.'[55]

Just such issues were raised on 15 March 1940, when a meeting to discuss the Army Group A attack was held at the Reich Chancellery. The gathering included Hitler, Halder, von Rundstedt and his competent but utterly conventional new chief of staff, Georg von Sodenstern. The latter had taken an immediate dislike to OKH's plan and was to have a considerable influence on his commander's deepening reservations about it. On 22 February, in a formal submission to von Rundstedt, von Sodenstern wrote:

> I am not convinced that even the reinforced panzer and motorized units will manage to force the crossing over the Meuse in the kind of breadth that is necessary for operational purposes. Yes, I doubt, to begin with, that they will be in a position to cross the Meuse River even only here and there, holding the bridgeheads thus gained until the following infantry division would be able to make room for an operational exploitation featuring the necessary breadth and depth ... But even if that should come off successfully, the panzer and motorized units by that time will be so 'exhausted' that sending them deep into enemy rear areas will no longer offer any chances of success.[56]

Also present at the meeting were the senior commanders of Army Group A's formations: Generaloberst Günther von Kluge commanding 4th Army, which included General Hermann Hoth's XV Panzer Corps consisting of 5th and 7th Panzer Divisions and an infantry division; 12th Army's General Wilhelm List; and 16th Army's General Ernst Busch. They were joined by General Paul von Kleist, the fifty-eight-year-old commander of a new formation, a panzer group, who was an upstanding Prussian cavalryman and an officer who 'never compromised with the Nazis or anyone else'.[57] It was Panzer Group Kleist that would lead Twelfth Army – to which it was subordinated – to the *Schwerpunkt* on the Meuse, and the formation was put in the hands of a traditionalist such as von Kleist because the High Command wanted the formation to be used with restraint and for Guderian to be controlled. The panzer group itself consisted of the 1st, 2nd, and 10th Panzer Divisions in Guderian's XIX Panzer Corps, 6th and 8th Panzer Divisions in Major General Georg Hans Reinhardt's XXXXI Panzer Corps, and 2nd, 13th and 29th Motorized Divisions in General Gustav Anton von Wietersheim's XIV Motorized Infantry Corps. Formed on 5 March to provide a distinct organization for the armoured spearhead, it consisted of 134,370 men and 41,140 vehicles including 1,222 tanks (which was half the total German number and were painted with a 'K' for Kleist for identification). If von Kleist's vehicles had been placed nose to tail on a single road, they would have extended over 600 miles.[58] It was just the sort of powerful concentration of panzer divisions that the traditionalists had feared, for at a stroke it made independent panzer operations far more likely and more viable.

While von Rundstedt, von Sodenstern and Busch, who did not understand tank warfare, all raised various concerns at the Reich Chancellery meeting with Hitler about the armour-led offensive, it was left to Guderian to represent the views of von Manstein and to argue that there should be no dilution of the plan's boldness. Halder recognized the concerns of both parties, but told the conference that, given the operation had been successfully war-gamed several times, 'We must resort to extraordinary means and bear the attendant risk.'[59] He added that the armoured spearhead should not only lead the infantry to the Meuse, but cross it and create a bridgehead before the infantry arrived. This, Halder opined, would make best use of the surprise appearance of the panzer divisions on the river, and help maintain the momentum of the spearhead's advance. In this way, he concluded, more opportunities would be created than if the panzer divisions were forced to pause. It was an opinion that won Hitler over and so it was decided that elements of Panzer Group Kleist would bounce the Meuse in a single push rather than waiting for the infantry to arrive. Halder noted in his diary on 17 March: 'The Führer now approves the preparations made and is manifestly confident of success ... Decision reserved on further moves after the crossing of the Meuse.'[60]

The detailed planning of the attack could now continue on a firm footing, although the conflicting demands of the panzer divisions and those of the infantry would be manifest throughout the process. In this vein, while List respected the decision that von Kleist's panzer and motorized divisions would lead his infantry army up to and over the Meuse, he did everything in his power to ensure that his subordinate's panzer group was kept on a short leash. This caused von Kleist's highly capable chief of staff, Oberst Kurt Zeitzler, endless difficulties. Perhaps the best example of this was the way in which List denied von Kleist the space that his divisions needed to advance by limiting Guderian's vanguard corps to just four roads in an attempt to slow its advance to the speed of the infantry. In fact, the decision had the opposite effect, because Zeitzler merely demanded that Guderian advance hard and fast from the outset, moving ahead of the infantry and thereby allowing them to use whatever roads they required. Reinhardt and von Wietersheim, denied the space they needed to attack abreast of Guderian, would follow immediately behind and then fan out as they reached the Meuse. It was anything but ideal yet Guderian recognized the importance of traversing the 105 miles from the German border to the river as quickly as possible, proclaiming to his officers: 'In three days the Meuse, on the fourth day across the Meuse!'[61]

The Allies had no idea that the Germans intended to send their main effort through the Ardennes and across the Meuse, and Gamelin was resolute in his belief that the enemy would attack on the traditional invasion route. They failed to seriously consider that the Germans might change their plans after the capture of their secret documents on 10 January largely because senior officers could not comprehend what an alternative plan might look like, and since the French were only primarily interested in the detail of what faced them north of the Ardennes, the picture of German movements and deployment they obtained was necessarily incomplete. Intelligence also helped to confirm their assumptions because it identified increasingly large German concentrations of tanks and motorized units east of Holland and Belgium. Gamelin therefore read the numerous reports about the developing strength of Army Group B and was more confident than ever that the enemy was about to fall into his trap. Such was his optimism that he sought to augment Plan D with the so-called Breda Variant by pushing formations beyond the Dyle, past the Scheldt and into the Netherlands to Breda (and no further than Tilburg) to link up with ten Dutch divisions. This 'enhancement' sought to ensure that the Dutch forces were not isolated, safeguard the important port of Antwerp and retain valuable territory and resources. To achieve this, Gamelin strengthened the French First Army Group on the Allied left wing with Seventh Army – the most highly mobile and capable French army – from the General Reserve near Reims. This was the very formation that the Germans feared might be in the ideal position to strike at the exposed southern flank of Army Group A after it had crossed the Meuse. On 12 March 1940 a directive to General Alphonse Georges, the pedestrian commander of the North-East Front which included First and Third Army Groups, formally adopted the Breda Variant as part of Plan D. Georges already harboured concerns about the Allies' ability to occupy defensive positions on the Dyle, and now this amendment demanded that Seventh Army advance up to 110 miles to Tilburg while the Germans needed to move only fifty-five miles. It was also a move that would have the effect of significantly reducing the threat to von Rundstedt's flank while significantly increasing the number of first-class formations that the Germans could encircle if his formation reached the Channel coast.[62]

Suddenly, the Breda Variant cast doubt on a basic French assumption. The British did not like it and Georges was moved to pronounce: 'This is an adventure. If the enemy should be feigning in Belgium, then he can manoeuvre elsewhere. We should therefore not employ our reserves for this operation! This is nothing more than a dream!'[63] Gamelin ignored this jibe and put it down to the signs of the strain that Georges was beginning to show. The commander of the North-East Front had been hit by four bullets during the assassination of King Alexander I of Yugoslavia in Marseilles in 1934 and latterly there had been questions raised about his ability to concentrate, his patience, and his nerves.[64] Colonel Jean Petibon, the head of Gamelin's staff at Vincennes, thought that Georges should have been replaced while the British military attaché in Paris, Colonel William Fraser, opined that he was 'not a fit man and that the weight of responsibility which would be his in war might be too much for him'.[65] Why Gamelin did not replace him may have had something to do with the lack of better alternatives or the fact that, with every passing day, the replacement of the man who had overseen the preparations of his Front with one who had not might have proved counter-productive. It may just be that the French Supreme Commander simply avoided his responsibility. Indeed, when he was asked in January 1940 about Georges's competency, he replied, 'We shall not know until the first clash comes. In 1914 there were many officers and men who failed, but old Joffre handled the situation with great firmness. Will the *Blitzkrieg,* when it comes, allow us to rectify things if they are the same? I must say I don't know.'[66]

As it was, the final Allied plan, one which assumed the Belgians and Dutch would invite the French and British to enter their countries if and when the Germans invaded, involved Seventh Army advancing into the southern Netherlands by the coast while, on its right, the BEF and French First Army rushed to the Dyle.

Having held the Germans for the requisite period, the Belgian defenders would fall back from the Albert Canal, which ran close to their border with Germany, to take up a position on the Dyle from Antwerp south to Louvain. On their right flank, nine divisions of the BEF were to defend 12.5 miles of front down to Wavre, while fifty divisions of First Army covered twenty-two miles to Namur. This French sector included the area that Gamelin considered the most dangerous avenue of approach – the Gembloux Gap. From Namur, Ninth Army's left flank was to move into Belgium to take up a position along the Meuse while its right remained stationary as the river ran through French territory. On Ninth Army's right, Second Army was also dug in on the Meuse from Pont á Bar, four miles west of Sedan, to Longuyon and acted as a hinge for the movement of First Army Group into Belgium and the Netherlands.

By the beginning of spring 1940, both the Germans and the Allies had plans that were being refined, with staff officers working on their details to ensure that they could be applied as efficiently and effectively as possible. Yet on both sides there were senior figures who questioned the ability of those plans to deliver what was required and were frustrated that decision-makers were failing to ask the right questions and look in the right places for answers. Such concerns, however, were trampled over by those in key appointments, the men of influence who seemed to retain a confidence in their schemes. They, of course, had anxieties of their own, private concerns of a type that always bedevil commanders on the eve of operations. Were the right personnel in critical posts and would they work well with their peers and subordinates? Were the right formations and resources assigned to the right sectors? How would the enemy react? And how would both plan and personnel survive the strain of contact with the enemy? Planning dealt with some of these issues, but other preparations were also needed to ensure that both sides were in the best possible condition for the campaign.

CHAPTER THREE

Final Preparations

THE PHONEY WAR WAS A LONG TEST for France's devotion to making the necessary preparations to fight Germany. As Daniel Barlone wrote in November 1939: 'No one talks of the war now. Winter is on its way and we are convinced that Hitler will not attack before the spring ... The whole world seems to be unruffled. Shall we really have this war? Or shall we remain facing each other, for years?'[1] Some argued that the war would not necessarily lead to the trading of blows and the prospects of confrontation would 'die away', but generally the population just wanted to 'get on with it'. At first, this caused anxiety across the nation and particularly in the north-east which, once again, was going to be at the forefront of any action. The government and military hierarchy nonetheless went about their business with an admirable briskness and poise as they enacted their plans. The system worked tolerably well once some early issues had been solved, and war production increased while mobilization produced more troops. The government also worked hard to promote calmness in the population by reassuring them that, despite the challenges ahead, France *would* win, as she had earlier that century. Anything that upset the continuing preparation for war was avoided; it was to be business as usual. Arrangements were, however, made for those living along the

Franco-German frontier to be moved to departments in the south of the country. Civil servants also drew up contingency plans for the evacuation of the population from the capital, but these would be put into action only *in extremis* and were not publicized. In fact, some 500,000 people left Paris of their own volition in the days after the declaration of war: most were frightened by the prospect of German air raids and had no concerns about jobs and money, but the majority heeded official advice and stayed put.[2] France settled into a quiet groove: it was at war but as yet there were only short, local skirmishes while commercial, political and everyday life continued largely as before. Indeed, during December 1939 the French Cabinet spent a considerable amount of time discussing the intricacies of family law.[3]

By the early spring of 1940, however, a dangerous lassitude had embraced France. Even though military commanders knew that better weather made a German attack more likely, the population seems to have been lulled into a state of false security. Journalist Alexander Werth wrote that 'Life in Paris became quite normal'[4] with the political merry-go-round still turning and on 20 March Paul Reynaud replacing Daladier as prime minister, although the latter remained minister of defence. Reynaud was a decisive man and had serious reservations about Gamelin's suitability for the job of Supreme Commander and, by extension, his plans and preparations. He immediately began to make arrangements to replace him when the time was right. In the meantime, he hoped that the German invasion would be further delayed so that France was strengthened not only by the production of more war resources but also by the perspicacity of his leadership. The troops at the front knew nothing of this and some were concerned by yet another change in government, with Daniel Barlone writing, 'The moral effect on the troops is bad ... Our enemies do not waste their time over parliamentary manoeuvres which are both unintelligible and disconcerting. Spring is now here, the time of trial is probably at hand and look what a government we have!'[5]

The troops commanded by Barlone, in common with many others along the French eastern border, found life extremely tedious during the Phoney War. Although the way in which an individual's time was filled very much depended on his unit, formation, sector and role, days tended to be dreary. For those deployed at the northern end of the Maginot Line to the North Sea coast, the critical task was to develop the Line's second phase of light defence works. This manual construction absorbed time and energy but was hardly designed to make the troops better soldiers or any military organization better at its primary defensive task. Initially, the novelty of the situation and fine weather allowed morale and motivation to remain robust. Even so, Barlone, who had been given command of a 2nd North African Division horse transport company just behind the Maginot Line in Lorraine, had observed in late August 1939: 'The men of the reserve come in without undue haste, without the enthusiasm of 1914, or even that of last year, being fully persuaded that they will be sent home in two weeks' time, and annoyed at not being able to complete the harvest.'[6] Unlike in 1914, when there were Alsace and Lorraine to retrieve, in 1939 there was no such motivation, leading Barlone to write: '[T]oday we desire nothing ... We know our land is safe from invasion, thanks to the Maginot Line.'[7]

The fighting spirit in Barlone's unit was not high to start with and soon, as in many comparable French outfits, it was eroded by monotony and chronic equipment shortages and, when winter came, by rain and darkness, frost and snow. Attempts to raise morale by allowing access to local estaminets, and arranging entertainment in the larger towns and cities, village film shows, games of football and the like were appreciated, but could do little more than only temporarily warm and lighten the hearts of damp, cold and bored troops. Recently mobilized reservist Pierre Roussel, serving five miles south of Sedan, noted in his diary during a particularly foul spell of weather in December 1939:

Life is bad at the moment. It is very cold. There is mud everywhere and even simple tasks are difficult in such conditions. We smoke and yarn when the weather is too poor to work, but most often we toil with frozen hands … We have almost forgotten why we are here. I think that prison might be preferable to this routine.

Men who had joined up to fight found that there was, in fact, very little fighting during this period of stand-off, with any military activity often being limited to patrols. 'We are forced labourers rather than soldiers,' wrote Roussel. 'I hardly ever see a rifle and only have the vaguest notion how our key weapons work and should be maintained.'[8]

The winter months were a difficult time for all troops living in the field who had to work long hours in poor conditions to ensure that their section of the line was fit for purpose. As the official history of the British 5th Division notes:

During the appalling weather conditions of the 1939–40 winter, first wet and muddy, then cold and hard, the division worked strenuously to improve their positions; digging deeper, revetting and wiring. Field and anti-tank guns, machine guns and other support weapons were cunningly concealed in the then fashionable disguise of houses, haystacks and chicken sheds … It was difficult, however, to believe that there was a war around the corner.[9]

The impact of the worsening conditions at the front, however, seems to have affected the second-rate troops far more than those in Billotte's First Army Group. Lieutenant Colonel Sumner Waite, an American observer touring French First Army, found morale 'splendid everywhere' and he noted that there was a clear desire throughout the ranks 'to do away with the threat of German domination for good and all'. He also made a point of emphasizing that the reservists gave the impression 'that they had been soldiering for years', and praised the 'keenness and enthusiasm of reserve officers as well as regulars', noting 'a gallant and pugnacious spirit was met at every turn. They're ready to meet the best the enemy has'.[10] Morale and motivation closely reflected a formation's fighting capability. Billotte's formations retained their fighting spirit over the hard winter months, while those further south struggled to maintain what little they had.

Gamelin's headquarters was aware that certain formations of the Ninth and Second Army seemed to lack the *esprit des corps* of their sister formations towards the coast, but would have been far more concerned had the reverse been true. Of course, the troops disliked the hard physical labour in such conditions, but the spring would surely see a change when the back of the work had been broken and the weather improved. Indeed, over the winter of 1939–40, far from being worried about conditions at the front or, more specifically, at that part of the front they assumed would meet the main German effort, the French High Command became increasingly confident. Continued improvements in rearmament, the progress on the second phase of the Maginot Line, good news about the improvements made to the Belgian and Dutch armies and their defences, all led to a sense of well-being at Vincennes – and also ushered in the refinement of the Breda Variant to Plan D.

Underlying everything was the increased size of the army, which had grown to ninety-four divisions by the spring of 1940, including five that were partly mechanized cavalry divisions, three that were light mechanized divisions (DLMs) and seven that were motorized infantry divisions. There were also three new heavily armoured divisions or Divisions de Cuirassiers de Réserve (DCRs), which were established for armoured breakthrough in the wake of the German victory in Poland. Smaller than the DLMs, they had 158 medium and heavy tanks and a single battalion of motorized infantry. Yet just as the capability of France's infantry divisions varied wildly, a note of caution must be expressed here: the DCRs only contained half the number of tanks that each was established to receive and the divisions lacked the balance in other arms that would enable them to be flexible and of high utility in a defensive confrontation. By May 1940, only 1st and 2nd DCRs were at anything like operational strength and, with no likelihood of an armoured breakthrough being required in the short term, they were held in reserve.

There is little doubt that the High Command drew assurance from the improvements that the French army had made since the outbreak of war, but digging in was not cost-free. Every hour that a soldier spent moving earth from one place to another was an hour not spent in training and an hour nearer to the German onslaught. Stringing barbed wire across your company's front was all very well, but it encouraged a mindset which relied more on the defensive properties of field works and less on a soldier's own military skills. Indeed, by the spring of 1940 Gamelin was presiding over an army that desperately needed shaping and emboldening. The training that would have helped to provide this, so often relegated to a subsidiary activity during the development of defences and commonly postponed or cancelled due to inclement winter weather, began in earnest during late March. Seventh Army, for example, undertook exhaustive training in terrain similar to that north of Antwerp where they were scheduled to meet the enemy, and the two DLMs under General Prioux practised engagements in territory similar to that they would find at the Gembloux Gap.

Yet in those areas where more substantial defences were required, such as that held by General Charles Huntziger's unimpressive Second Army before the Ardennes, the digging and building continued. Consisting of five divisions in two corps, Second Army held a sector of forty-seven miles on French soil, partly along the Meuse around Sedan but then along the far less formidable River Chiers heading east through La Ferté towards Longwy. The front included the Sedan sector, where developing defences on the west bank looked down on the open slope to the river on the opposite side. Yet it was not Sedan that Huntziger believed to be most at threat – on 7 May he declared, 'I do not believe that the Germans will ever consider attacking in the region of Sedan'[11] – but the area between the end of the Maginot Line and Sedan, the area known as the Stenay Gap. This large, flat, open valley, he perceived, could well be a route taken by the Germans in order to outflank the main defensive wall. Huntziger therefore positioned the competent XVIII Corps in the Stenay Gap while the less impressive X Corps defended the Sedan sector. Although 55th Division at Sedan itself was an unimpressive formation, General Pierre-Paul-Charles Grandsard, the X Corps commander, deemed it to be considerably stronger than 71st Division on its right flank. Indeed, Grandsard became so concerned at the latter's leadership and preparations in April that he took it out of the line and into reserve for remedial training and replaced it with 3rd North African Division. Thus X Corps relied for its counter-attacking ability on four independent tank battalions and a division that did not have its senior commander's confidence.

It was no coincidence that Huntziger's first exercise scenario in April 1940 was 71st Division leading a counter-attack by X Corps towards Sedan after the Germans had made a crossing from the town. The conclusion drawn from this valuable piece of work was that 55th Division had to significantly slow the enemy if the corps' counter-attacking force were to have the time that they needed to assemble, form up and strike back. If the 16,000 men of this division were merely rolled over, Grandsard's ability to assert his will on the battlefield would be extremely limited. A great deal was therefore expected of the four regiments of 55th Division, a Category B formation comprised largely of older reservists and almost wholly officered by them. In fact, 96 per cent of 55th Division's officers were reservists, although its regimental commanders were regulars. Commanded by General Pierre Lafontaine, it had arrived on the west bank of the Meuse at Sedan in October 1939, joining 147th Fortress Infantry Regiment and working assiduously thereafter to improve its defences which, to a large extent, were seen as a means by which to ameliorate its lack of fighting ability. Sedan was built largely on a loop in the Meuse which cuts deeply into the east bank. That loop also has the river flowing across its base, thus creating a large island in the middle of the river, surrounded on three sides by the east bank of the Meuse. As this would make the island vulnerable to the enemy if they reached the east bank, the French decided in November 1939 to withdraw their main line of resistance away from the river bank in this area. The line was eventually built as part of the second-phase Maginot Line constructions which commenced during the autumn of 1939.

Up to the end of April 1940, Second Army used enough concrete to cover thirteen acres to a depth of one foot.[12] At Sedan, Lafontaine oversaw building which included dozens of blockhouses intended to deprive the enemy of momentum. The defences were developed along the lines of X Corps orders, which stated: '[T]he defence will be organized into circular fighting positions or centres of resistance, capable of defending themselves when isolated, even if bypassed by enemy infantry and tanks. As a consequence, the fighting positions or centres of resistance will be interlocked with obstacles of terrain, woods, villages etc.'[13] Second Army also worked on a second line of defences some nine miles behind the principal line of resistance. The result was that Second Army spent twice as much time in construction work as it did in training. Although in terms of priorities for resources the Sedan sector continued to rank below the needs of the Stenay Gap, the ground opposite Sedan was a construction site throughout the winter and into the spring. While Lafontaine's large command bunker at Fond Dagot, five miles south of the Sedan defences, was completed by early May, 55th Division continued to be engaged in work completing their defensive works and was still waiting for vital items such as bunker doors and steel shutters for the embrasures.

When the weather improved and hours of daylight increased in March, 55th Division had begun to benefit from more training as Lafontaine established an intensive three-week programme instigated for regiments behind the lines. Yet even this rather late attention to a pressing need came with its own set of problems. When on 6 May 331st Regiment completed its training, for example, it replaced in the line 213th Regiment, which then went for training. The latter had been in the same position since October 1939 and knew its ground intimately, but 331st Regiment took over its sector with little more than an hour-long briefing, a file of important information and whisper of *'Bonne chance'*. To complicate matters even more, although every regiment had its own clear sector of command responsibility, each of the three sectors contained units from other regiments. This system did provide an element of continuity in each sector when a regiment was removed for training, particularly as units of 147th Fortress Infantry Regiment remained resolutely in occupation of the forward positions across the division's front, but it also fragmented the regiment when in the line and was a potential recipe for command and control chaos under pressure. All regimental commanders were well aware of this fact and also that they and their units would have to rely on field telephones and runners to communicate during battle. During the first week of May, field telephone communications cables still lay above ground and looped over tree boughs waiting to be put underground, where they would be safer from enemy bombs and shells.

The regiments were also only too aware of the deficit in their defensive firepower. Along 55th Division's front there were a mere fifty-six modern anti-tank weapons – approximately one third of what it should have had – and three light anti-aircraft batteries. They also lacked mines – Second Army had only 2,000 anti-personnel mines available for its formations' principal line of resistance – and X Corps had only 1,972 anti-tank weapons with which to cover both banks of the Meuse. 55th Division received 422 of them, forty-two per mile of front. According to doctrine, the deficiencies were to be made up by artillery firepower. The division was directly supported by seven battalions of guns and could also call on a further four if required, as well as two heavier batteries of X Corps artillery. By May this amounted to 140 guns, which was more than double the usual support for a division.[14] Lafontaine's satisfaction at having such artillery support would have been tempered, however, by Grandsard's confession to him that the X Corps' artillery was 'without the capacity and without the will for command':[15] 110 out of 280 of its NCOs had been relieved of their duties by May.

Despite the clear deficiencies in Second Army, and particularly X Corps, the formation gave Gamelin no cause for concern. The Supreme Commander visited Huntziger twice in nine months and on both occasions found nothing to be terribly awry.[16] He made suggestions for improvements to Second Army as he did to every formation he inspected, but they were suggestions rather than orders and, as such, were not always acted on. This was Gamelin's command style – he argued that at 'certain levels of responsibility, it is no longer a matter of giving orders but of persuading'.[17] It was a technique totally out of step with what was required and as a result the French army – and particularly Ninth and Second Armies – atrophied during the winter of 1939–40. Thus, although observing in mid-September, 'When the war really begins [in the west], it will come as a very rude awakening,'[18] Gamelin used the time available to temper the likely shock of a German attack extremely poorly. He was far too satisfied with merely increasing the size of the army rather than with developing the fighting capability of what he had, and he was guilty of naïve assumptions about German intentions which left his defences vulnerable. In short, the French Supreme Commander failed to provide the leadership and direction that was central to his role and which his army desperately needed.

Superficially, there was nothing wrong with the French army, and Sir Edmund 'Tiny' Ironside,* the bulky, British, 6' 4" tall Chief of the Imperial General Staff, wrote after a visit to the front in January 1940:

> I must say that I saw nothing amiss with it on the surface. The Generals are all tried men, if a bit old from our point of view. None of them showed any lack of confidence ... In 1914 there were many officers and men who failed, but old Joffre handled the situation with great firmness. Will the *Blitzkrieg*, when it comes, allow us to rectify things if they are the same? I must say I don't know. But I say to myself that we must have confidence in the French Army. It is the only thing in which we can have confidence.[19]

Alan Brooke had also made an age-related entry in his diary, having met Gamelin a few months earlier and written, '[He] struck me as looking old and rather tired.'[20] The British had their concerns about Plan D, the Breda Variant and the ability of the French to stand up to a German onslaught, with Brooke complaining, 'I am not happy about our general attitude, we are facing war in a half-hearted way ... I feel that the Germans would have been tackling the situation very differently',[21] but they were also acutely aware that they were the junior partner in France and had challenges enough of their own without getting involved in the business of their ally. It was therefore left to the civilian French deputy Pierre Taittinger[22] to raise concerns about the military state of play. Visiting the Ardennes front in his capacity as a member of the Parliamentary Army Committee during March 1940, he was shocked to find the critical sector of the 1870 campaign so poorly prepared for a German onslaught.

---

* John Buchan is said to have based his character Richard Hannay from *The Thirty-Nine Steps* on Ironside's early career in German South-West Africa.

On the day of his return, Taittinger submitted a report to the war minister and to Gamelin which stated:

> In this region, we are entirely too much taken with the idea that the Ardennes woods and the Meuse River will protect Sedan and we assign entirely too much significance to these natural obstacles. The defences in this sector are rudimentary, not to say embryonic.[23]

He was also unimpressed with the divisions defending the area, noting that the Sedan sector was a particular 'weak point', that he 'trembled' at the thought of it being attacked and going as far as to say: 'This place spells misfortune for our troops.'[24] A riled Gamelin informed Georges of the report, and the latter, somewhat taken aback by Taittinger's criticisms, asked Huntziger to reply. Huntziger was furious that a civilian had cast aspersions on the professionalism of the army – and no doubt also because these criticisms were being taken so seriously by his superiors – and perceived Taittinger's remarks as a personal attack. In a measured response, however, the commander of Second Army endeavoured to put the politician's mind at rest, stating that Belgian resistance and the natural obstacles of the Ardennes, together with the Meuse, needed to be taken into consideration when assessing the security of the sector. He concluded by saying, 'I believe that there are no urgent measures to take for the reinforcement of the Sedan sector.'[25] Everything was in hand.

Like the French, the BEF spent the period of the Phoney War putting on muscle, developing their sector of the border for defence and undertaking what training time and the weather allowed. Its commander, the fifty-three-year-old Lord Gort – John Standish Surtees Prendergast Vereker, sixth Viscount Gort – had been Chief of the Imperial General Staff at the outbreak of war but, having been replaced by Ironside, took to his new field appointment a robust working knowledge of the capabilities of the British army together with youth and vitality.[26] Yet despite a distinguished First World War in which he had been wounded four times, mentioned in despatches on nine occasions and awarded the Military Cross, the Distinguished Service Order with two bars and the Victoria Cross, some doubted Gort's ability to command a large organization and believed him to be limited 'in mind and personality'.[27] II Corps's Alan Brooke for one was concerned by his lack of wider focus and his inability to delegate, and wrote in his diary on 22 November:

> Gort is a queer mixture, perfectly charming, very definite personality, full of vitality, energy and joie de vivre, and gifted with great powers of leadership. But he fails to see the big picture and is continually returning to those trivial details that counted a lot when commanding a battalion, but which should not be the concern of the Commander-in-Chief.[28]

Brooke himself dealt with his superior with all the tact that he could muster, but continued to be frustrated by details about training schedules when there was a desperate need to sort out the command and control hierarchy with the French. Brooke's divisions and units were also constantly asking him when vital equipment was going to arrive. 15/19 King's Royal Hussars (KRH) was a cavalry regiment which would lead 3rd Infantry Division forward to the Dyle Line when the time came. The regiment's history, written by Guy Courage, who was a lieutenant in 1940, later stated: 'As far as equipment was concerned, the harvest of the fruit of twenty years' parsimony would find a scarce and rotten crop. Our only real assets were the sterling qualities of the officers and men, who, confronted with a desperate situation, willingly gave of their best.'[29] It was positioned near Lille, just a few miles from the frontier with Belgium, and 'settled down to a steady round of training and maintenance; time might be short but there was much to do'.[30]

The French High Command had a high degree of confidence in the BEF, something which was reflected in its position on the left flank of First Army, but although encouraging noises were made by the Belgians and Dutch about their own successful preparations, Gamelin did not have any real sense of their capabilities. Belgium, with a population of just 8.2 million, had experienced many invasions in its history, which was why there were so many fortifications along its eastern border. Many had been restored and modernized by May 1940, by which time the country had eighteen infantry divisions, two partly motorized divisions and two mechanized cavalry divisions: a total of 650,000 men and 270 largely obsolete light tanks commanded by General Raoul van Overstraeten. Yet despite Belgium's attempts to improve its armed forces over the past one or two years, the quality of training and equipment was poor. The air force consisted of 377 aircraft, half of which were also obsolete, and, to make matters worse, the country's air bases lacked the space in which to disperse the aircraft, leaving them clustered and vulnerable.[31] The Belgian plan for defence, despite the lack of joint staff talks, anticipated Gamelin's moves: the Germans would be delayed first along the frontier, then along a line ten miles to the rear before the main position along the Albert Canal from Antwerp to Maastricht and then down the Meuse to Dinant. Both the Albert Canal and the Meuse were studded with casemates and fortresses which, it was hoped and believed, would take days for the Germans to overcome, thus providing the French and British forces with the minimum of seventy-two hours to reach the Dyle position.[32]

As for the Ardennes, the Belgians did not consider them as a priority given their limited resources, while both they and the French made the dangerous assumption that the other would take responsibility for the area's defence. As it was, van

Overstraeten covered the area with a single army corps known as 'K' Group – named after its commander, Lieutenant General Maurice Keyaerts – which largely consisted of 1st Ardennes Light Infantry (Chasseurs Ardennais) Division, 1st Cavalry Division and some engineers. Once 'K' Group had delayed any German attack, it would withdraw not towards the French border but north behind the Meuse between Liège and Namur to reinforce the units defending that sector. Behind 'K' Group there were no substantial defences for sixty miles on an eighty-mile-wide front before the French border. Into that void, the French were preparing to push nothing more than their own delaying force, which consisted of five cavalry divisions, three cavalry brigades and light advance units from the divisions defending the border. The defence of the Ardennes in neutral Luxembourg was even less well-defined, with a mere thirteen officers, 255 armed gendarmes and 425 soldiers. Their role was to man the Schuster Line – named after its architect, Joseph Schuster – which consisted of frontier posts and to use iron gates at the bridges on the border with Germany together with barriers to block roads heading west and cause delay to the German advance. The area identified by the Germans for their main armoured attack was, therefore, defended by a collection of mobile light French and Belgian formations, some Luxembourg policemen and a number of road blocks. Even so, Gamelin maintained that the complex terrain was the equivalent of several heavy divisions and it would take the enemy five to nine days to penetrate the region and at least another week before he would be in a position to cross the Meuse.

The Netherlands did not offer a buffer zone to France as Belgium did, but the Allied High Command recognized that the more German troops that could be absorbed by the country, the easier it would be to hold central Belgium. The difficulty of defending the Netherlands, however, was its long border with Germany and lack of strategic depth, which left both the capital city of Amsterdam and The Hague, the seat of government and the Dutch royal family, just sixty miles from the frontier. The likelihood of a protracted fight was further undermined by a military left weak due to the nation's long-term neutrality. Despite the country's population of nine million, which was slightly larger than that of Belgium, just 300,000 men were called up and formed into eight infantry divisions in four corps, together with a motorized division, two independent brigades (A and B) and twenty-four frontier defence battalions.[33] The force had just forty aged tanks, 656 mostly horse-drawn artillery pieces, a few dozen anti-tank guns and an air force of 124 aircraft, of which half were modern.[34] By the spring of 1940, the professional head of the army, General H. G. Winkelman, and the commander of the field army, Lieutenant General Jan Joseph Godfried Baron van Voorst tot Voorst, were extremely concerned about the severe limitations of their small, poorly organized and trained force. As Dutch historian L. de Jong later wrote, reflecting on this period: 'The fact that the previous war [Great War] had spared us, had filled many of us with a curious belief that history would repeat itself ... So we hoped that the storm once again would not touch us, and if so, that our army would give a good account of itself.'[35] Plans were made, nonetheless, to use the advantages that the Netherlands had for its defence: a plethora of water obstacles and mechanisms for deliberate inundation.

Although the Netherlands lacked large fortresses, the country-side was peppered with around 2,000 machine gun-armed pillboxes which were incorporated into a defensive plan based on a 300-year-old system. With frontier troops holding a line on the border, the ground behind them east of Utrecht was to be flooded while troops manned defensive lines to the west. These included the forward Ijssel Line, with the Grebbe Line behind it in the north and Meuse Line, itself backed by the Peel-Raam Line, in the south. Along the coast, the key Dutch cities were protected by a final fallback position, known as Fortress Holland, from which it was planned, if necessary, to fight for three months while awaiting reinforcement. However, just like Belgium, the Netherlands made its plans more in the hope than the expectation that they suited Allied thinking. Although Gamelin's Breda push by Seventh Army sought to link up with Dutch divisions in the south of the country, this had not been co-ordinated with them. Indeed, even as the French were making plans for this controversial advance, the Dutch were becoming concerned that their southern flank might be exposed by any Belgian withdrawal from the Albert Line. As a result, Winkelman decided to abandon the Peel-Raam position when the Germans invaded, and tuck the wing of his force back to protect the southern part of Fortress Holland. This meant that if Gamelin's Seventh Army advanced to link up with the Dutch in the vicinity of Breda-Tilburg, it would in fact find itself vulnerable in a defensive void.

Given that they had handed Germany the initiative, there was little France and Britain and the neutral countries on Hitler's western frontier could do but prepare and await events. In many ways, however, although the strategic decision as to when to order the launching of the offensive was OKW's, the Wehrmacht's predicament was broadly the same as the Allies': it made preparations and waited for its orders to attack. By late March, formations began to be moved into position, resources gathered, plans were refined and final training took place. It was a delicate business for all the power that the Wehrmacht was husbanding, as Halder was keen to ensure that the correct balance was struck between Army Groups A and B. Although von Rundstedt's formation was the main effort, von Bock's formation was to facilitate its success. Indeed, Halder noted that the Army Group B attack must be 'staged in sufficient strength' and that the operation 'designed to contain enemy forces must be launched concurrently with our big offensive'.[36] Ensuring that balance between the two army groups was therefore essential, but throughout the spring the Germans continued to struggle to provide both with what their generals required. From November 1939, divisional commanders were asked to indicate the level of combat effectiveness of their formations in a monthly evaluation report so as to properly assess German fighting power.[37] This revealed a far from uniform picture, despite a gradual improvement, with peaks and troughs depending on new cohorts and the arrival of equipment. Thus, although heavy infantry gun ammunition production rose by 86 per cent during the Phoney War,[38] there remained great shortages and none more so than in all things required for motorization. As a consequence, only 10 per cent of German divisions were motorized and this remained an army highly dependent on horses.[*39] The strength of a typical infantry division was 17,000 men, along with 5,375 horses requiring fifty-three tons of oats and hay daily and the requisite amounts of water.

As Karl-Heinz Frieser comments, 'In terms of its structure, the German army resembled a lance whose point consisted of hardened steel; but the wooden shaft looked all the longer and therefore ever more brittle.'[40] Indeed, only half of the 157 German divisions were combat-ready by the spring of 1940 as Germany struggled to replenish depleted ammunition stocks and losses of tanks, trucks and aircraft incurred in Poland. A mere 1,000 trucks a month were being produced by the spring of 1940 as the tonnage of German imports fell by three-quarters which in turn drastically undermined industry's access to raw materials. As a consequence, the military had to use whatever vehicles they could. In 1938 the Wehrmacht already had 100 different types of lorries and 150 different types of motorcycle, and by the following year this number was added to by Czech and Polish vehicles as well as a further 16,000 civilian vehicles that had been commandeered. This papered over cracks but made securing replacement parts a logistical nightmare. Indeed, on 13 March 1940, von Bock noted of one of his armoured formations:

> I could not characterize 4th Panzer Division as fully attack-
> capable as it did not have a single serviceable command

---

* In the First World War Germany used 1.4 million horses and in the Second World War 2.7 million.

vehicle and all requests for additional vehicles and spare parts had come to nothing. Many of the panzer division's junior company commanders could never lead their companies in practice, because there is no way to train at the front. Training opportunities absolutely have to be provided.[41]

Meanwhile, by April fuel stocks were also causing concern as they had dropped two thirds since the beginning of the war. This situation had a dramatic effect on the formations preparing to go to war, with von Bock confiding to his diary: 'The fuel situation is alleged to be so tight that the motorized divisions aren't receiving enough fuel to train their drivers.'[42] The commander of Army Group B became so agitated that his concerns were not being taken seriously that he sent a senior member of his staff, Oberst Karl Gerber, to Berlin to find out whether his reports were being read and what was being done about them. The officer arrived in the German capital on 8 April to find that both OKW and the high commands for all three services were so busy with the launch of another invasion that nobody could afford the time to meet with him.[43]

At a vital time in the run-up to *Fall Gelb*, Hitler launched a campaign in Scandinavia. Although it aimed to be completely independent of *Fall Gelb*'s schedule and resources, its shadow fell heavily across preparations for it. *Fall Weserübung* opened against neutral and poorly armed Norway on 9 April.[44] Its aim, aside from increasing German control of the North Sea, was to ensure that Britain was not able to stop the supply of iron ore reaching Germany from Sweden via the Norwegian port of Narvik. And with the Luftwaffe interested in establishing airfields in Denmark, it too was invaded. The Norwegian episode was a humiliating failure for the British and French forces, which sought to land their troops to reinforce the defenders. Denmark capitulated within a few hours, and although some fighting continued in Norway until 10 June, its defeat had been all but sealed five weeks earlier. It was an operation that Hitler called 'not only bold, but one of the sauciest undertakings in the history of modern warfare'.[45] Yet although a painful kick to the Allied solar plexus, *Fall Weserübung* highlighted a number of German problems. Chief among these was Hitler's inability to recognize that in the chaos of war plans rarely survive contact with the enemy. His persistent anxiety and his desire to meddle in operational details was a source of considerable frustration to experienced military commanders who looked on at their Supreme Commander's lack of self-control with growing incredulity. General Walter Warlimont observed Hitler at close quarters at this time and later pointed to 'the impression of truly terrifying weakness of character on the part of the man who was at the head of the Reich', and Jodl noted 'a striking picture of agitation and lack of balance'.[46] When success had been gained, however, Hitler immediately became calm and basked in the glory of another victory as he turned his full attention – and apprehension – to offensive operations in the West.

Although it might be argued that the resources required by *Fall Weserübung* were a drain on those required for *Fall Gelb*, the campaign did help to further refine staff procedures and provided a useful boost to German morale at an important time. Von Bock, however, continued to receive reports from his subordinates bemoaning a lack of vital equipment and no doubt wondered what impact the fighting in Norway and Army Group A's elevation to becoming the main effort in the plan were having on his own formation. Yet he had to accept the fact that von Rundstedt was receiving the best troops and the most modern equipment, and that his panzer divisions were voracious consumers of highly prized assets and resources. One of the newest was Major General Erwin Rommel's 7th Panzer Division, which was established in mid-February. A bold infantry officer, Rommel believed that lessons he had learnt in the First World War about the need for speed, momentum and excellent communications made him well qualified to command an all-arms armoured division. His consisted of 218 tanks, of which half were Czech and the other half PzKpfw IIIs and IVs. It also had an armoured reconnaissance battalion, two rifle regiments (each of three battalions), a motorcycle battalion, an engineer battalion, an artillery component of thirty-six guns and seventy-five anti-tank guns. While deftly picking up the technical knowledge required to command armour, Rommel immediately made it his business to impress his personality on his new formation and took no time to dismiss one battalion commander who did not meet his high standards. By the spring, he was putting the formation through its final paces on exercise and remedying any errors by further training. Rommel particularly emphasized blanketing the enemy with fire, the impact of shock through rapid movement, traffic control drills, all-arms co-operation and communications. His slim figure, rapid movements and penetrating Swabian tones became well known around the division, where he turned up at unexpected times and in unexpected places to gain knowledge and raise performance. One biographer has described his personality thus:

> [B]risk, incisive, intolerant of slackness or infirmity of purpose, inventive, questioning, essentially business-like, enormously energetic. Rommel believed with passion in physical fitness, going for early-morning runs himself and [being] intolerant of flabbiness or inertia in his subordinates. He had always been impatient of others, whatever their rank, who failed to meet his own standards, and with the authority of a divisional commander his impatience was fortified … Rommel was by instinct a humane man, but his kindness never extended to toleration of inadequacy.[47]

He was above all a man of action, instinctive and not prone to over-analysis, and he was disparaging of 'unnecessary academic nonsense'.[48]

Corps commanders kept a watchful eye on their divisions, trying to ensure that, while they retained their own identity, they co-operated with their fellow divisions fully in their endeavour to achieve the wider aim. Rommel's corps commander Hoth found this difficult as the commander of 7th Panzer Division was so consumed with the preparation of his division and, Hoth found, had ambitions and a personality that were not always conducive to the team effort. Guderian would have had no truck with such a prima donna, partly because there was only room for one such individual in his corps and that place was already taken by himself. But both Guderian, at corps level, and Rommel, at division level, used the force of their characters and leadership to drive their formations on. Of the three divisions under Guderian's command, it was Major General Friedrich Kirchner's 1st Panzer Division that had been selected to lead the corps and, in so doing, lead Panzer Group Kleist, Twelfth Army and Army Group A. The formation moved into its assembly area near Cochem, twenty-five miles south-west of Koblenz, in March and began its final, rigorous training. Oberstleutnant Hermann Balck, the forty-six-year-old commander of the division's 1st Rifle Regiment, had great respect for Guderian, saying later that: 'He was very hard to get along with, and it's a tribute to the German army, as well as to Guderian's own remarkable abilities, that he was able to rise as high as he did within the German army.'[49] He recognized the energetic corps commander's hand in their training schedule, which sought to identify faults and correct them, and remarked:

Training was intensive and geared toward the future mission. Up to the breakthrough at Sedan, everything was practised down to the last detail in map exercises and every situation was run through in similar terrain also with live firing and air support. The Mosel [Moselle] River had to stand in for the Meuse River and I did not let up until every last man in my regiment knew how to handle rubber boats like an engineer.

I let the exercises run their course, completely and freely, to get everybody accustomed to independent action. This was the best preparation for an offensive that I ever saw.[50]

Mechanized infantry, meanwhile, practised attacking fortified locations while tanks refined their movement and both were supported by the Luftwaffe. Units rehearsed their tasks until these became second nature, and there was distinct training for units with special roles such as the combat engineers, who would be responsible for dismantling barriers and destroying bunkers. Like Rommel, Guderian was mindful not to break the morale of his formations, but he too pushed them hard. By early May, every panzer division had been put through a systematic training regime which would enable them to reach the limits of what a formation could achieve on the modern battlefield. They were, however, just one small part of the huge forces that had been drawn up by both sides for the coming campaign.

On the eve of battle, the German army was 4.2 million men strong, with a further one million in the Luftwaffe and 100,000 in the Waffen SS. Of this total, some three million were designated for the war in the West in 135 of 157 divisions: forty-five in Army Group A, twenty-nine in Army Group B, nineteen in Army Group C and forty-two in reserve. They were armed with 7,378 guns and 2,439 tanks, of which nearly 1,500 were Mk I and IIs, 349 were Mk IIIs and 278 were Mk IVs. The French army stood at 5.5 million men in 117 divisions, of which 2.24 million were in ninety-five North-East Front divisions with eleven in reserve. With the British, Belgian and Dutch contingents included, there were a total of 151 Allied divisions. Of these, fifteen French divisions, ten British divisions, twenty-two Belgian and ten Dutch divisions – a total of fifty-seven – faced the twenty-nine German divisions of Army Group B, while against the forty-five divisions of Army Group A there were a mere eighteen Allied divisions, with two Belgian divisions providing a delaying force in the

Ardennes. Altogether, the Allies boasted 14,000 guns and 4,204 tanks, of which 3,254 were French, including 300 SOMUA S35s and 274 Char B1s. The Germans had 2,589 operational aircraft in the west by May (including 1,090 bombers, 316 Stukas and 923 fighters) but while the French had 2,562 aircraft, a mere 879 were operational and at the front, with a further 1,687 held back in reserve. The RAF had some 384 operational combat aircraft in France on 10 May 1940, with another 1,500 held back in Britain. Thus, together with Belgian and Dutch aircraft, the Allies could muster 1,453 machines at the front on the eve of battle, while the Germans could call on 2,589.[51]

The time was coming when both sides would finally play their hands in what the great Prussian military theorist Karl von Clausewitz argued was an event that 'closely resembled a game of cards'.[52] War is indeed an unpredictable business. Chance and luck play their part, as do factors as various as morale and the weather. But the most effective armed forces are those which can respond quickly to the unexpected, deploy their resources skilfully and exploit opportunities. The fact that the Allies outnumbered the Germans in every key area except aircraft was not in itself important since *Fall Gelb* sought to avoid precisely the sort of drawn-out, attritional contest where such statistics might carry weight. Instead, the German aim was to take the initiative and hold on to it until a decision was reached, and from the late winter onwards Admiral Wilhelm Canaris, the experienced and capable chief of the Abwehr, the military intelligence service, prepared the ground. Rumours were carefully spread, intentionally indiscreet conversations were staged and some lines of communication were left insecure, all in an attempt to mislead the French. German intelligence, meanwhile, learned a good deal that was to its benefit from its agents and captured enemy personnel, and from monitoring radio traffic, counter-espionage and its secret listening posts. Gradually the Germans learned that the Allies were falling into their trap by expecting a mechanized Schlieffen Plan and had acquired a sound idea of their organization, troop concentrations and even of Plan D. The French put remarkably little emphasis on security at any level, with Daniel Barlone writing, '[C]ountry folk, inquisitive folk, and spies wander about continuously. No one makes any attempt to preserve any secrecy about our defences.'[53] The Germans consequently built up an accurate and detailed intelligence picture of the enemy and his deployments, and this was updated with the latest information gleaned from patrols and Luftwaffe reconnaissance.

The French made various attempts to secure information about enemy intentions which included material from Enigma, the principal German cipher machine which was used for encrypting and decrypting messages. With the assistance of Polish cryptanalysts in Paris and British code-breakers at Bletchley Park, the Allies learned a good deal about the Luftwaffe's plans and deployments for the coming campaign. It was thoroughly misleading information, however, not because the Germans knew that their code had been cracked – they did not – but because they had decided to favour Army Group B with the vast majority of air support in the initial stages of *Fall Gelb* in an attempt to mislead the Allies into thinking von Bock's army group was to be the main effort once the offensive began. The ruse was successful, for Enigma decrypts seemed only to confirm Gamelin's assumptions about German operational intentions.[54] Indeed, along with the information recovered from the captured German plans in January, the French High Command might well have felt confident about its predictions and been surprised to learn that its enemy was in fact extremely security-conscious. For despite appearances, the Germans put great effort into maintaining the integrity of their plans, which is why on 11 January OKW issued an order that 'No officer may learn of something to be kept secret if they don't absolutely have to have knowledge of it for official reasons'.[55] Officers were to learn what they needed in order to perform their duties, but nothing more and no earlier than absolutely necessary. Moreover, as an extension of this, the time between putting the army on alert for the offensive and it starting was gradually reduced from a week in the autumn of 1939 to just twenty-four hours by late winter.

Breaches of misleading Enigma traffic, Abwehr disinformation and Gamelin's belief that the Germans were limited in their choice of routes of attack, all combined to bamboozle the French as to the truth of Hitler's intentions. Indeed, such was the complacency that began to reveal itself within the upper echelons of the French army during the spring of 1940 that solid intelligence which ran contrary to received wisdom was unceremoniously rejected. German counter-intelligence officer Oberst Hans Oster, who opposed Hitler, provided considerable amounts of secret information to the Dutch military attaché, Colonel Gijsbertus Jacobus Sas. Although in and of itself, no single piece of information by Oster indicated that the French were wrongly deployed, when this material was properly assessed and cross-referenced with other intelligence, an unsettling picture began to emerge. Belgian reports indicated that the enemy was increasing his strength south of Liège, while one of the few aerial reconnaissance missions to return intact and with significant information identified German armoured and motorized formations just east of the border with Luxembourg. The French were also told that the intelligence services of Belgium and Switzerland had both received information which convinced them that the Ardennes would be the route for the main German effort. This was followed by a reliable French agent reporting in mid-April that German forces were gathering for an attack on the Sedan-Charleville-St. Quentin axis and that the offensive would open in early May and would seek to reach the Seine in less than one month.

French intelligence chiefs endeavoured to persuade Gamelin and Georges to listen, but failed. Georges's intelligence officer, Colonel Louis Baril, did show enough concern to induce his superior to correspond with Gamelin in mid-April about his worries that the Allied advance to the Dyle might leave them open to being outflanked to the south, and proposed an advance as far as the Escaut as a safer option. Such anxieties, however, were rejected by Gamelin as incomplete, inconclusive and the result of misleading information fed by the Germans. There was, it was thought, simply too much detailed intelligence indicating that the enemy's main attack would be through central Belgium.[56] During the first week of May, information that the German invasion was imminent came from more than one source. But even a summary received on 1 May 1940 from the French military attaché in Bern which stated quite categorically, 'The German Army will attack between 8 and 10 May along the entire front, including the Maginot Line. Point of main effort: Sedan',[57] was dismissed by Gamelin and Georges: any attack in the Sedan sector would surely be a diversion. The two men did become convinced, however, that the German attack was imminent for, although failing to identify the point of main effort, over the next eight days a host of French agents reported that the offensive would begin 'within days'.

In the final days before he gave the order for *Fall Gelb* to be launched, Hitler was understandably nervous. The staff of OKW sensed that, far from having total confidence in the invasion plan, he still hoped that the political fragility he had identified in his enemies would finally cause the downfall of their governments when the offensive began and that their populations would demand that an agreement be reached with him to end the war.[58] As it was, had Hitler known what was happening in London and Paris on 9 May, he might have felt even more convinced that his prediction would come true since both the British prime minister and the French Supreme Commander were on the verge of relinquishing their appointments. Having been so badly damaged by the outcome of the Scandinavian campaign, Neville Chamberlain was considering his position and would resign the next day, while in the French capital Reynaud had called a cabinet meeting to discuss the 'state of command'. At the meeting, the French prime minister spoke for an hour against Gamelin. It was, according to one of those present, like 'witnessing an execution'[59] and only Minister of War Daladier spoke up in Gamelin's support and even then just to say, 'I disagree'.[60] Reynaud's intention was quite simple – to force former premier Daladier out of the government and to sack Gamelin – and the meeting had started what he hoped would be a swift process for all concerned. Hitler, meanwhile, informed that the weather was due to be fine on the following day and for as far ahead as the meteorologists were willing to forecast, decided to launch *Fall Gelb*. At around noon, Keitel signed the order specifying A-Day as 10 May and X-hour as 0345 hours. Having received the high-alert signal warning that an attack was imminent, Rommel wrote a brief letter to his wife:

Dearest Lu,
We're packing up at last. Let's hope not in vain. You'll get all the news for the next few days from the papers. Don't worry yourself. Everything will go alright.[61]

General Kirchner at 1st Panzer Division received the same signal and within minutes his headquarters was a hive of activity as orders were received for units to prepare for a move to the border and its jumping-off points. Everything worked just as it had been rehearsed, with the advanced elements of the staff at the head of the division moving off at 1630 hours and the main body following thirty minutes later. Hitler, meanwhile, had boarded a special armoured train, *Amerika*, at a small, out-of-the-way station just outside Berlin and headed north. Such was the secrecy surrounding the journey that even his press chief, Otto Dietrich, thought he was going to visit shipworks in Hamburg, and his secretaries believed he was travelling to Norway and Denmark to visit the troops. The train travelled slowly northwards as the forward elements of the three army groups moved towards their attack positions and, just after 2100 hours, received the code word 'Danzig' confirming that the attack was to be unleashed at 0345 hours. One officer from 1st Panzer Division, Major von Kielmansegg, later recalled:

> The long columns of Panzer Group Kleist moved forward on three large routes, with the infantry primarily using trucks. The night enveloped us; not a single light could be seen. The march was slow and difficult. It was also very difficult to establish an itinerary permitting the forward movement of the column and the simultaneous joining of it by small detachments coming from all directions.[62]

Hauptmann Helmuth Mahlke was at his airfield at Hennweiler, just south of Koblenz, that evening. He commanded a Luftlotte 3 Stuka *staffel* (squadron) and had just been briefed in preparation for his first operational mission against the West. At 0600 hours on 10 May, his *gruppe* was to attack a French air base at Metz-Frescaty. Mahlke memorized the details of his target and went through a mental checklist. He later recalled:

> The preparations had been made. With nothing more to be done, we turned in early. But on this particular night it took me a very long time to get off to sleep. Thoughts of what tomorrow might bring were going round and round inside my head ... Had I done everything in my power to justify the responsibility placed on me? What was going to happen tomorrow, our first day of action? What did the future hold? What else could I have done – what else *must* I do – to make sure that all crews entrusted to my care got home safely?[63]

Just after midnight, *Amerika* changed tracks for the south-west and arrived at the station of Eifel near Euskirchen shortly before dawn. Cars drove Hitler and his party, which included Keitel, Jodl, Julius Schaub, his chief military aide, Schmundt, Dr Karl Brandt, his personal physician, and various adjutants, through hilly, wooded countryside to a new Führer Headquarters near Münstereifel called the *Felsennest* (Rock eyrie). As the party gathered in front of the main bunker, a rumble of distant shellfire broke the silence. Pointing to the sound, Hitler said simply: 'Gentlemen, the offensive against the western powers has just started.'[64]

CHAPTER 4

10 May – Forward

I N THE EARLY HOURS OF 10 MAY, a proclamation was issued by Hitler which was to be read by officers to all personnel on the Western Front. Nervous and already tired, their minds no doubt racing, the Reich's warriors listened intently. The last sentences were poignant:

> The battle which begins today will decide the fate of the German nation for the next thousand years. Now do your duty. The German people give you their blessing.[1]

Most remained silent when the message ended, but those in the SS cheered. The opening of *Fall Gelb* was epochal. After seven months of the Phoney War, the posturing, planning and preparation had come to an end. Europe would never be the same again and those involved felt it – some who were privy to *Fall Gelb* because they had no faith in it, others because they did. The opening moves, they understood, would be critical. Would the Allies fall into the trap or was Germany inviting disaster?

Gefreiter Otto Gull, an engineer in 1st Panzer Division, was at the vanguard of the attack and later recalled:

> I had no real sense of the general plan – that was for the generals – and only an outline of what our division had to achieve. We had been told the night before that all our training had been done to push us through the Ardennes and across the Meuse. That was our objective. We were given a vague idea that what we were doing was vital to the operation and that speed was vital. No time-wasting![2]

Gull would only learn later that the advance of his formation within Panzer Group Kleist was so dependent on the ability of Army Group B, as he described it, 'to lure the enemy bear from his cave and distract him'.[3] Von Bock's intention was to move as fast as his formations would allow him in order to undermine the opposition's defensive preparations and create an irresistible momentum. Although he lacked the mobile armoured assets of Army Group A, his task would be assisted by significant air power, which would undertake roles such as the insertion of airborne forces just minutes before the ground troops crossed the border at 0535 hours. Faced with significant fortified positions and water obstacles close to his start line, the commander of Army Group B was intent on making a major psychological impact on the enemy; if he managed as much, he might unhinge his opponent's defences and so avoid having to lay siege to his forts and waste time wearing down his positions.

Yet even if von Bock's primary objective was to engage the enemy in central Belgium using Sixth Army, his formations also had the tricky task of forcing the capitulation of the Netherlands. This would be conducted by Eighteenth Army under General Georg von Küchler. In the north, the main bulk of the Dutch forces would be engaged by 1st Cavalry Division while a simultaneous landing from barges near Enkhuizen turned the enemy. In the south, Lieutenant General Kurt Student's 7th Fliegerkorps (parachute and air-landing infantry) would strike initially to occupy a number of airfields to facilitate the arrival of more troops, and also attempt to capture the government, the Dutch High Command and Queen Wilhelmina. It was a move designed, according to Student, 'to severe the head from the snake'[4] by removing the nation's decision-making capability and which, it was believed, would lead to the collapse of its defences, undermine its will and create the conditions for Dutch capitulation. If the operation failed to achieve the desired result, other airborne troops were also tasked with securing bridges at Rotterdam, Dordrecht and Moerdijk to allow 9th Panzer Division to penetrate Fortress Holland on the third day of the offensive.

This attack south of Rotterdam, the main effort of Eighteenth Army, had little hope of achieving success unless the airborne forces could seize critical bridges before they were destroyed by the defenders. These troops, with their ability to be inserted into areas that were otherwise inaccessible, were central to the German ability to overcome the Netherlands quickly. Even so, the risks inherent in airborne operations, a very new way of applying force at specific points, were considerable: the method of insertion, the necessarily light armaments, the vulnerability to encirclement, the requirement for resupply and rapid relief – the list was a long one, reflected *Fall Gelb*.[5] The plan was the embodiment of a carefully considered high-risk, high-gain solution to Germany's strategic dilemma and so the use of airborne troops reflected the character of the offensive. On 27 October 1939, Hitler had summoned Student to Berlin for consultations about how airborne forces might best be used in an invasion of the West. The officer was quick to stress to his audience 'that one had to realize that paratroopers and the airborne arm were a completely new, untried and – so far as Germany was concerned – still secret weapon. The first airborne operation had to employ every resource available, and be delivered boldly at a decisive time and place.'[6] At this time, Hitler was merely looking for any means of dislocating the enemy and so invigorating Halder's early schemes. But airborne operations became more critical to the final version of his plan, for they became the key which would unlock von Bock's front, the means of adding early momentum and avoiding the laborious business of having to kick the enemy's barriers down.

The German attack on the Netherlands caught the Dutch by surprise despite the fact that the previous evening the Abwehr's treacherous Hans Oster had telephoned an anxious Gijsbertus Sas at the Dutch Embassy in Berlin and said simply: 'Tomorrow, at dawn.' Oster's information had helped keep the military authorities on high alert since the previous autumn, but the repeated German postponements of their invasion had made the Dutch wary of his warnings. As it was, they were caught unnecessarily unawares when the Luftwaffe began bombing their airfields in the early hours of 10 May. These raids were the first part of the German attempt to achieve superiority over the battlefield in order to safeguard the insertion of the airborne forces, protect the ground forces and allow the Luftwaffe to support the wider operation. Oberst Martin Fiebig's *Kampfgeschwader* 4 (KG4), for example, attacked the naval airfield at De Kooy north of Amsterdam, destroying thirty-five aircraft, and the air bases at Schiphol, where one third of the Dutch medium bombers were rendered inoperable, and at The Hague, where twenty-one fighters were accounted for. KG 4 then assisted KG 30 and KG 54 in attacks against Dutch ports and communications. These raids, together with losses to German fighters in aerial combat, led to the Dutch having just seventy dispersed aircraft operational by the end of the day.

The raids in the Netherlands were replicated in Belgium and France, where surprise was also gained and, in the face of insignificant anti-aircraft fire, considerable damage was done to facilities and aircraft before the latter could get airborne. With no radar or early-warning systems, those on the ground generally only began to realize what was happening when the bombs started to fall. Ordered to attack an aerodrome just south of Metz, the ground and air crew of Helmuth Mahlke's Stuka *staffel* were up well before dawn. The airfield at Hennweiler, some forty-five miles east of the border with Luxembourg, came to life at 0400 hours, the beams of the mechanics' shaded torches dancing around in the dark as the armourers attached 250 kg bombs onto the bellies of machines set out in ranks. After completing a visual check of his Stuka, Mahlke eased himself into the cockpit, was strapped in and tested the intercom with his rear gunner. Within minutes, the starter motors were jerked into life by a rapid turn of a mechanic's handle and Mahlke fired up the engine. Across the airfield, other pilots of the *gruppe* did the same and, he later recalled, 'suddenly the nocturnal quiet of Hennweiler was shattered by the thunderous roar of engines as thirty Ju 87s started up almost as one'.[7]

The *gruppe* flew in formation to the target area as dawn broke and crossed the border. 'Like a delicate veil,' Mahlke later wrote, 'the milky morning haze still shrouded the landscape below us. Nothing stirred. It was as if the whole countryside was in a deep slumber.' Mahlke, however, was as alive as he had ever been, his senses heightened as his Stukas closed in on the target and manoeuvred themselves into line astern as soon as the aerodrome was spotted. Then, having circled the area once, the aircraft began to dive on their individual targets like taxis peeling off from a rank. Mahlke hardly needed to think, his actions had become automatic:

A brief check: bomb switches in, radiator flaps closed, dive brakes extended, close throttle, drop the left wing and put the machine into an 80-degree dive. And suddenly the large airship hangar that was my target – and which had drifted into my bombsight with such apparent slowness only a moment ago – now came rushing up to meet me at a terrifying rate ... 2,000 metres, 1,500 metres – is the enemy flak still shooting at us? No time to worry about that now – 1,000 metres. At the height of 500 metres I pressed the bomb button as briefed. There was a slight jolt ... then the bomb was on its way. As we pulled out of the dive into a climbing left-hand turn, we watched it strike almost dead centre near the front of the hangar roof. My two wingmen also scored direct hits.[8]

On 10 May, the Luftwaffe managed to destroy over 140 French, Belgian and Dutch aircraft on the ground and in aerial combat but it recognized that the task of securing the skies was not over.[9] For the rest of the day, the air forces of all the belligerent nations endeavoured to assert themselves in order to disrupt the opposition's plans and gain information about its movements. The tenacity of the Dutch air force was to pay dividends in the immediate aftermath of the carefully choreographed insertion of 7th Flieger (Air) Division and 22nd Luftlande-Infanterie (Air-landing) Division into the Netherlands. Near The Hague, German paratroopers successfully secured three airfields but plans started to go awry with the arrival of the air-landing infantry. At Valkenburg, the first Ju 52 transport aircraft to land became stuck on the soft grass runway, which forced a further twenty-six to land on a nearby beach – many crashed and others were shot down by fighters. One Dutch pilot, Conrad Houtkooper, recalls:

> My ancient aircraft was a match for the slow transporters. I could not believe my luck when I managed to latch on to one of these beasts and was not followed by one of the Me 109s buzzing around to protect them. I managed to fire off all my ammunition in a couple of long bursts. One hit the starboard engine of the Ju 52 as it began to land. It burst into flames and crumpled and exploded in front of my eyes.[10]

By that evening, none of the three targeted Dutch airfields was under close German control and the attempt to take The Hague in a surprise attack had failed in a bloody vortex of burning aircraft and heavy casualties. It was recognized that the airborne troops would be overrun if left in situ, and so they were ordered to make their way to Rotterdam twenty miles to the south and there to reinforce colleagues engaged in the undermining of Fortress Holland's defences.

In Rotterdam itself, a remarkable *coup de main* had seen twelve seaplanes land in the middle of the city to allow two platoons of infantry to take the Wilhelms Bridge over the Nieuwe Maas. Further to the south, a series of bridges along a sixteen-mile road leading from Moerdijk – over the wide estuary and over the Rhine and Meuse rivers – to the city had also been seized following the capture of the airfield at Waalhaven. It was now up to German ground forces to advance up the road before the lightly armed airborne troops were overrun and the bridges destroyed. Dutch counter-attacks began that morning against the Wilhelms Bridge, but failed to dislodge the tenacious German defenders while Blenheim bombers from 2 Group RAF and Dutch artillery tried to stop their reinforcement by respectively attacking and shelling the airfield at Waalhaven, yet with only limited success.

Meanwhile, German ground forces pushed forward across the border with the support of specially trained commandos of the Brandenburg Battalion to capture bridges over the Ijssel in the north and Meuse in the south. Infiltrating over the border in small teams after dark on 9 May, these special forces sought to ensure that the break-in forces did not stall even as their offensive began. Most of the bridges were destroyed before the Brandenburgers had even reached the rivers – although in two instances they were blown up while the German troops were standing on them – but a railway bridge over the Meuse was captured intact and this severely compromised the forward Dutch defences. The crossing at Gennep was taken by an eight-man team led by Leutnant Wilhelm Walther. Dressed as Dutch military policemen, the Germans acted as if they were escorting enemy prisoners when they launched their assault and successfully overcame the defenders while removing the charges on the bridge. With the bridge cleared, an armoured train crossed the

Meuse and, followed by a troop train, penetrated ten miles in the direction of Breda and off-loaded a battalion of infantry.

The German advance caught the enemy in the midst of General Winkleman's pre-planned abandonment of the Peel-Raam Line but the attempt by 256th Infantry Division to link up with the forward battalion kept the Dutch forces in situ. The division lacked artillery support as it struggled across the Meuse via a single pontoon bridge, and the decision was made to attack without waiting for the guns. In confused hand-to-hand fighting with stoic defenders, the rather nervous German assault only began to make progress when a fortuitously timed Stuka raid was followed by the shells of a 105mm battery which had been hurriedly brought up. The Dutch line did not collapse, however, and it was not until mid-evening when the Dutch commander, Colonel Leonard Johannes Schmidt, ordered the position to be abandoned.

Further north, the elite SS Leibstandarte Adolf Hitler, a regiment of Hitler's personal bodyguard, led 227th Division's assault on the Dutch defences.[11] An initial punch forward found them at Zwolle by midday, but there the regiment stalled as the bridges over the Ijssel had been destroyed. Its 3rd Battalion eventually managed to force a crossing more than twenty miles to the south at Zutphen which allowed elements of the regiment to reach the Grebbe Line before the end of the day, but no breakthrough had been achieved. By nightfall, a smaller than anticipated number of Eighteenth Army formations had managed to establish themselves along the main Dutch defensive line, with all finding the enemy's tenacity in the inundated and obstacle-strewn terrain a considerable challenge to their progress. In the far north of the country, for example, 1st Cavalry Division was frustrated by 236 destroyed bridges. Indeed, some of von Küchler's divisions decided to temporarily abandon their attempts to cross the Meuse and Ijssel until the front became more stable. Von Bock had always recognized that operations in what he called the 'Dutch water-park' would be challenging and was not overtly concerned by the day's numerous setbacks. He had achieved sufficient success along the line to give hope for prospects on the second day of the offensive and, in particular, for making progress towards the southern end of the airborne corridor at Moerdijk.

While the northern part of Army Group B's offensive staggered into the Netherlands, the southern part sought to advance into central Belgium. Conducted by Sixth Army, it crossed a narrow corridor of Dutch territory defended by nothing more than border guards until running into the most southerly part of the Meuse Line, which incorporated the city of Maastricht close to the Belgian frontier. The roads through Maastricht offered an important route towards the Gembloux Gap for Sixth Army, but rather than concentrating on the city alone, the plan was to unhinge the defences in the area by attacking a broad sector of the Meuse and Albert Canal. Central to the sector was the fort at Eben-Emael. Standing six miles south of Maastricht, it acted as a strongpoint which, in conjunction with others in the vicinity, provided protection for the canal defences. It had been built in response to the German threat and stood proudly at the cutting edge of defensive technology. Completed in 1935 atop a low hill less than 100 yards from the west bank of the canal, it was a reinforced artillery position designed as much to deter the Germans as to hold out against an attack for any significant period of time. If attacked, its primary purpose was to provide artillery support for 2nd Grenadier Regiment of 7th Infantry Division, whose 2,600 men were stretched across a 5.6-mile front defending the canal. The fort was roughly the shape of an equilateral triangle, consisting of two subterranean levels and one above ground, with each separated by hermetically sealed armoured doors to protect them from infiltration. The fort boasted a 1,200-man garrison commanded by Major Jean Fritz Lucien Jottrand and thirty artillery pieces. These pieces included two 120mm guns with a range of 10.5 miles, sixteen rapid-firing 75mm guns with a range of five miles and a dozen 60mm anti-tank guns with a range of 1.8 miles. Its 360° defences were made up of ditches, trenches, minefields and barbed wire swept by thirty machine guns. Gamelin confidently expected Eben-Emael to hold out for five days but Jottrand was not so sure as his men were poorly trained and he had no confidence in the ability of the other forts along the front to mutually support each other.

Although Eben-Emael was supposedly impregnable, the Germans had obtained information about its defences which revealed that it was nothing of the sort. Chief among the chinks in its armour was a large, flat meadow on its concrete roof which, because the garrison used it as a football pitch, contained no obstacles. This, together with the fact that the position had a mere four anti-aircraft machine guns, provided the Germans with an opportunity to silence the position as part of a wider airborne operation to seize bridges over the Meuse and Albert Canal. Hauptmann Walther Koch's battalion-sized *Sturmabteilung* (Assault Detachment) was to use paratroopers in gliders to take three bridges over the canal which would be crossed by 61st Infantry Division while a mixture of eighty-five specially selected airborne infantry and combat engineers – Group *Granite* – were to land on Eben-Emael's roof, again in gliders. Commanded by twenty-three-year-old Oberleutnant Rudolf Witzig, who later called his men 'superior soldiers in every way',[12] the combat engineers were to break into the fort using a hollow charge, a new weapon which could blow through any known steel and ballistic concrete fortification, and then clear its three levels with the infantry.

Training had commenced in October 1939 without any real sense of when the operation would be launched. The airborne troops lived in a gymnasium at an airfield at Hildesheim, where they practised glider landings as well as methods and tactics specifically designed for their mission by Witzig. They trained twelve hours a day, six days a week. The *Granite* force was confined to camp, their letters censored and their cherished airborne insignia removed from their uniforms. Security was so tight that when three men decided to sneak out of camp for a cup of coffee at a nearby café, they were caught, tried and sentenced to death. 'Although the sentence was never carried out,' Witzig later explained, 'it does indicate how seriously the authorities took our security measures.'[13] Delays in the launching of *Fall Gelb* allowed the airborne soldiers more time to learn everything they needed to make their mission a success from lectures, sand tables, analysis of intelligence including aerial photographs, detailed engineering drawings of the fort – inside and out – to information gleaned from deserters from other Belgian forts. Each man was given a map of the fort in a small case, and the group even travelled to casemates in the Czech Beneš Line to practise their assault and so hone their techniques. By the time the attack came, each member of Witzig's unit could find his way around the fort blind-folded and knew the job of every member of his squad as well as he knew his own.

Group *Granite* took off in eleven DFS 230 fabric-covered gliders towed by Ju 52 transports at 0430 hours on 10 May. Nine landed on top of Fort Eben-Emael fifty minutes later after being released from their tugs eighteen miles from the objective. One of the two gliders that failed to reach its objective contained Witzig – it had been forced to land after its tow rope had snapped. Even as the young officer was making a remarkable effort to return to his airfield to restart his journey and join up with his men, the attack began. While the gliders were still skidding to a halt, the exit doors were opened and the paratroopers poured out. Having surprised the enemy, the eleven squads destroyed the fort's protective infantry weaponry and then fell on the guns – and particularly those facing the oncoming 61st Infantry Division. Within minutes, the fort's communications had been cut, its machine guns neutralized and some of its guns had been destroyed. With the garrison having fled to the sealed heart of the fort to lay fire on Walter Koch's units as they assaulted the bridges, Witzig's men began to blast open the protective steel doors and grapple with the fort's defenders and to silence the guns. Witzig himself had managed to return to his home airfield, where he ordered a reserve Ju 52 to fly to his stricken glider, reattach it and then tow it over the battlefield. Witzig eventually joined the battle at Eben-Emael three hours late and was told that the Belgian infantry had tried and failed to counter-attack the fort while the German paratroopers continued to fight to suppress its occupants. It eventually took until noon on 11 May to finally neutralize the remaining guns in the fort and so allow Koch's force, which had successfully taken two of its three allocated bridges, to relieve Witzig's men – twenty-four hours behind schedule. Over 1,000 men of the Belgian garrison were eventually extracted from the fort's bowels, including Jottrand, who had performed as well as he could under the circumstances; a further twenty-three had been killed during the battle and another sixty-two wounded. Six members of Group *Granite* lost their lives in the attack, and a further thirty had been wounded.*

The battle at Eben-Emael was, of course, just one tactical engagement occupying the German forces seeking to plunge into Belgium, but it was not the only one to fall behind schedule. Although Maastricht had surrendered quickly after being overwhelmed by German troops on the morning of 10 May, its bridge over the Meuse had been destroyed and so 4th Panzer Division's advance was delayed until 11 May while a replacement was built. Von Bock recognized the need to push forward as quickly as possible so as not to give the enemy an opportunity to settle into the Dyle Line, but he was satisfied with what had been achieved that first day and wrote in his diary on the evening of 10 May: 'I pushed where and however I could ... It is going well!'[14] The Allies, on the other hand, were equally keen not to delay their advance to the Dyle after the Belgians had sent the French government a request for assistance at 0650 hours that morning. Within a couple of hours, French and

---

* On returning to Germany, all the officers involved in the Eben-Emael assault attended a special ceremony at their base, where Hitler addressed them and awarded each a Knight's Cross. Other ranks were awarded the Iron Cross by General Albert Kesselring and promoted one rank – save for one man who, it was found, had carried a canteen full of rum into battle.

British reconnaissance units were pushing forward 'to the unbridled encouragement of the Belgian population'[15] and these fast-moving units reached the Dyle and conducted an initial reconnoitre of the area that evening, leaving the main body of the Allied force to link up with them over the coming days. Those divisions were moving forward by the early afternoon.

For Gamelin, Georges and Billotte, it was essential that the six divisions and several independent tank battalions of General Georges Blanchard's First Army moved into position swiftly in order to defend the Gembloux Gap. It was the task of Prioux's Cavalry Corps, with its two DLMs, to advance eighteen miles ahead of the Gap towards Liège to hold the Germans until at least 14 May between Tirlemont (Tienen), Hannut and Huy. Behind Prioux, in recognition of the critical importance of the Gap to the enemy, the Belgians had built some anti-tank obstacles consisting of steel bars and concrete blocks before the village of Perwez and protected them with mines and barbed wire. Meanwhile, to the north, the lead elements of General Henri Giraud's Seventh Army sped across Belgium parallel to the coast, heading towards Antwerp in an attempt to link up with Dutch forces in the Breda-Tilburg area. Their advance was swift and by 2200 hours reconnaissance units in armoured cars from the French 1st DLM arrived at the Dutch border to find total confusion. The Dutch commander responsible for the area, Colonel Schmidt, could not be found or raised on the radio and, the French were distressed to hear, the defenders were already in retreat.

Sandwiched between the two French armies, General Gort's BEF also moved east with three divisions forward and five in support to hold the line east of Brussels. The British lurched into action after something of a slow start. One army liaison officer, Philip Gribble, serving on the staff of Air Marshal Sir A. S. Barratt, the commander-in-chief of British Air Forces in France, noted:

> G.H.Q. seem to have been caught off their guard ... Quite a
> lot of people away on leave. The contrast between the real

thing and the opening phase of an exercise is very forcible....
[In the exercises] Intelligence summary trumps intelligence
summary. There is not a second to spare. And now the fact,
the real thing in practice. There is no news of our own
troops or aircraft. No messages, no intelligence summaries,
no telephone.[16]

Yet despite the lack of information, the BEF set off and made
good progress with the II Corps commander, Alan Brooke, finding
time to make a positive diary entry: 'Everything so far has been
running like clockwork and with less interference from bombing
than I'd anticipated – 3rd Division started off at 2.30 pm this
afternoon and by now its advance elements should be approaching
the Dyle.'[17] Providing reconnaissance for Major General Bernard
Montgomery's 3rd Division was 15/19 King's Royal Hussars (KRH).
The regiment had been engaged in some physical training that
morning when they learned from the BBC News on the wireless that
the Germans had invaded the Netherlands and Belgium. Lieutenant
Guy Courage later wrote: 'At first we could not believe our ears;
but it was true and, as we rushed out of our billets, questioning
and wondering, we knew that we should soon be in action and we
prayed that victory might be ours.'[18] The next few hours saw the
men make their preparations with maps issued, kit packed and
stowed in lorries, ammunition belts filled, equipment checked and
orders given. As they crossed the border that afternoon, Courage
noted that 'Excitement was on every face.'[19] A little later, the look
had turned to relief. Just after the regiment had passed through
Alost on the Escaut, the town was attacked by sixty Stukas.

Although its *modus operandi* was different in many ways to Army
Group B's due to the Maginot Line, von Leeb's Army Group C
had a role which also demanded that it exert pressure on the
enemy and pin and fix as many French divisions along its front

as possible. Thus on 10 May Seventh Army began to simulate an offensive against Switzerland which, Gamelin thought, might develop into an attempt to envelop the Maginot Line from the south. During the spring the Germans had fed their enemy a plethora of misleading information about the arrival of various elite formations in the sector in preparation for this deception and had made easily observable troop movements to emphasize its likelihood. The result was that, at the start of the campaign in the West, thirty-six French divisions were concentrated in the area of the heavily fortified Maginot Line facing only nineteen divisions of Army Group C on the German side. In this way, Army Groups B and C fixed the French where the Germans wanted them while Army Group A undertook its tacit move through the Ardennes and to the Meuse. It was to be led on a twelve-mile front by three divisions: Major General Rudolf Veiel's 2nd Panzer Division on the right, Major General Friedrich Kirchner's 1st Panzer Division in the centre and Major General Ferdinand Schaal's 10th Panzer Division on the left. These formations, von Kleist recognized, would have to be given the ability to break the rules of accepted operational behaviour if *Fall Gelb* were to succeed. Consequently, Guderian's leash sat loosely in von Kleist's hand. This, however, was a liberty not offered to von Kleist by his own superior, von Rundstedt. Anything that smacked of unnecessary risk and threatened to leave his three armies isolated would, the commander of Army Group A promised, bring about a prompt and aggressive reaction in order to bring the panzer group back under control.

1st Panzer Division's attack began at 0535 hours when a whistle blew and a squad of German soldiers rushed across the Sauer to disarm the Luxembourg border gendarmes. Engineers then began to deal with the concrete barriers on two bridges, one a little downstream over the Our, and to build three additional bridges across the rivers. It took just forty minutes for the bridges to be constructed, the Schuster Line of obstacles to be overcome and for the formation to start moving forward. Acting as Kirchner's trailblazers were a motorcycle company and three reconnaissance platoons in armoured cars supported by combat engineers, followed by the infantry of 1st Rifle Regiment and some artillery. The division advanced thirty miles and did not encounter any opposition before reaching the Belgian border at Martelange after three hours. Here, there was a thin line of Belgian border guards and behind them the light covering force offered by the two reinforced divisions of 'K' Group. Lieutenant General Keyaerts had established two thinly held and fragmented lines of resistance – amounting to a series of strongpoints – across the Ardennes: one forward and centred on Bastogne and running close to the border with Luxembourg, and the other behind along the Semois river close to the border with France. 1st Panzer Division's aim was to penetrate both on the first day and reach the high ground west of Neufchâteau to complete an advance on 10 May of around forty miles. The French, meanwhile, sent their own delaying force into the Ardennes consisting of the equivalent of five cavalry divisions, three cavalry brigades and some advance units from the divisions defending the border. Ninth Army sent 1st and 4th Light Cavalry Divisions and 3rd Brigade of Spahis while Second Army sent 2nd and 5th Light Cavalry Divisions and 1st Cavalry Brigade. Added to these forces were the reconnaissance squadrons of each of the divisions and corps in the two field armies.[20] How the Belgian and French forces were to work together, what their boundaries would be, who would be in command and a host of other questions had not been answered because Belgian neutrality had meant there had been no co-ordination between the two forces. The efficiency or effectiveness of this important delaying force had been severely compromised by circumstances and now, unbeknown to its commanders, its component parts were spread out over a wide front – outnumbered and outgunned – facing the *Schwerpunkt* of the main German effort. Guderian's corps, meanwhile, was expecting some opposition, somewhere and at some time and had been left in no doubt that there was no time for a gentle probing of the difficult terrain through which the formations were moving. Any delay, the three division commanders knew, would be deleterious to the achievement of the operation's aim and thus they kept in mind Guderian's adage: 'Punch with the fist rather than feel with the fingers.'

The combined power of the panzer divisions surging through the Ardennes notwithstanding, the German planners were well aware that in the close terrain relatively few defenders armed with explosives, guile and tenacity could make life extremely difficult. There was the possibility, particularly while Guderian's corps was endeavouring to arrange itself on a broad front due to its less than ideal echeloning, that the vanguard of the leading 1st Panzer Division advancing down a critical road could find itself thwarted by a few well-positioned Belgian defences. It was for this reason that airborne troops were to be inserted behind the border village of Bodange. Expecting Belgian resistance in the area, Operation NiWi (as in the towns of Nîves and Witry) was to cause chaos in the rear area, stop the defenders from being reinforced and also to thwart any attempts they might make to conduct a fighting withdrawal. Lacking Ju 52s for the mission, two companies of Oberstleutnant Eugen Garski's specially trained 3rd Battalion Gross Deutschland Regiment, an elite unit of volunteers drawn from every province of the Reich, and some combat engineers were instead to be delivered in two lifts by nearly 100 tiny Fieseler Fi 156 Storch liaison aircraft. These airborne troops were to capture two towns: a force led by Garksi was to take Witry, some 3.5 miles behind Bodange on 1st Panzer Division's route, and Hauptmann Krüger was to seize Nîves, 3.5 miles north of Witry on 2nd Panzer Division's route.

After crossing Luxembourg at an altitude of under 100 feet, the swarm of light aircraft began to land in Belgium at 0600 hours. At Witry, however, just five aircraft, including Garski's, landed where they were supposed to. A mixture of fog and small arms fire had sent the majority of the Witry-bound force off-course and it had mistakenly joined Krüger's group, only for the enlarged group to land in completely the wrong place at Léglise, 5.5 miles south-west of Witry. Krüger immediately endeavoured to link up with Garski at Witry but, having requisitioned a number of vehicles, ran into a Belgian patrol and some armoured cars. Eventually arriving in Witry at 1300 hours on foot, Krüger found that Garski and his nine men had successfully blocked the route out of the town leading to Neufchâteau. The successful arrival of this second wave had enlarged Garski's force just in time to beat off Belgian counter-attacks, which had for a time threatened to wipe them out. With his company now complete, Garski subsequently pushed forward to the rear of the Belgian defences at Bodange, where they arrived at around 1730 hours. Krüger's second lift, meanwhile, had arrived at Nîves earlier that morning to find themselves alone. Leutnant Obermeier took charge and blocked the Bastogne-Neufchâteau road before beating off several counter-attacks from Belgian and French troops.

Despite its chaotic application, Operation NiWi managed to successfully thwart enemy attempts in the area to move up important roads towards the Belgian border. Assisted by the scattering of Garski's force which suddenly turned up behind the front line, panicked reports reached French and Belgian commanders variously that 'a battalion', 'a regiment' and even a 'a division' had been inserted in the middle of the Ardennes. The effect of NiWi was to sow doubt into the minds of the defenders about where and in what numbers their adversaries might be found. In the context of events that were unfolding on 10 May, those defenders' confusion and concern were understandable. The operation did have a negative effect on the advance of 1st Panzer Division, however, since the Belgian units defending Martelange and Bodange could now not withdraw.

Situated just behind the Belgian border, 2nd Battalion Chasseurs Ardennais was put on high alert immediately after the first Luftwaffe attacks on the airfields. Their task was to block the route to Neufchâteau in complex terrain with narrow, curving roads and set themselves in two fortified villages. 4th Company was positioned in the border village of Martelange while 5th Company lay behind on the same road at Bodange. Both had covered the approaches to their villages with minefields in the fields and demolitions which made the roads immediately impassable to vehicles. Nevertheless, the preparations did little to stop 1st Panzer Division's motorcyclists first reaching Martelange, where they were immediately engaged by the enemy. Oberstleutnant Hermann Balck, the commander of 1st Rifle Regiment following on, was always grateful for the efforts of the motorcycle infantry and later testified that the combination of men and machines were able to 'get very, very quickly to the decisive point … [and so were] often out far in front of the tanks'. He added that, although 'restricted to paved roads and noisy, which made it difficult to do reconnaissance while on the motorcycle … [the machines would] move out very quickly in advance of the main forces in order to grab a bridge before it could be blown up. This happened time after time in the advance through France, and had a good deal to do with greatly speeding up the rate of movement of our main forces.'[21] Although on this occasion the bridge at Martelange had been destroyed before the arrival of the motorcycle troops, the reports that they provided Balck on his arrival allowed him to make important decisions immediately. First, the company-sized group of motorcyclists were to dismount and attack across the river in order to drive the enemy off a hill overlooking the village. It was a success. Using fire and manoeuvre – a German tactical procedure in which one squad of men moved under the covering fire of another, then reversing the roles – the speed and aggression of the attack was decisive and as the motorcyclists stormed up the slope towards the enemy, a number of the defenders began to flee. With this, the defences of Martelange quickly began to disintegrate and the men of 1st Panzer Division seized the opportunity to move forward without delay.

Two miles beyond Martelange lay Bodange, defended by Major Maurice Bricart's 5th Company Chasseurs Ardennais. Now aware that the Germans were behind him at Witry, Bricart recognized that his situation was extremely precarious. He expected orders to withdraw from 2nd Battalion, but they never came as Operation NiWi had cut communications between regimental and battalion headquarters, and then the company's explosion of a demolition charge had destroyed a field telephone line between battalion headquarters and Bricart. Thus, with no orders to withdraw and with the Germans to their rear in any case, the company was forced into a position where it would have to fight for its survival. The vanguard of 1st Panzer Division approached them after first pushing aside a screen of Belgians en route – thus announcing their imminent arrival – and immediately drew fire at around 1330 hours. The Germans were stopped first by a demolition which had cratered the road, and then by a destroyed bridge over a large stream. From here, the road led just to the south of the small village from where 5th Company overlooked it. The slope up from the stream was occupied by a platoon in some stout buildings, while another was in position just to the south of the road on some high ground – thus creating a killing zone between the two small units. The Germans later described the Belgian defences at Bodange as 'well-camouflaged and carefully fortified positions of fire. The defence was strong. Everywhere there were dense and deep rolls of barbed wire; the roads and trails were all blocked. It was not possible to go around them: that would accomplish nothing. It was necessary that we go directly over them.'[22]

As in Martelange, the Germans did not waste any time taking the decision to attack. While a company of infantry were to cross the stream and attack the village from the north, three companies of motorcyclists were to clear the high ground to the south and then use the road to link up with the NiWi troops as soon as possible. The motorcyclists took to the hill and, coming under withering fire from the village which had yet to be silenced, moved speedily on foot towards Garski's force. Meanwhile, the defence of Bodange by a depleted light infantry company continued to hold up the advance of an impatient panzer division. Although a battalion of artillery managed to get forward along the choked road and some field howitzers laid fire on the village's solid buildings, it was not until powerful 88mm guns were deployed that the defenders' grip began to loosen on the position and a battalion of infantry managed to close in.

Bricart's last message was at 1600 hours, when he reported that he had taken heavy casualties and that his ammunition was running low. Even so, it took another two hours for the Germans to start clearing the village and some bitter hand-to-hand fighting ensued. In the end, there were just twenty-six Belgian defenders left to surrender and Major Bricart died endeavouring to evade capture. The village finally fell at 1900 hours, five and a half hours after 1st Panzer Divsion had made its first approach. Even so, the formation was stuck fast for, as it later reported, 'all possible crossing points and tracks were completely destroyed. Detours were rarely found.'[23] Thus it was not until a new bridge had been built and mines cleared from the surrounding marshy ground at 2115 hours that vehicles finally began their progress forward again. Although the men of the motorcycle battalion had successfully linked up with Garski's men at 1730 hours, two companies of Chasseurs Ardennais had unhinged Guderian's schedule as they had contrived to stop 1st Panzer Division from reaching Neufchâteau on 10 May as planned.

It was a long, hot day for the German troops and while those relatively few involved in the fighting had obvious challenges, those stuck sweltering in cramped vehicles had problems of their own. For hour after hour, drivers, radio operators, gunners, loaders and commanders were tied to their tanks, trucks, self-propelled guns, armoured cars and a panoply of other motorized and mechanized vehicles. The corps had been pushed to its limits during training, and now it was being pushed to its limits on operations. Headaches and eye strain were common by the evening after a day of concentrating on the often tortuously complicated routes ahead and the instructions being given over the intercom to avoid demolitions and soft ground, to negotiate narrow bridges and evade other vehicles. Some men took breaks sitting on the outside of their tanks or perched precariously on bonnets, wheel arches or any other surface that gave them respite, a change of scene, an opportunity to stretch and to feel fresh air on their faces. One tank driver, Gefreiter Möllman, recalls: 'They clench their teeth. Stay awake at all costs! Roads, roads, roads – all the same. The men at their side talk to them, telling them anything that comes into their heads. Anything to stay awake.'[24] Guderian told his officers: 'I demand that you go sleepless for at least three nights if that should be necessary.'[25] As a consequence, the divisions were issued with 20,000 Pervitin tablets – known by panzer troops as 'tank chocolates' – which were an early version of crystal meth and used to help tank crews stay awake as they carved through the Ardennes and beyond. Adrenaline, however, would keep them wide awake until they needed to resort to drugs. As Otto Gull later explained:

> I find it difficult to believe that any man during those opening days was not anxious about what lay before him. There we were, often sitting waiting and vulnerable. We lived on our wits and on our nerves and disliked having to be idle while the infantry dealt with the enemy just in front of us. We just wanted to keep moving. It was frustrating.[26]

It was a frustrating day for Guderian as well, for all three of his divisions struggled to achieve any of the necessary momentum that day. While 1st Panzer Division encountered difficulties at Bodange, 2nd Panzer Division was also held up by a handful of defenders and it failed to take its first-day objective of Libramont.

10th Panzer Division, with two battalions of the Gross Deutschland Regiment attached to strengthen it for the protection of Guderian's flank, also fell short of obtaining its first-day objective. Advancing on two routes into Belgium, it came up against strong opposition offered by the French 2nd Light Cavalry Division in Etalle. Both 5th and 2nd Light Cavalry Divisions had pushed forward behind the Belgian 'K' Group that morning, their main body holding a line just beyond the Semois River with a focus on the main roads heading west through the area. Schaal's division took several hours to overcome the dogged resistance in Etalle which, among others, cost the lives of the commanders of both 2nd Gross Deutschland Regiment and 69th Infantry Regiment.

All Guderian could do was look on at events, encourage and hope that the second day of the offensive would be more kind. If his corps was to be able to bounce the Meuse on the move, he knew that the achievement and maintenance of momentum was essential. Without it, he feared that his divisions would stall on the east bank of the river and that all hope of mounting independent operations towards the coast would have been lost. As a result, he was driven to take risks and so, having identified a potentially weak spot in the enemy's line from intelligence reports just to the north of Etalle, sought permission from von Kleist for units on the southern of 10th Panzer Division's two routes to disengage, cut across the rear of the units on the northern route, which would pin and fix the enemy in that area, and infiltrate through the weak spot in terrain that the division's log called 'barely passable'. It put great pressure on the unsung heroes of the Ardennes thrust, the traffic police, who had to quickly find ingenious new routes for hundreds of vehicles, ensure that they were clearly marked and then manage the consequences. The complications of the proposal, together with the fact that the movement would remove the corps' flank protection units, meant that it took until dawn on 11 May for von Kleist to agree to the reorientation. He was won over by Guderian's argument that a static flank was far more vulnerable than a moving one and also by his insistence that it was the only way to ensure all three of his divisions would hit the Meuse at the same time. Guderian had also inadvertently ensured that, by shifting the southern part of Schaal's division to the north, all three of his divisions were now faced by 5th Light Cavalry Division alone.

The sluggish advance of Guderian's panzer corps on 10 May had implications for Army Group A's offensive. These were most evident at the front edge of the attacking divisions, but there were other, wider repercussions. By evening, a massive armoured and motorized tailback had built up from behind the German border across Luxembourg and into Belgium. A good deal of the problems had been caused by the decision made during planning by conservative forces in Army Group A to limit von Kleist's room for manoeuvre. As it was, he had to echelon his division with its lines of communication running back through the infantry armies, and so there were bound to be issues of bunching up and disagreements over which formation had priority over others on the very limited routes. These certainly surfaced on 10 May, for it took ten hours for a single panzer division to cross the German border, a situation that was not helped by Guderian's slow progress and saw 6th Panzer Division of Reinhardt's corps in the second echelon run into the tail of 2nd Panzer Division in the first. This meant that neither Reinhardt's corps, which was due to take up a position on Guderian's right, nor von Wietersheim's, which was to advance on Guderian's left, had room to deploy forward. Not only did this potentially affect the forward mass of Army Group A, it also left Guderian's flanks wide open to counter-attacks.

Yet despite the obvious and understandable anxiety caused by the enemy on the first day of the offensive through the Ardennes, such difficulties were not wholly unexpected and the Germans did not panic. Guderian and his commanders understood that the terrain favoured the defender and that the power of the panzer divisions could not be fully unleashed until they were properly massed and deployed in more favourable country. Halder had noted this in the Army Group A war games he had attended and, moreover, saw how the inability of Guderian to 'show his full hand' during this period would mean that the panzer divisions' infantry and not their armour would play the key role until a bridgehead had been established on the Meuse. He also recognized that in such circumstances, when the Belgian and French commanders facing von Kleist submitted their reports up the chain of command during the course of the day, the word 'armour' was unlikely to appear in them. This is just what Halder wanted, for the appearance of German infantry rather than armour in the Ardennes was far less likely to lead the Allies to question whether Army Group B was really the main enemy effort.

Indeed, at Gamelin's Vincennes headquarters on 10 May there was considerable relief that the German offensive had begun and that it appeared to be taking place just where it had been expected, with what looked like the main attack coming north of Maastricht. To this end, General Pierre Jacomet, the Secretary-General in the War Ministry, later noted: 'If you had seen, as I have done this morning, the broad smile of General Gamelin when he told me the direction of the enemy attack, you would feel no uneasiness. The Germans have provided him with just the opportunity he was awaiting.'[27] There were nonetheless reports of German forces advancing into and through the Ardennes. A 'large motorized column' was spotted by Third Army approaching Luxembourg city and Second Army identified a fifty-vehicle motorized column moving towards Bastogne, while aerial reconnaissance found about forty motorized vehicles moving west from Arlon, although this too was what the French had expected and certainly did not indicate a worryingly significant attack in the area. It was a belief reinforced by a Second Army intelligence summary received by Gamelin's headquarters at end of the day which concluded:

[E]nemy motorized elements have been pushed back by the Chasseurs Ardennais ... and have come in contact with our covering [force] elements. Belgian obstacles seem to have been sufficient to halt the progression of the enemy. THERE HAVE BEEN NO INDICATIONS OF ARMOURED VEHICLES ON THE ARMY'S FRONT.[28]

Other reports from the air force did nothing to dissuade Gamelin that this précis of the situation was not accurate. Although the information received from French aerial reconnaissance was severely limited by the 1,500 Luftwaffe machines maintaining a defensive air umbrella over Panzer Group Kleist and the formidable anti-aircraft assets of the panzer divisions themselves, it suggested that there was 'a secondary but extremely strong effort to the west of Luxembourg'. But Guderian's spearhead had not been identified and so the French continued to believe that the 'principal enemy effort would be in the region between Maastricht and Nijmegen'.[29]

The Allies thus continued to commit themselves to Plan D and threw themselves into the German trap. From the outset, therefore, the Germans out-thought their enemies, even if at this stage they were not necessarily out-fighting them. Although the Allies did score some local tactical successes on 10 May by causing the German airborne operations in the Netherlands some difficulties and slowing Guderian in the Ardennes, operationally OKH's plan to draw the enemy into central Belgium while masking the main effort through the Ardennes was unfolding tolerably well. Halder believed that a relatively encouraging first step had been taken, although he was also aware that many more such steps were needed before success could be anticipated.

Taking the events of 10 May as a whole, therefore, neither the Allies nor the Germans were particularly concerned by the way in which the campaign had opened. Both sides had made a solid start, with their plans being rolled out and the enemy reacting in a way that caused neither any great concern. Both Gamelin and von

Brauchitsch were experienced enough to recognize that, while few campaigns are won in the first twenty-four hours, great strides can be made towards losing them. The opening shots of the German invasion of the West had been fired and no side had obviously acquired the upper hand. The fate of the campaign was still in the balance, but senior commanders in both Paris and Berlin believed that the picture would become much clearer within the next seventy-two hours. They were right.

CHAPTER 5

11–12 May – To the Meuse

THE BAUWENS FAMILY had lived near the small Belgian village of Zammelen a dozen or so miles west of Maastricht for as far back as anybody could remember. They were not wealthy, but had a little land that fifty-two-year-old Maarten Bauwens farmed while his young wife, Margot, made some extra money teaching part-time in the local primary school. Their teenage children, Arnaud and Emma, were just getting out of bed and making their way to the kitchen for breakfast on the morning of 10 May when their father called for the family to gather around the wireless. The German invasion had begun. Maarten had noticed a good deal of air activity over the village that morning but had thought little of it. There had been plenty of unusual military comings and goings over the past few weeks and he was becoming accustomed to such activity. Now, however, the news that everybody had been dreading had been announced. The Germans had crossed the border and were engaged with the Belgian army. The air force was lending support but its resources had been badly damaged by earlier Luftwaffe raids.

Living so close to the border, Maarten knew that the time had come to make a decision about fleeing their comfortable home and, with it, the animals that so relied on them. In the end, it was

Margot who said that they should leave: the Germans were capable of vile acts – she remembered hearing about what they had done to Belgians in 1914 – and she would not abandon Emma to these Nazi monsters. Even as she made her case, a stream of people passed by the kitchen window on the road heading west and carrying whatever they were able in suitcases, boxes and wheelbarrows, and on bicycles. An exodus had begun and within the hour the Bauwens had packed a bag each, said farewell to their farm and livestock, and joined a growing number of people fleeing from an unseen enemy.

By the following morning, the Bauwens had walked over twenty miles. Footsore, tired and without any firm destination in mind other than to reach the French border, they tramped on. Maarten was already concerned that they had made a mistake and wondered what was to become of the home and animals that meant so much to him. Margot tried not to listen and instead attempted to keep the spirits of Arnaud and Emma as high as a few songs and the occasional joke would allow. By the evening of 11 May, the family had reached the Dyle at Louvain and there were ushered across a bridge by soldiers who, they later found out, were British. Now there were soldiers with lots of guns and what looked like little tanks between them and the Germans. For the first time since they had left Zammelen, the Bauwens felt a degree of safety.[*1]

Although most of the French population living close to the Maginot Line had been removed from the area prior to the German invasion, elsewhere they had not. While only some of those from southern Holland decided to flee their homes, there was a massive displacement of people from Belgium, Luxembourg and the French

---

* The Bauwens were eventually overtaken by advancing German troops and, taking the advice of a kindly officer, made a 100-mile return journey back to Zammelen. They arrived home on 1 June 1940 to find that it had been ransacked by German troops and that every single animal had gone.

border region after the announcement that the German offensive had begun. Most, invariably without men of military age, used whatever means of transport was available to move themselves and essentials away from whatever danger they foresaw. Accurate information was scant, but stories of bombers, tanks, airborne troops, fifth columnists and atrocities were rife and gave urgency to the civilian movement which clogged the roads and impeded the movement of the belligerents in the fine, hot weather that was to last throughout the campaign.[2] Guy Courage, a junior officer in the 15/19 KRH, noted that on 11 May the trickle of Belgian refugees coming through the lines on the Dyle had become a constant stream, demoralized and disorganized. Their number included the Bauwens. Courage recalled:

> It was a most pathetic sight, which could not fail to move the most hardened heart – carts drawn by weedy horses, hand carts, wheelbarrows, a few cars, and all sorts of 'soapbox vehicles', piled high with precious belongings, were pushed or pulled along the roads to the west by refugees. The people were, of course, all women, old men and children: on they plodded, mile after mile along the straight, dusty road, going they knew not whither and caring little what became of them.[3]

The governments of the Netherlands, Belgium and France had made no plans for the evacuation of such vast numbers of people and so their movement was unco-ordinated and unplanned. Gradually, some order was established, with certain roads being kept solely for the use of the military and routes being signposted to ease the congestion, but no official information was provided, although the refugees were increasingly directed towards Paris.

At Sedan, there had been an orderly evacuation of civilians just before dark on 10 May after it became clear that the town could well be a German objective. Those living in the town left by train, soon followed on the roads by the rural population. As elsewhere, once the inhabitants of one town or village left, there was a domino effect as those of the towns and villages they passed through were encouraged to do the same. Many left in haste with a few warm clothes and a little food and drink, but without any serious thought about what would be required. One fourteen-year-old girl, who left Amiens in the Somme department of France with her mother, sister and her sister's baby, recalls: 'We did not take much, just what we could carry. We just dropped everything and took off. We were so scared.'[4] They shut the front door and began walking along with thousands of others in the opening scenes of a human tragedy that is often overlooked in the light of the dramatic military events that were unfolding around them.

By and large, the troops ignored the refugees – there was little that they could do for them in any case – but there were some in uniform from regions most obviously affected by the German invasion who could not help worrying about their families. Most, however, were more concerned about what these people were fleeing from. The displaced offered little information, and as one soldier later wrote: '[T]he one constant statement on their lips was, "No one could stand the bombing on the Albert Canal pillboxes." We drew our own conclusions and anxiously awaited the coming Hun.'[5]

The tide of German field grey and black had begun moving west again by dawn on 11 May, having had little rest. The period after dark on the 1940 battlefield was not a time that the belligerents commonly sought to fight in, but it did provide an opportunity for other activities. On both sides these undertakings were organized, managed and overseen by officers and non-commissioned officers and completed during and after some food, and before snatching a couple of hours' sleep. Perimeter defence, sentry duty, reconnaissance, refuelling, rearming, weapon and vehicle maintenance, writing reports, orders groups, briefings – there was a host of essential undertakings that, unless properly catered for and carried out, rapidly undermined a unit's fighting capability and increased its vulnerability. One of Balck's 1st Rifle Regiment men, a twenty-two-year-old rifleman named Gerd Ritter, later wrote:

> There was little sleep – we slept where we fell, on our packs – little time for anything really. Often we had to be told to eat or else we could drift off standing up. The intensity was unremitting from the first day to the last. A blur of marching, fighting, weapon maintenance – we didn't know where we were or when it would end.[6]

The experience of an airborne soldier of Student's, Peter Meier, was much the same. He got no sleep at all for three days while fighting in Rotterdam and recalled:

> We were prepared for a lack of rest and constant night-time activity. As a paratrooper I was trained for it because our situation often involved being surrounded and waiting for reinforcement or relief … In Rotterdam on the night 10-11 May, the fighting was sporadic but it could be intense. After a tiring night it was a boost to see the sun rise in a clear blue sky.[7]

The job of those airborne forces in the Netherlands on 11 May was essentially a straightforward one – to hold on until the arrival of the ground forces. General Winkelman's task as Dutch Commander-in-Chief was similarly unambiguous – to eliminate the potentially fatal German penetration of Fortress Holland. The counter-attacks that were launched by the Dutch against the German airborne forces that day, however, all failed in the face of fierce resistance from a technically superior enemy. In Rotterdam, despite being reinforced by an infantry regiment, the Dutch made several unsuccessful attempts to oust Meier and his colleagues from their perimeter around the Wilhelms Bridge and a bombing raid mounted to destroy the structure also failed. At the other bridges further south, a number of gallant Dutch actions were also beaten off with the assistance of waves of Stukas. Similar outcomes also wrecked Dutch attempts to overwhelm the airborne troops on the three Dutch airfields near The Hague who had failed to extract themselves and head towards Rotterdam. The situation was, Peter Meier later explained, less difficult for the German airborne soldiers to contend with than for the Dutch fighting them:

> We had been mentally and physically trained for such difficult scenarios. Being encircled was something that we had practised time and time again. How often had the Dutch tried to oust an enemy fighting for his life from an objective that he would die for? Not once, I would think. So, I looked on at the growing number of enemy corpses surrounding our position with rather less surprise than the enemy did. We were supremely motivated while the Dutch found that the defence of their country was beginning to collapse around them.[8]

For the Dutch and the Allies, the news from the Netherlands on 11 May was indeed disheartening. Not only had the defenders withdrawn from the Peel-Raam Line, thus leaving the French Seventh Army without a host when it arrived in the Breda-Tilburg sector that morning, but the Grebbe Line to the north was also crumbling under intense pressure from troops who had advanced to the Zwolle-Zuphten area the previous day. Before first light on 11 May, a ferocious German artillery bombardment was followed by an attack by two battalions of the SS Leibstandarte Adolf Hitler. Leaving 227th Infantry Division to attack towards Amersfoort, the regiment was sent south-west to link up with 9th Panzer Division, which crossed the Meuse on the morning of 11 May and then threw itself towards the Moerdijk Bridge and Rotterdam. In so doing, the panzer division's reconnaissance force ran into Seventh Army around Tilburg. The resultant contact led the vulnerable yet important French formation to begin a withdrawal back to Antwerp under intense Luftwaffe pressure; it was an ignominious end to the Breda Variant, which had been – and would continue to be – of far greater benefit to the Germans than to the Allies. The extraction of Seventh Army ended any possibility of a French counter-attack south of Rotterdam, and with the SS Leibstandarte Adolf Hitler having broken the Grebbe Line defences during that afternoon – the Dutch troops only just preventing a rout[9] – and 1st Cavalry Division forcing the Dutch back in Friesland to the west of the Ijsselmeer, by the end of the day Fortress Holland was being squeezed from all landward sides.

The dominance of the Luftwaffe over the Netherlands proved to be of great importance to Eighteenth Army on 11 May. It facilitated close air support of both the defensive efforts of the airborne troops and the offensive efforts of those formations looking to dismantle the Dutch defences. It also brought home the threat posed by the German overwhelming of Fortress Holland. As one Rotterdam resident has testified: 'We feared German bombing raids above all else. The idea of our city being crushed like a Dutch Guernica was a real worry. Our eyes were constantly looking skywards for the first signs of any sort of attack.'[10] Across the front, the Luftwaffe sought to further establish its dominance of the skies. While there were some repeats of missions to destroy aircraft and airfield facilities, most of the action now took the form of aerial combat.

Adolf Galland was a German fighter pilot who had served in Spain and Poland. Although a non-flying *geschwader* adjutant at this time, he talked himself into an Bf 109E and took to the skies around the Maastricht sector. He later said that his first kill, a Belgian Hurricane, 'was child's play'. Attacking his enemy from above, Galland was not spotted and recalled:

> I was neither excited nor did I feel any hunting fever. 'Come on, defend yourself!' I thought as soon as I had one of the

eight [Hurricanes] in my gun sight. I closed in more and more without being noticed. 'Someone ought to warn him!' ... I gave him my first burst from a distance which, considering the situation, was still too great. I was dead on the target. The poor devil at last noticed what it was all about. He took rather clumsy avoiding action which brought him into the fire of my companion. The other seven Hurricanes made no effort to come to the aid of their comrade in distress but made off in all directions. After a second attack my opponent spun down in spirals minus his rudder. Part of the wing came off. Another burst would have been a waste of ammunition.[11]

The Allied air forces also took heavy losses in their attempts to stem the German flow of men, vehicles and materiel by targeting the bridges over the Albert Canal and Meuse. The Germans had anticipated this and ensured that each was well-protected with anti-aircraft guns. A Blenheim squadron of 2 Group RAF attacked the bridges at Maastricht causing little damage. One pilot who took part in the raid that day recalled: 'Running in, we were in the middle of the biggest barrage I could possibly imagine. I do not know to this day how some of us ever got through it for there didn't seem to be an inch of sky that was not covered with flak.'[12] Later in the day, one Belgian squadron lost eleven of its twelve aircraft in a single mission against the same bridge.

Even so, the Germans did not have it all their own way, for on the morning of 11 May ten Stukas of Sturzkampfgeschwader 2 were shot down while attacking ground forces between Namur and Dinant despite the protective presence of fighters. Generally, however, the Luftwaffe quickly became a constant menace to the Allied ground forces, who wondered how the enemy was being allowed such freedom. Henry de la Falaise, who was serving with the 12th Lancers in the vanguard of the BEF, felt extremely vulnerable and noted that 'Everyone is beginning to feel uneasy and even mortified about the unexpected and total absence of British or French planes' and, after being targeted, was angered when 'Some of them insultingly make barrel rolls and loops over our heads'.[13]

All along the line, troop concentrations and movements were targeted and the Stukas made a considerable psychological impact on those unfortunate enough to be attacked by them. One such soldier later wrote, 'If anybody said he wasn't frightened when the Stukas were around, he was a liar – anybody!'[14] And as Second Lieutenant John Dixon explained:

> To be dive-bombed by Stukas was a nerve-shattering experience. With their cranked wing shape, they could drop like a stone from the sky, position their bomb accurately and with the howling mechanism in operation on the dive, those on the ground were forced to scatter in terror.*[15]

But the Luftwaffe was not simply involved in close air support on 11 May. On just the second day of *Fall Gelb* attempts were begun to stifle Allied reaction to the Germans' offensive moves, and plenty of these deeper interdiction missions were conducted against the British and French formations moving up to their Dyle positions; they not only sobered the enthusiasm of the troops but also caused considerable destruction, disruption and delay. Charles-Michel Lépée was a truck driver supporting an infantry regiment in First Army and had just crossed the Senne twenty miles south of Brussels when his column was attacked. As he later explained:

> The aircraft came from nowhere and before I knew what was happening a vehicle was thrown up into the air in a massive explosion right before my eyes. Debris fell onto my own vehicle, smashing the windscreen and causing me to swerve off the road in order to avoid the burning wreck. The

---

* The 'howling mechanism' was the so-called Jericho Trumpet, a propeller-driven siren attached to the aircraft's undercarriage legs which produced a scream as the Stuka dived in order to undermine enemy morale.

truck hit a drainage ditch and immediately fell onto its side. I broke my shoulder and was to have fifty stitches in two ugly face wounds. I counted myself lucky, however, as I later heard that six drivers had been killed in that one incident.[16]

Reports from both the French formations and the Luftwaffe during this period only confirm the success the Stukas were having in both targeting enemy columns moving towards the front and making those moves more tentative and dispersed and, in some cases, forcing them to be undertaken only during the hours of darkness.

Despite being attacked from the air, the BEF and French divisions pushed forward against a growing tide of refugees and through a series of small, indistinguishable Belgian towns and villages. News had reached various units about the scale and early success of the German invasion, but details remained scant and rumours were rife. It was with some relief, therefore, that the main bodies of the divisions began to meet up with their forward elements already on the Dyle during the evening of 11 May. They immediately began to prepare their defences in a process that would take days rather than hours: guns were sited, minefields laid, trenches dug, observation points established, troops deployed, and headquarters established in a frenzy of activity. Montgomery's 3rd Division began to arrive in force at its planned sector at Louvain to the east of Brussels after a thirty-six-hour journey. 15/19 Hussars immediately pushed forward to set up an outpost on a ridge five miles to the east of the river and a standing patrol was sent another six miles forward to make contact with any Belgian troops that might be in the vicinity, and also to warn of any approaching Germans. Before they could move off, however, contact was made with Belgian 10th Division, which was heading towards Montgomery's formation.

Rather than holding the Albert Canal for several days as Gamelin had anticipated, the Belgians had managed around thirty hours since, after the fall of Eben-Emael, the German Sixth Army had advanced beyond Tongeren, south-west of Maastricht. During

September 1939: Adolf Hitler arrives in Poland. The officers behind him include Halder, von Rundstedt, von Brauchitsch, Keitel, Rommel and von Manstein.

Hitler at OKH headquarters in Berlin with three of his generals (*left to right*): Keitel, von Brauchitsch and Halder. Keitel placed great trust in what he perceived to be Hitler's genius; von Brauchitsch and Halder did not.

Above left: Franz Halder and von Brauchitsch at OKH headquarters having just heard of Hitler's plans to undertake a campaign in the West. They were horrified. *Above right:* General Fedor von Bock, the commander of Army Group B, was originally tasked with the main effort in the West, but his role had been reduced to secondary one by the time this photograph was taken.

General Gerd von Rundstedt, commander of Army Group A (*left*), and his Second Army commander Maximilian von Weichs (*right*). Von Rundstedt allowed his subordinates as much freedom of action as possible during the campaign.

Heinz Guderian (*left*) with Georg-Hans Reinhardt, photographed in 1938. Both were panzer corps commanders in May–June 1940.

Below left: General Erich Hoepner, whose corps fell on Liège, fought at Gembloux and then pushed on to Dunkirk. *Below right:* General Ewald von Kleist: a conservative officer, but the first commander of a German panzer group that contained five panzer divisions during *Fall Gelb*.

Above left: General Friedrich Kirchner, the commander of 1st Panzer Division, whose leadership drove his formation forward at the spearhead of Guderian's panzer corps. *Above centre:* General Erich von Manstein, whose offensive concept captured Hitler's imagination. *Above right:* French prime minister Paul Reynaud, who came to office just a couple of months before the German invasion.

General Maurice Gamelin, the French Commander-in-Chief (*centre*), and General Lord Gort, the BEFs Commander-in-Chief (*left*), on 13 October 1939.

Chateau de Couroy, France, 5 November 1939: Winston Churchill, the First Lord of the Admiralty, talks to General Lord Gort. Lieutenant General Henry Pownall stands on the right.

Bethune, France, 23 April 1940: General Alphonse Joseph Georges, the commander of North East Front, inspects men from the BEF's Royal Inniskilling Fusiliers accompanied by General Lord Gort.

A German armoured fighting vehicle factory. A prototype Neubaufahrzeug B is being refitted, with a Pz Kpfw.III Ausf. A. and several Sd.Kfz. 251 halftracks in the background.

French troops prepare defences along the French border during the long, cold winter of 1939–40.

At an airfield near Arras, a pilots' briefing takes place before a Junkers Ju 87 'Stuka'.

One of the best fighters in the French air force, the American designed Curtiss H75C-1 (or P-36 'Hawk'). It accounted for a third of French air-to-air kills during the campaign.

Leutnant Joachim Meissner, Oberleutnant Rudolf Witzig and Hauptmann Walter Koch – the victors of Eben Emael – listen to Hitler.

10 May 1940: a Bren Carrier passes across the Belgian border from France at Herseaux as locals look on apprehensively.

the afternoon, General Walter von Reichenau's formations looked to push on to the Dyle by attacking north-west towards Antwerp and south-west towards the Gembloux Gap. The 10th Division had therefore endured a torrid twenty-four hours – it was tired after its withdrawal and had been shaken by numerous Luftwaffe attacks – and the discombobulated Belgians initially mistook Montgomery's men for German parachutists and opened fire on them. It was a situation typical of the confusion that existed at this time, with one set of troops pulling back, another set pushing forward and neither knowing about the presence of the other until contact was made.

Although the Belgian fusillade stopped when the British made it clear that they were friendly forces, Alan Brooke, the astute commander of II Corps, soon became so concerned about 10th Division's disinclination to co-operate with him that he went to see the Belgian commander-in-chief, the thirty-eight-year-old King Leopold, at Belgian GHQ in St. André, just outside Bruges. He received little support from the monarch or his military aide General van Overstraeten and was tartly informed that, as far as they were concerned, the 10th was a Belgian division, on Belgian soil defending the Belgian capital and would not be dictated to by the army of a foreign power – no matter how well-meaning. Brooke left the meeting not only concerned about the integrity of 3rd Division's sector in the light of what he'd been told, but also the competence of the Belgian High Command.[17]

Guderian, meanwhile, having fallen behind schedule on the first day of the offensive, was keen to make up for lost time on 11 May and to ensure that his corps crossed the Semois River, which was close to the French border and the last natural obstacle before the Meuse. With the corps' divisions also manoeuvring themselves into a position whereby they would be able to arrive on the Meuse simultaneously, there was now considerable pressure on 2nd Panzer Division to move particularly quickly on the right of the corps as the Semois, the French border and the Meuse were all located to the front of Veiel's formation. By dawn the forward screen of French 5th Light Cavalry Division had begun to make contact with the three German divisions and to undertake a fighting withdrawal back into the main body of the formation. By mid-morning there was intense infantry fighting along the Libramont-Neufchâteau Line. 2nd Panzer Division looked to take Libramont as quickly as possible in order to surge on, but its tussle in the town lasted for several hours and was only concluded after some vicious house-to-house fighting forced the French to withdraw back to the Semois. It was a delay that the division could ill afford and by the end of the day it remained several miles short of the river.

In contrast, 1st Panzer Division proved too powerful for its adversaries on 11 May. The formation had its tank regiment up front, the only one of Guderian's divisions to do so, but although this gave Kirchener's attack a sense of menace and immense firepower, it was far from ideal for the battle it faced in Neufchâteau that morning. Nevertheless, in a sensible attempt to utilize the strength of his armour rather than showcase its weaknesses, the commander decided to encircle the town rather than try to blast his way through it. It was his great good fortune to strike at a weak point just south of Neufchâteau where the 5th Light Cavalry Division's 11th Cuirassier (Dragoon) Regiment and 60th Reconnaissance Battalion met. Tearing a hole in the defences, the tanks broke the French line after an hour of fighting and pushed deep into the enemy's rear while Balck's 1st Rifle Regiment, which was following up, moved into the town to clear it. As they did so, the armour forged on, rolling over the French artillery before threatening the headquarters commanding Neufchâteau garrison in the village of Petitvoir. Panic ensued.

The speed of the German attack had caught the French off guard and now vehicles hastily withdrew alongside fleeing, riderless horses, the sight of them alone being enough to ensure that pandemonium gripped the French rear area. The German armour then faced the challenge of how to attack the village housing the enemy's headquarters without resorting to the infantry. A plan was quickly formulated and put into action: 2nd Panzer Regiment continued to draw the attention of the defenders in the village while 1st Panzer Regiment outflanked them. It worked and shortly after 1500 hours, with the defenders' withdrawal route blocked, Petitvoir surrendered and in that same moment the co-ordinated defence of Neufchâteau became untenable. One last message from the headquarters informing the garrison that they had been outflanked by panzers was all that was required to spark the mass capitulation of the French garrison in Neufchâteau to Balck's men.

The men of 5th Light Cavalry Division began to cross back across the Semois in small parties during the late afternoon of 11 May and continued to arrive after dark. Here the remnants of the division joined with a single battalion from French 55th Infantry Division commanded by Captain Picault. Moving up behind them quickly, 1st Panzer Division arrived on the Semois at Bouillon before dark and immediately attempted to take two bridges that remained intact because the French had not expected the enemy's arrival so soon. Both were blown just as the armour approached them but, keen to cross the river before dark, Kirchner ordered Oberst Johannes Nedwig's 1st Panzer Regiment, elements of 1st Rifle Regiment and a wave of Stukas to plaster the opposite bank with fire. Under this cover, an infantry company led by Hauptmann Friedrich Freiherr von Kressenstein used a ford to get to the west bank, where his men then began to infiltrate the French positions. A misdirected Stuka attack against Nedwig's tanks together with a French bombardment from heavy artillery located to the rear of Sedan forced von Kressenstein's withdrawal, but his infantry moved back into Bouillon under the cover of darkness to find that the French had already left and at that moment were falling gratefully back across the Meuse. At the end of a successful day, 1st Panzer Division's log read:

A feeling of superiority over our western opponents arose in the division on this day – a day in which it encountered for the first time French forces along the second Belgian resistance line. The division has reached its goals planned for it on the second day – far in advance of its sister divisions – without regard for its flanks and in spite of the slow progress of the day.[18]

In fact, 1st Panzer Division had taken more than its own objectives on 11 May for, having spotted an opportunity to seize another crossing point over the Semois at Mouzaive, this too was taken. Mouzaive lay in the sector designated for 2nd Panzer Division but as Veiel's division had been delayed at Libramont and then by 2nd Moroccan Spahi Regiment, Oberst Karl Keltsch, the commander of 1st Panzer Brigade, used his initiative and threw a reinforced 1st Motorcycle Battalion into the gap between the Semois and the rear of the Moroccans. The bridge at Mouzaive was taken just after midnight and from there the motorcyclists pressed across the river to create a bridgehead. Kirchner immediately contacted corps headquarters for permission to use the site as a second crossing point and Guderian readily agreed. The bridge at Mouzaive was to have massive operational significance for, unbeknown to Keltsch, Kirchner or Guderian, it lay on the boundary between the French Second and Ninth Armies. In the immediate term, however, Keltsch's quick thinking had led directly not only to the panic and unauthorized withdrawal of 2nd Moroccan Spahi Regiment and its parent 3rd Spahis Brigade, but also to that of 5th Light Cavalry Brigade – and thus its troops at Bouillon – after it realized that its left flank was being exposed. The Semois front collapsed early on 12 May, therefore, not because it had been prodded by 1st Panzer Division several hours earlier, but because of the speedy appreciation and exploitation of an opportunity by Oberst Keltsch.

The third of Guderian's formations, 10th Panzer Division, successfully completed its re-routing on 11 May. Although the drive of the left flank through the rear of the right flank and out the other side had slowed the westward drive of Schaal's units, the fact that the Semois River was closer to the formation in this sector, allowing it to reach the obstacle more quickly, was a reassurance to all concerned. In the end, the complicated movement proved to be unnecessary due to the withdrawal of 5th Light Cavalry Brigade, but a crossing was taken at Mortehan by the early hours of 12 May – albeit it with the tanks lagging ten miles behind. It was at this point that the Gross Deutschland Regiment – a formation that had been temporarily attached to the division – was moved back to corps reserve in preparation for its attachment to 1st Panzer Division for the crossing of the Meuse. With Guderian beginning to reorder his corps for this undertaking and content with how events were unfolding, it was with some anger therefore that he learned from von Kleist that Berlin was concerned the corps was not paying enough attention to the protection of its southern flank. Although managing to diffuse the situation by saying that 29th Motorized Division would soon arrive to assume that very role, Guderian became acutely aware that his superiors might already be losing their nerve. Indeed, he fully expected that, as his corps' advance developed and its flank became more exposed, so they would become increasingly anxious. He was prepared, however, to do whatever was within his power to protect his corps from what he saw as any unwarranted interference.

Guderian knew that his corps was vulnerable while it was still deploying but, even though the opposition had managed to cause some local difficulties, he was relieved that these had not been exploited by the arrival of Allied aircraft, which could have done great damage to his strung-out divisions. The reality was, though, that Allied air power was being directed at what was believed to be the main German ground effort – itself still supported by the main Luftwaffe effort – to the north. What aircraft there were across the Ardennes and protecting French Second Army came from Air Group 23, which had received orders on the morning of 10 May to bomb any German columns that were spotted, but not to hit any buildings. Thus, towns and villages – just the places where enemy vehicles could be seen after they had emerged from cover amongst the trees and which also acted as choke points – could not be targeted. When the Allied aircraft did manage to engage the enemy, they were swatted away with contempt. One attack by light bombers of the British Advanced Air Striking Force was launched against a German column in the Ardennes. Eight sluggish and vulnerable Battles managed to avoid the protective air cover and even the anti-aircraft fire, but were met by a hail of machine-gun and small arms fire which brought three down. Of the thirty-two Battles that took to the air that day against a variety of targets, thirteen were shot down and the rest were damaged.[19]

But it was not only strike aircraft the Germans were careful to defend themselves against; it was also the reconnaissance machines that could have revealed the true extent of the Wehrmacht's commitment to the Ardennes. As one German officer later recalled:

> Again and again, I cast a worried look up at the bright blue sky; my division now presents an ideal attack target because it is not deployed and it is forced to move slowly forward on a single road. But we could not spot a single French reconnaissance aircraft.[20]

Indeed, the aerial unit supporting the French Second Army had maintained a weak presence over the battlefield and raised no concerns in its daily report on 11 May. It identified four three-mile-long enemy columns in Belgium, but this was not seen to be anything other than what was expected in the area. Even so, it was information which, when seen alongside other intelligence gathered that day, could have provided an early warning of German intentions. In the end, documents from a dead German soldier identifying his unit as the elite Gross Deutschland Regiment and a radio intercept detecting the presence of 1st Panzer Division were regarded as perplexing rather than evidence of anything more sinister. The reports from French commanders at the front were confused, contradictory and spasmodic. While the vast majority referred to actions against enemy infantry, only the battle at Neufchâteau involved German tanks. Second Army informed First Army Group of a 'panzer presence' on the afternoon of 11 May, and followed it with a detailed report to Billotte that evening saying that it had been 'heavily pressed at Neufchâteau by heavy tanks in the beginning of the afternoon ... Lost one [artillery] battery which destroyed three tanks armed with large cannons'. [21] Yet although this threat was not replicated across the Ardennes front, largely because only 1st Panzer Division deployed its tanks on 11 May, the French High Command signally failed to react to the evidence with which it had been presented: its blinkered focus remained on Army Group B.

That attention on von Bock's formation continued into 12 May as the situation in the Netherlands deteriorated significantly south of Rotterdam due to the advance of 9th Panzer Division. Reconnaissance units from the formation punched forward from dawn and by noon had linked up with cheering airborne troops at the Moerdijk bridgehead. This achievement successfully ended any opportunity that the Allies had to reinforce Fortress Holland from the south without a contest. General Winkelman hoped that the British might send three divisions by sea with which he might launch a counter-attack, but London refused, stating a 'lack of reserves'. The Netherlands was to be unceremoniously abandoned, and Winkelman knew it. With pressure mounting in Belgium and the French border threatened, he accepted that the British and French had other pressing demands on their resources. He also understood that in such a situation, the time would soon come when a decision would have to be made about whether the Netherlands continued to fight and thus tied down German resources in Holland, or whether the nation capitulated and allowed the enemy to concentrate his fighting power against the Dyle.

For the time being, the Dutch continued to fight. If 9th Panzer Division could be stopped from advancing to Rotterdam, then there might yet be a hope of conducting a protracted defence from Fortress Holland. The day, however, was Germany's. Despite continued counter-attacks against the Moerdijk Bridge and efforts to make it impassable by turning the artillery on the airborne troops, these remained intransigent and elements of the panzer division gradually established themselves in force. Compounding the situation was the collapse of the Grebbe Line after SS Leibstandarte Adolf Hitler had rolled through a series of enemy positions on a two-mile front. With this the Germans looked to make further inroads into the Dutch defences and to make continued resistance from Fortress Holland untenable. To facilitate this, OKW formed 9th Panzer Division, SS Leibstandarte Adolf Hitler and 254th Infantry Division into a new corps which would strike at Rotterdam and then become the manoeuvre group which would pursue the French Seventh Army as it withdrew towards Antwerp. Rotterdam would be forced into submission by some of 9th Panzer Division's tanks and infantry with close air support. Time was, however, of the essence if Seventh Army was to be pressurized by ground forces and so the Luftwaffe began to make preparations for bombing raids against Rotterdam, which was still full of civilians. If the enemy continued to be stubborn, high explosives would blow the fighting spirit out of him.

Throughout 12 May the Dutch government continued to discuss its limited options, which all agreed looked 'bleak in the extreme'. The Allied High Command also recognized the fact and prepared themselves for the reorientation of Eighteenth Army towards central Belgium within the next couple of days. That morning King Leopold, van Overstraeten, Daladier, Georges, Billotte and Gort's chief of staff, General Henry Pownall, met near Mons. The mood was tense, businesslike and frank. The Belgian contingent were keen to assert that its army had fulfilled the demand to delay the Germans for long enough for French and British divisions to move forward. The French and British could hardly agree, but such a meeting was not the place for recriminations as Gamelin wanted Leopold to assent to his forces being brought under French command. The king agreed and with that details were confirmed for their part in the defensive line running from Antwerp, along the Dyle and down to Namur.

None of those present openly expressed whatever concerns they may have had about the campaign thus far, although the difficult position of the Netherlands was acknowledged, and the German movement through the Ardennes was mentioned only in passing. Meanwhile, with the first phase of operations completed, King Leopold issued the following proclamation to his troops:

Soldiers,

The Belgian Army, brutally assailed by an unparalleled surprise attack, grappling with forces that are better equipped and have the advantage of a formidable air force, has for three days carried out difficult operations, the success of which is of the utmost importance to the general conduct of the battle and to the result of the war. These operations require from all of us – officers and men – exceptional efforts, sustained day and night, despite a moral tension tested to its limits by the sight of the devastation wrought by a pitiless invader. However severe the trial may be, you will come through it gallantly. Our position improves with every hour; our ranks are closing up. In the critical days that are ahead of us, you will summon up all your energies, you will make every sacrifice, to stem the invasion. Just as they did in 1914 on the Yser, so now the French and British troops are counting on you: the safety and honour of the country are in your hands.

Leopold[22]

On the afternoon of 12 May, a series of critical engagements began in central Belgium. The Battle of Hannut was part of a wider Sixth Army attack against the Allied line and was to last for two days. Its progress was tracked closely by Gamelin and the High Command because it was fought at the gateway to the Gembloux Gap. Leading the way were 3rd and 4th Panzer Divisions of General Erich Hoepner's XVI Panzer Motorized Corps which ran into a twenty-mile-wide defensive position occupied by Prioux's Cavalry Corps some eighteen miles beyond the main defensive line. Prioux's corps lacked the number of formations to provide a depth that would hold two concentrated panzer divisions for long, but it had to hold them long enough for First Army to strengthen the defences behind them and for 1st and 2nd DCRs to move into position to act as a final stopping force if required. The panzer divisions were resupplied for their attack by air as the lines of communications over the rivers to their rear were congested with all manner of units and the bridges were under frequent Allied air attack. It was a testament to the work of OKH's chief logistician, Major General Eduard Wagner, whose flexible planning and preparations across the front allowed for resupply up to 190 miles beyond railheads. As a consequence, Hoepner's formations were in better condition to fight the battle than the French, who were still busy preparing their defences and whose lines of communication – regularly attacked by the Luftwaffe – stretched all the way back to the French border.

Hoepner concentrated his two divisions against 2nd and 3rd Light Mechanized Divisions (DLM). The Germans had a quantitative superiority of 623 tanks against 415, but 498 of the German total were PzKpf Mk Is and IIs, leaving only 125 Mk IIIs and IVs to be used against the French SOMUA and Hotchkiss tanks.[23] Lieutenant Robert La Bel of 11th Regiment, 3DLM observed the massing German armour through field glasses from his Hotchkiss H39 parked beneath an apple tree:

I saw an extraordinary show which was played out about three kilometres away: a panzer division shaping itself for battle. The massive gathering of this armoured armada was an unforgettable sight, the more so that it appeared even more terrifying through the glasses. How many were there? It was not possible to tell from so far away but they were numerous and their guns seemed to be potent ... Some men, probably officers, walked to and fro gesticulating in front of the tanks. They were probably giving last-minute orders to the tank commanders, the head and shoulders of whom I could see between the two open parts of the turret hatches. Suddenly, as if swept away by a magic trick, they all disappeared. No doubt 'H'-hour was approaching. A dust cloud soon appeared on the skyline, disclosing the enemy move.

La Bel's desire 'to give the Boche a kick in the face that he will remember and which will send him reeling back to his homeland'[24] was not, however, matched by the French ability to provide it.

Hannut was the largest armoured clash the world had seen to date – and was to be the largest of the campaign – and was a great test of the belligerents' fighting methods, leadership, technology, command, control and training. Initially the firepower of Prioux's tanks caused the enemy considerable losses. It did not take long, however, for the Germans to realize that the Mk Is and IIs could not be used to take on the French armour and instead the panzer regiments tried to avoid engagements and to out-manoeuvre the enemy. The French proved themselves to be sluggish, slow to react and predictable against such tactics, while the Germans were mobile, lithe and unpredictable. The confrontation seemed to be a microcosm of the two sides' operational capabilities, with the Germans achieving armoured mass where it was most needed and so managing to overwhelm a large number of qualitatively superior French tanks.

Sergeant Major Georges Hillion of 4th Squadron Cuirassiers was in a Hotchkiss H39: 'My first target!' he later recalled, 'I fired and saw the direct hit.' However, his tank then stalled. 'A shell burst through my turret,' Hillion continued, 'I was wounded in the face and left arm; blood covered my face and I could not see any more from my left eye.' The tank fought on, shell after shell crashing into it. But the 40mm armour protected Hillion and his driver until an anti-tank round pierced it and before long further resistance became impossible as the interior filled with smoke. Blinded in his left eye, Hillion clambered out of the tank dragging its machine gun, was thrown to the ground by the impact of another shell and came to in great pain. 'I opened my right eye,' he later said, 'and saw a tank rolling over both my legs, the edge of the track just under my knees.' His driver had been killed in the exchange and his regiment lost twenty-four Hotchkiss tanks that day.[25]

Altogether, the panzers showed better tactical awareness, focusing on obtaining a critical mass and then winning each individual fire-fight, only firing when stationary, zigzagging to make difficult targets, keeping the sun behind them when manoeuvring into the flanks and rear of the enemy, and linking their efforts together with first-class radio proficiency. One German tank commander remarked that the French armour at Hannut was 'leaderless, purposeless, poorly led, tactically inferior'.[26] Doctrine, the design of their tanks and a lack of radios severely undermined the ability of the French to cope with the enemy's speed of thought and action, while their failure to concentrate themselves against the most likely attack routes allowed the Germans to develop significant local superiority. The latter's strengths, especially when married with excellent co-operation with other arms, allowed them to penetrate the French positions, although not to break through them. Hauptman Ernst von Jüngenfeld, commander of a 4th Panzer Division tank company, later wrote: '[The day was] hard and bloody, many a brave *Panzermann* had to lay down his life for the Fatherland, many were wounded and a large number of our tanks was lost, in part to shells and in part to breakdowns.'[27]

The first day of the Battle of Hannut was a tumultuous confrontation that held the French transfixed for Gamelin believed that its outcome was a critical precursor to Gembloux and the continuing integrity of the Dyle defences. The attention of the German High Command was also held by the battle, for if the French defeated Hoepner, then Army Group B's attempt to fix the Allied formations in central Belgium was threatened, whereas if Hoepner succeeded in pushing on to the Gembloux Gap, German prospects remained good. Because of this, events in the Ardennes were of at least equal importance to those taking place west of Maastricht. The continued advance of von Rundstedt's Army Group through the Ardennes was critical, but this was not a task that was the sole preserve of Panzer Group Kleist.

To the south of Hannut, Panzer Corps Hoth led Fourth Army forward not only to protect the north flank of the main effort, but also to break the French Ninth Army line as it moved forward to take up a position on the Meuse. Hoth thus ordered his 5th and 7th Panzer Divisions to advance as quickly as possible in order to reach the river before the enemy's defences were set. This was just the sort of direction that Erwin Rommel liked. In the days and weeks that followed, the maverick general was to gain himself the reputation as one of the finest and boldest divisional commanders in the Wehrmacht while his formation, much to Rommel's delight, became dubbed 'The Ghost Division'. 7th Panzer Division made rapid progress, making short work of the Belgian defences and the delaying efforts of 1st and 4th Light Cavalry Divisions in a manner very similar to Guderian's divisions. Rommel was always energetic, ensuring that forward momentum was achieved by avoiding unnecessary contact and being on the spot to make important decisions to ensure that no opportunity was missed. It was an exhausting style of command and on just the second day of battle he wrote to his wife:

> I've come up for breath for the first time today and have a moment to write. Everything wonderful so far. Am way ahead of my neighbours. I'm completely hoarse from orders and shouting. A bare three hours' sleep and an occasional meal. Otherwise I'm absolutely fine. Make do with this, please, I'm too tired for more.[28]

Rommel had indeed outstripped 5th Panzer Division and during the morning of 12 May Hoth put Oberst Paul Hermann Werner's 31st Panzer Regiment under 7th Panzer Division's command in order to broaden its attacking front. That afternoon, Werner's Detachment was sent to Yvoir on the east bank of the Meuse where aerial reconnaissance had identified an intact bridge. It had been prepared for demolition but it had not been destroyed as civilian refugees were using it. It was protected by a platoon of Ardennes Light Infantry and part of a French infantry battalion when Leutnant Heinz Zobel's armoured assault team consisting of two armoured cars and a panzer platoon raced forward and reached it before the defenders knew what was happening. Lieutenant de Wispelaere pushed the button of an electronic detonation ignition system, but there was no explosion. Despite coming under fire from German tanks and approaching infantry, he managed to detonate the explosives manually. The bridge heaved and crumpled into the river below a cloud of dust.

Although thwarted at Yvoir, Werner despatched a number of motorcycle infantry patrols to look for an alternative crossing site. Two miles to the south one patrol found a weir and lock system which connected the island of Houx to both banks of the Meuse. Although it was an obvious crossing point – indeed, it was the place where the Germans had crossed the river in August 1914 – responsibility for the area fell on a boundary between French formations which were only just arriving. IX Corps' 18th Infantry Division and II Corps' 5th Motorized Divisions, joined by 1st Light Cavalry Division as it withdrew from the Ardennes, were in a poor position to fend off a major attempt to cross the river and could hardly believe that the Germans had managed to advance so far, so fast. At dusk, the defenders were still confirming their boundaries and moving units into position along the front.

18th Infantry Division took command of the Houx sector, but it was a 5th Motorized Division battalion that was used to defend the area around the island, although its commander failed to occupy the island itself. After dark, therefore, a few of the German motorcycle infantrymen managed to cross the river, the first soldiers from Army Group A to reach the west bank of the Meuse. It was only as this small group probed forward to ascertain the enemy's strength that they came under fire and were forced to ground. Reinforcements sent by Werner, however, managed to expand the tiny bridgehead, assisted by a French decision to wait until daylight to counter-attack. In the meantime, a panzer company led Rommel's 7th Panzer Division to Dinant, just a couple of miles south of the island and where both bridges were found to have been destroyed. As Rommel prepared his division for an assault crossing the following morning, he was informed of the pin-prick that had been made in the French defences at Houx. Encouraged, he ordered 7th Panzer Division to begin its attack at dawn.

Yet despite Rommel's not inconsiderable success on the evening of 12 May, it was the progress of Guderian's corps at the *Schwerpunkt* that most occupied Halder's mind. Having crossed the Semois in two places, 1st Panzer Division led the charge south with Kirchner, encouraged by his corps commander, keen not to give the French time to settle into the Meuse defences. Making use of their two crossing points while new bridges over the Semois were constructed by the engineers, Keltsch's 1st Panzer Brigade and a battalion of infantry led the attack from Mouzaive, while a group commanded by Oberst Krüger containing the majority of Balck's regiment and supported by two tank platoons led the main body of the division out from Bouillon.

South of the Semois, the terrain was tortuous for the attacking forces – so much so that, in trying to find a route south from Mortehan, 10th Panzer Division had moved onto the route designated for Kirchner's advance. Krüger found a different but more meandering road which also contained several large demolitions requiring attention by the engineers. While waiting for the advance to proceed, the column came under accurate artillery fire, which caused casualties among the staff of 1st Rifle Regiment. When Krüger's attack continued, it was greatly advantaged by Keltsch, who was already putting pressure along the road to Sedan and forced the French cavalry back and into a line of blockhouses and pillboxes camouflaged as residential homes approximately three miles before the Meuse. The German divisions spent much of the late morning and afternoon fighting through these mutually supporting positions in close terrain. The most stubborn proved to be centred on a pillbox at La Hatrelle which contained an anti-tank gun and machine guns and was secured by mines. Krüger's group attacked it several times during the mid-afternoon with various combinations of tanks and infantry but failed to make an impression. After nearly four hours of obstruction, a single panzer succeeded in firing a round through the pillbox's gun embrasure. This was followed by an infantry assault which finally silenced the occupants. That evening, the last French defenders gave up on their attempt to delay the advancing Germans and fled into Sedan to cross the bridges that had been kept intact for their withdrawal at around 1900 hours. As the leading elements of 1st Panzer Division entered the town that evening, they heard a series of explosions which told them that these bridges had finally been destroyed.

By nightfall, Kirchner's division was establishing itself in Sedan and preparing for its assault crossing of the town which, at that time, was expected to be the following morning. It did so in close proximity to the river because of the protection offered by the town's buildings, a luxury not afforded to 10th Panzer Division, whose crossing point was out of the town in more open countryside. As a consequence and in order to thwart observation by the enemy, its assembly area was one or two miles from the Meuse in the wooded fringes of the Ardennes. The forward units of Schaal's division reached their destination, the village of Givonne two miles north-east of Sedan, just as Sedan's bridges crashed into the Meuse. The last division to arrive in position was 2nd Panzer Division which, finding its crossing point at Mouzaive being used by 1st Panzer Division when its lead elements arrived on the Semois just after dawn and that a bridge at Membre had been destroyed, set about constructing a new bridge at Vresse. This was completed in the mid-afternoon and Veiel immediately sent his motorcycle infantry forward to the industrialized area of Donchery on the east bank of the Meuse from where his division would launch its assault. The rest of the division was held up in awful traffic jams which led back many miles east of the Semois and meant that by nightfall the majority of the division was still four miles short of the Meuse.

Behind Guderian's corps there continued to be a hideous congestion of formations which were struggling to wriggle free of the confines imposed on them by List and the terrain. It included Reinhardt's 6th and 8th Panzer Divisions and attached 2nd Motorized Division which, rather than being mere follow-up forces, had the task of crossing the Meuse in the Monthermé sector on 13 May between Guderian's and Hoth's corps. 6th Panzer Division's war diary for that day reported:

> The Division was ripped apart during the attack by parts of the 2nd Panzer Division, along with 16th, 23rd, 24th and 32nd Infantry divisions that pushed in between. In the afternoon and evening there was little clarity about where the advancing groups and their individual formations were

located. It was also impossible to get accurate information by radio because such communications were limited due to the great distances and radio interference.[29]

The corps strained every sinew to get into position, but as soon as its units struggled free of the traffic jams and onto its own routes, it then had to overcome enemy obstacles and the terrain. At one point it was even bombed by some errant He 111s which left twenty dead and twenty-six wounded. Thus, although elements of 6th Panzer Division were to arrive on the Meuse during the early hours of 13 May, 2nd Motorized Infantry Division did not arrive at Nouzonville four miles south of Monthermé until 14 May and 8th Panzer Division did not reach the Meuse until 16 May. The echeloning of Panzer Group Kleist had led to 2nd Panzer Division and Corps Reinhardt falling behind schedule too and so, rather than seven panzer divisions being on the Meuse on the morning of 13 May, there were only five and there was a gap in their centre. Halder watched and waited, applauding Guderian's unconventional and unprecedented 170-mile advance but concerned about whether he would have the power to make a successful crossing on the following day and whether two panzer corps would be enough to punch through the enemy's defences and into the open ground beyond.

OKW hoped that the French remained unaware that what was building on the Meuse was the main German effort. They did. Reports from Ninth and Second Armies to Billotte and Gamelin on 12 May continued to point at the enemy's advance south of Maastricht as being a secondary offensive and suggested the planned delaying operations should hold them. Intelligence officers at both army headquarters continued to receive information from various sources that ran contrary to the main thrust of the submissions they were receiving from the front, but these continued to be treated as unexplained anomalies. One aerial reconnaissance mission conducted during the early hours of 12 May, for example, identified columns of enemy vehicles advancing with their lights blacked out. Another aircraft was sent up during daylight hours to verify the sighting. It limped back to base full of holes after running into a hail of fire from the ground as the pilot confirmed the presence of the German columns. Second Army reported enemy tanks advancing towards Sedan along with vehicles carrying vast amounts of bridging equipment. There were even aerial photographs of the ensuing bridge-building and of vehicles driving across the Semois at Bouillon. But all such intelligence was ignored, partly because of the weight of evidence suggesting that nothing was amiss in the Ardennes and partly because the armies did not want to alarm an already tense High Command, which at that time was preoccupied by the Battle of Hannut. Indeed, although Gamelin's chief of staff noted on the evening of 12 May that German forces in the Ardennes were 'making contact in some places with the forward elements of our fortified line', he added, '[but in] contrast, to the west of Maastricht, his advance has noticeably decreased.'[30]

Sedan itself had been quiet for the first two days and the French troops there had assisted with the evacuation of civilians from the area. Although they had been put on alert, there had been no air raids and nothing to unduly concern them. The men of 55th Infantry Division spent their time in preparation, making sure that their positions were as strong as possible, checking communications and weapons, ensuring they had the necessary supplies and running through likely scenarios. There was a feeling abroad they were soon going to taste the war at first hand, and they were pleased to learn that they would do so while grappling with the enemy's secondary effort. Their first sight of the Germans came during the evening of 12 May shortly after the last units of 5th Cavalry Division had run across Sedan's bridges and into friendly lines. A little later David Boyer, a young soldier manning the division's forward defences, had an unsettling experience. He later recalled:

157

I was already extremely anxious at the sight and sound of the Germans just across the river and was at my post waiting for orders when a man from 295th Infantry Regiment ran past. He was stopped by my officer, who asked him what was going on. The man stood to attention and said that he had just returned from fighting the Germans with the cavalry and was looking for his company's lines. The Lieutenant immediately asked him what he had learned of the enemy. The man spoke just two sentences, saluted and left. He said: 'There are many of them, they have tanks and flamethrowers. We are dead men.'[31]

CHAPTER 6

13 May – Crossing the Meuse

D AVID BOYER DID NOT SLEEP AT ALL during the night of 12–13 May. He felt sick and could not dislodge from his mind the image of that man from the 295th nor his dire warning. Boyer's officer deliberately sought him out later that evening with the intention of reassuring him. In his experience on exercise, he said, soldiers always over-exaggerated and no matter what, the defences that they had built together could withstand the attack of an entire army. He advised his charge to get a couple of hours' rest and not to worry. All would be well.[1]

Less than half a mile away, 1st Panzer Division was planning, preparing and positioning its various units. During the night Guderian had produced an outline corps plan for the divisions so that they might begin their own more detailed planning. A mere three pages long, it was immediately recognized by the division staffs as being very similar to a corps exercise run in late March and provided the divisions with plenty of scope. At 1600 hours 1st Panzer Division would attack from Gaulier, 2nd Panzer Division at Donchery, and 10th Panzer Division from the eastern fringe of Sedan, a front of just five miles and containing some 60,000 men and 22,000 vehicles in its depth. 1st Panzer Division had a particular advantage because after one such exercise run less than two weeks before, the division's operations officer, Major i.G. Walther Wenck, had ordered twenty-five copies of the final attack orders he had drafted to be run off. On 13 May, Wenck issued those copies with changes merely to the timings and locations.[2]

By daybreak, Kirchner and Schaal's divisions were making good, if somewhat frantic, progress with their preparations while their units continued to arrive in the assembly areas. The fact that it was still the leading units of Veiel's formation that were arriving in Donchery during the morning was of some concern to Guderian. As one French officer wrote after the war: 'What a chance to acquire imperishable glory ... by smothering at birth the German offensive and transforming all these mechanized and armoured units into scraps of burnt and twisted metal.'[3] Unfortunately, it was a chance the French did not take. Launching an assault on a major river obstacle without an operational pause was always going to be difficult, but the French had no idea that this is what the Germans were going to attempt and as a consequence made no major effort to undermine their preparations. The French artillery lobbed shells into the divisional areas and at anything that moved, but their weight of fire merely inconvenienced the Germans and there were no air strikes or any spoiling attacks. As 1st Panzer Division engineer Otto Gull later commented:

> It was as if the enemy had not expected our arrival. In training we were told to expect the worst and had learned to do our work under the most appalling conditions. Now, here we were on the Meuse and other than some nasty artillery concentrations there was nothing to suggest that the enemy were ready for us. I drew great strength from this.[4]

After receiving overnight reports about the arrivals at Sedan, Second Army informed superior headquarters that 'the enemy had arrived in force' on the Meuse and that they included 'significant numbers of tanks'.[5] In mid-morning this was followed by a French air reconnaissance mission which informed Georges's headquarters that a significant enemy movement up to the Meuse had occurred during the night of 12–13 May and clearly stated that 'Everything confirms a large German effort on the Bouillon-Sedan axis.'[6] André Beaufre, an operations officer at Gamelin's headquarters, collated the latest information from the Ardennes sector and transferred it onto a map. To his horror, he could only conclude that the main German effort was not, in fact, towards the Gembloux Gap but towards Sedan. Georges's headquarters came to the same, stultifying deduction at about the same time. There was no panic, however, because it was believed that the Germans would take several days to gather what they required to attempt a crossing of the Meuse. It was an assumption that was not immediately challenged and re-tested because Gamelin, Georges and Billotte were focused on the continuation of the Battle of Hannut and the establishment of the Allied formations along the Dyle Line.

Although inexcusable in the circumstances of a developing wider campaign, the French generals' preoccupation with events east of the Gembloux Gap is at least understandable because, having withstood Hoepner's attack on the previous day, on 13 May Prioux's line cracked. With the assistance of Wolfram Freiherr von Richthofen's VIII Air Corps providing close air support, the French were sent into withdrawal. It was an appalling setback for Gamelin, who had anticipated such an eventuality only after the Belgians had held the enemy for several days on the Albert Canal and Prioux had managed the same behind them. Instead, the Sixth Army was motoring *en masse* towards the Gembloux Gap and incomplete Dyle defences on just the fourth day of the offensive. Billotte took some comfort from the fact that Prioux's divisions had inflicted a loss of 160 tanks on Hoepner at a cost of 105 of his own machines. His comfort was misplaced, however, for within forty-eight hours mobile workshops had repaired 111 of the 'lost' German tanks and they immediately rejoined their divisions.

The situation in central Belgium was concerning for the Supreme Commander and it looked set to deteriorate further after news arrived of setbacks in the Netherlands. On the morning of 13 May, Winkelman advised the Dutch government that he considered the general situation to be critical. With German tanks poised to advance on Rotterdam from Moerdijk and infantry divisions pressing beyond the Grebbe Line, the general was not confident of prolonged successful resistance. The Cabinet's reaction was to flee to England and there, joining the Dutch royal family, establish a government in exile. A dismayed Winkelman was to remain in the Netherlands, co-ordinating the nation's resistance, avoiding unnecessary casualties, until such time as he believed the situation hopeless, whereupon he was to surrender. It was a huge responsibility for a military man, but Winkelman understood that if the Netherlands was to have an independent future, then he must assist the Allies by ensuring that the German forces were tied up in and around Fortress Holland for as long as possible.

As it was, 9th Panzer Division had restarted its offensive from the south side of the Moerdijk bridgehead just after dawn. Leading with four tank companies, the Germans pressed on to the Moerdijk Bridge itself, swatting aside all Dutch attempts to thwart them. As the first panzers rolled across, the last operational medium Dutch bomber – a Fokker T.V. – dropped two bombs on the bridge. In another forlorn scene of Dutch courage against the odds, one of the bombs hit a supporting pillar but failed to explode and the bomber was immediately shot down. Subsequent attempts to destroy the bridge by artillery fire from guns whose crews remained at their posts even when under intense Stuka attack, also foundered. To add insult to injury, last-ditch attempts to inundate the area also miscarried as the inlet sluices were not only too small but failed to open.

The German armour moved steadily north, to the very great relief of some airborne troops who were at the end of their supplies, and took Dortrecht. The Dutch continued to throw themselves at the corridor that the armour was creating but were kept under intense aerial bombardment and failed to achieve anything more than a temporary tactical impact. Lacking any useful information about the broader operational situation, the Dutch were forced to act in an unco-ordinated fashion which severely undermined their efforts. As one Dutch soldier has remarked, 'We were not always sure who was friend and who was foe. Often we had no idea who was on our right and left flank, all we knew is where the enemy was and that we had to attack. There was little co-ordination, but we did what we could – but it was not enough.'[7] Yet sometimes the Dutch did not even know where the enemy was, and at one point the defenders mistook the red air recognition cloths strapped to the German tanks as orange Dutch flags and were mercilessly gunned down as they approached the vehicles.

As 9th Panzer Division pushed on to Barendrecht Bridge – the last before reaching the Rotterdam suburbs – the Dutch defence became increasingly desperate and more fractured. Even so, an initial attack by a platoon of German tanks saw the leading three fall to 47mm anti-tank fire, but such was the obvious strength of the units following on behind that the defenders abandoned the bridge. In Rotterdam, the Wilhelms Bridge was held by just fifty remaining airborne troops ensconced in nearby buildings and they were being extremely hard-pressed. An attempt by two companies of Dutch marines to oust the defenders and destroy the bridge lasted several hours. The armour arrived just in time to stop the perimeter being overrun. Peter Meier had been wounded in his left arm by a Dutch grenade when the tanks opened fire on the marines. 'I sank to my knees and thanked God,' he later recalled, 'I had twenty rounds left and had already unsheathed my combat knife in preparation for one last stand ... It had been a real ordeal at that bridge.'[8] But the bridge was now secured and an entry point had been made by 9th Panzer Division into the very heart of Fortress Holland.

The advance to Rotterdam was accompanied by further progress elsewhere in the country: in the far north 1st Cavalry Division had managed to work its way through to the mouth of the Ijsselmeer while along the rear of the Grebbe Line infantry supported by Stukas tried to fight its way through difficult inundated terrain against the Dutch rearguard. Some success was achieved east of Utrecht and the defenders fell back yet again to the outer defensive lines of Fortress Holland protecting The Hague. As one Dutch infantryman later testified:

> While we held our line, we always believed that there was hope. During the first three days of the invasion, we fought well even if we knew that without reinforcement we could not hold out indefinitely … We were subjected to heavy artillery bombardments, merciless infantry attacks and when we retreated back towards Utrecht on the 13th, murderous Stuka attacks. It was then that we began to lose hope. In fact, it flooded away.[9]

The battle for the Netherlands was fast reaching its denouement by the afternoon of 13 May, but even as Winkelman considered whether a final defensive effort was in the best interests of the people of the Netherlands, a new phase in *Fall Gelb* was opening on the Meuse south of Maastricht. Having created a very small bridgehead at Houx overnight, three rifle battalions from 5th Panzer Division crossed the weir in single file at 0530 hours to reinforce and expand it. By this time the French had woken up to the threat posed by the link that the Germans had found to the west bank and covered it with fire, causing heavy casualties. An after-action report stated: 'The dead are floating in the water. The wounded desperately clinging to the lock gates. They call for help but nobody can help them.'[10] Commanders on the spot ordered their men to continue the attack and get to the opposite bank of the river as quickly as possible in order to deal with the defenders from the rear. Gradually, the defenders' fire diminished and the attacking infantry pushed on to take the village of Grange, which acted as an anchor for the bridgehead. From this firm base, the Germans pushed a further 2.5 miles, plunging deeper between the two French corps, and approached the village of Haut-le-Wastia, which stood on high ground. The French fought tenaciously throughout 13 May and into the next day to hold onto the tactically important position while their armour tried, and failed, to push the men of 5th Panzer Division back into the Meuse. With increasing numbers of attackers with heavy weapons filing into the bridgehead during the course of the day, it became increasingly secure, but the French had resisted well after a poor start and had not collapsed. The intensity of the fighting at Houx, however, undoubtedly advantaged Rommel's assault across the Meuse as he would otherwise have found the enemy concentrating purely against his division.

7th Panzer Division had two crossing sites. The main one at Leffe on the northern edge of Dinant had good road communications on the west bank, while a secondary one south of Houx not only lacked adequate roads but was also overlooked by high, rocky cliffs which provided the defenders with a superb view. Even so, Rommel was determined that the enemy should not be able to concentrate all his fighting power against a single crossing site and so at dawn 6th Rifle Regiment and 7th Motorcycle Rifle Battalion began their crossing from the significantly inferior location. Fortuitously, the site was shrouded in mist as the first rubber boats started their 100-yard crossing but, noticing movement, the defenders raked the river with fire and were soon joined by artillery sited at a castle at Bouvignes. The Germans returned fire with two light artillery battalions and some spasmodic Luftwaffe support, but the assault teams knew that success depended on the infantry themselves clearing the defenders from their rocky eyries.

Rommel strode along the bank and later called the scene before him 'none too pleasant' and watched helpless as a damaged rubber boat drifted past with a badly wounded man clinging to it, screaming for help and near to drowning. He did what he could, however, to provide encouragement and leadership to his troops in their endeavours. As the mist lifted, he immediately ordered that the house on the east bank be set on fire to provide smoke cover and so the assault continued. Rommel left in a PzKpfw Mk IV to visit his primary crossing point just as soon as the infantry had a critical mass of troops on the west bank and were beginning to infiltrate forward.

At Leffe, Rommel arrived to find the crossing being undertaken by Oberst Georg von Bismarck's 7th Rifle Regiment under heavy fire. As the general observed the scene, his aide-de-camp, Hauptmann Hans-Joachim Schraepler, was wounded at his side by shell splinters. Rommel was unharmed, but the incident was a reminder of the cost that had to be borne if commanders were to conduct their business in the front line.[11] Yet Rommel, like many others, believed that to be able to make swift and informed decisions an officer had to be at the point of the action, and that the alternatives were unthinkable. In fact, as if wishing to provide an immediate illustration of his indispensability in the line of fire, he took personal command of 2nd Battalion for a short time. With the infantry having managed to get a company onto the west bank but the troops following faltering, the general screamed orders in an attempt to kick-start the reinforcement. He even crossed the river himself in one of the first boats, partly to be able to give direction to the assault that was developing on the other side of the Meuse, but also to show that he would not ask his men to do something that he himself was not prepared to do.

Few who were at Leffe on 13 May would disagree that Rommel did not play an important personal role in the establishment of 7th Rifle Regiment's bridgehead that morning. For the remainder of the day, he remained on the eastern river bank – largely at the crossing point south of Houx where enemy artillery fire continued its disruption – encouraging his troops. On one occasion he waded waist-deep into the river to assist engineers building a bridge and, when the bridge was completed, Rommel was one of the first across in his command tank.

By the evening, 7th Panzer Division had established two bridgeheads which were now being connected and also linked to that achieved at Houx. It was an extremely impressive achievement as any opposed crossing, particularly one made on the move, was a high-risk enterprise. The fact that the French were poorly set counterbalanced some of those challenges but in lesser hands the assault could easily have stalled. A significant counter-attack before the Germans were well established across the river could have had a momentous impact, but the French were not only slow to react to the initial crossing at Houx, they were also tardy in informing the chain of command about their deteriorating situation while they established exactly what was happening where and to whom.

At noon the IX Corps commander, General Julien-François-René Martin, was finally in a position to order a counter-attack consisting of an infantry regiment, a company of tanks, some scout cars and four artillery battalions. As the infantry was slow to arrive, the armour attacked 5th Panzer Division without them. They made good progress and advanced to within a mile of the crossing point before a precipitate decision was made to suspend the thrust when darkness fell due to the tanks' vulnerability without infantry support. A languid counter-attack towards Dinant by II Corps also ended in failure after slow reaction times were, once again, compounded by sluggish assembly and a timely Stuka raid. Although the intention was for the enterprise to be restarted the following morning, the Germans were careful to ferry ever more troops, armour and heavy weapons across the Meuse during the night via their newly constructed bridges and so by dawn the French had missed their opening.

This meant that they had lost two very important opportunities to strike back at the Germans while they were in an unusually vulnerable situation. These were to prove to be just the first of several similar episodes, all stemming from a chronic French inability to react in a timely fashion to German initiatives. To make matters worse, the situation at Dinant and Houx was not properly communicated up the Allied chain of command. With each successive recipient of such information wary of the tendency of subordinates to over-exaggerate situations, Georges eventually told Gamelin that 'a battalion had got into trouble' near Houx.[12] In reality, for the cost of 182 casualties, Rommel had a firm footing on the west bank of the Meuse and, along with 5th Panzer Division, provided Hoth with an excellent springboard from which to launch operations to the west.

The breaching of the Meuse line on the right flank of Army Group A was just one of three that were planned. Another was to be attempted forty-five miles south of Dinant by Reinhardt's second echelon corps which, because of the difficulties that its formations had getting to the Meuse, was represented on the river in the early hours of 13 May by Kempf's 6th Panzer Division alone. By dawn it had been decided that the assault crossing to Monthermé would take place at 1600 hours, the same time as Guderian's attack at Sedan, thus giving the formation the time that it needed to make its preparations. It was a tricky proposition, for the Meuse in this area is set in a deep gorge and Monthermé occupies a tight loop in the river, one which made it easy for the enemy to be cut off, and it was defended by a well-organized colonial infantry battalion from 102nd Fortress Division. Reinhardt later wrote:

> The terrain really scares you. The only road leading to
> Monthermé snakes down ... into the deeply cut Meuse valley
> ... The riflemen are having trouble climbing down the steep

slopes leading down to the Meuse river while manhandling their heavy weapons. The rubber boats have to be taken down to the Meuse in the armoured personnel carriers because it was impossible to carry them down.[13]

Kempf would ideally have liked the Luftwaffe to provide some close air support and interdiction to assist his division, but he had been told little was available as Guderian's divisions had priority. When during the course of the battle some Stukas did turn up, the division was horrified to watch as the dive-bombers mistakenly attacked their own troops, leading to the destruction of several guns and thirty casualties.[14] For the most part, however, Kempf was forced to rely on the division's own guns both for the preparation of the battlefield and also in support of its assault forces. Some of those guns belonged to the eighteen tanks of 1st Company 11th Panzer Regiment, which was commanded by Oberleutnant Dr Franz Bake and covered the assault crossing of 4th Rifle Regiment.

The first two attempts to get the infantry across the Meuse ended up in a bloody mess, but the third crossing was a success after a key French machine-gun position in a café was spotted and destroyed by accurate tank fire. With infantry on the west bank and moving into the town, tanks immediately began to cross at a weir that had been spotted a little earlier by an eagle-eyed reconnaissance patrol. By placing himself in one of the first groups of vehicles that crossed the Meuse – one of which moved slightly off the narrow route and sank up to its turret – Kempf was able to organize his units quickly and give orders to his command team on the east bank to release specific assets to aid the advance. Engineers, meanwhile, set about making one of the poorly demolished bridges useable again. The clearing of the town was an infantry task, but the tanks were on hand to offer firepower where it was needed to remove stubborn positions. Meanwhile, the French sealed off the town by occupying a pre-prepared defensive line running across the neck of the urban salient which had been occupied by the Germans.

What was needed now was the arrival on the Meuse of one of the corps' other divisions in order to dilute the French concentration against 6th Panzer Division and provide a threat to their rear area.

It was not without reason that Reinhardt's post-war account of his campaign in France was titled *In Guderian's Shadow* for in the Sedan sector, even as Monthermé was being attacked, Guderian's three divisions were crossing the Meuse at the *Schwerpunkt* centred on Sedan. Von Kleist had wanted a crossing several miles further west, in the broad Sedan sector but where there were fewer river obstacles, to make progress beyond the Meuse while pushing the corps closer to Hoth and facilitating an attack on the boundary between the French Second and Ninth Armies. Guderian, however, ignored direct orders and presented his superior with a *fait accompli* by heading for and finally arriving in Sedan itself. Guderian's argument for his choice was that it offered 1st Panzer Division more cover for its assault crossing than the alternative further west, but thinking ahead he also recognized that ten miles south of Sedan was some high ground – Mont Dieu – which, if captured, would make an ideal hard protective edge to his southern flank as his corps swung west.

Ironically, having told von Kleist on 12 May that, if he wanted his corps to reorientate to the west, he would have to postpone his crossing by twenty-four hours, on the morning of 13 May Guderian reflected on the fact that a delay might have been useful to him as his artillery was emerging from the woods at a worryingly slow rate. The 141 guns contained within his three divisions were a vital component in the corps plan for the break-in and break-through battle as he expected the French to enjoy a 3:1 gun superiority. As such, his scheme demanded that 1st Panzer Division take the majority of the heavy guns from 2nd and 10th Panzer Divisions as they arrived in order to concentrate them and so enhance the likelihood of a break-in by Kirchner. In preparation for this,

Guderian had put a huge effort into developing a precise sequence of firing on a detailed target map which aerial reconnaissance would keep updated right through to the end of the day before the assault. That fire plan was then to be applied in co-ordination with the Luftwaffe for the attack.

The level of air-ground co-operation that Guderian sought was unprecedented, but it had been trialled by him in Poland and he had learned a good many lessons doing so. Consequently in early May, Guderian and Generalleutnant Bruno Loerzer, commander of II. Fliegerkorps, had developed the 'rolling raid' in which only a few Luftwaffe formations would attack at any one time, but small raids were repeated throughout the day in order to permanently neutralize the enemy artillery, target bunkers and create such chaos as might break the will of the defenders. Guderian was therefore furious to learn at his meeting with von Kleist on 12 May that his superior had intervened and ordered the commander of Luftflotte 3, General der Flieger Hugo Sperrle, to change his plans. His orders were to provide a long preparatory raid to prepare the battlefield and then a conventional brief and concentrated bombing attack immediately before the infantry crossed the river to force the enemy deep into his defences. It was a fundamental alteration to Guderian's carefully considered arrangement and matters were further jeopardized by the fact that, just hours before his assault was due to be launched, his guns were still struggling to get into position.

Guderian could only hope that the guns which did arrive, when combined with von Kleist's new air plan, would be enough to allow the 1st Panzer Division, reinforced with Gross Deutschland Regiment, to crack the French defences open and make a breakthrough by seizing high ground immediately south of the river and, with 2nd and 10th Divisions on its flanks, push to a line running between Chéhéry and Chaumont, then punch through the final French defences and pivot west with the corps's left on Mont Dieu. The first but critical step was for the divisions to get across the river and break into the enemy's defences. After some superb traffic control, the guns of 1st and 10th Panzer Divisions arrived in enough time to be positioned and sighted, although those of 2nd Panzer Division were still arriving as the attack began. In the final hours before 1600 hours, plans were briefed, unit preparations were completed and troops checked their equipment. The French shelling remained relatively light, but the ground running down to the river became increasingly full of burning vehicles, nearby buildings were set on fire too, and casualties were taken by troop concentrations close to the river in both Sedan and Donchery. It made for an anxious wait until the attack began.

The French too were apprehensive at dawn on 13 May, although they had no idea that the Germans intended to attempt an assault crossing that day. The defenders of the Sedan sector needed every minute available to prepare because they were lacking both manpower and weaponry. With 147th Fortress Infantry Regiment and 11th Machine Gun Battalion included, 55th Infantry Division should have been 16,712 men strong but had lost nearly 25 per cent of its strength through Pentecostal holiday leave and only a small number had returned when Sedan was threatened.[15] The division was further hampered by its unfinished defences, lack of anti-tank guns and mines and also a gap in its defences across a 2-mile stretch of river opposite Gaulier at Glaire. Thus, at the most obvious crossing place at Sedan – the place where 1st and 2nd Panzer Divisions looked to attack the west bank of the Meuse – there was no interlocking fire and there were no mines following the decision to move the principal line of resistance back in this sub-sector in order to shorten the line overall. The commander at Sedan, General Lafontaine, believed that he had several days in which to enhance his defences and welcomed the news that the corps reserve, 71st Infantry Division, would arrive on his right flank during the night of 13–14 May and so reduce his area of front by one third. His pleasure at this increase of manpower, despite the thoroughly disruptive impact the arrival of this formation would have after months of careful organization in the area, gives a good indication of Lafontaine's concerns.

The German commanders had all put themselves in the place of their French counterparts. Their understanding of their enemy's doctrine, his army and circumstances, led them to conclude that the French would be slow to react to the nascent threat emerging from the Ardennes and that an immediate attempt to assault the Meuse, despite its inherent risks, was essential if their own vision was to be fulfilled. Halder had therefore watched developments with great interest and knew that the campaign had reached an important and delicate point on 13 May. Having read the morning reports, he noted: 'Group Kleist bunched together near Sedan, intends attacking at 1600. Plan of attack rather complicated ... Outcome of Meuse drive will decide if, and when, and where we would be able to take advantage of [our] superiority. The enemy has no substantial mobile forces in the rear of this front, no more than three armoured divisions at best, but he does have a very well integrated railroad system.'[16]

Guderian was under huge pressure, but if there was a German general who was suited to excelling under such a burden, it was the commander of XIX Corps at Sedan. Even as Halder was writing, on a clear, warm and sunny day, the Luftwaffe suddenly vanished over Army Group B and concentrated almost totally against the Sedan sector. With the guns of the three divisions still arriving and being positioned, the air attack began. It was a devastating surprise to the French, who not only learned during its course that the Germans were about to make an early assault across the Meuse but also found themselves under the largest concentration of aircraft so far mustered in the war. In total around 1,500 machines, largely from Luftflotte 3, supported Panzer Group Kleist, with the vast majority of them at Sedan. The German aerial force included 600 bombers, 250 dive-bombers, 500 single-engine and 120 twin-engine fighters, most of which flew several sorties on 13 May. The impact of the Luftwaffe's attack was better than Guderian could have imagined for, as he watched the opening raids from Hill 266 south of Givonne that afternoon, he realized that it was his plan that was being put into action after all. Loerzer, Guderian found out when he called to thank him later that day, had decided that von Kleist's order had reached him from Luftflotte 3 'too late' not to have caused confusion and so stuck with the original plan.[17] Good fortune, not for the first or last time in the campaign, was on Guderian's side.

The rolling raid that Guderian and Loerzer had designed for Sedan focused on zones which were sub-divided into areas of between 275 and 550 yards and contained specific targets along the Meuse and then the defences immediately behind them – the depth of 55th Infantry Division. It came in five phases. During the morning, there were harassing missions carried out along the Sedan sector front, then from noon dive-bombing and the bombing of specific targets until twenty minutes before the river assault, when there was a huge raid against the loop in the Meuse at Sedan. At 1600 hours and for ninety minutes after, the raids moved away from the river bank to deeper targets, with Stukas hitting rear-area positions and the artillery, and then, finally, from 1730 hours until dusk, there were interdiction operations to seal off the rear area by targeting reserves approaching the battlefield. The day was to see 1,215 bomber and dive-bomber sorties flown against the area to be attacked by 1st Panzer Division alone.

Lieutenant Colonel Pinaud, commanding 147th Fortress Infantry in the main attack area of the Frénois sub-sector, later testified:

> The bombardment was particularly heavy on the principal line of resistance, Sedan railway station, and on Torcy where numerous fires were started … [At noon] the aerial

bombardment intensified and was interspersed with lulls until [1800 hours] … [T]he entire area, but particularly the principal line of resistance, was shrouded by a thick cloud of smoke. The attacks were implemented by successive waves, each including around forty bombers while fighters strafed the ground.[18]

The deployment of wave after wave of steeply diving and screaming Stukas against second-rate troops so affected a significant portion of the men cowering under the onslaught that they were rendered militarily useless. Only the brave and foolhardy and the psychologically unhinged discharged their rifles and machine guns at the aircraft. There was just a single, unsuccessful attempt by seven French aircraft to become involved in the battle and only one light anti-aircraft battalion at Sedan. One of its gunners, Hugo Novak, later said: 'All hell seems to have broken loose … The enormous air pressure causes glass panes to rattle and crack.'[19] It was during the second and third phases of the Luftwaffe blitz that the bombing increasingly focused on 1st Panzer Division's area of main effort and the defenders' will and ability to resist really began to erode. Deafened, winded and disorientated by the explosions, the French struggled to know what to do among the devastation. Some bombs created craters forty-five feet across and twenty-one feet deep.

David Boyer of 55th Infantry Division found himself in the middle of the maelstrom:

> The air attack was far worse than my imagination could have ever have invented. After a night of worrying about what might happen, I found that I could not escape the bombs. I was in a reinforced trench linked to a bunker and felt as unprotected from the bombs as any man that day. I remember a bell being rung when the first aircraft approached and we were supposed to take cover. This meant cowering in our trench and praying. The first attack lasted around five

minutes, and I thought that it was all over, but moments later another raid began, and then another and another until they merged into one nightmare lasting hours. One bomb landed by my trench and collapsed a section of it burying my sergeant ... The moments of silence were as frightening as the explosions as I could hear screams of pain, but no movement or sense that we were doing something to defend ourselves. We were defenceless ... In the minutes before the [German] attack, the explosions were so frequent that one could not distinguish between the individual blasts. I was deaf and could hardly breathe. I tried to make my body as small as possible, my hands over my head, my world shaking and swaying. I sobbed.[20]

The Luftwaffe's attack was so long and so intense that those who might well have been able to withstand a raid of conventional duration eventually succumbed to its power. One staff officer testified: 'When the dive-bombers came down on them they stood the noise – there were hardly any casualties – for only two hours, and then they bolted out with their hands over their ears.'[21] In the final minutes before the river assault, the aerial bombardment rose to a crescendo. Watching the scene from the east bank, Unteroffizier Prümer of 3rd Battalion 1st Rifle Regiment later reported:

What we now got to see during the next twenty minutes is one of the most tremendous impressions of this war. Squadron after squadron approaches at high altitude, deploys into a line formation and then the first aircraft comes diving down perpendicularly, followed by the second, the third, and so on, ten, twelve aircraft pouncing simultaneously like predatory birds on their quarry, releasing their bomb load right over the target ... The explosion is immense each time and the noise is deafening. Everything is blurred ... The enemy is hit here by an enormous annihilation strike and still more squadrons keep coming on, climbing to high altitudes in order to dive steeply down with the same objective, that is, to bust the Sedan invasion gateway wide open. We stand there and watch events as if transfixed.[22]

David Boyer remained physically uninjured, even through the final twenty minutes, but when the raids suddenly moved on to targets behind the front line, he had been stripped of his ability to act as a soldier, later recalling: 'When it ended, it took me several minutes to stand. My world was silent and my view obscured by smoke which, as it cleared, looked like I had been transported to 1916 Verdun – and then they came at us. I raised my hands hoping more to be shot than taken prisoner.'*[23]

In common with the great German 'hurricane' artillery preparations of 1918, the greatest impact of the Luftwaffe's attack was psychological rather than physical. Indeed, only fifty-six men were listed as casualties during the raid,[24] very few bunkers were destroyed and few guns were put out of action. As Guderian and Loerzer knew, German aircraft were not capable of the sort of reliable precision bombing required to consistently destroy small targets but their plan recognized the impact of intense and unrelenting bombing on a soldier's fighting effectiveness. Nevertheless, the air attacks, gradually intensifying artillery bombardment and then tank fire from across the river in the twenty minutes before the river assault did enough physical damage to severely undermine French co-ordination and defensive capabilities. Several bunkers and machine-gun positions were destroyed before the first German rubber boats touched the water and the field telephone lines of many 55th Infantry Division units were cut, which was of great advantage to the attackers.

---

* As it was, Boyer was captured and spent the rest of the war as a PoW.

1st Panzer Division's 1st Rifle Regiment was to attack with two battalions up-front, crossing the Meuse and landing at Glaire. On its left, Gross Deutschland Regiment with one battalion up-front would attack to Torchy. The regiments' tasks were to create a wedge into the French defences and establish a bridgehead. Supporting Balck's Rifle Regiment was a battalion of engineers which not only controlled their movement across the river in forty-four large and sixty-six small rubber assault boats, but also provided specialists in bunker destruction. They had worked together on numerous exercises, during which time they had practised crossing similar rivers against a similar defence on many occasions. Thus, when at 1600 hours the engineers crewing 1st Rifle Regiment's boats had failed to arrive, it took just ten minutes for Balck take stock of the situation and order the infantry to do the job themselves.

As the first wave of boats started their short journey across the Meuse – supported by fire from their tanks, anti-tank guns and assault guns – they came under fire from those French positions that had managed to recover from the mauling meted out by German bombs and shells. Machine-gun rounds splashed into the water around the vulnerable attackers and some hit their mark, sinking the light craft and making casualties of many on board. But the attackers had inadvertently found what might be called the Glaire Gap, and they could not be stopped. Encouraged by their junior leaders, the German infantry and engineers moved quickly on French positions and began silencing them with a mixture of small arms fire, smoke bombs, hand grenades and flamethrowers. Some positions fought to the death and some fought until their fate was sealed, but many saw the Germans coming towards them and fled to the rear. The strong-point at Les Forges, for example, fought up to the moment it was overwhelmed before its commander, Lieutenant Lamay, ordered a withdrawal 650 yards back to Bellevue and occupied a bunker left empty by its fleeing occupants.

The initial attack around Glaire had made a successful lodgement on the west bank of the Meuse by around 1700 hours and the three battalions involved immediately fought to develop it further. 1st Rifle Regiment was rallied by Balck, who was soon joined by Guderian, who had crossed with the second wave. The general's presence was noted by a captured French junior officer, Second Lieutenant Verron, whose forward bunker had been taken by surprise after hand grenades had rattled down the air vents and were followed by an infantry attack. Fearing the enemy's next move, Verron surrendered and was taken by a sergeant to a high-ranking German officer – probably Guderian – who was crouching over a map and talking into a radio. The general scanned Verron from head to foot and barked out an order before motioning for the confused prisoner to be led away.

The Germans pushed on ruthlessly, seeking to maintain their tempo, the initiative and advantage they had gained by their preparation of the battlefield. The 1st Panzer Division journal says: 'One bunker after the other, anti-tank guns, machine guns, and field fortifications are taken in individual combat and through the personal example of all the leaders who advance in front of their men.'[25] One such leader was Oberleutnant Günther Korthal, who commanded the assault platoon of 3rd Company of the engineer battalion. Failing to find either his company commander, battalion commander or Balck, he linked up with another platoon and led the group forward, fighting tenaciously throughout the day as he worked methodically through the complex defensive system of the principal line of resistance. Other units did the same. Although charging at the enemy had its place at certain times and in certain places, a degree of finesse was required to overcome the French defences, one that necessitated close, quick verbal orders, equally close co-ordination and mutual support, all of which had been developed to a pitch of excellence over months of hard training. It was not until 1830 hours, therefore, that Korthal destroyed two bunkers at the Bellevue intersection a mere one and a half miles from their crossing point at the loop in the river, and turned west along the west bank of the Meuse.

The Germans now began to engage the French positions on high ground that confronted the crossing of 2nd Panzer Division at Donchery and dominated the flat, coverless launch point for Veiel's units. This was the place where Lafontaine expected any attempt to cross the river to take place, and so the defence here was particularly strong and included artillery support from the neighbouring 102nd Infantry Division. 2nd Panzer Division had started its assault at 1730 hours due to the late arrival of their units, but had faltered in the face of French firepower in the hours since. Without the benefit of an intense air attack on its front and deprived of its heavy artillery – the division was left with just twenty-four light guns which arrived an hour after the assault began – the formation encountered more opposition opposite Donchery than had been offered south of Sedan. Yet the advance of Korthal's group so undermined the French defences by silencing several bunkers and casemates that the division was still able to cross the Meuse on 13 May. Indeed, by 2030 hours, the first of Veiel's infantry and engineers clambered onto the west bank, thus creating a vital lodgement that was rapidly reinforced after dark, and began pushing forward at around midnight.

As Korthal went about his vital work, Gross Deutschland Regiment attempted to fulfil its role as the eastern part of 1st Panzer Division's wedge into the French defences. With Balck's men on their right flank, the men from Gross Deutschland sought to make progress into and around the extension of Sedan on the west bank of the Meuse known as Torchy. After traffic jams had forced the regiment to march the final six miles on foot under French artillery fire (which killed one of the battalion commanders), its leading battalion was then ordered to begin its assault with very little time to organize itself. Even so, the first companies grabbed their boats, only to be prevented from putting them into the water by a wall of French fire. Despite the supporting fire of 150mm cannon from the Heavy Weapons Company, it was not until the powerful and extremely accurate 88mm anti-aircraft guns were brought forward that two critical French bunkers were destroyed by shells entering their embrasures and the infantry found it possible to start across the river. Some managed to get within twenty yards of the west bank, but a cleverly placed machine gun fired into the flank of the assault and thwarted any landings.

Seeing the problem, the engineer in charge of the crossings on the east bank sent as many boats across the river as he could in a single wave and this ploy allowed some men from 2nd Battalion's 7th Company to land and then silence the machine-gun position. They made their way forward and the strongpoints at Pont Neuf and Cimetière fell before the attack stalled again in front of the western edge of Torchy as fire from the area ripped into the German left flank. 3rd Battalion was therefore detailed to cross the Meuse and conduct a building-clearance operation that was to last for much of the rest of the day while 2nd Battalion endeavoured to move south. By 1800 hours, 6th and 7th Companies were supporting each other as they took on the French principal line of resistance.

It was most often the courage, aggression and tactical awareness of very small groups, however, that contributed to the success of the final attack. At Bunker 104, for example, a diversionary frontal assault fixed the attention of its two machine guns, while another attack outflanked the position by moving quickly through the cover provided by an orchard and several bomb craters. The final approach was made by two men who moved carefully towards the bunker to create a second, closer diversion, while a third man ran forward to drop a grenade into one of the bunker's six ports. After the ensuing explosion, the occupants ran out and surrendered, with several yelling, 'Shoot!' The attackers refused and when the French were asked by an officer why they were asking to be shot, he was informed that they had expected to be tortured before being killed.[26]

Bunker 104 was found to have fired 10,000 rounds before falling to Gross Deutschland Regiment at 1830 hours. It was a linchpin in the strongest French line in the sector and other bunkers began to fall once it had been captured. This was not achieved without considerable German casualties being taken, including those sustained from a French anti-tank gun in a bunker that was disguised as a barn. Gradually, however, the line began to lose its cohesion as gaps were created in the defenders' interlinked arcs of fire, which allowed for infiltration. Such successes further undermined the defenders' ability to co-ordinate their defence as the Germans sought to make each bunker deaf, dumb and blind. Indeed, Captain Carribou, who had responsibility for the defences south of Torchy from his headquarters on the northern edge of the Bois de la Marfée, found his sub-sector in a state of collapse at around 2000 hours. Having personally spotted the fact that his left flank had become exposed as the advance of Gross Deutschland Regiment had caused the infantry to flee, he was then informed that the Germans were also breaking through on his right by Second Lieutenant Loritte, who had been captured by the Germans but managed to escape despite being badly wounded. Carribou immediately ordered that all official documents be destroyed and, while repositioning his headquarters to the rear, ordered Loritte and the other troops that had converged on the area to join the defence of this wooded area under Captain Vitte. These troops were soon involved in the defence of Hill 247, which overlooked the woods, but could not stop it falling and were forced into a fighting withdrawal and also swept up Carribou's headquarters. They found the defences there incomplete and that the men in place lacked information about what was happening. A firm position was not established until the village of Chaumont had been reached two miles to the south of Hill 247 at dawn on 14 May.

After a difficult start, Gross Deutschland Regiment had managed to make an important breakthrough by the end of 13 May, but its ability to achieve this owed much to 10th Panzer Division's attack towards Wadelincourt. It was this advance by Schaal's men that had undone Carribou's right flank and then helped to put Hill 247 in a pincer. In common with its sister divisions, however,

10th Panzer's crossing of the Meuse had not been trouble-free. Just getting their boats onto the Meuse at their two crossing points had been tortuous because there was 800 yards of open ground leading to the river and the assaulting forces suffered heavy casualties as they moved towards the water. 86th Rifle Regiment attacked close to the eastern edge of Sedan while 69th Rifle Regiment tried to make a crossing two miles along the river towards Pont Maugis. Indeed, a huge barrage hit the engineers just as they were unloading their equipment from trucks for the latter assault and destroyed eighty-one of the regiment's ninety-six rubber boats.[27] Like 2nd Panzer, Schaal's division was not as well served in either air or artillery support as 1st Panzer Division and this had important consequences for a formation which also drew fire from both 71st Infantry Division as it moved into position on Lafontaine's right and the guns of X Corps. Having suffered such a loss of assault craft and attracting such a fusillade of French shells, 69th Rifle Regiment abandoned its attempts to cross the Meuse at its designated point at 1700 hours and joined its sister regiment closer to Sedan.

The initial crossing of the Meuse by 86th Rifle Regiment was conducted under intense machine-gun fire and failed everywhere except for a team of five assault engineers and six infantrymen led by Walther Rubarth. An engineer like Korthal, Feldwebel Rubarth had a vital tactical role to play on a shoulder of the main effort that was to have operational significance. Having put a small bunker out of action soon after landing on the French side of the river, the team cut through some barbed-wire entanglements and seized the next bunker from the rear. Rubarth later wrote: 'I use an explosive charge. In a moment, the force of the detonation tears off the rear part of the bunker. We use the opportunity and attack the occupants with hand grenades.'[28] As a white flag appeared, cheering was heard from the beleaguered troops waiting to cross from the opposite bank and the group pushed on to silence another three bunkers before running into the principal line of resistance. There was now a 300-yard gap for the infantry following on behind, and these men duly moved forward and attacked. Rubarth's team joined a company of infantry and he first stormed a machine-gun position and then, dropping over a railway embankment covered in wire, his team attacked a bunker from both sides. Rubarth later recalled: 'One Frenchman, who had left the bunker and aimed [his weapon] directly at me, was rendered harmless with a hand grenade.'[29] Having blasted the bunker doors open and forced the surrender of its occupants, the group moved on to take another two bunkers and in so doing cracked open the main line of defences.

The dismantling of the French defences allowed the 10th Panzer Division infantry to lunge forward into Wadelincourt and forced the defenders commanded by Captain Leflon to withdraw to a pre-planned stopping line which he found empty. These French troops continued to move south and only stopped when they linked up with Carribou's in Chaumont. While 86th Regiment took their objective, Hill 246 just to the south of Wadelincourt, which fell to them at 2100 hours, Rubarth and his team had been working their way down the principal line of resistance towards Frénois. The last bunker he secured was No. 8 *ter*, halfway towards the village and well into the 1st Panzer Division's area of operations. With this, the company of 86th Rifle Regiment following Rubarth's team stormed up Hill 247 to assist Gross Deutschland Regiment in taking the position and the French principal line of resistance fell. For his excellent work on that day, Rubarth was to receive a commission and he also received the Knighthood of the Iron Cross.*

Balck's 1st Rifle Regiment were also the grateful recipients of good work on their flanks, for without it they might well have stalled at Frénois. Korthal's destruction of the two bunkers at the Bellevue intersection at around 1830 hours opened a vital area of the front, allowing Frénois to be by-passed by the forward companies. The village was eventually taken at around 2010 hours by follow-on troops after the French fire support provided

---

* Rubarth was later killed in action in Russia on 26 October 1941.

from atop Hill 247 was ended by the Gross Deutschland Regiment and 86th Rifle Regiment's pincer on the position. The battalion commander of the 331st Infantry Regiment defending Frénois, Lieutenant Colonel Foucault, later complained that he had no idea what was happening because his communication had been cut during the air raids. This situation had been replicated across the platoons, companies, battalions and regiments of the division while Lafontaine's communications with Grandsard had also been degraded by the Luftwaffe. Throughout the day, 55th Infantry Division units felt isolated and lacked information, which encouraged poor decision-making, rumour and fear. As a result, there were both unauthorized local withdrawals and swift capitulations. By the evening, the cracks that had been created in the French line had been expanded to create potential for Guderian's corps not only to secure a significant bridgehead by consolidating their gains, but also to follow up on their success and deepen their lodgement. Balck's regiment had an important role in this in the centre of the corps and he intended to capture La Boulette (Hill 301) – the site of von Moltke's 1870 command post – and the Bois de la Marfée (Hill 336) to complete his breakthrough.

By 2100 hours and with dusk approaching, the exertions of the day – and the previous three or more days before that – began to affect all three German divisions. It was a natural reaction to the success that had been achieved and had partly been fuelled by the adrenaline of such a challenge. Yet while the troops may well have been encouraged to learn that the enemy was in withdrawal – one or two units were even beginning to dig in for the night and eat some food – commanders recognized that the battle was at a critical stage. Overnight it was essential not only for the divisions to construct the bridges that would allow tanks, vehicles and heavy weapons to cross the Meuse, but there also needed to be the space on the west bank to deploy them. Commanders also recognized the need to exploit the French withdrawal. The enemy had to be put under unremitting pressure and prevented from establishing strong defences, and the front line had to be pushed as far away from the river as possible prior to the inevitable French counter-attack. As a result, German officers and NCOs had to try and motivate their men to get to their feet and continue their attack in a southerly direction in the gathering gloom. In 1st Rifle Regiment, when the omnipresent Balck was informed by subordinates that their men were too exhausted to move, he replied: 'Fine. Whoever wants to stay here can stay here. I'm leading the attack on the next village.'[30] With that, every man got to his feet and Balck led them forward towards Hill 301.

The battle that followed has been described by Captain Litalien, the 331st Infantry Regiment company commander defending the high ground:

> The [enemy's] fire progressively increased in intensity, and we had great difficulty containing the German advance [which was] very superior in numbers, and which finally progressed even more rapidly despite the unleashing of final protective fire by every automatic weapon. At [2230 hours] the Germans were thirty metres from the centre of resistance … [and] completely overran the left and began to move on the right …[31]

Litalien's withdrawal was immediately followed up by men of 1st Rifle Regiment's 2nd Battalion, who took forty-one prisoners before signalling to division headquarters:

> At 2240, 1st Rifle Regiment took commanding heights just north of Cheveuges. Last enemy bunker in our hands. Complete breakthrough. Elements 1st Rifle Regiment sent towards Chéhéry and high ground to the east of the village.[32]

The onrushing infantry subsequently developed a salient approximately one mile wide to the south and had reached the outskirts of Chéhéry by midnight. Soon after Hill 301 had fallen, a company-strong unit defending Hill 336 just to the south-east feared being outflanked and had withdrawn to a position between Chéhéry and Bulson by dawn but lost sixty men in doing so. By this time, 2nd Panzer Division's 2nd Rifle Regiment had grafted itself onto the right flank of 1st Panzer Division and advanced to take much of the high ground overlooking Donchery and in so doing created a narrow shoulder on Guderian's right. 10th Panzer Division created something similar on the German left flank by taking Hills 246, 247 and the village of Wadelincourt. It was a move that left Guderian's corps in possession of all the high ground immediately south of Sedan. Kirchner's satisfaction at the day can be seen in the formation's log that night which noted that it was the 'best day' so far for 1st Panzer Division which:

> [S]ucceeded in being the first to cross the Meuse, to punch a hole in the defensive line of the French and to tear through a defensive zone believed by the French to be impenetrable … The importance of this penetration had been pounded into every man from the moment the division was attached to the XIXth Army Corps in Cochem.[33]

The achievement of Guderian's corps which allowed 1st Panzer Division to fight through 5.5 miles of French defences in just eight hours should not be underestimated. It was a great vindication of German preparation, planning, training, doctrine, leadership and fighting spirit. The disaster that had befallen X Corps and 55th Division was equally immense and revealed French weaknesses in all the areas where their enemy had shown strength. The differences between the two sides can be seen in the actions of Kirchner and Lafontaine during the afternoon and evening of 13 May. While the commander of 1st Panzer Division was a model general officer going about his business of command and control, organizing and co-ordinating the various elements of his division through radio communication and, where necessary, personal visits, the commander of 55th Infantry Division was completely out of touch with rapidly developing events. Shielded in his command post at Fond Dagot five miles from Frénois, its communication with his regimental commanders fractured, his own knowledge of the unfolding battle woefully incomplete and his ability to command, control and assert his will on the battle fatally weakened, Lafontaine was impotent and virtually useless. In a report he wrote soon after the battle, he explained that although he had a broad understanding that the enemy had managed to 'infiltrate rapidly, bypassing and taking from the rear our strongpoints', he had also heard 'alarmist information coming from the front and rear' while 'orders from unqualified cadres or coming from an unknown source' led to some infantry units making disorganized withdrawals, some artillery batteries putting their guns out of service and some columns withdrawing 'far to the rear, creating bottlenecks on the roads and a feeling of panic in the rear'.[34]

The 'panic' to which Lafontaine refers had been a very real phenomenon during the evening of 13 May at the time the principal line of resistance was broken. From around 1900 hours, when some of the French troops that had been resisting the enemy's onslaught began a semi-orderly withdrawal, others fled the battlefield and caused great alarm from Bulson southwards with their overblown stories of battle and warnings of imminent annihilation. An officer was despatched from Fond Dagot to Bulson to ascertain what was happening further forward and returned to tell Lafontaine that the division had broken and that troops – on foot, in vehicles and many without weapons – were in retreat. They included gunners from north of Chaumont who had been swept along in a tide of southbound troops, their will already undermined by shells that had exploded near their positions and had been incorrectly identified as having been fired by tanks. Both the headquarters of Lieutenant Colonel Dourzal, commander of a group of X Corp's heavy artillery at Bulson, and Colonel Baudet, commander of 55th Division artillery just to the south, believed the rumours that panzers were close by and, rather than attempting to verify the information, withdrew and so lent credence to it. The panic manifested itself to the division commander and his staff at Fond Dagot and left them King Canute-like as they attempted to stop the inundation. Lafontaine himself stood, revolver in hand, before two trucks blocking the road down which the troops were withdrawing. His men tried not to meet his eye or those of other officers who stood shouting at the hundreds of troops to stop and make a stand. Very few, if any, obeyed and most dissolved into the darkness, with some eventually being spotted sixty miles to the rear.

With no knowledge of any troops remaining between him and 1st Panzer Division, Lafontaine ordered his headquarters to withdraw to Chémery and its documents to be destroyed, leaving him incommunicado and without any control over his units at 2000 hours when Hill 247 fell. The impact of 55th Division's reverses was great and led to the recently arrived 71st Division withdrawing for fear that its left flank would become exposed along with Colonel Poncelet's headquarters of X Corps' heavy artillery. It was an error of judgement that Poncelet immediately regretted and, shamed by his part in the disintegration of the French defences, he took his own life on 24 May. It was a mass withdrawal which left those 55th Infantry Division units still in place without any means of communicating their existence to the chain of command and to their fate. Lieutenant Colonel Pinaud's headquarters just south of Chaumont did not withdraw until dawn on the following day. Throughout the night he and Lieutenant Colonel Lafont commanding 331st Regiment to the west were left to their own devices as they endeavoured to try to pull together a defensive line running from Cheveuges to Bulson. The meagre troops under these officers did their best to resist the Germans until the next morning, but were finally forced to withdraw after they found that the enemy had seeped through the holes in their line during the night.

The stand taken by Pinaud and Lafontaine raises the question of what might have been achieved had Lafontaine been able to provide the two officers with a regiment's worth of infantry. While there is little doubt that 1st Panzer Division would undoubtedly have been successful in breaking through, this would most likely have been more slowly and more expensively achieved. Indeed, the shoulders of Guderian's bridgehead remained narrow during the night of 13–14 May and, had 71st Division remained in situ on Lafontaine's right flank, the prospects for a counter-attack within a couple of miles from the German crossing points would have been reasonable. As it was, the X Corps front fell back under moderate German infantry pressure, making any attempt to strike back much more difficult. The key question by midnight on 13–14 May was whether Guderian could strengthen his hold on the west bank quickly enough before the French attempted to push his divisions back into the Meuse.

But while Guderian drove his troops on to even greater efforts at Sedan, Gamelin still seemed to be working under the misapprehension that it was the developing challenge to the Dyle Line that demanded his concentration and focus. His report concluded: 'It is not yet possible to determine the zone in which the enemy will make his main attack.' The summary ended with a handwritten line – probably by General Louis Koeltz, the head of Gamelin's operations staff – which read, '[Overall] impression [is] very good.'[35] Georges hardly helped the situation for, despite all the information made available to him, he described the afternoon's events at Sedan as nothing more than a 'rather serious pin prick'.[36] Von Bock, meanwhile, noted in his diary, 'The French really do appear to have taken leave of their senses.'[37]

CHAPTER 7

14–15 May – Counter-Attacks and Exploitation

WHILE THE FIGHTING south of Sedan on 13 May became less intense after dark, the rear areas of the two opposing corps were thrown into a frenzy of activity. The French were responding to a completely unexpected situation, while the Germans, having created that situation, were moving into a series of well-rehearsed drills. Gefreiter Otto Gull, an engineer with 1st Panzer Division, had slept an average of three hours a night since 9 May. He later recalled:

> Sleep just was not an option, there was always something to do and we were exhorted to ever greater feats of endurance. We were constantly reminded how important we were to the offensive and that the lives of comrades were in our hands. It was a huge responsibility, we thought, but in the end we just did what we were told.[1]

Gull was well aware that the huge opportunity created on the Meuse could not be allowed to expire. Central to this was Guderian's plan to get his panzers across the river in order to add valuable protection to the infantry but also, when the time was right, to be in a position to thrust out of the bridgehead. 1st Panzer Division's tanks were waiting in their tree-covered assembly area at Corbion eight miles north-west of Sedan. During 13 May their crews and supporting mobile workshops undertook some much-needed vehicle maintenance, rested, rearmed, refuelled, reorganized and waited for orders to start moving forward in anticipation of the completion of the bridges. In the meantime, a pontoon ferry was constructed at Gaulier during the evening of 13 May so that vital weapons and supplies could be received on the west bank. The cargo included anti-tank guns and their ammunition in anticipation that the French might try to drive an armoured wedge through to Sedan against the lightly armed infantry. This ferry was absorbed into a heavier bridge, which became operational at midnight. Priority was initially given to the remaining anti-tank guns and artillery interspersed with vehicles containing resupplies of ammunition and other essentials for the infantry. The construction of the bridges for 10th and 2nd Panzer Divisions, however, began considerably later due to the difficulties that they had encountered getting a foothold across the Meuse and as a result their bridges were not open to traffic until dawn on 14 May and first light on 15 May respectively.

1st Panzer thus had an important role in protecting the corps while the other two divisions created their own arteries with the west bank. Pushing their anti-tank guns forward and positioning their light artillery pieces on the reverse slopes of the high ground south of Sedan, Kirchner remained offensively minded but ensured that he had made adequate defensive preparations should they become necessary – and he was certain they would. As his infantry made a concerted effort to push forward again at dawn on 14 May, they found the remnants of 55th Infantry Division which amounted to two battalions with three anti-tank platoons on a 4.5-mile front from Chérey across to Chaumont, then to Noyers-Pont Maugis and from there down to the Meuse.

On the division's left flank across the narrow River Bar was the remains of 5th Light Cavalry Division, while on their right was 71st Infantry Division.

By this time, the French High Command had a far better understanding of the threat posed by Guderian after more detailed reports had been received and absorbed. Although still awaiting evidence that would confirm that events at Sedan were the German main effort, Gamelin and Georges immediately saw the implications if it was. The Supreme Commander retained his composure but Georges, it seems, did not. The commander of the North-East Front spent most of his time at a 'personal command post' in Château des Bondons at La-Ferté-sous-Jouarre thirty-seven miles east of Vincennes. There, in the early hours of 14 May, a staff officer, André Beaufre, and Major General Aimé Doumenc, the French Army Chief of Staff, found a sombre scene. Beaufre later wrote:

> The room was barely half-lit. Major Navereau was repeating in a low voice the information that was coming in. Everyone else was silent. General Roton, the Chief of Staff, was stretched out in the armchair. The atmosphere was that of a family in which there has been a death. Georges got up quickly and came to Doumenc. He was terribly pale. 'Our front has been broken at Sedan! There has been a collapse … ' He flung himself into a chair and burst into tears. He was the first man I had seen weep in this campaign. Alas, there were to be others. It made a terrible impression on me.[2]

From this point on, Gamelin spent a good deal of time at Georges's headquarters providing support and reassurance and taking the decisions that he could not rely on his subordinate to take. It was a hugely inefficient and awkward arrangement that could and should have been avoided considering the weakness that Georges had shown before 10 May. As it was, from 14 May the Supreme Commander had to shoulder the burden of a senior general suffering a nervous breakdown and, despite his other responsibilities, he was concerned not to leave Georges for too long. Gamelin later wrote of his incapacitated subordinate: 'Right from the start of the crisis he was overwhelmed. He did not know how to organize his work, became submerged in details and exhausted himself to no avail.'[3]

While the High Command endeavoured to conjure with the broader implications for the German emergence at Sedan, local initiatives were left to Grandsard's X Corps headquarters at La Berlière. Over the course of the winter, the corps had practised a table-top response to a major river crossing at Sedan on several occasions and just three weeks before had held a map exercise which mirrored the situation faced on 13–14 May in many respects. In these rehearsals the X Corps reserve was to occupy a position from Chéhéry through Bulson to the edge of the woods south of Haraucourt and launch a counter-attack in the centre to drive the enemy into the Meuse, giving time for Second Army's XXI Corps, which was released during the afternoon of 13 May, to move up from the south to add more weight: a classic *colmater*.

Grandsard's written orders were sent to the two infantry regiments and two tank battalions by motorcycle despatch riders and informed them that they were to attack at dawn on 14 May. Both groups struggled to get forward and into position through fleeing troops from 55th Division during the evening of 13 May. On the left, Lieutenant Colonel Labarthe's 213th Infantry Regiment got to a position between Chémery and Maisoncelle by 2300 hours and dug in as 7th Tank Battalion drove through the night to reach them. On the right, Lieutenant Colonel Montvignies-Monnet's 205th Infantry Regiment and its already attached 4th Tank Battalion, meanwhile, dug in to the west of Flaba. Both groups, therefore, would need to make their final moves to the start line just north of Chémery-Maisoncelle-Villers during the last hours of darkness. The great difficulty for these attacking units, however, is that they were not being managed and lacked any information after having received Grandsard's orders.

The X Corps commander had telephoned Lafontaine to order him verbally to take command of the counter-attack – with written orders to follow – just before the 55th Division commander moved his headquarters to Chémery. Indeed, Lafontaine later argued that he moved his headquarters to better co-ordinate the counter-attack, but this was refuted by X Corps, which recognized that the divisional commander was incommunicado just when the counter-attacking groups needed encouragement, orders and direction to ensure that they were in the planned positions to attack at dawn. Yet even though he arrived at Chémery that night, Lafontaine failed to take charge of the counter-attack because he demanded written orders from Grandsard. In search of them, he tried to reach Grandsard's headquarters through the choked roads, only to find when he arrived that the corps commander was not there and that his deputy, Colonel Cachou, was en route to Chémery with Lafontaine's written orders. Lafontaine arrived back at his headquarters before Cachou arrived and continued to wait for the written orders, even though they had already been received verbatim over the telephone in his absence. Time was running out if the counter-attack was to face only German infantry lacking firepower and still the French general vacillated, a slave to a procedure, the product of a system that was just not configured for rapid decision-making on a mobile battlefield, and a man of responsibility who feared applying his own common sense and rejected the pressing need for immediate action.

After finally receiving Grandsard's one or two sentences of written orders, Lafontaine at last issued his own at 0500 hours, some nine hours after he had first been placed in charge of the counter-attack. Unbeknown to the French, their push from Bulson though the Bois de la Marfée and to the Meuse would now be a race against the German armour to claim the high ground. The first of Kirchner's tanks had moved to Gaulier through traffic jams and French shelling during the night, and they crossed the bridge at 0720 hours, spearheaded by 2nd Regiment of 1st Panzer Brigade. Gull had worked on the construction of the bridge and later testified:

> Our eyes stung with the effort of staying awake ... There were one or two mishaps along the way with heavy equipment due to fatigue, but seeing the panzers cross was a wonderful sight. We cheered, shouted good luck to the tank crews, who waved an acknowledgement back ... The division now felt that it was really on its way.[4]

The tanks' appearance on the west bank was a great relief to the German infantry, who since first light had begun to penetrate the weakly held French line north of Bulson. As part of this move 1st Rifle Regiment had taken Chéhéry and pressed on to the River Bar at Omicourt while Gross Deutschland Regiment followed them past Cheveuges in order to by-pass some stubborn opposition at the Bois de la Marfée and sought to attack towards Bulson. Orchestrating these movements was Kirchner standing atop Hill 301, keeping his eye on the infantry moving below him to his front, eagerly awaiting the arrival of the armour from his rear and watching the high ground around Bulson for signs of enemy armour. He and Guderian both knew from aerial reconnaissance that two mobile divisions were heading towards the area – these were from Second Army reserve – but also expected a more local counter-attack of the sort that Grandsard and Lafontaine were endeavouring to develop.

Had the French launched their X Corps initiative at dawn as planned, they would have caught their enemy reorienting his infantry and without any armour. As it was, 7th Tank Battalion was spotted organizing at Chémery at 0700 hours. Once again, the Germans reacted immediately and sent an advance detachment of two Gross Deutschland Regiment anti-tank platoons and two armoured scout cars under the command of Oberleutnant

Helmut Beck-Broichsitter to delay them. At 0730 hours, while 205th Infantry Regiment and 4th Tank Battalion continued their lamentably organized movement into their forming-up area, 7th Tank Battalion and 213th Infantry Regiment began its counter-attack. It was launched just as the leading units of 1st Panzer Regiment arrived on the west bank of the Meuse. The trepidation with which this under-strength push was mounted can be seen in Labarthe's response to Lafontaine's orders: 'This is a mission of sacrifice that you ask of my regiment.'[5]

As a single company of French infantry and another of tanks were sent to seize Connage, two tank companies were sent in support of Labarthe's infantry but were tied to the speed of its reluctant trudge towards Bulson. They were all observed by German aerial reconnaissance aircraft, which reported their findings back to Kirchner and Guderian. It was this information that led the first German panzer unit, a company of 2nd Panzer Regiment commanded by Oberleutnant Krajewski, to advance with the 'greatest possible speed' on the road to Chéhéry before branching off to the south-east to Bulson. The panzer company won the race to the ridge by just a couple of minutes. Krajewski's after-action report said:

> Cautiously, we drove through Bulson, which had been evacuated by the enemy, and slowly, riding single file, we approached the Hill [322] a few hundred yards south-west of the village. Heavy fire commenced the moment the first panzers reached the hill. Our two lead panzers took several direct anti-tank gun hits and burned.[6]

Krajewski's own tank was one of those that took a French shell on its front armour and he was forced to scramble out and find some cover. The enemy had caught Krajewski's armour in a pincer, and Second Lieutenant Penissou has offered a French perspective on this opening engagement:

> Three German tanks move towards Fond Dagot. They are taken under fire by the 25mm's at around 500 meters. The first is hit and bursts into flames: the second in turn is hit and bursts into flames: the third is immobilized and hit with about fifteen 25mm shells.[7]

The outnumbered German tanks fought bravely until just one tank was left mobile but held on long enough for Oberleutnant Friedrich von Grolman's panzer company to arrive. These tanks plugged the gap and, when another company arrived along with units from the Gross Deutschland Regiment, the Germans struck back. While the panzers lent fire support, the German infantry attacked 213rd Infantry Regiment in positions they had taken up around Fond Dagot. Penissou said of the situation by noon:

> We are surrounded and engage the enemy from all sides. The small arms fire is heavy. The crew of the 25mm [gun] fall dead or wounded beside their weapon. We are completely encircled and the ammunition is almost exhausted.[8]

Meanwhile, the French infantry and tanks heading for Connage managed to advance through a screen of German defenders just north of Chéméry, but then ran into Beck-Broichsitter's anti-tank team at the road intersection just east of the village at 0900 hours. The position consisted of a hedgehog of six 37mm anti-tank guns which offered all-round protection, with the two armoured scout cars offering an element of mobility. The French attack was led by their thirteen tanks, with the infantry following immediately behind. The anti-tank guns had considerable success after waiting for the enemy armour to approach to within a couple of hundred yards, and then aiming at each machine's weak spot. Even so, part of the infantry-tank group managed to work its way into Connage as the remainder endeavoured to outflank the hedgehog position and was on the verge of success when two companies of 43rd Assault Engineer Battalion arrived and hit back. This critical holding operation provided the time for a company of German tanks to arrive and begin to push the French out of Connage and back towards Chémery and then beyond just as Labarthe's attack was in withdrawal from Fond Dagot.

It was a success that had been so swift that the fall of Chémery had not been communicated to the Luftwaffe, which launched a Stuka attack on the village just as German commanders were meeting by the church to discuss their next moves. It killed the commander of 43rd Assault Engineer Battalion and three officers from 2nd Panzer Regiment and seriously wounded several others including the commander of the panzer brigade. But other German air raids hindered the advance of French reinforcements and the withdrawal of Labarthe's troops throughout 14 May, and led the regiment's commander to later write:

> During the course of the day, squadron after squadron of enemy dropped their bombs ... without being harassed by one of our own aircraft ... This was a baptism of fire for the 213th Infantry Regiment. The troops were very affected by the whistling bombs and the sight of the casualties.[9]

The dive-bombers also targeted Lieutenant Colonel Montvignies-Monnet's 205th Infantry Regiment and supporting 4th Tank Battalion which had finally attacked east of Maisoncelles at 1045 hours, just minutes before Labarthe began his withdrawal from Fond Dagot. The forward movement of this secondary advance lasted just fifteen minutes before it too was forced to withdraw and by noon Montvignies-Monnet's men were facing a German reaction which demanded that they fight for their very lives. They eventually managed to extract themselves from this precarious situation and link up in the mid-afternoon with 213th Infantry Regiment and the sorry remnants of 55th Division in a line two miles south of Chémery protecting the high ground around Mont Dieu. Labarthe and his entire staff were taken prisoner, his regiment having suffered 50 per cent casualties as had 7th Tank Battalion, along with three-quarters of its machines. Montvignies-Monnet, meanwhile, had completely lost control of his formation and was later picked up by the military police in Verdun, initially on suspicion of desertion, supposedly seeking orders from superiors.[10]

With the first, limp French counter-attack having been beaten back, Guderian, standing on Hill 301 with Kirchner, thought the success 'almost a miracle'.[11] Throughout the activity south of Bulson, 1st and 2nd Panzer Divisions used their completed bridges to fill the expanding footprint south of Sedan with more armour, artillery, combat support units and vital supplies. The Allies, understanding how important these crossing points were to the Germans, spent much of the day trying to destroy them. General Billotte appealed to General d'Astier de la Vigerie, the commander of the air force in the northern operations zone, for support in this task, saying to him: 'Victory or defeat will depend on these bridges.'[12] Indeed, with no more bridging materials to replace destroyed bridges, Guderian's corps would have been placed in a precarious position had their arteries across the Meuse been severed. Anticipating the need for their defence, the Germans moved anti-aircraft teams crewing 303 guns into position during the night of 13–14 May and the following morning.[13] These would provide a considerable defence, but with a heavy enough concentration of aircraft the Allies could still hope to achieve an important success. It was to Billotte's great dismay, therefore, that although 152 bombers were available (of which 109 were from the RAF), problems in their co-ordination led to them being diluted in twenty-seven separate attacks of between ten and twenty aircraft, with Allied fighters flying 250 supporting sorties.

The attacks began at 0530 hours and continued until midnight on 14–15 May. The German anti-aircraft gunners coped well with them and were supported by fighters flying 814 sorties, which meant that only a small proportion of the bombers reached the Sedan area.[14] One German officer who watched the Allied attempts to punch through to the bridge at Gaulier later wrote:

> Again and again an enemy aircraft crashes out of the sky dragging a long plume of smoke behind it, which after the crash of the succeeding explosion remains for some time perpendicular in the warm air. Occasionally from the falling machines one or two white parachutes release themselves and float slowly to earth. In the short time that I am at the bridge, barely an hour, eleven planes were brought down.[15]

The largest raid of the day took place in the late afternoon by the RAF when seventy-three Battles and Blenheims attacked, protected by twenty-seven French fighters. It was a disaster, with forty of the bombers shot down and leading the Official RAF History to note: 'No higher rate of loss in an operation of comparable size has ever been experienced by the Royal Air Force.'[16] One British pilot, Flying Officer Sarll, recalled: 'I do not think anyone who did not experience what we were called upon to perform this day could ever visualize the tremendous courage of our people, so many of whom died.'[17] That courage was also noted by the Germans, with Oberst von Hippel, the commander of a flak regiment, later recalling:

> We could not help admiring the guts displayed by our opponents in attacking the bridges again and again despite all their losses and the fierce flak fire, and even shooting from planes already on fire, wounding some of our artillerymen.[18]

The total Allied aircraft losses on 14 May at Sedan were fifty-three bombers and fifty fighters. Many more aircraft were badly damaged, and some of these could not be returned to action. The backbone of the Allied bomber fleet, therefore, had been broken in a defensive action which was to prove of considerable benefit to the Germans in the days and weeks of the campaign that followed.

Throughout the Allied air raids, whatever delays there were to the continued use of the bridges were short. Guderian made a point of standing on various bridges during the attacks, at one point with a rather dubious von Rundstedt, in order to encourage continued traffic crossings. As a consequence, the bulk of Guderian's corps – 600 German tanks, 60,000 men and an impressive 22,000 vehicles – passed into the bridgehead on 14 May. This put the formation in an excellent position to exploit the offensive movements it had also made that day as it partially reorientated itself westwards. While Gross Deutschland Regiment and part of its armour was dealing with the X Corps counter-attack, the remainder of 1st Panzer Division attacked west and crossed the Bar and Ardennes Canal at Omincourt at 0730 hours. Had the French managed to outflank Connage with the left wing of their counter-attack, this development would have been imperilled, but they had been pushed out of the village and then out of Chémery, and so Kirchner's troops were also able to make crossings towards Malmy at 1230 hours.

Together, these successes allowed 1st Panzer Division to push 6.5 miles with the infantry-dominated Kampfgruppe Krüger to the village of Singly on the left and three miles with the armour-heavy Kampfgruppe Nedtwig to Vendresse on the right. Further north, 2nd Panzer Division made a similar movement across the Bar and Ardennes Canal for, although its own bridge at Donchery was not due for completion until the following morning, ferries and the Gaulier bridge allowed its units to cross the river during the afternoon of 14 May. Splitting into two parts in a manner very similar to Kirchner's division, one group pushed four miles to Flize on the Meuse while another on its left flank thrust three miles to Sapogne. Neither division's attacks were without difficulty. Both formations were tired, their lines of communication stretched and they had taken accumulative losses which affected their immediate offensive outlook: Nedtwig, for example, had lost a quarter of the tanks under his command by the end of the day.

Although the defence by 3rd Spahi Brigade, 5th Light Cavalry Division and 53rd Infantry Division was tenacious and had some tactical value, Guderian's move to the west had wrongfooted the French. They were not anticipating a breakout from the Sedan bridgehead so early and, when it came, they assumed that it would head east to outflank the Maginot Line. As a result, only 10th Panzer Division's advance conformed to their expectations. Schaal managed to get a single panzer regiment into the bridgehead on 14 May which, together with his infantry, managed to overcome some stiff French resistance at Noyers during the morning, and continued its advance as the French began their wider withdrawal during the afternoon. At this point the division still needed confirmation that Guderian wanted it to push on to take the high ground of Mont Dieu half a dozen miles to the south in order to provide protection for the bridgehead and the rear of 1st and 2nd Panzer Divisions. Although an assessment of intelligence concerning the potential threats to the corps in the short and medium term initially pointed to the possibility of Schaal's division being able to turn west itself and leave the defence of the southern flank to 29th Motorized Division, within hours the risk posed by the two divisions from Second Army that had been spotted heading to the area proved too great for Guderian to ignore. Thus, in the early hours of 15 May he ordered 10th Panzer Division to seize the high ground of Mont Dieu at Stonne assisted by Gross Deutschland Regiment.

Despite the reports he was now receiving from the sector, Gamelin still failed to fully grasp the immensity of the situation that was confronting the Allies at Sedan, referring to it as 'merely a local interlude' at noon on 14 May.[19] Throughout the day, he continued to battle roads clogged up with refugees and military vehicles to be with Georges. Meanwhile staff officers at both Vincennes and La-Ferté-sous-Jouarre continued to rely on motorcycle messengers to send and receive messages of all types. It was extremely common for these messengers to be held up by the choked roads and by Luftwaffe attacks, which were increasingly targeting anything that moved along them. Scores of these motorcyclists were killed or seriously wounded in accidents, and particularly at night, as they attempted to deliver messages as quickly as possible. Yet despite their best efforts, it was not uncommon for the required – and time-sensitive – written orders of commanders to take two days to reach them and then be carried out. As officer and historian Marc Bloch argued, 'From the beginning to the end of the war, the metronome at headquarters was always set at too slow a beat.'[20]

Such communication problems exacerbated the doctrinal requirement for written orders and the close control of operations, but the reality was that commanders had a poor 'grip' of the battle and that the French were drifting irrevocably from being able to influence events at Sedan. Yet with Huntziger confirming to his superiors that General Jean-Adolphe-Louis-Robert Flavigny's two counter-attacking divisions were on their way to the sector, Gamelin and Georges felt confident the Germans could be contained. Flavigny was commonly regarded to be France's leading armoured warfare commander and his 3rd Motorized Infantry and 3rd Armoured Divisions were prepared to counter what had always been considered to be the main threat offered by an enemy crossing at Sedan: a turning of the Maginot Line. In this sense, 10th Panzer Division had been offered by Guderian as bait in a trap that the French were only too willing to take, and so Second Army's counter-attack was consequently drawn away from his westerly thrust. Huntziger even moved his headquarters – including 2,638 staff – from Senuc thirty miles to Verdun in order to be better placed to organize the defences against the expected German turn east. But as soon as appropriate forces had arrived south of Sedan, Schaal's division would be relieved and could join its sister divisions in their attack towards the Channel coast.

Flavigny's counter-attack was planned to be conducted along with 1st Cavalry Brigade, 5th Light Cavalry Division on the left and 2nd Light Cavalry Division, 1st Colonial Infantry Division and elements of 71st Infantry Division on their right. Although there were question marks about the military capability and strength of some of these formations, together the force concentrated some 300 French tanks against the bridgehead and Flavigny recognized that the earlier he attacked, the greater the likelihood he would be able to push Guderian's force back into the Meuse. The counter-attack was initially to have started in the late morning of 14 May in the immediate wake of X Corps' own, over the same ground and at a time when only 1st and some of 10th Panzer Divisions had crossed to the west bank. Yet there remained a question over whether the French force was capable of striking a blow against the Germans for Flavigny was not only concerned about the co-ordination and co-operation of the divisions but also the fact that his main strike force, General Antoine Brocard's 3rd Armoured Division, lacked most of its combat support, twenty of its 158 tanks and all of its anti-tank weapons, and had no radios. Even so, it was an essential element in the French scheme, but when the division arrived at its Le Chesne assembly area at 0600 hours, Brocard then needed time to refuel and reorganize before moving the final six miles to the start line. This laborious but essential process forced a frustrated Flavigny to postpone his attack until 1400 hours, a less favourable start time as 2nd Panzer Division's tanks had begun to cross the Meuse by the early afternoon and Guderian's troops had already crossed the Ardennes Canal in force. Yet even this later hour asked too much of the attacking divisions, for orders only made slow progress through the immense command bureaucracy, which meant that some units did not receive them until 1300 hours. So the attack was postponed again, this time until the evening, and then, with Brocard's force still tinkering and vacillating in the wake of X Corps' failure and with dusk approaching, it was put off until the next day.

By this stage, Flavigny had moved on from being irritated by the delays to infuriated. He recognized during the evening of 14 May that he had missed the opportunity that was so beguiling twelve hours earlier as Guderian's force had split and wondered whether a counter-attack might prove to be a futile gesture in the circumstances and that failure might leave Mont Dieu and the Maginot Line extremely vulnerable. The day had taught him that 3rd Armoured Division very likely lacked the morale and capability to take on the responsibility that it had been given and that German speed of thought and action had allowed them to retain the initiative. Having discussed the situation with Huntziger and in recognition of the threat that the Germans posed whether they continued their attack west or began to push east, Flavigny dispersed his force in defensive positions. There would be no Second Army counter-attack at Sedan, there was no major counter-attacking force in the General Reserve and 14 May slipped by as a day of missed opportunity. This was the apogee of French feebleness, revealing the cost of divisions whose quality varied widely, incoherent command, sluggish movement and lack of offensive spirit. While Flavigny may have seen the need for rapid action, he had no means to achieve it and this was fatal on the 1940 battlefield.

By nightfall, there was a considerable bulge in the French line twelve miles wide and nine miles deep. 71st Division defended the eastern side of the bridgehead, with 1st Colonial Division and 2nd Light Cavalry Division around La Besace together with the remnants of 55th Infantry Division, while 3rd Armoured Division and 3rd Motorized Division looked to protect Mont Dieu and Stonne. To the west of the Ardennes Canal, the Second Army's 1st Cavalry Brigade and 5th Light Cavalry Division took the front to a point just short of Omont from where 152nd Infantry Regiment, the first part of General Jean de Lattre de Tassigny's 14th Infantry Division to arrive, held the line. This formation was part of a new Sixth Army that was being formed to strengthen the join between Second and Ninth Armies to protect the route to the crucial communications hub of Rethel. Beyond 152nd Infantry Regiment, and taking the line in a westerly facing bulge north to Charleville Mézieres on the Meuse, were Ninth Army's 3rd Spahis Brigade, 53rd Infantry Division and 102nd Infantry Division.

This was a defensive front which, for want of a better plan, would see the French formations contain the Germans, wear them down and then, as the enemy's expedition withered on the vine, strike back. Guderian, however, had every reason to avoid being contained and, recognizing that his actions would determine the shape of German plans now that the Meuse had been crossed, sought to conduct an independent operation. While 10th Panzer Division provided protection by fighting for the high ground south of Sedan, 1st and 2nd Panzer Divisions would continue to drive west towards Rethel. Thus, while his superiors argued about whether von Kleist's spearhead should wait for the marching infantry to catch up, Guderian's intention was to have made such progress as to present them with a fait accompli. In the early hours of 15 May, a circumspect von Kleist approved the move.

The continuance of Guderian's attack would not only see his corps take another large step forward towards his longer-term goal of pushing through to the Channel coast, but would also close the gap between his divisions and Reinhardt's corps crossing the Meuse at Monthermé and then Hoth's corps at Dinant. Together, this mass of panzer divisions, he believed, would have far greater ability to burst through behind the Allied troops pinned in central Belgium than if they fought their own isolated battles while waiting for the infantry armies. On 14 May, having managed to cross the Meuse and occupy Monthermé, Kempf's 6th Panzer Division – its sister 8th Panzer Division was still closing on the river – endeavoured to fight out of the town and surge forward. However, being trapped in a built-up area in a loop of the river drastically reduced the division's ability to concentrate its force and retain its mobility while, effectively acting as the cork in a bottle, a battalion of the competent 102nd Fortress Infantry Division's 42nd Colonial Infantry Regiment plugged the exit.

The deployment of French air power against the trapped Germans at this point could have been devastating for Kempf, but no aircraft were available due to the attacks on the Sedan sector. Left to apply its infantry to loosen the French defences, 6th Panzer Division gradually made some important infiltrations which by dawn on 15 May meant that two battalions were working hard to expand and would lead to a breakthrough later that morning. Further north in the Dinant sector, Hoth's 5th and 7th Panzer Divisions were not quite so hemmed into their conjoined bridgehead and both probed forward on the morning of 14 May. Max von Hartlieb's 5th Panzer Division finally secured the fiercely defended Haut-le-Wastia two miles from the river while 7th Panzer Division's 7th Rifle Regiment commanded by Georg von Bismarck advanced to take Onhaye. It was at this stage that the two division commanders clashed when, with just one military bridge having been constructed at Leffe due to a lack of bridging equipment, Hartlieb asked Rommel if he could pass his tanks over the 7th Panzer Division bridge to reinforce his formation. Rommel responded that because 5th Panzer Division lacked boldness and its panzers always lagged behind, he would agree only if he was authorized to take those tanks under his command. Hartlieb was furious but when he informed Hoth about the situation, the corps commander recognized the offensive advantage that this would give 7th Panzer Division and acceded to Rommel's petulant demand. He liked and even encouraged Rommel's boldness, but that did not mean that he approved of his subordinate's vainglorious approach.

The family squabble within Hoth's corps was unsavoury but inevitable considering Rommel's character and ambition, but it was soon overshadowed by an apparent emergency in his division.

Shortly after 0800 hours Rommel was informed that a radio message had been received – 'Bismarck encircled in Onhaye'[21] – just before all contact with him had been lost. The situation bore all the signs of a French counter-attack and worried not only Rommel, who had not anticipated such a swift and strong enemy reaction, but also Fourth Army headquarters when it was informed. Rommel responded to the situation without hesitation and immediately ordered all his armour across the Meuse to break the encirclement. Rommel's personal group followed the spearhead column as it rushed towards Onhaye so that he might be on the spot to command a response to the German encirclement, but his PzKpfw Mk III was targeted by a French anti-tank gun en route. Hit several times, the tank slipped down a slope as the driver took evasive action. Bleeding heavily from a shell splinter wound on his cheek, Rommel tried to engage an enemy gun with the tank's main armament but the turret would not move as it was wedged into the soil. The general ordered that the vulnerable tank be abandoned and, once he was outside it, it became clear that the column had suffered a number of losses, with one subaltern reporting to him, 'Herr General, my left arm has been shot off.'[22]

It was another close escape for the cavalier Rommel, who shortly after was told that Bismarck had not in fact radioed 'encircled [*eingeschlossen*] in Onhaye' but 'arrived [*eingetroffen*] in Onhaye'.[23] Rommel nonetheless continued his attack, advancing to Sommière with Hartlieb's panzers, breaking the main French defensive line in the sector and pushing his armour to Morville, eight miles west of the Meuse. Yet although Hoth had succeeded in opening up the French line at Dinant, the very possibility that the French had seemed to be launching a swift counter-attack unsettled some senior officers and particularly those who were concerned about the panzer divisions mounting their own independent operations. The 'Bismarck Fright' had revived some long-standing fears and was used as evidence of the folly in allowing the panzer divisions to bolt forward 'off the leash'.

The French had meanwhile tried to respond to the Dinant crossings, but in common with the response at Sedan, their counter-attack was plagued by a mixture of incompetence and practical difficulties. At midnight on 13–14 May, 1st DCR, commanded by General Bruneau, had been dispatched from Charleroi, just twenty-five miles away from Rommel's penetration. The forward elements of the division, however, only reached an assembly area north of Flavion, some ten miles west of Dinant, at around 2100 hours on 14 May due to the congested roads and some units getting lost. Nevertheless, the Ninth Army commander, Corap, sent a message to Bruneau: 'You must counterattack this evening with all that you have. That's a formal order.'[24] Unbeknown to both men, and to Rommel, the leading elements of 1st DCR and 7th Panzer Division's 25th Panzer Regiment at Morville were just three miles apart. Had Bruneau been able to carry out Corap's order, he would have been able to cause a great deal of damage to Rommel's relatively flimsy armour, but 1st DCR's Char B1s could not move anywhere because they had run out of fuel and needed to reorganize. With the attack postponed until Bruneau's force was ready, another fleeting but important opportunity for the French had gone begging.

In retrospect, Rommel's breakthrough on 14 May, when considered together with that achieved by Guderian and the growing threat at Monthermé, could not have looked more like the main German effort. Yet intense action to the north continued to supply what seemed to be compelling evidence to Gamelin that this was not necessarily the case. On the morning of 14 May, the Allied High Command felt that a critical point had been attained in the defence against Army Group B with the Germans reaching the Gembloux Gap and the Netherlands on the point of being overrun. The Dutch were, indeed, under unrelenting pressure: in the north the Germans were threatening to break through and envelop Amsterdam while in the east there was a withdrawal from the Grebbe Line back to the incomplete defences of Fortress Holland, this pursued by German ground and air forces with a tenacity and ferocity which belied their tiredness. It was in the south, however, that the invaders posed the greatest immediate threat as 9th Panzer Division prepared to cross the Meuse into the centre of the city over the Wilhelms Bridge.

Yet the continued resistance of the Dutch was becoming a source of great frustration to the Germans, particularly when it was compared with the remarkable developments on the Meuse and the success in central Belgium. On 13 May, therefore, the commander of Eighteenth Army, General Georg von Küchler, set out his intent to his subordinates: 'Resistance in Rotterdam should be broken with all means, if necessary threaten with and carry out the annihilation of the city.'[25] Hitler agreed and in Führer Directive No. 11 stated: '… the speedy conquest of the Fortress Holland is to be facilitated through a deliberate weakening of the [air] power operated by Sixth Army.'[26] As a result, Heinkel He 111 bombers of Kampfgeschwader 54 were shifted north away from their support of operations in central Belgium in order to force a Dutch capitulation.

There was considerable discussion about what Küchler meant by 'annihilation' as the ground forces were concerned by the thought of having to fight through piles of Rotterdam rubble containing innumerable civilian corpses against an enraged enemy. Even so, the word played on the worst Dutch fears and so it was employed when a messenger was sent to the Dutch commander of Rotterdam, Colonel Pieter Scharroo, demanding the city's capitulation or promising that the 'severest means of annihilation' would be employed. Although the deadline for a decision passed on 14 May, negotiations were still continuing when nearly sixty Heinkels were not called back and dropped 1,308 bombs on the city which destroyed its centre, killed 814 civilians and made 80,000 homeless in the resultant fires.[27] A second attack was cancelled when Scharroo capitulated just minutes before its aircraft dropped their bombs.

The Germans were in no mood to enter into protracted dialogue with their enemies for they had no time to waste as commanders attempted to turn operational success into final victory. Whatever stood in the way would be destroyed. It was a ruthlessness that became increasingly obvious to those that sought to deny the Germans and was immediately recognized by their enemies. Indeed, the loss of Rotterdam and the rapidly deteriorating situation across the country left Winkelman with precious few options. He could order that the fight continue even though the enemy were in the process of advancing into the body of Fortress Holland, but he also appreciated the ultimate futility of such attempts. Thus, having heard that the Germans were threatening the destruction of Utrecht and Amsterdam too and with a mandate to avoid unnecessary suffering, Winkelman decided that the Netherlands would surrender the next morning – 15 May. The Dutch troops west of Breda – approximately two battalions of army and navy personnel – were exempt from the surrender as they were fighting under the command of the French and were gradually withdrawn onto Belgian soil and to Ostend. Although a tiny force, their presence was welcomed by the Allies as the Germans swiftly followed the Dutch capitulation with a reorientation that saw Eighteenth Army's XXVI Corps attack into northern Belgium.

The collapse of resistance in the Netherlands was hardly greeted with great enthusiasm by Gamelin and the High Command, but it did at least allow them to focus more intently on the struggle for the Gembloux Gap, which had been at the heart of French defensive planning ever since the building of the Maginot Line. This critical area was protected not only by Blanchard's French First Army but also the two weakened and withdrawing DLMs of Prioux's cavalry corps. The Battle of Gembloux began on the afternoon of 14 May when 4th Panzer Division mounted an attack even before 3rd Panzer Division had arrived as Hoepner wished to make the most of the formation's momentum and so exploit

French disorganization. What followed was a brutal confrontation that reflected the importance of the Gembloux sector to both sides. Although the eventual arrival of 3rd Panzer Division assisted its sister division, there was no immediate breakthrough since 2nd and 3rd DLMs held the enemy five miles in front of Blanchard's men, who used the opportunity to dig in faster and deeper. The appearance of the three divisions of Sixth Army's IV Corps, however, gave the Germans such a superiority of numbers that Prioux had no option other than to withdraw behind Blanchard's main positions that evening and to leave the approaching enemy to the artillery. Prioux's Corps was one of the few Allied success stories during the first week of the German campaign: it successfully delayed the advance of Hoepner's two panzer divisions, inflicted significant damage on them and allowed a critical position in the Dyle Line to be reached and prepared. Although the corps was undoubtedly assisted by excellent preparation for its semi-independent role, its application and capability was rarely, if ever, seen in any other French formation during the campaign.

On 15 May, however, the engagement of the Dyle Line infantry by Army Group B would be complete and a new phase in the campaign would begin. Indeed, increasingly undermined by the advance of Army Group A's outflanking panzer divisions south of Gembloux, Billotte's headquarters had on the evening of 14 May ordered Blanchard to prepare for a retreat. The reality of the German trap that the French had marched into had finally dawned. For the Allied soldiers and civilians whose knowledge of unfolding events was limited to what they could see and embellished with stories and wild rumours, the end of the fifth day of the campaign was as confused as it was distressing.

Although Captain Daniel Barlone of 2nd North African Division wrote in his diary about the fate of the Netherlands, 'Fortunately our *poilus* have no more idea where Rotterdam is than Peking, so this news does not worry them,'[28] there is little doubt that tales of collapse and the fall of great cities was percolating through to soldier and civilian alike. Government radio broadcasts and press briefings were solemn, but rarely gave a faithful sense of the implications of what was befalling a relatively small corner of north-west Europe. Alexander Werth, a Russian-born British journalist living in Paris, was not taken in by the broadcasts of Ludovic-Oscar Frossard, the French minister of information, who asked that the population be patient for success: '"Verdun lasted six months," he says, "the Somme as long …". Are these valid arguments? Haven't the French Ministers realized yet that this type of war is *different*?'[29]

Meanwhile, for those senior officers, politicians and other interested parties who were following events across France and Belgium, what was happening was both confusing and distressing. Georges, the commander of the North-East Front, was showing obvious signs of strain, but he was not the only one. The British army liaison officer at the headquarters of British Air Forces in France made a diary note of a meeting held at this time with attendees who included Air Marshal Barratt and Generals Vuillemin and Billotte:

> The conference was a tragic affair. Most of the French officers were in tears, some quite openly sobbing at having to admit the shame they felt in acknowledging the appalling fact that the French had walked out of their fortified positions without any attempt at genuine resistance. This is a very bad affair.[30]

Yet even if the tension of the situation was permeating through the upper echelons of the French High Command, this was not translated into the political collapse in Paris and London that Hitler had thought likely. Although Neville Chamberlain was replaced as British prime minister by Winston Churchill on 10 May, this was an event that coincided with the German invasion but was not caused directly by it, and the change not only stabilized the country but also made it more resilient and tenacious. Something had almost happened in France, where Reynaud had revealed a clear desire to remove Daladier from his cabinet and Gamelin from command, but the German offensive had temporarily forced the prime minister to postpone his manoeuvrings and place what faith he had in the incumbent Supreme Commander.

As it was, by 15 May Churchill had already shown signs of being a strong and pugnacious leader and he had coped well with the early pressure put upon him. But he did find that he spent increasing amounts of time trying to extract information from the French and reassuring them. Indeed, on 14 May Reynaud had sent a remarkably jittery telegram to him, saying: 'The situation is really very serious. The German Army has pierced our fortified lines south of Sedan … Between Sedan and Paris there are no more fortifications comparable to those.'[31] This revealed just the sort of pessimism that Churchill could not abide and it was compounded the next morning when he was woken to take a telephone call from the French leader, who told him, 'We have been defeated … We are beaten; we have lost the battle … The front is broken near Sedan; they are pouring through in great numbers with tanks and armoured cars.'[32] Although Churchill's military knowledge led him to respond that the Germans were extremely unlikely to be able to sustain such an advance, it was clear that the situation was grave, and in an attempt to test the temperature in France, learn the truth about events and buoy up Britain's ally, he prepared to make a trip to Paris on 16 May.

If it had been left to Guderian, the situation about which Churchill would be briefed when he met Reynaud would have been one of unremitting woe. The panzer commander, however, was as aware as anybody that even if the fate of France rested in the hands of many, the decisions of the few would have a disproportionate impact on the outcome. The few that most concerned Guderian included von Kleist, von Rundstedt and Hitler. This triumvirate simply would not countenance a carefree thrust to the west: like Churchill, they did not think that panzer forces had the ability to sustain such an advance, and they retained long-standing concerns about French counter-attacks and the turning of the Maginot Line. As a result, Guderian had reluctantly split his force in two but continued his attack with the support of Halder, who saw the very great benefit of maintaining the initiative rather than waiting in a small bridgehead for the arrival of the infantry. Both men were aware, however, of the nervousness in some quarters that mounted every extra mile the panzer divisions advanced from the Meuse.

10th Panzer Division had the significant challenge of pinning and fixing a numerically superior enemy south of Sedan by attacking and holding the high ground at Mont Dieu. Guderian's aim was for Schaal's division, backed by the arriving 29th Motorized Division, to distract the French long enough to hand over to the advancing foot infantry and then rejoin the offensive. In the meantime, its objective on the morning of 15 May was to seize a long line from the Ardennes Canal west, on to the heights of Mont Dieu – including Stonne – then down to a bend in the Meuse south of Villemontry. The next two days saw 10th Panzer Division and the attached Gross Deutschland Regiment involved in some extremely intense fighting as the French sought to deny the Germans the high ground. The epicentre was the elevated village of Stonne, a small collection of farm buildings which was protected by units of 3rd Armoured Division and won and lost several times by both sides before the matter was concluded.

The Germans attacked at dawn on 15 May, using a battalion of Gross Deutschland Regiment, supported by a company of anti-tank guns, a battalion of tanks from 8th Panzer Regiment and men from 43rd Assault Engineer Battalion on the flanks. Stonne fell to the Germans after some frenetic close-quarters fighting which led to all units taking casualties, seven tanks among them. Fearful that the Germans could now observe their lines, the French were ordered to strike back immediately and, using their heaviest tanks, briefly retook the village. Unwilling to allow the French time to settle, grizzled Gross Deutschland units took Stonne for a second time in the late morning – and so the die was cast for a battle of tenuous holds.

The French attacked again at 1100 hours, using three companies of tanks to lead several hundred infantry into the village. 1st Battalion Gross Deutschland Regiment and twelve anti-tank guns were waiting. Three guns commanded by Oberfeldwebel Hans Hindelang had just arrived and were being sighted in the south-west corner of the village by a water tower when three Char B1s fell on the position. The guns opened fire and saw their rounds bounce off the advancing armour which continued to fire their machine guns. One of the anti-tank guns was destroyed, its commander and gunner were wounded and the remainder of the crew killed. The lack of penetration offered by the German guns frightened the defenders and led to some of the infantry withdrawing, but the gunners held their positions, hoping to penetrate a weak spot on the tanks. Describing the first success for the anti-tank guns, a participant later testified:

> The fire of the three heavy tanks threatens to wipe out the anti-tank section. But it remains in position. One moment one of the colossuses crosses the front. The left gun commander, Corporal Giesemann, discovers in the middle of its right side a small-ribbed surface; apparently it is the radiator! It is not much bigger than an ammunition box. He aims at it. A tongue of flame shoots out of the tank.[33]

A second tank turned and destroyed Giesemann's gun, but the weakness in the armour had been noted and the final gun, withdrawn by Hindelang to better cover by some buildings, struck the other two tanks in the same area. The three burning tanks were a beacon of hope for the German defenders, and their destruction forced the French to withdraw. They returned, however, and retook the village at noon.

These were the first blows in a fight that was to last three days and was to see Stonne change hands seventeen times. The village became a running sore for Flavigny, who continued to attack along Mont Dieu to deny the Germans the high ground, but was in no position to attempt a breakthrough, not least because of the increasing German strength that was flooding south of the Meuse. The increasing solidity of the Sedan bridgehead also gave Guderian firmer foundations for his attempt on 15 May to turn his advance into something of critical operational significance. Standing in the way was Sixth Army under General Robert-Auguste Touchon, an effective if rather hidebound commander, with XXIII Corps on the right consisting of 14th Infantry Division, 36th Infantry Division and with 2nd DCR moving into position, and XXXXI Corps on the left largely made up of the remnants of 5th Light Cavalry Division, 3rd Spahis Brigade and 53rd, 102nd and 61st Infantry Divisions. These two hastily organized corps were weakly joined fifteen miles west of Charleville Mézières and had the task of holding Reinhardt as 6th Panzer Division emerged from Monthermé and Guderian and his two divisions pushed towards Rethel. Touchon's ad hoc formation was in an invidious position as it had the important job of being the glue that held together two failing armies but was stretched even as it was being inserted and long before its front had hardened.

15 May was a day of heavy fighting for both 1st and 2nd Panzer Divisions in extremely close terrain. Kirchner's remained the main effort as he continued with his two-pronged advance with the infantry of Kampfgruppe Krüger having to struggle hard for La Horgne. Here elements of 3rd Spahis Brigade had done good work fortifying the village and for the first time since 10 May, 1st Rifle Regiment just could not find a way through the defences. It led to one of the most ferocious contested engagements of the entire campaign between two aggressive and well-led formations. After a series of attacks had failed to make any progress despite some desperate hand-to-hand fighting, Balck came forward to

lead his men and encourage them to new feats of endurance and achievement. In an immense effort, the German infantry rallied and, despite lacking the supporting fire of tanks and artillery due to the nature of the terrain, gradually began to infiltrate and outflank the Spahis' positions. La Horgne fell that afternoon, but the defenders had done a first-class job in slowing 1st Rifle Regiment, which suffered more casualties in the struggle for the village than they were to receive on any other day of the campaign. Balck later declared:

> I fought against all foes in both wars and I was always in the thick of it. Rarely did anyone fight as outstandingly as the 3rd Spahis Brigade. Its commander, Colonel Maré, was captured having been wounded ... Out of the brigade's twenty-seven officers, twelve were killed in action, seven were wounded, along with 610 Spahi dead or wounded. The brigade had ceased to exist. It had sacrificed itself for France. I gave orders that prisoners we took be given especially good treatment.[34]

The *kampfgruppe* then headed to the last defended villages before more open ground. Baâlons posed little problem for Balck's 3rd battalion, but that evening his 1st battalion strained every weary sinew to try and overcome the strong defence at Bouvellemont. Having taken heavy officer casualties in La Horgne, units bounced off the French positions and clearly lacked the drive to take the enemy on. Balck observed this weariness with understanding but dismay and feared that their preference was to eat, sleep and reorganize before launching a full-blooded attack the next morning. Dressed in a windproof smock, a grubby scarf tight to his neck and carrying a knotted stick, he wandered around his units, talking to his commanders and explaining that there was nothing to be gained by waiting until dawn and a great deal to lose because the enemy would only be reinforced. Grimy-faced and with red-rimmed eyes, he exhorted his men to attack before nightfall, saying, 'Gentlemen, we are attacking or we are simply giving victory away ... if you do not want to go on, I will take the village myself.'[35] Once again, he obtained the desired reaction for, as he led the attack alone, he turned after 100 yards to see his officers right behind him, and they turned to see their men right behind them. Balck later recalled:

> Men and officers, who just a few seconds earlier were at the end of their tether, passed by me. Nobody was thinking of seeking cover. Everybody rushed on ahead. Our fixed bayonets glistened in the setting sun. There was no stopping us. From everywhere came the sound of wild cheering as a thin line of completely exhausted riflemen pushed into the village. Bouvellemont was ours.[36]

The infantry were joined that evening by men from Kampfgruppe Nedtwig who had advanced well that morning through Terron and Omont. The fight for Chagny – less than two miles from Bouvellemont and defended by cavalrymen and a battalion of 14th Infantry Division – came next. Here the Germans were tank-heavy and the unit had been informed that a French counter-attack was possible from the south. Both mitigated against swift success and, despite efforts throughout the afternoon, Nedtwig was forced to withdraw his tanks back to Omont for the night. The prospect of attacking Chagny again the next day was not a welcome one for anyone concerned, not least because they feared that the enemy would have been reinforced and, with so little opportunity to manoeuvre in such dense terrain, they would again be forced into a frontal attack. It was, therefore, only as the result of a stupendous effort by the drained infantry infiltrating during the night of 15–16 May – and doubtless assisted by the fall of Bouvellemont – that Chagny was taken.

— ◻ —

Although 1st Panzer Division's two *kampfgruppen* had failed to burst the front open and reach Rethel on 15 May, Guderian was aware of the significance of what had been achieved by exhausted troops in difficult terrain. When he visited Kirchner early the following morning, he was keen to emphasize his belief that the hole which had been punched in the French line would release a great amount of pressure. 2nd Panzer Division had made better ground to the north in terrain more conducive to movement and the deployment of its firepower, and it had quickly established bridgeheads beyond the River Vence at Boulzicourt and Poix-Terron, just three miles from Kirchner's right wing. Despite some desperate defence by elements of 14th, 53rd and 102nd Divisions, by the middle of the afternoon 2nd Panzer Division had also taken the last high ground. In so doing they forced the enemy off the best defensive terrain and into a withdrawal back towards Rethel. It was this that had inadvertently assisted 1st Panzer Division's capture of Bouvellemont and Chagny that evening. Yet although a new defensive position was being formed by 14th Infantry Division around Rethel to contain Guderian, the northern front was collapsing. 2nd DCR would have added considerable ballast to that position, but significant transport problems meant that it was struggling forward and so arrived in its positions piecemeal north of Rethel between Guderian's corps on its right and Reinhardt's corps on its left.

It was Reinhardt's advance that caught the eye on 15 May. Kempf's 6th Panzer Division managed not only to fight its way out of the tiny Monthermé bridgehead that morning, but then stormed forward thirty-five miles to advance via Liart towards Montcornet. Once again, it had been the good work of engineers and infantry taking French bunkers in a manner very similar to that seen on the west bank of the Meuse at Sedan on 13 May that pierced the defences after around four and a half hours of intense and close-quarters fighting. The torch was then handed by Kempf to an ad hoc unit, Pursuit Detachment von Esebeck, an all-arms grouping including battalions of tanks, motorcyclists and engineers supported by artillery, anti-tank and anti-aircraft guns, to exploit the success and push into the enemy's rear. Having crossed the Meuse on a new bridge, von Esebeck pushed forward in the middle of the afternoon and so paralysed the enemy that his troops had only to engage in skirmishes as they went. Indeed, one staff officer's overriding memory of the advance was that of the bellowing of unmilked cows belonging to farmers that had left the beasts to their fate.

It was a thrust that threw the French into a spin and certainly influenced the decision of XXIII Corps to withdraw to Rethel as the rampaging panzer division tore between the two corps of Sixth Army that had been brought in to strengthen the front between Second and Ninth Armies. The defenders were sent scuttling back and the bridgeheads created by Guderian and Reinhardt were merged on 2nd Panzer Division's extreme right flank. With this thrust, Reinhardt ensured the survival of Panzer Group Kleist as an operational independent organization. The continued bottling up of 6th Panzer Division at Monthermé would undoubtedly have been used as evidence to end the experiment, and with this in mind von Kleist had ordered the division to do whatever it could to stay ahead of the infantry army that had come up to the east bank of the Meuse. This was why Reinhardt, having received orders from Twelfth Army to assist 3rd Infantry Division across the Meuse just to the south of Monthermé, then said that it was impossible to do so as Kempf had already, and instinctively, set off on his exploitation. Consenting to orders and then evading them was to become increasingly common among panzer division and corps commanders in the coming days. It was not just the Allies that were being out-manoeuvred, it was the conservative forces within the Wehrmacht that would take any opportunity to rein in the opportunistic panzer forces. For the time being, however, von Rundstedt saw merit in retaining the independent role of Panzer Group Kleist – but always with one eye on threats to its flanks.

It was just such a threat that had blundered towards Panzer Group Hoth, and specifically Rommel's 7th Panzer Division near Flavion, on the night of 14 May. Although any success it achieved would only be tactical, General Bruneau's 1st DCR represented the last French hope to thwart Hoth's attempts to strike west and so significantly broaden the attacking front of Army Group A. While 25th Panzer Regiment rested and reorganized south of Flavion during the night of 14–15 May, just a few miles to the north French 28th and 25th Tank Battalions – comprised of Char B1s and Hotchkiss H39s respectively – waited for fuel and made preparations to strike the next morning. Then, at 1000 hours on 15 May, the predatory 25th Panzer Regiment came across its still supine enemy and attacked. It drove a wedge formation into the middle of the group and then fanned out. Within moments, French troops were scattered, vehicles were ablaze and black smoke filled the air. The German tanks were outnumbered, but keeping calm was something that had been drummed into their crews, with one of those involved, Hans Becker, later saying: 'When you are involved in combat and the banging starts around you to the right and to the left, then it's as if the human mechanism is switched off. All you can think of is – watch out! [Make sure] that nobody can shoot you. If you don't, the other will shoot, and you are a goner!'[37] Rommel's tanks did not fully commit to the battle, but by the time that 5th Panzer Division's 31st Tank Regiment arrived on the scene from the north-east at 1100 hours, considerable damage had already been inflicted. Seizing the opportunity to move on, Rommel immediately withdrew his armour, leaving 5th Panzer Division to complete the rout while he pushed on to Philippeville.

Rommel's departure left Werner's 31st Panzer Regiment considerably outnumbered, out-gunned and out-armoured by the French division – 170 Char B1s and H39s against 30 Mk IIIs and IVs and 90 Mk Is and IIs – but over the course of the afternoon, the heavier tanks were out-thought and out-fought by the nimble German armour. Well led and once again closely co-ordinated through first-class radio communication, the more powerful of the German tanks combined well with anti-tank guns which had been rushed into the area to expose and target weak spots. Stuka raids, meanwhile, stopped more French tanks from entering the battlefield and also those that sought to leave it. By the evening, with scores of his tanks blazing wrecks and others running out of fuel, Bruneau ordered a withdrawal of his thirty-six remaining machines. The carnage they left behind was numbing, as one of the survivors recalled:

> I could not think or feel that evening. We drove into the darkness in more ways than one. I was never the same man again. I left myself on that battlefield, among the glowing hulks of broken machines, the charred bodies of men that I knew well.[38]

By the next morning, 1st DCR had been diminished to a mere sixteen tanks. It had been eviscerated in less than ten hours by two German tank battalions.[39]

Even as 31st Panzer Regiment was in the throes of completing its task – which meant that Hartlieb's division only managed to advance a handful of miles on 15 May – 7th Panzer Division was speeding ahead with its tanks in the lead, followed by lorried infantry and artillery. Rommel later wrote: 'It was my intention to ride with 25th Panzer Regiment so that I could direct the attack from up forward and bring in the artillery and dive-bombers at the decisive moment.'[40] The line of advance was agreed with his chief of staff and artillery commander and briefed to officers during an Orders Group at which they all marked their maps, whereupon the advance began at an average speed of 40 mph. The division moved forward with little thought for its flanks because it sought to shatter the enemy's cohesion – and it did, Rommel noting that the division passed:

... fully armed French motorcyclists coming in the opposite direction, and picked them up as they passed. Most of them were so shaken at suddenly finding themselves in a German column that they drove their machines into a ditch and were in no position to put up a fight.[41]

Had the Allies been able to get sufficient aircraft into the air over the sector at this time, they would have had little difficulty locating the column for, as Rommel wrote, 'the dust cloud behind us was enormous',[42] but the sky was as clear of enemy aircraft as it was of clouds. By the end of the day, 7th Panzer Division had advanced so successfully that it was several miles beyond its objective, having reached the outskirts of Froid-Chapelle. It was a plunge deep into the enemy's rear area that was fully in keeping with Rommel's aim of avoiding unnecessary fighting in order to further both the cause of Hoth's corps and his burgeoning reputation as a panzer commander. Which was more important to him was, at times, difficult to discern.

It was only on 15 May that Gamelin truly understood that he had been caught in the Germans' trap as their panzer divisions began to break out to the south of his main force. Along the Franco-German border, nineteen divisions of Army Group C continued to attack and pin thirty-six French divisions to the Maginot Line, but although the situation now tempted Gamelin to redeploy them, he could not for fear of a German attack through Switzerland on 16 or 17 May. This particular, and brilliant, ruse had been developed by Hitler's propaganda minister Goebbels with the Abwehr and succeeded in stretching the enemy's mental and physical resources while enabling the Germans to keep the strategic initiative.

Meanwhile, the great deception of central Belgium continued to play out. But by this stage, Gamelin could not simply disengage from Army Group B in order to deal with the developing threat of Army Group A. By 15 May, the critical task that fell to the French High Command was to act quickly to ensure that their forces were not so fixed by von Bock that those of von Rundstedt were free to outflank them. All along the Dyle, French, British and Belgian forces were being engaged by strong but not overwhelming German forces. The BEF had three divisions on the Dyle and all came under extreme pressure on 15 May. 2nd Division was on Gort's right and was hit particularly hard by the attacks launched in von Bock's main effort emanating from Maastricht. The fighting was intense as the Germans endeavoured to cross the Dyle and establish themselves on the west bank.

All along the line, in battles reminiscent of those fought by their fathers during the First World War, the German infantry attacked the British trenches after brief but powerful artillery barrages. 2nd Battalion Durham Light Infantry, for example, had a torrid time denying German 31st Infantry Division a bridge-head at Gastuche. Twenty-five-year-old Second Lieutenant Dick Annand's 16 Platoon of B Company took the brunt of the attack that morning, suffering heavy casualties but remaining in place as Annand and his NCOs kept order and led by example. Annand led two counter-attacks personally before being wounded. The battalion came under increasing pressure during the afternoon, however, and after dark the Germans made another attempt to oust the defenders with a strong assault. Annand personally endeavoured to disrupt them and, armed with hand grenades, went forward to cause mayhem despite his wounds. Remarkably, he survived, and for his leadership and personal gallantry – which included retrieving his wounded batman from the battlefield in a wheelbarrow – on 15 and 16 May he was awarded the first British Victoria Cross of the Second World War.[43]

During the course of 15 May, the Allied line on the Dyle was nonetheless infiltrated after the river was crossed in several sectors, forcing the defenders into a withdrawal while the Germans constructed bridges and established themselves on the west bank.

Von Bock's aim at this point, and which he had made clear to subordinates, was to make steady progress forwards by threshing the opposition like a combine harvester in a summer field, not allowing the enemy to avoid contact and certainly not attempting a breakthrough. The ambition continued to be the pinning, fixing and destruction of the enemy in situ, so allowing Army Group A to affect its outflanking movement. For this reason, the Battle of Gembloux was less about Hoepner bursting through the French line, and more about an attritional push to remove vital enemy assets from the battlefield while retaining the integrity of the wider German front.

The French frontline divisions of First Army had been well served by Prioux's Cavalry Corps, having been given vital time to prepare their defences, including digging in and sighting their artillery, but now the fight was theirs. Hoepner attacked on the morning of the 15th, throwing his weakened panzer divisions across a four-mile front without waiting for the support of the infantry divisions marching up behind him and in the hope of catching the enemy less well prepared. In the van of the ensuing storm General Albert Mellier's elite Moroccan Division performed excellently, defending the village of Ernage and flanked by motorized infantry divisions.* The Stuka attacks preparing the battlefield had less impact here than they did in Sedan as the defenders were more resolute and understood that such raids had a bark significantly stronger than their subsequent bite. This meant that when the panzer divisions advanced, they were caught in a killing zone of artillery fire and interlocking defences which remained manned and co-ordinated. With field telephone wires buried deeply and communications as good as such a system would allow, the French felt far more comfortable in their defences than they had facing Guderian on 13 May. The attack stalled and Hoepner's decision to attack without

---

* That day the Moroccan Division lost 2,000 men, with one of its frontline battalions suffering 90 per cent casualties and another reduced to four officers and thirty-one men out of 700.

extra infantry support was seen to be misguided after continued attempts to throw metal and flesh against the French were rebuffed, causing heavy casualties and tank losses. The attack was suspended that afternoon with the prospect of resuming it the next morning with the support of two infantry divisions. The order, however, was not received by all 3rd Panzer Division units and, against the odds, 3rd Rifle Regiment managed to achieve a lodgement in the French line and by evening had broken the main line of resistance.

The French had nothing with which to respond as Prioux's remaining armour had been dispersed within the front line to reinforce the individual tank battalions there.[44] Yet even if Hoepner had wished to complete his success by turning behind the enemy to undermine the integrity of the line, the recent battle had so weakened his two divisions that they were no longer strong enough to do it. Hannut and Gembloux had combined to reduce the corps' strength by well over one third, with 4th Panzer Division boasting a mere 137 armoured fighting vehicles, including just four Mk IVs, by the end of the day.[45] The corps was in dire need of the attentions of its mobile field workshops and of resupply, reorganization and rest. Its achievement had been central to both Army Group B's success and to the continuing success of *Fall Gelb*, but now that the Dyle Line had been engaged, the load would be shared more evenly along the front.

The Battle of Gembloux was *Bataille Conduite* epitomized – a battle that the French could control because they were prepared and expecting the attack. It showed exactly why the Wehrmacht had been so keen to avoid such frontal attacks and was concerned that they had seemed to be *de rigueur* for the main effort during early invasion planning. It also revealed that in certain places the French did have the wherewithal to confront German methods and that in different circumstances, if it had been forced to undertake frontal attacks, the Wehrmacht may well have struggled to gain any momentum. As it was, the French fought along the Dyle with more than one eye on what was happening on their southern flank and, rather than launching strong counter-attacks to restore positions on the Dyle and at Gembloux, the Allies were forced to withdraw from the river in order to maintain the cohesion of their line.

This move, in fact, coincided with Gamelin being informed, 'Very strong [German] motorized column advancing in the direction of Montcornet, with nothing much remaining between Paris and the panzer divisions.'[46] The news confirmed his worst fears that the Germans were outflanking Billotte's force, and reports suggested that attempts to thwart that thrust had failed, with Ninth Army struggling to cope. Its commander, Corap, had been sacked by Georges that morning – he was the most senior of the thirty-five officers who were relieved of their duties during this period – and replaced by General Henri Giraud. The unfortunate Giraud arrived at his new headquarters on the afternoon of the 15th to find that his army was disintegrating, with the strength of the German thrust from Maastricht threatening his left flank and that from Sedan smashing his right. The state of Ninth Army was confirmed to Gamelin that evening when a Lieutenant Colonel Guillaut, despatched from Gamelin's personal staff to ascertain the situation, reported to him the 'lamentable state in which he had found the [Ninth] Army headquarters – like a lifeless corpse – entirely ignorant of the situation of the army's divisions'. Guillaut added that he was aware of positions where whole units were missing because 'from the moment the Germans appeared, everyone had run away'.[47]

In such circumstances, Gamelin directed Billotte to order a phased disengagement from the Dyle position and he did so more in reaction to the threat offered by Army Group A than the pressure exerted by Army Group B. It was to take place under the cover of darkness over the next four nights, and would see a complicated withdrawal by troops of four nations while they remained in contact with the enemy and would use the Rivers Senne, Dendre and Scheldt as phase lines. It was a decision that grasped the reality of the situation for the first time. It recognized that Billotte's force had to be protected, that a hard front had to be formed south of von Rundstedt to protect Paris, and looked to future counter-attacks into the flanks of the well-extended German formations to restore the situation.

Yet Gamelin was thoroughly pessimistic; the unexpected and unthinkable had happened, and his forces were on the back foot and barely coping with the enemy's offensive. The Supreme Commander's plans and French strategy had been unhinged by *Fall Gelb* and there was no doubt that the Germans held the initiative. That evening, Gamelin admitted defeat to Daladier in a telephone call outlining the situation across the front that left the minister of war 'stupefied' and shouting, 'No! What you tell me is not possible! You must be wrong! It's impossible!' He demanded an immediate counter-attack, only to receive a terrible response from Gamelin: 'With what? I don't have the reserves.' There was a pause. 'Then the French Army is finished?' asked Daladier. 'It's finished,' the Supreme Commander replied.[48]

CHAPTER 8

16–20 May – Crisis of Command and the Coast

T HE PARIS THAT WINSTON CHURCHILL ARRIVED IN on the morning of 16 May was emptier of people than usual but filled with rumours about the character and nature of Germany's invasion. There were stories of fifth columnists engaged in sabotage, German parachutists in rural districts, atrocities committed by ideological zealots, panzers rampaging around Soissons, broken troops fleeing the front, the government quitting Paris – a mixture of truth and fiction that cloaked the French capital in a dark anxiety that suffocated its sun-drenched streets. The British prime minister and his military advisers, Generals John Dill and Hastings Ismay, felt the claustrophobia and they were shocked by what they learned from their visit.

As bundles of documents were being incinerated on the lawns outside the French Foreign Ministry, Gamelin provided an erudite summary of the military situation to his foreign guests as they sat, furrow-browed, with Reynaud and Daladier. Churchill later recalled: 'Utter dejection was written on every face. In front of Gamelin, on a student's easel, was a map about two yards square, with a black ink line purporting to show the Allied front. In this there was drawn a small sinister bulge at Sedan.'[1] Gamelin said that it was not clear whether the Germans would push to the coast at Abbeville or turn towards Paris, but what was apparent was that the panzer divisions were moving fast. Churchill then asked a question: 'Where is the strategic reserve?' Gamelin's reply was no surprise to Daladier. There was, he said, no strategic reserve. A long silence followed while the British tried to take in the information. Churchill later wrote:

> I was dumbfounded. What were we to think of the great French Army and its highest chiefs? It had never occurred to me that any commanders would have left themselves unprovided with a mass of manoeuvre ... I admit this was one of the greatest surprises I have had in my life.[2]

As Churchill flew back to England, he began to discuss with his colleagues the options that Britain had available to assist the French and, of course, the British Expeditionary Force. Should more troops be sent across the Channel, and what about more aircraft? But there was also an understanding that the primary role of the government was the defence of its own people – a responsibility not lost on Reynaud and Gamelin – and that, in the final analysis, Churchill had to ensure that if France fell, he had the necessary assets to protect the British mainland. Being able to continue the fight was essential, and the French government recognized this as well because they had already taken steps to ensure that, if and when the Germans arrived in the capital, they would find no official documents and that the vital organs of government had moved out of harm's way.

It was a lonely and anxious Reynaud who wondered how much longer he would continue to attract the support required to prolong his leadership of a nation in such peril. The French prime minister had attempted to assert his authority but found that his ability to do so was consistently undermined by fickle colleagues and fast-moving events. In no area was this truer than in his attempt to maintain calm in Paris. On the afternoon of 16 May, he said in the Chamber:

> There are absolutely absurd rumours going round. People are saying that the government wanted to leave Paris; this is not true! People are saying that the enemy has new irresistible weapons when our aviators are covering themselves in glory, and our tanks outclass those of the Germans in the same category.[3]

Yet the people of Paris increasingly lacked faith in the words of politicians and officials – weren't these the same people who had told them that French defences were 'impenetrable' and that France was too strong for Germany? – and began to think about taking responsibility for their own destiny. Paris itself remained quiet and although thousands had left the city, the majority stayed despite the arrival of the first bedraggled refugees from the Netherlands, Belgium, Luxembourg and the border regions. The authorities were quick to try and move the foreigners on, for they feared that their demoralizing stories would affect Parisians, but they need not have worried: these particular refugees had left their homes well before they could have had contact with either the Germans or dispirited French troops. To this end, Eugène Dépigny, who worked in the *mairie* of Paris, wrote: 'In spite of their destitution, [the refugees'] evident anxiety and suffering, these lonely individuals did not look hunted in May.'[4] Those who were to leave their homes in the middle of the month, however, would take weeks to reach Paris and when they arrived, their stories were terrifying.

Defending Paris was a central part of the developing French plan now that Billotte's First Army Group was undertaking a withdrawal while Second and Ninth Armies desperately sought to work with Sixth Army to block the German main effort. To stabilize the situation west of the German breakthrough while ensuring that the capital was protected required Touchon's force to fall back on the Oise and Aisne to establish a blocking position from Rethel west to the Somme and link up there with Seventh Army. This was a campaign-affecting decision as it would break the link between First Army facing Army Group B and Sixth Army facing Army Group A, leaving just a few fragmented units before the Germans and the Channel coast, and the only hope of re-establishing that link lay in attacking the open flanks of Panzer Group Kleist as it advanced.

But the defence of Paris was not Gamelin's sole concern because the invaders had also created an option to outflank the Maginot Line with a pivot from Mont Dieu. To deal with this potentially fatal blow, the left wing of Second Army fell back. This allowed Huntziger to shorten his line while maintaining contact with the enemy around Stonne – where the battle raged until 25 May – and concentrate his Second Army forces at the end of the Maginot Line around La Ferté. In the days that followed, the French were put under extreme pressure here as the Germans made a big show of concentrating around 250 artillery pieces in this narrow sector to feign an important breakthrough attempt. As a result, troops from the Maginot Line who could have been transferred to defend against the main German effort were kept in place to counter the threat of the Line being outflanked at both ends, and the La Ferté sector defending the front around Sedan was reinforced.

The success of this German deception reduced the potential pressure on Guderian's westward advance on an eighteen-mile front, leading Halder to write, 'Our breakthrough wedge is developing in a positively classic manner. West of the Meuse our advance is sweeping in, smashing tank counterattacks in its path...'[5] Even so, the wedge looked extremely vulnerable as it began to achieve a head of steam and pull away from the infantry divisions traipsing behind. It was happening so fast that even some of the more sceptical German commanders found themselves reacting instinctively to the situation. Von Rundstedt and Hitler, for example, were concerned about the southern flank but so amazed by the advance and its potential that they had initially been willing to see it develop. Even so, they were not so anesthetized by success that they would not react adversely to suspected threats and their imaginations were increasingly febrile. Guderian, Hoth and Reinhardt were aware of this but continued to push as hard and as fast as possible in the belief that it was the only way to dislocate the enemy and protect the wedge. This was reflected in the log of 1st Panzer Division for 15 May which stated: 'Now it is important to thrust forward without consideration of casualties and exhaustion before the French have had the opportunity to set up again. There is no time for half-stepping now.'[6] It did not take long, however, before von Rundstedt began to feel uneasy at the build-up of French forces on the Aisne. Thus, despite the sixty-mile gap that had opened up before Army Group A, on 16 May its commander stopped anything other than reconnaissance troops crossing a line from Beaumont to Montcornet and ordered that the Sambre-Oise Line fifteen miles further west could only be broken with his personal permission.

To the north, von Bock was keen to maintain the tempo of his advance and co-ordinate it with von Rundstedt's. With the Allied armies having begun their withdrawal, Hoepner's 3rd and 4th Panzer Divisions moved through the Gembloux Gap while a squadron of 2 Group RAF dropped 250lb bombs in an attempt to slow them. The Germans were ready and waiting for, as the twelve Blenheims approached their target in close formation, they ran into a flak barrage that immediately turned one aircraft into a falling ball of flames.[7] The barrage stopped and moments later fifteen Bf 109s dived on their prey. One of the RAF crew, Sergeant T. J. Watkins, who was himself shot down in the attack, later recalled:

[The fighters] were having a field day shooting bombers out of the sky. Sergeant Grierson's Blenheim belched flames from its mainplane and two others were falling out of the sky, a mass of brilliant yellow and red fire and acrid smoke. In a matter of seconds almost the entire formation was shattered, fluttering to earth in a welter of fragments.[8]

Eleven aircraft and thirty-three crew were shot down, leaving just one Blenheim able to return to base. It took a little while for those waiting on the ground to realize what must have happened and then, in the words of the official history of 2 Group, 'Mesmerized, the ground crews made their stunned way back to the hangars and bore the shock for the rest of their lives.'[9]

Meanwhile, the two panzer divisions continued their advance, gradually dropping south to eventually come up on Hoth's right flank and under Army Group A's command for the final push to the coast. That corps continued to observe Rommel with a mixture of admiration and apprehension as he did all that he could to lead the German advance as far and as fast as possible, and such was his mindset that he was not afraid of ignoring or deliberately avoiding direct orders to do so. Indeed, this period of the campaign was later dubbed by Hitler as 'Rommel's private offensive', one which, he told the general, caused him a sleepless night or two as corps, army and army group had little idea where the 'ghost division' was and what it was doing.

Crossing the border into France at 1800 hours on 16 May, Rommel's formation prepared to take on those defences that had been prepared during the second phase of Maginot Line construction, some of which Guderian's corps had already passed through after their crossing of the Meuse farther to the east. Despite orders from Fourth Army to attack 'only if the weakness of the garrison promises a sure success',[10] Rommel did not wait for detailed orders from Hoth and advanced towards the defences in the direction of Avesnes. He later justified such actions by saying:

'The officers of a panzer division must learn to think and act independently within the framework of the general plan and not wait until they receive orders.'[11] On this occasion, his boldness was rewarded.

Rommel's aim was to pierce the outer French defences by surprise in daylight, before mounting a division-sized attack on the bunkers of the main line of resistance under the cover of darkness. The first attack was launched at 1830 hours on 16 May and the arrival of the Germans was a surprise to French units from 84th Regiment of 101st Fortress Infantry Division. Rommel later recalled: 'Suddenly we saw the angular outlines of the French fortification about 100 yards ahead. Close behind it were a number of fully-armed French troops, who, at the first sight of the tanks, at once made as if to surrender.'[12] However, once the defenders realized what was happening they fought well from their bunkers, knocking out two tanks and causing casualties in the supporting infantry. 7th Panzer Division was not in the least disconcerted by this robust response and, showing excellent all-arms co-operation and formidable aggression, attacked under the cover of a smoke barrage. In the murk, engineers set to work with their flamethrowers, grenades silenced pill-boxes and high explosives blasted a route through obstacles. Tanks offered direct covering fire, some managing to shoot shells into the embrasures of casemates, while the infantry stormed forward to lend the sappers support and the artillery laid fire down into the enemy's immediate rear area.

As dusk turned to night, 7th Panzer Division fought their way into and then through the main fortified zone and cleared significant steel hedgehogs that were blocking the road west of Clairfayts. Once those roads were open, the panzers led the way, firing their machine guns as they moved, closely followed by the motorcycle infantry and then the reconnaissance battalion. By 2300 hours the leading group was a mile south of Solre-le-Château and Rommel later wrote:

The flat countryside lay spread out around us under the cold light of the moon. We were through the Maginot Line! It was hardly conceivable. Twenty-two years before we had stood for four and a half long years before this self-same enemy and had won victory after victory and yet finally lost the war. And now we had broken through the renowned Maginot Line and were driving deep into enemy territory. It was not just a beautiful dream. It was reality.[13]

The only position that had to be cleared by this time was that occupied by the French artillery, which began to target the armoured column. Unlike guns supporting Lafontaine's division at Sedan, they stood firm, emboldened by the defence offered by the infantry, and forced Rommel to storm them, the guns of his tanks firing on the move 'from all barrels' despite the lack of accuracy this would entail. The intended psychological effect was achieved, the artillery line crumbled quickly, some of its crews gunned down and run over by the rampaging armour, and Rommel now had the opportunity to drive deep into the enemy's rear. It was at this point, drunk with his night-time success and feeling invulnerable, that the 7th Panzer Division commander ignored orders stating 'No breakthrough!'[14] and sped on towards Avesnes.

Rommel was anxious to avoid contact with superior headquarters during this 'unauthorized phase'. He later explained that his lack of communication was due to 'radio failure', conveniently ignoring the division's superior equipment. It seems that while Rommel could receive communications from his command post back at Froid-Chapelle, he could not contact it. He was also keen to avoid contact with the enemy, but this was sometimes unavoidable as, for instance, on the occasion his leading units ran into French 5th Motorized Division, which was resting along the road. The panzer division seized the opportunity, its tireless commander standing in his command vehicle barking orders into the radio, and wreaked destruction, chaos and havoc over six miles. The attack lasted minutes before the panzers in the vanguard continued their advance and entered Avesnes at midnight, pushed through it to some high ground, and then paused for the waylaid armour and motorcycle infantry to catch up.

When the vanguard of the panzer division heard the sound of engines, they initially believed that their colleagues had made better progress towards them than expected, but then realized that these were enemy tanks. They were, in fact, the last sixteen machines belonging to 1st DCR and these were swiftly taken on by the German armour that had just emerged from Avesnes a mile or two from their leading group. A bloody engagement followed which continued until dawn while Rommel's small group, consisting of two tank battalions and three motorcycle platoons, pushed on to successfully take an important bridge over the Sambre at Landrecies eleven miles away. The speed of the advance so confused the French that they were unsure whose tanks these were. While administering a fuel depot in Landrecies, Marc Bloch recalled a brother officer's interest in some tanks after noticing that they were painted an unusual colour and moving away from the front. It was only when he made a move to find out what was happening from their commander that he was told by a comrade that they were German tanks.[15]

Those Frenchmen who did approach the armour were told to lay down their weapons and walk east. Most did so without a murmur and problems were caused by whole units wishing to be taken prisoner. There was one French lieutenant colonel, however, who approached the German command echelon and was in no mood to take orders. Rommel later wrote: 'His eyes glowed with hate and impotent fury and he gave the impression of being a thoroughly fanatical type.' The colonel began to walk east, but Rommel thought that he might try to escape and so ordered him into his tank. He refused and so 'after summoning him three times to get in, there was nothing for it but to shoot him'.[16] As it was, the spearhead group crossed the bridge at Landrecies, leaving a unit behind to protect the valuable structure, and finally stopped its advance when it reached the hills east of Le Cateau at around 0630 hours.

It was only when a satisfied Rommel had his eyes on Le Cateau with his fragmented division spread out over twenty miles that he re-established radio communications with his furious corps commander. Rommel claimed not to have received the order to advance no further than Avesnes, despite the operations officer having radioed 'Stop immediately' on several occasions, and said in mitigation that he had endeavoured to gain permission to advance from corps but, on receiving no reply, had used his initiative. Having spoken to Hoth, Rommel suddenly wondered where the rest of his division was, not least because his leading group needed fuel and ammunition. Heading back in a signals vehicle with a PzKpfw Mk III to Avesnes to re-establish contact, he became aware of how long, narrow and vulnerable the corridor he had created was. On his journey he came across around a dozen French lorries. They did not try to escape, and nor did their drivers try to destroy their vehicles but instead allowed themselves to be led back to Avesnes by the general. On his arrival in the town, he handed over his prisoners and ordered that the division move forward without delay to support the isolated group just east of Le Cateau.

By late morning, the division was moving forward once again. Rommel had broken through the French defences for the cost of 115 casualties and had taken 10,000 prisoners, captured 200 tanks, thirty armoured cars and twenty-seven guns.[17] He had destroyed the ragged remnants of 2nd Corps of Ninth Army, completed the demolition of 1st DCR, run over several other formations and secured a bridge over the Sambre. In an extraordinarily audacious advance of forty-five miles in twenty-four hours, Rommel had pursued a high-risk, high-gain policy and it had come off. At the end of it, one of the general's biographers explains: 'He clearly felt that nothing could stop him, that 7th Panzer Division was irresistible, could win the war single-handed.'[18] Meanwhile, Rommel ensured that Hitler's adjutant, Schmundt, was kept well briefed about events and the fact that both a representative from the Propaganda Ministry and the editor of the Nazi newspaper *Der Stürmer* were attached to the division is revealing. This whirl of vainglorious self-publicity had caught the attention of Berlin, and Rommel's superiors were placed in the difficult position of not knowing whether to reprimand him or reward him. In the end, Rommel received a Knight's Cross – the highest order of the Iron Cross – for his personal bravery and an advance 'of decisive significance for the whole operation'.[19]

The noteworthy aspect of the German advance at this stage in the campaign was not just that 7th Panzer Division achieved outstanding success, but that it was replicated elsewhere. Although both Corps Reinhardt and Corps Guderian did not advance all of their divisions to the Oise, by 0700 hours on 17 May 1st and 6th Panzer Divisions had both created bridgeheads on the west bank of the river and had therefore advanced as far west as Rommel. This had been achieved after the two divisions had converged on Montcornet during the morning of 16 May and set the agenda for a meeting between Guderian and Kempf in the town. They decided to continue their attacks and organize how these would proceed using their on-the-spot knowledge of what was a developing opportunity to side-step the orders of von Kleist and, in so doing, thoroughly undermine him.

By the time that von Kleist had approved von Rundstedt's order prohibiting a push beyond Montcornet, two of his divisions were already well beyond it, with the corps commander travelling with 1st Panzer Division, and they kept on moving westwards. It seems that the Germans were suffering considerable 'communication difficulties' as the exploitation phase began since Guderian, despite his emphasis on excellent communications, did not receive the order. It took a staff officer until just before 0100 hours on 17 May to deliver by hand this important information to the corps commander, by which time he was creating a bridgehead west of the Oise. This task was completed six hours later, when 2nd Panzer Division was twelve miles behind on his right flank. 6th Panzer Division also created an Oise bridgehead some thirteen miles to the north of Kirchner's while 8th Panzer Division was finally crossing the Meuse some twenty-five miles to the rear. Von Kleist's pleasure at this success was certainly tempered by his understandable indignation at Guderian for not only failing to use the chain of command to organize the advance to the Oise – particularly as it included the division of another corps – but also, he suspected, wilfully ignoring orders. To von Kleist it was not just the old way of fighting that was being stood on its head; the generals who favoured the new methods seemed to revel in disobedience masquerading as the application of initiative while they failed to pay due respect to the time-honoured command hierarchy.

Both von Rundstedt and von Kleist had tried and failed to keep the panzer divisions under control on 16 May and had come away with a distinct feeling their fears were being realized and that individual division and corps commanders were putting themselves before the team. This was a critical issue, they argued, that did not just affect the efficiency and effectiveness of the main effort but put *Fall Gelb* in jeopardy because they believed that a significant French counter-attack was in the offing. Halder did not feel that such concerns were viable and fought hard to avoid an instinctive and conservative reaction. His own anxiety at the situation can be seen in his diary entry for 17 May:

> Rather unpleasant day. The Führer is terribly nervous. Frightened by his own success, he is afraid to take any chance and so would rather pull the reins on us. Puts forward the excuse that it is all because of his concern for the left flank![20]

Halder tried to put Hitler's mind at rest, saying that Luftwaffe reconnaissance revealed no such threat, and he was supported in this view by Oberst Ulrich Liss, the chief of the Foreign Armies West section of Army Intelligence. Even so, the German Supreme Commander could not bring himself to believe that the French were impotent and wished for the infantry to be brought up.[21] Von Brauchitsch and Halder were writhing at Hitler's interference in such operational matters, with the latter arguing that to 'tie up any of its strength on the southern flank' would be a mistake as this would undermine the striking power of Army Group A, and advocating building a defensive front there later with following troops.[22] Far from thinking about defence, Halder wished to develop the offensive and, now that the breakthrough had been achieved, to take a step closer to von Manstein's original plan by conducting a limited advance south-west in order to stop the French from establishing a defensive position on the Somme and Aisne towards Compiègne 'with the possibility of subsequently wheeling the right wing in a south-eastern direction past Paris'. Halder believed that 'A great decision must be taken now!'[23] Yet the mood was not conducive to the development of such a radical idea: quite the opposite.

Issued on 17 May, Führer Directive No. 12 placed Hitler at the heart of operational decision-making and stated: 'The bulk of the Panzer formations will not cross the line Le Cateau-Laon to the West.'[24] Hitler directed that, for the southern flank to be strengthened, von Kleist's thrust would stop and move into defensive positions while Twelfth Army moved forward to create a protective barrier. Field officers throughout the chain of command thought that this decision was not merited considering the situation that had been achieved and those in 1st and 2nd Panzer Divisions believed that this 'flank psychosis' was contrary to everything that Guderian had said about the ability to ignore threats on the flanks by maintaining the initiative and disrupting the enemy with a hard, fast and deep advance.

Halder's reaction to Hitler's decision is recalled in his diary:

> The Führer unaccountably keeps worrying about the south
> flank. He rages and screams that we are on the best way to
> ruin the whole campaign and that we are leading up to a
> defeat. He won't have any part of continuing the operation
> in a westward direction, let alone to the south-west, and still
> clings to the plan of a north-western drive. This is the subject
> of a most unpleasant discussion at Führer Hq. between the
> Führer on one side and [von Brauchitsch] and myself on
> the other.[25]

Halder recognized that a hard-won operational opportunity
which could have a strategic impact was being spurned by those
who lacked the military sense to see that continued exploitation
was required rather than stultification. Just as the French were
developing a defensive front along the Aisne and the Somme, OKH
lamented, so Hitler had aspirations to do the same. Nevertheless,
the Supreme Commander had justified his decision during a visit
to von Rundstedt's headquarters at Bastogne on 17 May, details
of which were noted in the Army Group A War Diary by von
Sodenstern in which he emphasized 'the significance the southern
flank has not only for the operations of the whole Army, but also
politically and psychologically'. He continued:

> Under no circumstances must a setback occur at this moment
> anywhere, a setback that would give a fateful rise [in spirit]
> to our adversaries, not alone to the military, but above all
> to their political leadership. Thus, the decision, for the
> moment, rests not so much in the rapid forward push to the
> Channel, but much more … in the speediest establishment
> of absolutely *defensive* readiness on the Aisne … and later on
> the Somme … Toward this purpose all measures are directed
> even if time is lost temporarily in the push toward the West.[26]

It was a decision that handed the Allies the time and the space they needed and, if only temporarily, it gave away the initiative.

The pressure of the situation began to spill over into the relationships between commanders. At a meeting between von Kleist and Guderian at a Montcornet airstrip at 0700 hours on the morning of 17 May, the panzer group commander's anger spilled out. Such was his fury that he neglected to even greet his corps commander and instead immediately admonished him for disobeying orders. Guderian, as cool as only a man who believed that he was in the presence of an inferior could be, immediately asked to be relieved of his command. Von Kleist accepted without hesitation in unsavoury circumstances which were not conducive to level-headed decision-making. Recognizing that the situation was unravelling, von Rundstedt characteristically despatched List, the commander of Twelfth Army to whom Panzer Group Kleist had been subordinate for two days, to act as peace-maker. Guderian was quickly reinstated and duly informed by List that he had been authorized to launch a 'reconnaissance in force' on the condition that he would not move his corps' command post forward from its current location at Soize, just east of Montcornet.

It appeared, however, that the lead that had been attached to Guderian's corps was of the extendable type and he took this flexibility as a personal victory. As a result, he would not kowtow to senior officers who, it seemed, could not be trusted with what he had achieved, and he even decided that in future he would issue orders using field telephones back to his corps command so that they could not be tracked by superiors as they would have been over an open radio net. What was more, 10th Panzer Division was returning back into the corps area after it had been released from the fighting at Stonne by the advance of Twelfth Army infantry divisions. The team was back together, and Guderian had every intention of moving forward whenever the opportunity presented itself. His attack would slip neatly into Halder's clarified campaign plan, which had been accepted by Hitler: Army Group B would continue to push the Allied forces back to the coast while Army Group A, its southern front having been protected, would endeavour to prevent the Allied formations dropping south by advancing to the mouth of the Somme. The resultant pocket would then be squeezed while preparations were made for a thrust south-west towards Paris. For this, von Rundstedt would not only receive Hoepner's corps but also XXXIX Motorized Corps commanded by Generalleutnant Rudolf Schmidt. Both were to be placed under Hoth's command to create Panzer Group Hoth.

By the end of 17 May, Guderian's 'reconnaissance in force' was working west of the Oise while the remainder of his panzer formations complied with Hitler's directive and took a much-needed opportunity to rest, rearm, refuel and reorganize. At this time, Guderian's lines of communication were stretched, vulnerable and an obvious target. The difficulty for the Allies, however, was as it had been since 13 May: getting what resources were available to where they were needed in a timely fashion to do something useful with them. It was a situation that was made more difficult with every passing day as French units were being chewed up and confidence – from Gamelin downwards – ebbed away. It was thus left to a young, dynamic officer to see the opportunity presented by the enemy's operational pause and the need to act quickly and decisively. Colonel Charles de Gaulle, who had been given command of the newly formed 4th DCR on 15 May, sought to succeed where 1st, 2nd and 3rd DCRs had failed. Even though only three and a half battalions of tanks had arrived and he lacked supporting infantry, the ambitious officer, who had been a long-term advocate of armoured warfare, spotted another fleeting opportunity and attacked two days later from exactly the area that had been the cause of so much angst among senior German commanders, the southern flank. De Gaulle had scant information but nonetheless ordered his units to strike at the enemy's stretched and poorly defended lines of communication.

On the morning of 17 May, a single French Char B1 emerged unseen from Crécy – eight miles from the Oise – and simply drove up to 1st Panzer Regiment, which was surprised but reacted quickly to halt the enemy's bold probe. Meanwhile, as Guderian was on the verge of resigning during his meeting with von Kleist, de Gaulle's 100-tank main attack was put in from a position several miles to the south-west of Montcornet. The French armour shot up some German trucks in an assault that was wholly unexpected by Kirchner, who was in the process of trying to establish exactly where each of his units were. For a while it looked as if de Gaulle's tanks would sever 1st Panzer Division's line of communications but the situation was brought under control by the prompt action of Johann Graf von Kielmansegg, a junior supply staff officer, who personally organized a defensive position using local troops, some tanks undergoing repair and a handful of anti-tank and anti-aircraft guns that were moving through the area at the time.

A significant engagement ensued in which the French tanks endeavoured to break through even though they lacked infantry and artillery support and had no radios with which to co-ordinate their movements. They had nonetheless made a noteworthy impression on their harassed enemy, who struggled to bring the requisite firepower to bear on the roving machines before the arrival of a hastily arranged Stuka strike seemed to lead directly to a French withdrawal. Close air support was not used as a matter of course during a panzer division's exploitation phase as the Luftwaffe concentrated on missions designed to undermine the enemy's operational mobility and will, but it could still be requested when required, as it was near Montcornet. Yet despite the French breaking off their attack in what seemed to be a clear reaction to the arrival of the German dive-bombers, de Gaulle's decision to withdraw had instead been prompted by the threat posed to his right flank by units from 10th Panzer Division speeding towards the battlefield.

De Gaulle's sally towards Montcornet became little more than a mere tactical irritation to Kirchner, one which led to twenty-three French tanks being destroyed and one or two hours of disruption for 1st Panzer Division. In the mind of Guderian, it did not change anything. Although those few hours on the morning of 17 May revealed what might have been had the French been able to mount a larger counter-attack, it was in fact the diminutive size of de Gaulle's attack which meant that it was not spotted but gave no cause for operational alarm when its true potential became clear. Although the naysayers leapt on the French infraction as further evidence of the threat to the southern flank, Guderian believed that its lack of strength and the way in which it was contained was evidence that movement trumped immobility. There was, of course, a strong element of ego in what Guderian sought to achieve, but he never lost sight of the potential fragility of *Fall Gelb* and this is why he felt that the Montcornet halt order was such a mistake.

On 18 May, Hoth, Reinhardt and Guderian used strong advance combat teams to tidy up their line along the Escaut as the limitations on their advance continued to be enforced. 7th Panzer Division took Cambrai on an advance which had covered 175 miles since 10 May and 6th Panzer Division captured the entire staff of Ninth Army in a Le Catelet hotel and just missed seizing its commander, Corap. 2nd Panzer Division, meanwhile, had taken St. Quentin while 1st Panzer Division had also crossed the Oise and was moving on Peronne. In this way, as the infantry sought to close the gap with the forward armoured formations, all three panzer corps created positions from which they could immediately launch their advances over the old Somme battlefields just as soon as OKW gave the order. For Halder, that release could not come soon enough with Army Group B having achieved the major success of having captured both the vital port of Antwerp and Brussels, the Belgian capital, on 18 May. Now, OKH believed, the time was ripe for the panzers to effect the encirclement of those Allied forces that could be trapped between the Somme and the Escaut, using the massed armour to strike between the two rivers.

Indeed, it was from the sides of this developing corridor that Gamelin saw the opportunity of a counter-attack in what he considered was likely to be the final opportunity for the Allies to salvage something from their precarious position. The French Supreme Commander's ability to act, however, was not only undermined by the difficulty in finding the resources for such an endeavour, but also by Georges's decline into ever greater ineffectiveness and the French prime minister's revitalized attempts to remove him. Matters came to a head on the afternoon of 18 May when Reynaud made a personal visit to Georges to assess the situation for himself. It was a decision that thoroughly undermined Gamelin's position and, to make matters worse, the prime minister was accompanied by his new deputy, the eighty-four-year-old Marshal Philippe Pétain, who had replaced the sacked Daladier.

Reynaud had been given a sense of what he might find at the headquarters, and he found the place struggling to function effectively under the joint strains of enemy action and an ineffectual commander. He and Pétain returned to Paris convinced that there needed to be changes at the top of the army, and the prime minister himself was determined to take hard decisions before it was too late – what, after all, did he have to lose? He knew that he would have to act fast as even at this stage his generals could not tell him whether the main threat was to the turning of the Maginot Line, a southward plunge towards Paris, a race to the Channel coast or a combination of all three.

The success of the withdrawal through Belgium back to the Scheldt, however, at least gave a little breathing space for the Allied High Command. It was a complicated procedure requiring excellent co-ordination under great pressure and one which stretched even the first-class formations under Billotte's command to the limits of their capability and endurance. A junior staff officer at First Army headquarters, Maxime Dufour, had the testing job of compiling reports that provided the chief of staff with an idea of what formations were where. He later recalled:

> The situation was changing hour on hour, and sometimes minute by minute ... Information arrived by despatch riders and field telephone. It was only when there was a lull in communication from a division that we began to get concerned for its situation. No message for a couple of hours often meant that it was under heavy attack. By the time we knew what was happening and reacted, several hours had often passed ... Generally, however, the divisions withdrew in good order.[27]

Alan Brooke's II Corps also coped admirably but he noted how difficult the situation was for all concerned, writing on the evening of 18 May:

> I was too tired to write last night and now can barely remember what happened yesterday. The hours are so crowded and follow so fast on each other that life becomes a blur and fails to cut a groove on one's memory.... Michael Barker [the commander of I Corps] [is] in a very difficult state to deal with, he is so overwrought with work and the present situation that he sees dangers where they don't exist and cannot make up his mind on any points. He is quite impossible to cooperate with. He has been worse than ever today and whenever anything is fixed he changes his mind shortly afterwards.[28]

Like H. C. Lloyd, the commander of 2nd Division, Barker was, in fact, in the grips of a nervous breakdown that sleep deprivation only served to hasten. Tiredness, no matter what arm a soldier was in or what army's uniform he wore, was ever present on the ninth day of the campaign. Henry de la Falaise recalled his Sergeant

Ditton 'fast asleep, all crumpled up in a heap at the bottom of the [Morris armoured] car and wedged somehow between all the paraphernalia which clutters it, his head on an ammunition case'.[29] Some were so tired that they fell asleep while eating. One British troop commander did so into his plate of eggs, leading an observer to scribble in his small diary, 'Young Andrew is still asleep in the same position, his face smeared with egg yolk.'[30]

In such situations, as the Germans also understood, the training, leadership and discipline of formations came to the fore and none, according to Brooke, performed better than Bernard Montgomery's 3rd Division. Its King's Royal Hussars Regiment had a particularly difficult time as they endeavoured to make a fighting withdrawal from the Dyle and across the Senne to allow the infantry the time they needed to reach the Dendre. Under constant aerial reconnaissance which brought down accurate artillery fire and finding their radios jammed by German interference, the regiment was then attacked by enemy tanks. Guy Courage later wrote, '[We] never stood a chance. The enemy was behind and in front of us with vastly greater numbers, with artillery; his speed of movement and his use of anti-tank guns, many of them horse-drawn, well up in front impressed themselves on every mind.' By the end of the day, the regiment had two thirds of its strength. Courage continued, 'That evening we gathered in a field ... our thoughts were grim and black. It was so difficult to realize the extent of our losses ... [M]any troops had vanished without trace and those of us who had managed to cross the river gradually knew little more than our own small part of the tale. Wild rumours were rife.'[31] The entire division found itself under great pressure which did not let up after the Dendre had been crossed. In a brief note made in his diary about the process of his 3rd Division's withdrawal to the Escaut on 19 May, Montgomery wrote: 'Disengaged in daylight ... Used artillery to effect a break-away ... Used a lot of shells ... Whole DIV back on L'Escaut line by dark. A very tricky operation.'[32]

— ☐ —

Fedor von Bock was keen to keep the Allies under unremitting pressure as their formations slipped back towards several Channel ports, but Halder recognized that the advantages of this would be undermined if Army Group A failed to make its own advance to the coast in order to complete the encirclement. It was with great relief, therefore, that on the morning of 19 May, OKW gave its permission for the continuance of the panzers' advance westwards the next morning. As 10th Panzer Division continued to move up on the southern flank to take over responsibility for its defence from Kirchner's men and as 3rd and 4th Panzer Divisions completed their own move into line from the north, in between them the other six armoured divisions of the three panzer corps established themselves on the line Cambrai-Péronne-Ham ready for the new advance. That evening, Halder wrote in his diary as he mused on plans for 20 May:

> The breakthrough wedge is developing in a satisfactory manner. Follow-up proceeds as planned. Bulk of enemy forces lately operating in Belgium probably straddle Belgium border. Our big tank drive in direction Arras (starting 0700) consequently will squarely hit the bulk of the retreating enemy. It will be a big battle, lasting several days, in which we have the advantage of initiative, while the enemy has that of heavy concentration. But since all the psychological factors work in our favour and we have the benefit of a superior and tremendously effective air force, I am certain of success.[33]

The big battle in the Arras area which Halder was clearly expecting would be conducted by Panzer Group Hoth in order to protect Reinhardt and Guderian as they entered the twenty-four-mile-wide corridor between the city and French Seventh Army, which was establishing itself on the Somme. During the 19th, de

Gaulle had made another attempt to use his 4th DCR to strike at 1st Panzer Division's flank and it was swatted away with little difficulty, but Army Group A remained determined to avoid the enemy slicing across von Kleist's divisions and reconnecting the two parts of the Allied army.

Winston Churchill had also seen the opportunity that had presented itself, writing to Georges on 19 May: 'The tortoise has protruded its head very far from its shell. Some days must elapse before their main body can reach our lines of communication. It would appear that powerful blows struck from north and south of this drawn-out pocket could yield surprising results.'[34] Gamelin, however, finding on the morning of 19 May that Georges was no longer capable of command, drafted the orders for the counter-attack himself. Known as *Instruction Personnelle et Secrète No.12*, it detailed a push south by Billotte, who could call on BEF and First Army divisions around Arras, and Touchon's extremely thinly stretched Sixth Army attacking north from the Somme. Gamelin ended his *Instruction* with the words 'Everything now is a question of hours',[35] and although he was clearly endeavouring to imbue his scheme with a sense of urgency, he too was sacked by Reynaud shortly after its promulgation.

Gamelin's replacement, the charismatic General Maxime Weygand, had impressed Reynaud on their first meeting and it was no secret that the prime minister favoured the seventy-four-year-old over Gamelin. As a member of the French negotiations delegation, Weygand had been present at the signing of the armistice by the Germans in a railway carriage at Compiègne in 1918. By 1931 he was Chief of Staff of the French Army and Vice President of the Supreme War Council before retiring in 1935. Even so, he was recalled to active service at the outbreak of war and returned to France from Syria to assume command of the Orient Theatre of Operations.[36] As it was, on his return from a visit to see Georges on the afternoon of 19 May the fatally weakened Supreme Commander was not entirely surprised to find Weygand at his headquarters or to receive official notification of his replacement later that evening. Gamelin cleared his desk and left his office for the last time the next morning. The new man had refused a handover and, having indicated to Gamelin that he would cancel *Instruction No.12*, closed the door behind his predecessor and set to work making his own assessment of the situation.

The British looked on incredulously as the French High Command seemed to implode. At the start of what was to prove to be a spiralling decline in the relationship between the two allies, Ironside had said on 17 May that the situation was shaping up to be 'the biggest military catastrophe in history'[37] and three days later he had no reason to alter his opinion. In such circumstances, contingency planning for the evacuation of the BEF was entirely sensible. Gort's headquarters had begun the process on 18 May and since then had become convinced that it was time well spent. Even so, Churchill was not willing to authorize the lifting of the British divisions from French soil until it became a military imperative and he still had hopes of a successful attack from Arras by the BEF. To which end on 20 May Ironside travelled to France to meet with Gort and, bypassing the French chain of command, he ordered him to launch a major attack in order to link up with the French forces on the Somme. Gort immediately said that he thought such an attack to be impossible in the circumstances: seven of his nine divisions were on the Escaut and he believed the French to be in no position to lend any support. In the end, however, recognizing the sense in trying to do something, Gort agreed to a limited attack from Arras using two reserve divisions and a tank brigade but emphasized again the precarious position of the French.

With Gamelin sacked and Georges useless, Ironside immediately went on to see Billotte and Blanchard to find out what they were capable of. The imposing British general later wrote of the meeting:

I found Billotte and Blanchard all in a state of complete depression. No plan, no thought of a plan. Ready to be

slaughtered. Defeated at the head without casualties …
I lost my temper and shook Billotte by the button of his
tunic. The man is completely beaten.[38]

A furious Ironside had to goad the commander of First Army Group
into action and made him promise that he would support Gort's
attack by ordering an attack towards Cambrai. Billotte agreed to
ensure that the two divisions of General René-Félix Altmeyer's
V Corps, supported by Prioux's Cavalry Corps consisting of the
remnants of 2nd and 3rd DLM and the recently added 1st DLM
from Seventh Army, would play their part. Ironside left France
unconvinced that the French would act and made it his business
to ensure that any plans for a counter-attack did nothing to
destabilize the work that was being done on the BEFs preparations
for evacuation. He was wise to do so, because, unbeknown to
Ironside, Altmeyer was also in a fragile mental state. He told Major
Vautrin, a French First Army liaison officer to the BEF, that he
believed his troops had no fighting spirit and was willing to take
the consequences of disobeying an order by refusing to attack as he
'would not continue to sacrifice his army corps, which had already
lost half its personnel strength'.[39]

Even as the British were attempting to extract themselves from a
tight corner, the Germans were seeking to make it even tighter.
On the morning of 20 May, while Hoth advanced towards a
confrontation around Arras, Guderian sought to reach the coast
along the Somme and Reinhardt pushed between the two in the
centre of the corridor. Hoth made a careful advance, because like
Halder he recognized that a major confrontation was likely at Arras,
a vital anchor to the Allies' line, as the enemy defended his open
flank. Thus, as Rommel moved towards the city from Cambrai he
had to retain his self-control. With 3rd and 4th Panzer Divisions
having only just crossed the French border and the Sambre, and

5th Panzer Division being attacked by elements of First Army as it crossed the Scarpe, the general knew how vulnerable his division was. As a result, when enemy raids began to affect his lines of communication, he was cautious and ensured that they had been contained and cleaned up before progressing. As he approached Arras from the south, the division was engaged by British troops defending the city, three battalions of Major General Roderick Petre's 12th Division, which ensured that Rommel's advance was a difficult one. On 20 May, 7th Panzer Division suffered more casualties than it had crossing the Meuse and Rommel understood that he needed to be watchful as his division continued to skirt round the city.

Better protected and moving through the central channel of the corridor was Reinhardt's corps. 6th Panzer Division ran into some British troops from 36th Brigade of Petre's 12th Division who provided it with some considerable resistance at Doullens. Ultimately, however, Brigadier George Roupell's formation could not hold the Germans and Kempf broke through that evening with 8th Panzer Division on his right ready to outflank Arras to the west. The advance of Guderian's corps in the southern sector of the corridor also ran into scattered elements of Petre's 12th Division which fought hard as well but were ultimately unable to do no more than temporarily hinder the advance. 1st Panzer Regiment of 1st Panzer Division raced thirty-five miles and seized Amiens and a bridgehead over the Somme from a battalion of the Royal Sussex Regiment in the early afternoon. 2nd Panzer Division on Kirchner's right flank made an even more remarkable drive and thrust of fifty-five miles – along the route taken by Henry V to Agincourt, across the old Somme battlefield and into the Allies' rear.

Although there were few enemy to cause 2nd Panzer difficulties, the combination of sun and dry ground did. Standing in the turrets of their tanks, commanders were plastered with dust and their eyes became red and painfully swollen as, unlike the motorcyclists, they were not issued with goggles. One of the men in Leutnant Wold-Max Ostwald's reconnaissance troop wrote of his officer: '[He] cools his driver's eyes with a wet handkerchief, although he can hardly keep his own eyes open, and tears are rolling down his blackened, dirt-streaked face.'[40] Anything, in fact, to ensure that his vehicle could keep moving, since a stop, no matter how short, was prohibited. The only limit on the division's advance was its logistics and, as Oberleutnant Dietz noted in his diary, there was concern about this as the leading units pushed on:

> The Battle Group Commander is travelling behind the lead tanks. His expression is grave. There must be something in his calculations that is not quite right. Every now and again he measures with his thumb the distance travelled against what is still to be covered. The Panzer regiments have reported their fuel will last just as far as Abbeville. What then? What could he do with immobilized tanks outside a heavily fortified town?[41]

In the end, the commander need not have worried. The division did not run into any enemy as they closed in on the mouth of the Somme and reached Abbeville that evening with just enough fuel to spare at 2030 hours, while at 0200 hours, 3rd Battalion 2nd Rifle Regiment reached the coast west of Noyelles.

Now that 2nd Panzer Division had reached the Channel, the door had been closed on an Allied withdrawal across the Somme. Jodl reported in his diary entry for 20 May: 'Führer is beside himself with joy. Talks in words of highest appreciation of the German Army and its leadership … Return of territory robbed over the past 400 years from the German people, and other values.'[42] The Netherlands had capitulated, Belgium would follow, fifteen Allied divisions had been lost and the entire northern wing of the Allied army, forty-five divisions including its elite formations, had been encircled between the two German army groups in a giant pocket some 120 miles long and eighty-five miles deep. It contained the remnants of the Belgian Army, the BEF, French First Army Group and some elements of French Seventh and Ninth Armies. Yet although the Germans had achieved a significant and substantial military success in just eleven days, there was satisfaction across the Wehrmacht but no celebration – the job was still unfinished.

By midnight on 20–21 May, Hitler's forces had a tenuous hold on the coast, but his panzer divisions' lines of communication were stretched and exposed while there remained a threat to them from Arras and the French Seventh Army on the Somme. There was also the huge pocket of Allied troops to be reduced and decisions had to be taken about how this task should be balanced with the need to turn through 90 degrees in order to cross the Somme and Aisne in the next phase of operations. That afternoon, Halder had at least secured agreement at a conference that there would be a new operation – *Fall Rot* (Case Red) – which would thrust into the French interior. Planned by the General Staff, the necessary preparations for the offensive were made without delay. In the meantime, the immediate threats posed by the Allies would be countered while the wedge that had been driven to the coast was strengthened and von Bock exerted pressure from Belgium.

That night, while the German generals moved into position for a new day of offensive action and planned their *coup de grâce*, their Allied counterparts were left dazed but increasingly aware that, with their backs against the sea, only courage could bolster their now limited optimism. At the headquarters of the British Air Forces in France, the army liaison officer despaired:

It looks like the end already. Can this really be true? The thing is farcical; it is an anti-climax without equal. I find it impossible to believe, but we cannot get away from the facts. As instructed in orders, I have destroyed all my private and official papers. Everything is burned. It is one of those acts we read of in tragedies – something that we never expect to undertake ourselves. It is more than the papers we have burned, for with them we have burned nearly everything that remains of hope.[43]

For the French army, which was now in the ponderous hands of Weygand, whose findings on 20 May were rapidly making him as pessimistic as Gamelin had been, the activities of the British had suddenly taken on greater significance. Would Churchill stick by the French to the bitter end and send reinforcements, or would they fall back on the Channel ports and evacuate? On the morning of 20 May, the British prime minister had finally recognized that an evacuation might become necessary and reluctantly directed that '... as a precautionary measure the Admiralty should assemble a large number of small vessels in readiness to proceed to the ports and inlets on the French coast'.[44] The responsibility of planning and organizing an operation capable of plucking the BEF from the Channel coast fell to Bertram Ramsay. The fifty-seven-year-old vice admiral, who had been lured out of retirement by Churchill the previous year and given command of the Dover area of operations, now faced a challenge that would draw deeply on his calm and methodical personality. Working from rooms carved into the famous white cliffs under Dover Castle during the night of 20–21 May, Ramsay and his team started to gather the vessels required for *Operation Dynamo*. As he did so, eighty miles away across the Channel at his headquarters near Lille, Gort was desperately endeavouring to find enough troops to launch a counter-attack from Arras.

CHAPTER 9

21–24 May – Arras, Weygand and the Halt Order

DURING THE EARLY HOURS of 21 May, Emmanuel Marcel, an infantryman in 143rd Regiment of First Army's 32nd Infantry Division, was nursing wounds that had been inflicted on him by 5th Panzer Division. He could not remember anything about the incident which had left him with a raging headache and an open wound the size of his palm that revealed part of his skull above his closed eye. He was told that he had been breaking from cover with his section when a German shell landed among them, throwing Marcel into the air. He was the only survivor. As Marcel would later explain:

> The man who described to me what had happened was from a neighbouring platoon and had viewed the scene while providing covering fire from a copse of trees. This man was wounded minutes later in the same bombardment after a shell exploded in the trees and left him with large chunks of wood in his shoulders and lower neck. He looked like

a ghost but we tried to chat to keep our minds from our predicament.[1]

A dazed Marcel and his comrade, who drifted in and out of consciousness as the night wore on, were at a casualty clearing station in a large farmhouse where their wounds had been assessed and, after some superficial treatment, they were waiting transportation to take them to a field hospital. It was a traumatic wait with the moaning of the delirious, the cries of pain from several and, Marcel remembered, the names of unknown women – presumably the loved ones of the wounded – drifting across the stinking, airless room. The man opposite Marcel, his shattered right leg bound in blood-soaked bandages, sobbed 'Mama' quietly to himself. Marcel was desperate to leave the claustrophobic cell, testifying:

> I thought that I had been left in the room to die and so, despite my wounds, I tried to stand. Before my legs had straightened, I slumped to the floor. Somebody came over and gave me a canteen of water and told me to stay put as the transport had arrived. My head was in a whirl when the orderlies came in the room and started to remove the stretchers. When it was my turn, I laid back and asked the man holding the handles near my head, 'What's the news?' He replied: 'Gamelin is gone. Weygand is in command. It's all over.' I said nothing. It was over? So soon? Where was the counter-attack that we were promised?*[2]

The attack to which Marcel was referring had been the talk of his regiment in recent days and they had anticipated a 'great armoured advance south towards the Somme'[3] by a concentration

---

* Marcel was taken prisoner at the field hospital on 30 May and was found to have a fractured skull. He recovered from his wounds in a German PoW camp, where he remained until April 1945.

of French tanks that were supposedly gathering around Arras. It is impossible to know whether the regiment had been told about Gamelin's intentions, its officers had made certain assumptions or the attack was merely a rumour, but what is beyond doubt is that Weygand had immediately postponed the counter-attack outlined in *Instruction No. 12*. While Gort had been prompted by Ironside to make an offensive effort out of Arras with his very limited assets on 21 May, the new French Supreme Commander continued to vacillate as he remained wedded to the operational tempo of 1918, and this despite all the evidence to the contrary provided by the German advance since 10 May.

After breakfast on 21 May and as Guderian consolidated his southern flank and lodgement on the coast, Weygand flew north for a meeting with Allied commanders. He landed at Calais, which was considered a suitably safe distance from the fighting front, and took a waiting car that was to drive him to his destination in the Belgian town of Ypres. With time of the essence but the roads from the coast filled with troops and traffic, Weygand did not manage to start his discussions with King Leopold until mid-afternoon, but while Billotte arrived later, Gort did not arrive at all. The absence of the British commander at the conference mattered not only because Weygand immediately questioned the loyalty of France's ally, but also because he had decided that there would be a counter-attack across the Somme corridor with the BEF acting as its spearhead. In order for the British to provide the required concentration of troops at the vital point, a contraction of the front was required and this, Weygand proposed, could be achieved if the Belgian army abandoned most of the remainder of Belgium by withdrawing to the Yser. Leopold refused, saying this would be an act of betrayal to his people, but he did offer the compromise of moving back to the Lys. Weygand accepted and, in the absence of Gort, began to work on the details of the attack with Billotte.

Although Weygand waited until around 2000 hours in the hope of seeing the British commander, he must have left Ypres feeling that there was a tension between his plan, which leant heavily on the BEF, and what he believed to be an increasing lack of British commitment to continuing operations. As it transpired, the French Supreme Commander was driving back to the coast – at the start of a return journey to his headquarters after a crucial twenty-six hours away – when Gort arrived in Ypres. He had not snubbed Weygand but had spent the day trying to find out where the meeting was taking place after a telegram had failed to reach him. Billotte was still in the town, however, and so briefed Gort about Weygand's scheme. His response was non-committal: the plan made sense, but he considered that, with the situation changing with every hour, it might not be possible. This was a view partly shaped by reports that Gort had received about the counter-attack that had been launched at Arras that day.

7th Panzer Division had the task of completing their advance around the south and west of Arras while the remainder of Panzer Group Hoth sought to break through French First Army to the east. The aim was to isolate and then unseat the Allies from the city before turning north into what was, on 21 May, an open flank between Arras and the coast. In this task Rommel's division was to be supported on his left flank by the untried SS Totenkopf Division. Formed in October 1939 from concentration camp guards, the division brought ideological zeal and fanaticism to France and was keen to prove itself. As it was, by the time that the British attacked at 1500 hours on 21 May, the main body of both German divisions were advancing on a three-mile front with its right flank just two miles south of the city. Rommel was advancing warily, but not tentatively, and had ordered his commanders to move quickly in order to provide as fleeting a target to the enemy as possible. Accordingly, he ordered that 25th Panzer Regiment would lead the attack, followed by his armoured reconnaissance regiment to hold the road open and create a link with the two rifle regiments that followed. The formation's right flank was screened by artillery but no close air support was planned.

The British aim was to reach the River Cojeul six miles south of the city and so decapitate the advancing enemy force. With Billotte having informed Gort that Altmayer's V Corps force would not be ready to lend any support until 22 May, it was left to a pitiably small British force to take on two German divisions. This force, commanded by Major General Harold Franklyn, was divided into two columns: 4th Royal Tank Regiment (RTR) led by 6th Battalion Durham Light Infantry (DLI) on the left and 8th DLI led by 7th RTR on the right. Thus, eighty-eight British tanks were to act as the spearhead against 7th Panzer Division, while sixty tanks from the battered remains of 3rd DLM were to engage SS Totenkopf Division on Franklyn's right flank. No air cover was available, the attack had been hastily developed and there had been no time for reconnaissance. Gort did not have much hope for the endeavour: the tiny force, the lack of preparation time and the failure of every French counter-attack since 14 May did not bode well. Even so, the plucky thrust at Arras on 21 May was destined to have considerable – and unexpected – operational significance.

The attack by 7th RTR and 8th DLI did not start well and revealed the lack of co-ordination inherent in the endeavour when, on crossing the Scarpe, it was shot up by the French tanks to its right. Then, shortly after, the British tanks lost contact with the infantry when they mistakenly split down parallel routes, only for 7th RTR to drift into the left-hand column's sector. Throughout the attack the armour struggled to ensure that it was where it was supposed to be because, as Trooper 'Butch' Williams has recalled, 'We had no map of the area, nor any idea of the objective, neither had we been allowed to net in the radio.'[4] 8th DLI was not in fact reunited with its tanks again until they reached the village of Wailly, three miles south-west of Arras, which had just been occupied by a battalion of Rommel's 7th Rifle Regiment. Much of the German armour, accompanied by the division commander himself, had already moved through to the west of the city and so the arrival of the British tanks initially caused some considerable concern. Rommel was immediately informed of the attack and with Leutnant Most, his ADC, drove back to find that the British had 'created chaos and confusion among our troops in the villages and they were jamming up the roads and yards with their vehicles, instead of going into action with every available weapon to fight the oncoming enemy. We tried to create order.'[5]

The British tanks had been held up initially outside Wailly by a howitzer battery and Rommel surveyed the scene from Hill 111 in the middle of his rapidly developed defensive line. He later wrote:

> With Most's help, I brought every available gun into action at top speed against the tanks. Every gun, both anti-tank and anti-aircraft, was ordered to open rapid fire immediately and I personally gave each gun its target. With the enemy tanks so perilously close, only rapid fire from every gun could save the situation. We ran from gun to gun ... All I cared about was to halt the enemy tanks by heavy gunfire.[6]

Several British Matilda Mk Is were knocked out, but rounds bounced off the Matilda Mk IIs, which continued to creep forward, destroying the anti-tank guns. Leutnant Most fell at his general's side, mortally wounded, with Rommel later writing, 'Blood gushed from his mouth, [he] was beyond help and died before he could be carried into cover beside the gun position. The death of this brave man, a magnificent soldier, touched me deeply.'[7] The attempted breakthrough was eventually stopped by a mixture of the guns of a nearby artillery battery, 7th Rifle Regiment's reinforcement of Wailly, and the motorized element of SS Totenkopf, which had closed up to the west of the village.

The British left flank of the attack, 4th RTR and 6th DLI, made better progress and engaged the 6th Rifle Regiment a little over a mile south of Arras either side of Agny. East of the village, the Germans had hurriedly established an anti-tank gun blocking position, but the Matildas rolled right over this and, leaving the DLI to tackle the German infantry, linked up with tanks advancing to the west of Agny. Together, this armoured battering ram advanced a further three miles towards Mercatel and on a three-quarter mile front thumped into the rear of 7th Rifle Regiment.

Meanwhile, on the far left of 4th RTR's attack east of the village of Beaurains, reconnaissance officer Second Lieutenant Peter Vaux was leading the advance. Three hours after crossing the start line, they attacked a group of 6th Rifle Regiment lorries, infantry and anti-tank guns. It was so successful, Vaux later recalled, 'We really didn't see why we shouldn't go all the way to Berlin at the rate we were going.'[8] The advance was soon stopped, however, by a line of infantry, artillery and 88mm anti-aircraft guns Rommel had ordered to form behind Tilloy, Beaurains and Agny and which successfully prevented a breakthrough by 4th RTR along its attacking front.

Peter Vaux's account of the line's fortunes east of Beaurains is chilling. Having been sent by his commanding officer, Lieutenant Colonel Fitzmaurice, to encourage a lone French tank that had appeared to their rear to join the group – which its commander refused to do – Vaux endeavoured to rejoin the advance. He approached a hayfield containing around twenty British tanks, including that of his colonel, which were being engaged by those powerful 88mm guns. Moving through 'A' Squadron, Vaux instinctively felt that something was not right and later said:

> I thought it very odd that they weren't moving and they weren't shooting, and then I noticed that there was something even odder about them – because their guns were pointing at all angles; a lot of them had their turret hatches open and some of the crews were half in and half out of the tanks, lying wounded and dead – and I realized then, suddenly, with a shock, that all these twenty tanks had been knocked out, and they had been knocked out by these big guns and they were, in fact, all dead – all these tanks. In the grass I could see a

number of black berets as the crews were crawling through the grass … and getting away – those who were not dead.[9]

Recognizing that he was now a target, Vaux needed to act quickly. While reversing to allow the tank's machine gunner to depress the weapon enough to engage the treeline in which the enemy were ensconced, a German rifleman took aim at Vaux's head, resting his weapon on a kitbag. The British Officer's adjutant, Captain Cracroft, in another tank spotted this and, Vaux later recalled, 'pulled out his revolver and, quick as a flash, he shot the chap in the throat. It must have been a jolly good revolver shot, and it saved my life.' Having raked the woods with its machine gun, Vaux's tank withdrew under heavy fire, leaving its commander to ruminate on what he had just experienced:

[M]y heart sank because I realized what had happened: there were all those tanks that I knew so well – the familiar names – Dreadnought, Dauntless, Demon, Devil; there were the faces of these men with whom I had played games, swum, lived with for years – lying there dead; and there were these tanks – useless, very few of them burning but most of them smashed up in one way or another. And as the Adjutant and I drove back up to the top of the hill, one realized that this really was it. This was a tragedy. This was the end of the 4th Tanks as we knew it. In that valley, the best of crews, our tanks, our soldiers, our officers were left behind.[10]

By the evening, the Allies were in withdrawal, hounded by 300 Stukas. Having failed to break through, Franklyn wanted to disengage his force before nightfall while he still had the semblance of a force to disengage. His attempt, however, was undermined by 25th Panzer Regiment, which lunged towards Arras from its advanced position near the 3rd DLM start line. While the German tanks failed to block the withdrawal routes due to the sterling work of a handful of anti-tank guns and the courage of some British and French tanks in the gathering gloom, it certainly upset the Allied equilibrium at a sensitive time. By the time the fighting petered out at midnight on 21–22 May, Franklyn was fraught but pleased to have completed a 'short-armed jab'* at the enemy without being wiped out.

Consulting their maps, both Franklyn and Rommel would have seen that the front line at the end of the battle closely resembled what it had been at the beginning – but with the miserable addition of corpses, burning vehicles and piles of twisted metal. The British lost 100 infantry casualties and forty tanks, the French twenty tanks and the Germans 400 men, scores of vehicles, twelve tanks and a similar number of guns.[11] The counter-attack was a chastening experience for both sides, but while the Anglo-French effort might only be said to have stalled one or two German divisions for a few hours and temporarily protected the Allied right flank, the day was soon to have more far-reaching implications for the invasion. During the afternoon of 21 May and over the days that followed, Hitler and some of his more circumspect generals also pored over maps and entered into conjectural discussions about what the Allies might have achieved. One of those generals was Gerd von Rundstedt, who later wrote:

> A critical moment in the drive came just as my forces had reached the Channel. It was caused by a British counterstroke southward from Arras toward Cambrai, on 21 May. For a short time it was feared that our armoured divisions would be cut off before the infantry divisions could come up to support them.[12]

Why von Rundstedt was quite so concerned can be found in Rommel's desire to protect his reputation – and even develop it – by

---

* A description used by Franklyn to Peter Vaux – letter to author 20 February 2009. Author's Archive.

reporting to his superiors that he had been attacked by 'hundreds of British tanks and five divisions' as opposed to considerably less than 100 tanks and two battalions of infantry.

Arras offered a salutary warning that immediately began to fester in the minds of some German officers because they overestimated what the Allies were capable of at this point in the campaign. While it was true that Churchill, Ironside and Gort, Weygand and Billotte were all endeavouring to take the opportunity that the Somme corridor presented, by the end of 21 May the chances of mounting a well-resourced and co-ordinated counter-attack had significantly diminished as the Allies sought to maintain their cohesion while they continued their withdrawal and to establish a defensive line from Arras to the coast. With Guderian's divisions trying to turn the open flank, Panzer Group Hoth exerting great pressure on the British contingent at Arras and against First Army, while Army Group B pushed against the BEF and the remains of Leopold's army in Belgium, the Allies were stretched and barely coping. Churchill himself was in a quandary for, although he wished to see the Allies strike back before the Germans reached the Channel ports, he was concerned that he was waiting for something that was impossible and imperilled the BEF. In an attempt to ascertain what was and what was not possible, the British prime minister flew to Paris on 22 May, to be greeted by unfounded rumours that Gamelin had shot himself. Here he agreed to the 'Weygand Plan', which was very similar to that cancelled two days earlier but now had a clear form: a pincer attack against the Somme corridor. Formations from the newly formed Third Army Group under General Antoine-Marie-Benoît Besson and consisting of Frère's Seventh Army on the left and Touchon's much diminished Sixth Army on the right would strike north to Amiens, while First Army struck south from Arras.

Churchill could not ignore the fact that the situation remained unpropitious for any Allied attempt to deal the Germans a blow.

Indeed, on 22 May the delayed counter-attack by Altmeyer's V Corps and Prioux's Cavalry Corps at Cambrai turned out to be a damp squib. Although it managed to struggle to the outskirts of the town in Hoth's rear, the French formations were ejected by rapidly concentrated Luftwaffe attacks – including some by squadrons of obsolete Henschel Hs 123 biplane dive-bombers – and 88mm anti-tank guns firing at point-blank range. Britain had been asked to provide more RAF support over France for several days, but now the French became insistent that it was essential. Weygand endeavoured to prise Fighter Command from Churchill's hands at their meeting on 22 May, claiming that its presence would make all the difference. The British understood the impact this transfer might have, but they were far from convinced that it would be decisive, and Churchill could not help remembering his Gallipoli experience and the lessons that military history taught about not reinforcing defeat. As a result, he agreed to nothing, despite being aware that the French would see it as yet more evidence of British selfishness. Indeed, British aircraft had become a symbol of hope to the French, with Alexander Werth noting after conversations with his Parisian neighbours: 'They all agree that the R.A.F. is magnificent. Curious how during the last few weeks the R.A.F. has become more popular in France than the French Army.'[13]

The RAF had indeed become more visible as General d'Astier de la Vigerie husbanded his own aircraft for the protection of Paris while 2 Group struck operational targets which mirrored those being targeted by the Luftwaffe: roads, railways and troop concentrations. There was not a single British squadron that did not understand how much the ground forces were relying on them to slow the enemy's advance and consequently the intensity of operations increased with every passing day. Flying a Blenheim, Flight Lieutenant Webster received orders on 22 May to attack a column of German vehicles that had been spotted approaching the battlefield:

We were leading and flying really low – literally climbing over hedges and passing between trees ... Ahead of us and running directly across our flight path was a road crammed with AFVs upon whom we unloaded our 250-pounders before they saw us coming ... At the same time we spotted a similar convoy on a parallel road to the first, a few fields farther on, so we continued straight on, intending to let them have our 40-lb anti-personnel bombs. Whereas the first lot seem to have been taken completely by surprise, the second were wide awake and gave us a right old pasting as we came in. It was a very hectic and noisy few seconds with one particularly loud bang right under my seat accompanied by a strong smell of hot, angry cordite.[14]

Webster duly landed his burning aircraft in a French field and joined a group of refugees on the road and headed towards the coast. By 22 May, 2 Group had lost forty-four Blenheims and 108 crew killed, with many more wounded or missing in action. Ground crews worked in shifts around the clock to get badly damaged aircraft patched up and airborne as quickly as possible as the pressure mounted on squadrons to fly increasing numbers of sorties each day.[15] As another pilot, Peter Mansfield, later testified:

We had little idea what impact we were having on the campaign – if any – but we knew that things were not good on the ground and we did our bit. We were told that this railway and that column had been put out of action, which was good for our morale, but what we really wanted to hear is that the army had counter-attacked and turned the situation round. Sadly, that was not to be.[16]

Although initially postponed for several days in order to prepare and deploy its strike force, the Weygand Plan was never launched as the Allied situation continued to deteriorate. Although Arras had been identified as the springboard for the northern pincer of the counter-attack, Gort found it impossible to hold the city and protect the vulnerable flank back to the coast. Moreover, co-ordination of the Allies' effort was becoming increasingly difficult as the time, space and resources that they had at their disposal were reduced hour on hour. It was further undermined by the death of General Billotte, who on leaving Ypres on the evening of 21 May had been involved in a traffic accident when his car hit a refugee lorry in the darkness, leaving him in a coma from which he never emerged. Yet despite the significant hole that Billotte's accident left at the heart of the command structure in this vital sector, with a lethargy that was representative of the pedestrian French response to any crisis, the new First Army Group commander, General Georges-Marie-Jean Blanchard, was not appointed Billotte's successor for three days.

While the French continued to immerse themselves in a dangerous mixture of indecisiveness and hope and the sceptical British looked more to the salvation of evacuation with every step they took back towards the coast, the battlefield shrank and became increasingly congested. One of the many challenges that the belligerents were faced with was trying to go about their business with civilians in their sights. A mobile circus was caught in an artillery exchange near the Belgian town of Tournai which injured many of the animals, causing the elephants to charge around and roar amongst the blasts and smoke. They were joined by the mentally ill who had been released into the town, where they roamed vulnerable and frightened but barely noticed by hundreds of locals desperately trying to escape a scene from perdition. This was the fate potentially waiting for all those who had decided not to leave their homes and who now found themselves in the middle of a battlefield. Douglas Manning, a British gunner in support of 3rd Division, recalls being given an order to stop firing despite the fact that the enemy could clearly be seen advancing towards them:

Our officer said that the village that we were gradually demolishing still contained civilians, that women and children had been seen by our forward observer running from the buildings. The Germans did not seem to have the same ethical concerns as we did in such matters and I personally witnessed the sad sight of the bodies of women and children lying under piles of rubble. They had been caught in a hell that they could not escape, like mice in a trap.[17]

Elsewhere, refugees continued to trudge west, where Hans Becker of 7th Panzer Division spotted a large group waiting to cross a dusty track in the wake of the fighting at Arras and was sympathetic to their plight:

I thought to myself, what if you had to leave your house and farm and didn't know when you would return, and ended up looking like this. This had an effect on me. 'Ç'est la guerre,' as the French would say. But the sadness was if someone returned later and saw that his house was destroyed. What must this person be thinking? He must be really angry with the Germans![18]

The Reynaud government was in fact endeavouring to stem the tide of refugees for their own safety, but also to reduce the burden of responsibility that it felt to assist them and to stop their numbers from clogging up the same roads that the military were relying on. As a result, an official government communiqué told the population to stay in their homes, saying:

The Germans ... wish to create panic among populations to incite them to leave towns and villages – even those which are situated far from the combat zones. Their aim is in this way to block roads and hinder the manoeuvre of the Allied forces. Our military operations are being slowed down as a result. German planes are taking advantage of this to bomb and gun down both military personnel and civilian evacuees indiscriminately. Such bomb attacks are considerably aggravating the sense of panic in the population.[19]

There was a good deal of truth in this, for with the shift of the Luftwaffe to operational targets had come deliberate attacks on refugees. Initially, the German raids sought out military columns, which were attacked despite the awareness that refugees shared the roads, but before long some pilots began to target civilians in an attempt to cause chaos and fear. The Lebeouf family – a mother and her two young children – had left their home in Reims on 19 May and were attacked on 21, 22 and 23 May. Diane Lebeouf, who was just twenty in 1940, later recalled:

> We left in a hurry with just a suitcase between us and a bag with some food. We spent the first night with another family, sheltering in a barn but were back on the road early the next morning. We joined hundreds of others shuffling along the dusty road heading west ... Then up ahead we saw people running, and then screaming. They ran into the woods or just threw themselves onto the verge as bullets ripped into the earth around them. There were no casualties, but some would not come out of the woods while others – often old men – shook their fists at the sky ... It was a lone aircraft, but on the second day it was a group of three and they swept the roads twice. Five people were killed – two were children, and several others were wounded. We did what we could for them. I thought about taking to the country lanes, but in the end thought that there was safety in numbers, particularly as we heard that German troops were getting close.[20]

Another family was undertaking a similarly fraught journey having left Albert on the Somme. Julia Lapointe noted in her diary: 'Children are tired. We are thirsty and finding it difficult to get food ... Everybody is finding the march very difficult and are concerned to see soldiers with no rifles walking with us. Still, we have been told that Pétain is now in government. There is hope still!'[21] Indeed, Pétain's appointment as deputy prime minister had been well received in France, although London was cynical as he had long been known to be against the war and 'defeatist'. But the victor of Verdun had already managed to deliver a triumph out of a seemingly hopeless situation in the First World War and now Reynaud said that the Marshal was 'putting all his wisdom and strength at the service of our country. He will remain there until we are victorious.'[22]

In spite of everything, France maintained a sense of hope, and in the wake of the Arras counter-attack OKW seemed intent on giving the Allies the vital breathing space that they yearned for to establish the defensive pocket forming around the Channel ports. Hitler used events on 21 May to chide Halder and argue that as a politician he read the operational situation better than the experienced military professionals. He also quoted von Kleist, von Kluge and von Rundstedt, who all remained concerned that the panzer divisions remained extremely vulnerable. As a result, the panzers were paused for twenty-four hours after the commencement of Franklyn's counter-attack because, von Rundstedt ordered, the priority was 'first of all to straighten out the situation at Arras'[23] before any attack might be mounted on this particularly vulnerable sector of the line.[24] In the meantime, 2nd Panzer Division prepared to attack Boulogne, 1st Panzer Division readied itself for a lunge towards Calais, while 10th Panzer Division, which might have been used to strike into the soft Allied flank towards Dunkirk, was instead ordered into reserve. Reinhardt's divisions, meanwhile, were to continue their attack on Guderian's right, while Hoth's dealt with Arras and the surrounding area during the pause to the west.

Halder and Guderian were extremely frustrated by what they believed to be an unnecessary pause over exaggerated fears about a counter-attack at a time when von Kleist's divisions were poised to strike behind the Allies to deny them the ports that offered the possibility of reinforcement and evacuation. The intelligence that OKH was reading indicated that the enemy was barely keeping his front together, that his troops were demoralized and, as a consequence, they were ripe for the plucking. Hitler, however, revelled in his intuition and squandered the chance to unhinge the Allied defences. The survival of the Allied pocket depended on a successful defence of the Channel ports. While Ostend was seen as expendable in view of the likely Belgian withdrawal back to the Yser, Boulogne and Calais were most immediately in danger but regarded as vital support to the central port of Dunkirk during this period. Allied plans, therefore, were to send formations out to the western ports to prepare their defence while a defensive line was developed along the line of the La Bassée and Aa Canals emanating from Gravelines, less than ten miles west of Dunkirk and stretching south-east to St Omer, Béthune and then, after Arras had been evacuated, down to Douai. Thus, for as long as Arras continued to offer resistance and the panzers were paused to the west, the Allies could rush troops into defensive positions.

On 22 May, Rommel was still licking his wounds and reorganizing while 5th Panzer Division came up on his right flank and 20th Motorized Division had arrived and was poised to attack through the city itself. The aim was to widen the corridor to make an Allied counter-attack to link up with French troops on the Somme far less likely. It worked, for on the following day Hoth's divisions pushed north heading towards Béthune and forced British 5th and 50th Divisions in what one officer called 'a nightmare withdrawal'[25] towards Ypres. They nonetheless resisted with great fortitude to slow the panzer divisions, knowing that their colleagues needed every hour that could be provided to firm up the west flank and allow the BEF and French First Army to withdraw out of a salient, its nose resting on Valenciennes. This bulge in the line had been formed by a synchronized advance by several German divisions with von Bock's Sixth Army pushing from the east. Its aim was to encircle seven enemy corps and promote the rapid collapse of the Allied pocket.

Even as Hoth was pushing north through Arras, Gort was using the diminishing length of his front line to release formations to strengthen the line north of the city to the coast. This included 2nd and 48th Divisions, which were moved to the La Bassée and Aa Canals, while units were also sent to Boulogne and Calais with orders to hold them to the end: Gort recognized the likelihood that the Germans would isolate them and deal with the towns piecemeal and that there was merit in tying up as many of the enemy forces for as long as possible. If the Allies had one unifying intention during this period, it was to sacrifice the lesser for the greater. Thus, if a unit had to fight to the point of annihilation in order to benefit the mass of formations elsewhere, it was done.

Boulogne was garrisoned by 1,100 French naval personnel commanded by Commandant Dutfoy de Mont de Benque, who, having lost control of his men, a significant proportion of whom were wandering the streets drunk on 21 May, decided to withdraw back to Dunkirk. Meanwhile two Guards battalions – the *crème de la crème* of the BEF and recently arrived in France – had been sent to reinforce him. Known as much for their discipline and tenacity as their military skills, the units of Brigadier William Fox-Pitt's 20th Guards Brigade arrived at the port on the morning of 22 May just after the last French sailors had left and found the town being bombed and burning. The Guardsmen immediately set about establishing just the sort of defences that Guderian feared they would. The Irish and Welsh Guards together amounted to 1,962 men supported by the brigade anti-tank regiment and an attached anti-tank battery. The town had also seen the recent arrival of around 1,500 men of the Auxiliary Military Pioneer Corps (AMPC) who had been sent to Boulogne for evacuation. Although largely unacquainted with fighting, being an organization that handled stores and engaged in road-building and construction projects, they immediately became a reserve, along with some similarly untrained French and Belgian units, for the 7.5-mile perimeter around the town.

Fox-Pitt's force was attacked by 2nd Panzer Division even as they were digging in. Now that von Rundstedt's pause order to Guderian had expired, the formation had worked its way through a regiment of the French 21st Infantry Division, which had rushed into position as a screen, and then fell on Boulogne. The Irish Guards were the first to be engaged in a two-mile sector to the south-west of the town. After a careful reconnaissance, the Germans probed forward in the early evening. Sergeant Arthur Evans of the Irish Guards' anti-tank platoon remembers an artillery bombardment preceding the arrival of the first tanks:

> I could clearly see the tank commander's head above the open turret with his field glasses to his eyes. We opened fire and the tank rocked as we scored two direct hits. The crew baled out and abandoned it. Soon a second appeared and that too, was effectively disposed of.[26]

Nevertheless, the brave defence of the Irish Guards was not enough to stop the Germans reaching Boulogne. Although a few units from 21st Infantry Division managed to fight their way through to the town during the evening, the Germans infiltrated and probed throughout the night and the battle continued to rage. Early the next morning, 23 May, the attack continued with a concentration along the coast from the south in an attempt to create an encirclement. One hundred and seven men of the Irish Guard's 4th Company took the brunt of the attack and held the line, but at the cost of ninety-eight casualties. The Germans were more successful with a push against the eastern part of the town held by the Welsh Guards during which they managed to open up a gap between the two British battalions. This was filled by 800 nervous men from the AMPC, but the pressure exerted on the perimeter that morning had caused considerable casualties and forced the defenders into tighter positions around the port, which immediately led to bitter, close-quarters fighting. One German infantryman, eighteen-year-old Marc Leicht, recalled a bloody and passionate struggle, with heavy casualties on both sides:

> We fought with bayonets and rifle butts and elbowed our way into positions, often to lose them again in mad counter-attacks. The enemy came at us screaming and battered us down. We did the same – and so the battle continued.[27]

That afternoon, the First World War destroyer HMS *Vimy* arrived at the quayside as it was being shelled to evacuate the wounded and also disembarked a naval demolition team tasked with disabling the port facilities. The vessel passed orders to Fox-Pitt that he was to hold Boulogne at all costs. In this task, he was now supported by several other Royal Navy destroyers, which lobbed 4.5-inch shells into the columns supporting the German troops fighting in Boulogne. The co-driver of one ammunition truck fled when the first of them exploded in a field one hundred yards from his vehicle. The driver, Gerd Reismann, a twenty-three-year-old from Hamburg who had already been injured in an accident with a Mk III panzer a week earlier, recalled:

> It was dangerous and, as a replacement, I am not surprised he ran. It was his first time in action and the power of the explosions so close could be felt. The truck was showered with dirt, and some pieces of the shell casing ripped through the canvas covering the load area, and peppered my door. Why didn't I run? I was too tired and was convinced sooner or later that I would die. Why not now, honourably? At least it would be quick.[28]

Reismann drove past several burning vehicles and others that had been reduced to barely recognizable mangled metal to where his MG 34 ammunition and hand grenades were off-loaded. He later said:

> While I was pleased to see the back of those deadly boxes, I knew that they were gratefully received by the infantry … Looking at the smoke over Boulogne and [hearing the] rat-a-tat of small arms fire, I was glad to be turning away. It looked and sounded like hell.[29]

The Germans continued to make progress which, although it could be measured in yards, began to fragment the defences and rendered the British ability to withstand continued assault highly unlikely. In a decision that was based more on compassion than sound military thinking, Churchill made the decision to evacuate as many of 20th Guards Brigade as could be embarked before the enemy overran the remaining defenders. During a lull in the fighting – one instigated by the German infantry withdrawing a safe distance in anticipation of a Luftwaffe raid to render the port unuseable for an evacuation attempt – commanders organized their units for a withdrawal in a way that would allow as many of their men as possible to go down to the quayside.

That evening, while more than sixty German bombers attacked, the evacuation began. A modern French destroyer was sunk, but the arrival of twelve Spitfires overhead managed to protect two British vessels that were tied up while their crews urged Fox-Pitt's men aboard. Even so, the commander of HMS *Vimy* was mortally wounded and the commander of HMS *Keith* was killed during the air raid and eventually a decision was taken to depart for Dover while the ships were still able to do so. Although some 4,368 men – including French and Belgian troops – were lifted from the port, some 400 British troops and nearly all who had arrived from the French 21st Infantry Division were left behind. In a remarkable defence, those who remained in Boulogne continued to fight until they were overwhelmed on the morning of 25 May.

The action at Boulogne was representative of many that were taking place across the front as the defenders tied up German resources, caused casualties and took the initiative from the enemy. All were courageous and, while they seemed like futile attempts to thwart an opponent of great strength, should be seen more as parts of a co-ordinated action that allowed for a perimeter to form around Dunkirk and for evacuation plans to be advanced. The very idea of lifting troops off the French coast rather than reinforcing them was an anathema to many of the French decision-makers, who declared the British self-interested and seemed unable to see the sense in salvaging as many troops as possible from the pocket, not only to protect Britain but also to act as a cadre to strike back at the Germans elsewhere in France. The British were, perhaps, as selfish as the French were illogical, but at least London's position had the virtue of ensuring there could be long-term resistance to Hitler, no matter what the outcome of the current German offensive.

Nevertheless, Churchill later regretted his decision to evacuate Boulogne and, when it came to Calais, he was determined that 'fighting to the finish' would mean exactly that. By 24 May, 10 Panzer Division was bearing down on the ancient coastal town while other formations exerted pressure on the newly established British canal-line defences between Gravelines and Béthune whose creation had only been allowed by the panzer pause of 21–22 May. Panzer Group Kleist, including Schaal's division, took on the Allied west flank with Guderian attacking north of St. Omer and Reinhardt either side of Aire. Panzer Group Hoth used Hoepner and General Rudolf Schmidt – now commanding a corps that included 5th and 7th Panzer Divisions – in an advance either side of Béthune. Both Guderian and Reinhardt seized crossings over the Aa Canal on 24 May which left 1st Panzer Division less than ten miles south-west of Dunkirk, the last port with the facilities for a major evacuation. But as they were on the verge of completing the encirclement of approximately one million Allied troops, the panzers were halted once again.

The reason for this decision can be explained by the continuing concern about the vulnerability of the thirteen divisions in the two Panzer Groups north of Arras. Although it was Hitler who formally ordered the infamous Halt Order, it was von Kleist who on the morning of 23 May had expressed his concerns to the commander of Fourth Army, General von Kluge. Von Kleist wrote:

> The Group now lacks the strength to mount an attack to the east against a strong enemy after losses taken after fourteen days of fighting which include half of all tanks. It should be noted that if the enemy launches a strong attack the Panzer Divisions are poorly suited to defence.[30]

With this ammunition to hand, it did not take much to persuade von Kluge and von Rundstedt to conclude that the campaign had moved on from an armoured pursuit to an infantry struggle and, as such, required another pause to bring forward more divisions for both attack and defence. The result was an order issued to the mobile elements of Army Group A to wait on the canal line until 25 May while the infantry closed up. Only von Kluge's II and VIII Corps, pitched against the nose of the Allied salient protruding forward from Lille, were allowed to attack. OKH and the panzer commanders vehemently disagreed with the decision, not least because their own information and instincts could not be reconciled with the belief that there were 'strong enemy forces' ready to upset any attack against the Allied west flank. Indeed, Halder commented in his diary, 'The enemy's fighting power probably does not amount to more than local resistance,' and 6th Panzer Division's war diary noted:

> In contrast to combat operations in the past, the tempo of the advance, dictated by operational considerations, has become slower than the tactical conditions would have permitted. The Division could have attacked out of the bridgehead it had been able to win with full force at dawn on 24 May against an inferior enemy to the east.[31]

Guderian himself could hardly understand what might have led to such an order, later reflecting:

> We were utterly speechless. But since we were not informed of the reasons for this order, it was difficult to argue against it. The panzer divisions were therefore instructed: Hold the line of the canal. Make use of the period of rest for general recuperation.[32]

Meanwhile, the OKH looked on incredulous and, fearing that the continuation of such a conservative approach to operations might cripple the ability to attain a strategic victory, intervened. Halder and von Brauchitsch no longer had faith in von Rundstedt and this led to von Brauchitsch acting in a most uncharacteristic fashion. At midnight on 23–24 May, von Rundstedt was informed that Fourth Army was being transferred from his command to Army Group B the following evening. This was officially justified as being required to unify the direction of operations under Army Group B for the last phase of the encircling battle while Army Group A, with one panzer division and both Twelfth and Sixteenth infantry armies, would provide flank protection along the Somme.

Halder did not agree with this decision: he was concerned that von Bock would not be able to exert his will over the panzer commanders at vital times in the battle as he had not had the time to establish full command and control over his new army and communications with it. Halder also believed that von Brauchitsch should have bitten the bullet and, rather than causing an inevitable friction between the two army group commanders, 'coordinate[d] the efforts of the various elements converging on the pocket, under his own command'. The chief of the general staff believed that von Brauchitsch had been weak and wrote, 'He seems to be glad to let someone else take the responsibility. But with that he also foregoes the honours of victory.'[33] As a protest, Halder let the written order for the transfer of Fourth Army to Army Group B be promulgated without his signature.

Halder was not the only one angered by von Brauchitsch's actions. When Hitler found out about the order the next morning, he was determined to make the commander-in-chief pay for his lack of respect for the chain of command. He not only rescinded the order but visited von Rundstedt's headquarters at Charleville in the late morning of 24 May and thoroughly undermined von Brauchitsch by asking the commander of Army Group A to decide for how long the panzer divisions should be paused. The famous Dunkirk Halt Order was issued in Directive No.13 by OWK and followed by details from headquarters Army Group A. The result was to stamp Hitler's authority on the military – the men who had told him that his ambitions in the West were unobtainable and yet now were trying to sideline their superior – and to give von Rundstedt a free hand.

In the meantime, faith was placed in the Luftwaffe to apply pressure on those Allied troops in the Dunkirk pocket, and particularly around the ports, where the ground forces could not. Despite the increase in the RAF presence and the vagaries of the weather, Göring – so very eager to please – had convinced Hitler that the air force could do what the armoured forces, limited by the sandy terrain and waterways, would find difficult after such a long period in action. It was an opportunity that Hitler leapt at as an opportunity to preserve his force prior to the turn south-west in the next phase of operations, but the Luftwaffe itself was not convinced, despite Göring's blandishments. General Albert Kesselring, commander of Luftlotte 2 supporting Army Group B, and Generalmajor Wolfram Freiherr von Richthofen, commander of Fliegerkorps VIII, both believed that the mission that had been assigned to their aircraft looked like a classic task for ground forces and that the over-stretched Luftwaffe, which had lost 810 aircraft totally destroyed between 10 and 24 May, was not well placed to carry it out and was actually in more need of respite than the panzers.[34] As for von Bock, he could not understand why he was now being asked to push to the coast when other panzer divisions were better placed to have a decisive impact and noted in his diary that the Halt Order would 'have very unpleasant consequences for the outcome of the battle I am fighting!'[35] Even von Kluge, who had wanted time for his infantry formations to close up, argued that the pause was misguided.

Militarily, the Halt Order certainly made little sense, but it was about far more than operations and strategy. According to Hitler's Luftwaffe adjutant, Nicolaus von Below, 'the English army had no significance for him' at Dunkirk[36] and his motives for stopping the panzers were entirely to do with asserting his dominance. Von Brauchitsch met Hitler during the afternoon of 24 May and was admonished for his actions and left the presence of the Supreme Commander in no doubt that he had lost the right to direct the employment of his own field armies and that alterations to the command structure were in Hitler's gift alone. The commander-in-chief of the army had been brutally and publicly emasculated. Despite his recent disagreement with von Brauchitsch, Halder was livid not only at his colleague's treatment by OKW but also by the way in which the headquarters was now interfering in operations. Reflecting on the Halt Order, he wrote:

This is a complete reversal of the elements of the plan. I wanted to make AGp.A the hammer and AGp.B the anvil in this operation. Now B will be the hammer and A the anvil. As AGp.B is confronted with a consolidated front, progress will be slow and casualties high. The air force, on which all hopes are pinned, is dependent on the weather. The divergence of views results in a tug-of-war which cost more nerves than does the actual conduct of operations.[37]

Tactically, the pause as Army Group A transformed into an unwilling anvil led to some reversals as the bridgeheads across the Aa Canal had to be evacuated since they had become so vulnerable. SS-Obergruppenführer Sepp Dietrich, despite being the commander of the SS Leibstandarte Adolf Hitler, one of the most loyal formations in the German order of battle, was so infuriated at the illogicality of what was being done that he took unauthorized action and occupied a hill on the east bank of the canal as an act of defiance. Dietrich's direct superior, Guderian, took no action.

A humiliated von Brauchitsch returned to his own headquarters that evening to find that Halder and the Chief of the Operations Staff, i.G. Hans von Greiffenberg, had been busy. In a marked escalation in the private – but increasingly public – war that OKH was fighting against OKW, von Brauchitsch's headquarters had sent a radio message to Army Groups A and B which gave their commanders some flexibility within the Halt Order. The deliberately vague communication informed von Rundstedt and von Bock that '... the go-ahead is hereby given for the continuation of the attack up to the line Dunkirk-Cassel-Estaires-Armentières-Ypres-Ostende'.[38] It acknowledged that, unless there was immediate action, the BEF and French First Army would have an opportunity to withdraw from the Lille salient and begin an evacuation from the coastline. Both army group commanders immediately recognized what was happening but while von Bock acted on it, von Rundstedt refused to pass it on to Fourth Army – whose operations he alone handled – considering that more time was required for 'closing up'. Old tensions that had remained submerged in less exacting circumstances had come to the surface at a vital time and were now threatening to tear the German command apart just at a point when they needed to exploit their hard-won gains.

For their part, Weygand and Gort recognized that they needed some sort of sensation in order for their frail position not to become a disastrous one – and the Germans seemed intent on handing it to them. At the front, Alan Brooke noted in his diary: 'Nothing but a miracle can save the BEF now and the end cannot be very far off! … It is a fortnight since the German advance started and the success they have achieved is nothing short of phenomenal. There is no doubt that they are most wonderful soldiers.'[39] Counter-attack plans had not been able to turn the situation and it looked increasingly likely that evacuation from the Dunkirk sector was the only realistic proposition for the Allies' beleaguered troops. But although the relationship between the French and the British was deteriorating as quickly as that between OKH and OKW, the two armies were still working together and, with the RAF lending increasing support, withdrawal and defence continued. By the end of 24 May, the Lille salient was being emptied of Allied troops, leaving those who remained there to fight on until they were killed, wounded or overrun. While their commanders did what they could to facilitate men's safe removal from an extremely precarious situation, Gort and Blanchard were at a loss to understand why the German panzer divisions had not moved in for the kill.

CHAPTER 10

25 May–4 June – Withdrawal and Evacuation

B Y THE THIRD WEEK of the offensive, despite Hitler's inter-ference in operations and internal command frictions within the Wehrmacht, there was no doubt who was winning the campaign. Even so, the awful and worsening situation of the BEF, French and Belgian forces in the coastal pocket did not mean that there was nothing left to fight for. On the contrary, the surrounded Allied forces were increasingly motivated by their predicament to fight for every yard of ground, with the British further spurred on by the prospects of an evacuation that Churchill now deemed vital 'to the furtherance of the defence of the British mainland', and to allow the French time to strengthen their defences along the Somme and Aisne. It would be naïve to think, however, that, regardless of any strategic or operational factors, troops were not also fighting for their survival.

French R35 tank driver David Schneider, who had been in Breda on 11 May as part of Seventh Army but by 24 May was armed with a rifle as part of a composite unit in First Army, remembered:

Surrender was not an option. Before we had properly contacted the Germans, there was fear of the unknown, but ever since we had been fighting them – and particularly as we got closer to the sea – there was an unspoken agreement that we would fight until we could fight no more. It was clear to us that along the line, we all relied on each other. Any breach would spell disaster. Every soldier I knew would not be the man to cause that breach. Verdun was won by stubbornness, not flight.[1]

For his part, a British soldier in the 10th Hussars remarked that he was very aware that the heavy hand of the past was on his shoulder as he fought, explaining, 'We had to measure up to our fathers of 1914–18.'[2]

It was not uncommon for units to have little idea of the broader context of their situation, only to know that what they were doing was of value. Andrew Hardcastle, a rifleman with 5th Division's 2nd battalion Wiltshire Regiment, has said: 'Evacuation was spoken about. We did not know whether it was possible and we certainly did not know whether our battalion would be one of the ones lucky enough to sail off to safety. We fought because we were told to do so, because we had our pride and our mates to consider ... In the end, our withdrawal was brilliantly organised, if tough – a great achievement.'[3] Indeed, the movement back towards the coast was a remarkably accomplished affair considering the circumstances. The retreat from the Dyle Line had been extremely well handled and now the Dunkirk pocket was consolidated, this phase in the Allied campaign stood in stark contrast to the ineffectiveness of the French forces defending against Army Group A that had been either shattered or pushed aside to the south. With the Royal Navy offering an exit from the perimeter and the BEF's command and control remaining robust, Gort began to calmly grip the situation in a way that other senior commanders had failed to do. Although Brooke's opinion of the BEF's commander had been poor during the 'Phoney War', now under the pressure of the German attack, Gort's instinctive leadership, fighting spirit and resilience came to the fore.

Stoicism and leadership were critical to the survival of the troops in the Allied pocket, who had suffered days of hardship. A new fighting resolve emerged just in time, for the Germans were on the brink of operations aimed at squeezing the pocket out of existence. Although those panzer commanders ordered to discontinue their attacks were displeased to do so, by the second day of their pause they could not but agree that their formations had benefited from some rest, resupply and attention to their vehicles. Yet even though von Kleist had reported that half of his tanks were out of service before the Halt Order, few tank commanders believed that their situation was so poor as to require any sort of postponement to their operations. Reflecting on this, von Bock wrote in his diary: 'The English continue their evacuation from Dunkirk, even from the open beaches! By the time we finally get there they will be gone! The halting of the panzer units by the Supreme Command is proving to be a serious mistake!'[4]

As it was, the Allies had a fifty-six-mile front from the Dutch border and along the Lys to the French frontier manned by seven Belgian corps, albeit of greatly different strength and capability. These were struggling and 'beginning to break' after being made to give up their capital and then driven back towards the coast. The two divisions of Belgian I Corps which were on the right of their line and linked up with the BEF were particularly stretched. Gort reacted immediately, but without seeking the authority of the French, to plug the gap with his 5th and 50th Divisions, fresh from Arras. Even so, the pressure on the Belgians was unremitting and led the British to fear a collapse on their left.

Meanwhile, the bulge in the Allied line had been reduced in depth during 25 May as three French corps withdrew behind the River Scarpe and the west flank of the perimeter gained strength. By this time, British 2nd, 44th and 48th Infantry Divisions were in position from La Bassée northwards to where units of the French 21st Infantry Division held the line at the coast around Gravelines. The units of these dispersed divisions established themselves on the terrain that was best suited to defence, but although attempts were made to ensure that gaps in the line were covered by fire, this was not always possible and, indeed, not every formation knew exactly what ground was being held on its flanks, far less the unit responsible for its defence. As a result, the holding of various strongpoints behind the forward defences was essential because Gort recognized that enemy infiltrations would eventually lead to a withdrawal. In preparation for this, a series of fortified positions had been established. These were often based on towns, as was the case at Cassel and Hazebrouck, and the aim was to slow the enemy's advance while preventing the collapse of a flank that was precariously close to Dunkirk. By 25 May, however, Panzer Groups Kleist and Hoth were poised to knock that flank in and four Allied divisions faced seven panzer divisions, four motorized divisions, two of which were SS, an SS motorized regiment and an infantry division.

It should be remembered, though, that elements of two of Guderian's divisions received no rest during this period. Although Boulogne fell to 2nd Panzer Division on 25 May, Calais had only just been surrounded by 10th Panzer Division. The town had been bombed and continued to be so as the first British troops from 1st Armoured Division sailed into the port on 22 May. This force, commanded by Brigadier Claude Nicolson, included the tanks of 3RTR, an under-strength battalion of the Queen Victoria Rifles, 1st Battalion The Rifle Brigade and 2nd Battalion King's Royal Rifle Corps, but it lacked artillery and important equipment. The northernmost part of the town was defended by a small force of French naval reservists and volunteers commanded by Capitaine de Frégate Carlos de Lambertye and this left the rest to the British. The 3RTR tanks (twenty-one light tanks and twenty-seven cruisers) had not been prepared to go straight into battle, which meant that their guns were still coated in mineral jelly and had not been calibrated, and their radios had not even been tested. To make matters worse, there were no maps of the area and no orders for commanders other than to 'hold the town'. Lieutenant Colonel Reginald Keller, the commander of 3RTR, later said: 'A great deal of valuable time was wasted owing to my not knowing who or what Brigadier Nicolson was and why I had come under his orders and what I was supposed to be doing.'[5] 10th Panzer Division would have made short work of such a poorly organized enemy in open countryside, but Calais was of great advantage to the defender with its seventeenth-century Vauban fortifications, which could absorb shelling and bombing and dissuaded frontal attacks. Having withdrawn into the town on 24 May and been surrounded, Nicolson's force prepared for an evacuation that had been agreed in principle for the next day, but the French protest in the wake of Boulogne's early abandonment and the prospect of Nicolson's force being able to hold their ground, encouraged Churchill to change his mind. By the time that an 'open-mouthed' Keller had been informed about the change of plan, he was halfway through the demoralizing task of destroying his tanks.

After a rapid change in plans, organization and deployments, the Anglo-French force realigned themselves for the sort of siege warfare that was more redolent of a bygone age. Perhaps this was just as well, since it was at this point that Philip Gribble, the army liaison officer at the headquarters of the British Air Forces in France, could only note that the French were 'helpless in the face of the unorthodox black magic of the German High Command'.[6] Either way, the result was a noisy, destructive struggle which saw the German heavy artillery blast the defenders and occasionally follow up with engineer and infantry assaults. Nicolson refused to surrender, despite his impossible position, and in keeping with Churchill's requirement, replied to the suggestion he do so, 'No, I shall not surrender. Tell the Germans that if they want Calais they will have to fight for it.'[7]

The RAF lent what support it could by attacking targets of opportunity. 2 Group's Order of the Day for 25 May read:

> It must be impressed upon leaders that risks must be taken in this emergency to find the really important targets, then attack them. It must now be accepted that the day has passed when attacks can be launched at definite targets as a result of previous reconnaissance. This is due to the rapidity of movement of enemy forces. In view of the critical situation of the B.E.F. it is essential that all attacks are pressed home with vigour.[8]

While the bombers grappled with the Luftwaffe and the panzer divisions' anti-aircraft units to reach their targets, Royal Navy destroyers were brought into position to lend some fire support. Indeed, Oberstleutnant von Jaworski was so incensed by the rounds falling among the panzers outside Calais that he ordered the driver of his Mk III into a firing position and, after several rounds, landed one that eventually sank the vessel in question. From then on his tank sported a large, childlike image of a boat applied to the turret in white paint to record and publicize the kill. The episode neatly encapsulated the British difficulty in engaging the enemy because the Germans maintained the initiative despite their ill-timed pause in offensive operations against Dunkirk. The Allies were constantly trying to fend off their attackers and found that they rarely had the resources they needed, or where they wanted them. Captain David McCullen, who was working on the staff of 48th Division, confirmed as much in his diary:

> Chaos is usual in war, but we are finding it difficult to do some of the most basic things because of a combination of the enemy artillery, air attack and [the division's] own dispersed and fractured structure. Moving and communicating are terribly difficult and I spend most of my time trying to find out who and what are where.[9]

This might be compared to the testimony of a transport officer with 10th Panzer Division, Hauptmann Jan Hoch, who wrote:

> Having moved to the coast we were well set. Our units were organized and well-supplied but we were frustrated by Calais, which I believed could be screened and left alone. However, I believe that our division was not seen as essential in the push into the British because we had such strength already in place … The defence of Calais was nothing less than heroic. We had great admiration for those defending the old town against our power. Had we seen more of such devotion to duty, our division may not have made it as far as it did, as quickly as it did.[10]

Late on 26 May, Calais finally succumbed to the power of 10th Panzer Division and the German bombers. De Lambertye died that day from a heart attack while touring his positions and the resilience of the defending troops had, like the gallant French commander, been broken. Winston Churchill later wrote of the battle:

> Calais was the crux. Many other causes might have prevented the deliverance of Dunkirk, but it is certain that the three days gained by the defence of Calais enabled the Gravelines waterline to be held and without this, even in spite of Hitler's vacillations and Rundstedt's orders, all would have been cut off and lost.[11]

This overstates the case because, as Hoch reflected, the Germans already enjoyed numerical superiority against the west flank of the Allied pocket, but there is no doubt that Calais revealed an intent and a stoicism that would be reflected elsewhere around the perimeter. Indeed, David McCullen noted in his diary during the battle: 'The flames of Calais are a beacon that invites us to ever greater efforts.'[12]

— ▯ —

Resilience, wherever it could be found and however it could be promoted, was in great demand around the perimeter because the Germans were on the cusp of restarting their armoured offensive. In the early afternoon of 26 May, OKH received notice that, after a visit to the front, von Rundstedt had decided to recommence the offensive by von Kleist and Hoth. That same afternoon, von Brauchitsch met with Hitler to discuss the military situation and the commander-in-chief boldly outlined his belief that von Rundstedt's protracted pause had done considerable damage to the prospects for subsequent operations and the German ability to achieve a strategic victory. Von Brauchitsch returned 'beaming', Halder notes in his diary, having heard at first hand from Hitler that he believed that von Rundstedt had paused for too long and that the Luftwaffe had not achieved what it had said it would achieve. As a consequence, an order was promulgated which stated: 'The Führer has authorized the left wing to be moved within artillery firing range of Dunkirk in order to cut off, from the land side, the continuous flow of transport (evacuations and arrivals).'[13] It was not, therefore, an order without limitations, but it did at least give the panzer commanders the opportunity to move forward again. The relief felt in OKH was palpable, for the situation was still advantageous if operations were now moved on quickly and aggressively.

The potential for the Allies to be overwhelmed within a matter of days was not lost on Churchill, who, having kept a keen eye on Ramsay's preparations, decided that the time was right to evacuate the main body of the BEF. During the morning of Sunday 26 May minister of war Anthony Eden informed Gort of the verdict in a message which said: 'In such conditions only course open to you may be to fight your way back to west where all beaches and ports east of Gravelines will be used for embarkation.'[14] Operation Dynamo, the evacuation of British and Allied troops – twelve

British, twenty-eight French and twenty-two Belgian divisions – was to start without delay.[15] Few now believed that there would be a major French counter-attack that would fundamentally alter the operational picture. Philip Gribble wrote in his diary:

> The confusion is indescribable. The situation must resolve itself in the course of the next few days. Personally I feel that the psychological moment for the attack has been passed. I hope that this apparently unjustified pause will ultimately prove to have been due to the foresight, patience and self-control of great generalship.[16]

He was to be disappointed, for the French were barely coping with the situation and the British were focusing on the need to extract as much of the BEF as possible. John Colville, Churchill's assistant private secretary, returned from a much-needed weekend break to find that the mood had changed in his absence:

> At Downing Street I was distressed to find the situation much blacker than when I left on Friday. It appears a grave deterioration has taken place in the last forty-eight hours: the BEF, unable to force their way southwards, have got to retreat to the coast as best they can and re-embark for England from whatever Channel ports remain open to them. The French seem demoralized and there is now serious fear that they may collapse. The Cabinet are feverishly considering our ability to carry on the war alone in such circumstances.[17]

On 26 May, the Belgian left flank withdrew to the outskirts of Bruges just half a dozen miles from the coast while their right flank in the Ypres-Menin sector had been broken. The British were in an invidious situation on the right flank for they had to hold the shoulders of the Lille salient in order for its formations to escape the closing jaws of the German trap and in doing so shorten their front and prepare a new defensive line behind the Belgians in anticipation of their capitulation. It was an operation that had to be closely co-ordinated with the formations of French First Army for, if the shoulders of the salient collapsed, it would lose its head. In such circumstances, the prospect of a British evacuation order filled the French with a sense of dread. Blanchard did not hear about Churchill's decision until 28 May, but in the meantime the first BEF units withdrew back towards Dunkirk. Although bombing had put the docks out of action, the East Mole, a 1,400-yard-long and five-foot-wide wooden sea wall which protected the harbour, could still be used for embarkation, as could the outer harbour wall. Ramsay's emissaries were further aware that there were sixteen miles of coastline stretching east from Dunkirk that also could be used for evacuation as its gently sloping beaches could be used by shallow-draught craft to transfer troops to vessels waiting in deeper water. The area also boasted a defendable hinterland which incorporated the towns of Nieuport, Furnes and Bergues, which were connected by a canal that was between forty-five and sixty feet wide. Other waterways, a central flooded area just behind the defences and dunes provided a further impediment to any attacker, while small resorts along the coast provided ideal bases for command and control. This perimeter was approximately thirty-five miles long and, while just three miles deep at its eastern end, was more than twice that at its western end around Dunkirk. As Private Alexander Wilkins, an infantryman in the 1st Division's 4th Battalion Green Howards, later said:

> It was gratifying to be told that preparations were being made for us to be evacuated. It did spur us on through some very dark hours, but we all knew that there was plenty of hard fighting to do before we set foot on a boat – the Germans would make sure of that.[18]

— ¤ —

The two German panzer groups south of Gravelines resumed their attack at 0800 hours on 27 May, three days and eight hours after they had been ordered to stop. Having crossed the British-manned canal defences with little difficulty, von Kleist and Hoth both then encountered stout defence as they approached the BEF's strongpoint line. These British divisions protected the eastern flank of a corridor used by I Corps to move towards Dunkirk during the night of 27–28 May and continued to do so during the following night. Meanwhile, on the western flank, the more dispersed British positions began to fall back as they were overwhelmed by superior enemy numbers. At Hazebrouck, for example, which was defended by a battalion of the Oxfordshire and Buckinghamshire Light Infantry, there was an intense battle on 27 May. As the enemy fell on the town intent on removing the defenders as quickly as possible, the battalion's orders were simply to 'Hold at all costs'.[19] A German bombardment that morning was quickly followed by an infantry attack supported by light armour and air support. The under-gunned Ox and Bucks defenders stood their ground in fortified houses using whatever they could to slow the enemy. Medic Les Allan later recalled: 'The Germans were infuriated that they were being held back. They were anxious to push past us. So the bombing was terrific. [The Stuka was] deadly when used against men armed with just rifle and bayonet.'[20]

It was just this sort of fighting that led Halder to note 'stronger resistance than expected' in his diary after reading the morning reports, but he added, 'We must bear in mind that a total of four enemy armies are packed into this pocket and that there is nothing left for them but to fight back as long as there is any ammunition; it must give out eventually.'[21] That afternoon the house-to-house fighting in Hazebrouck continued and British casualties grew at an alarming rate. Les Allan did what he could to help, which meant putting himself in great danger since he was armed with nothing

The Ardennes: two light and under-armed German tanks emerge from the woods. Both the PzKpfw II, in the foreground, and the PzKpfw I following on behind were obsolete.

Sedan, 14 May 1940: the pontoon bridge over the Meuse at Gaulier being used by 1st Panzer Regiment, with a PzKpfw II and III patrolling the west bank.

A French army signals post in an underground shelter. The doctrine of 'Methodical Battle' allowed commanders to rely on the telegraph, field telephones and couriers.

Below left: Sergeant Walther Rubarth, who led a small team of assault engineers at the head of 10th Panzer Division's 86th Rifle Regiment during the afternoon of 13 May 1940. *Below right:* Hermann Balck. Although pictured here later in the war when a general, in 1940 Balck was the outstanding commander of 1st Panzer Division's 1st Rifle Regiment.

15 May 1940: German tanks advance across featureless Belgian terrain before Gembloux.

Below left: Heinz Guderian in his command and communications halftrack (Sd.Kfz 251/3), equipped with an Enigma machine. *Below right:* Rommel (in the foreground) pictured with his corps commander, General Hermann Hoth, on 7 June 1940 at Eplessier, south-west of Amiens.

French tank crews run to their Renault D2 (model 1935) tanks. It is likely that this unit is part of de Gaulle's 4th DCR.

Below left: Rommel and a group of officers from 7th Panzer Division study their maps at an 'Orders Group' during *Fall Rot. Below right:* A poignant moment as Heinz Guderian receives the charred remains of a captured French Army standard during the latter stages of the Battle for France.

1 June 1940: British troops march through Dunkirk during a German bombardment.

St. Valéry, 12 June 1940: having just been taken prisoner along with 46,000 Allied troops, Major General Victor Fortune, the commander of 51st (Highland) Division, glowers at a preening Rommel.

Surrendered Belgian troops being goaded by Wehrmacht troops on horseback.

Below left: French refugees heading south in June 1940. Although accompanied by their dog and some blankets piled on top of the bicycle, the family would appear to have few other provisions for their journey. *Below right:* In the wake of the fighting in the Maginot Line, two Schutzpolizisten (uniformed police) visit a damaged bunker.

An unescorted low-level attack by an RAF Fairey Battle on a German transport column.

14 June 1940: German infantry march through Paris near the Arc de Triomphe. Civilians watched, some in tears, as the occupiers began to take control of the 'City of Lights'.

German infantry and armour pushing deeper into the heart of France during June 1940.

After the campaign had concluded, Marshal Philippe Pétain greets Hitler, watched by Hitler's interpreter, Paul Schmidt, and Foreign Minister Joachim von Ribbentrop.

more than a Red Cross-emblazoned armband and a haversack, but he had to make some difficult choices with his dwindling medical supplies. He came across one man in the entrance to a cellar whom he knew to be a Private Johnson and noticed that the young man had suffered 'awful head wounds. His face was all torn open. There was blood everywhere. His jaw and skull were bashed in. I just kicked him out of the way. You soon realize you have to help those who can be saved, not those who are virtually dead.'[22] (As it transpired, Johnson survived both his injuries and the war, and he and Les Allan later met at a reunion.)

Officers also put themselves in harm's way as they tried to visit positions for vital information about enemy progress and their own defences, but also to encourage their men. One company commander, Major Elliott Viney, not wishing for two boxes of his precious cigars to fall into enemy hands, handed out their contents to everybody he met on one of his regular rounds. Small comforts were much appreciated as the day wore on and it became clear that reinforcements were very unlikely to appear while ammunition stocks diminished and casualties continued to mount. One of those mortally wounded by a German shell was the battalion's thirty-three-year-old commanding officer, Major Brian Heyworth, which left Viney to organize the unit's diminishing defences. By the early evening the situation for the British in Hazebrouck was critical and with the Germans pressing towards it, Viney ordered the evacuation of the blazing battalion headquarters, which left around 100 men with two Bren guns and very little ammunition trapped in its large walled garden. Although a portion of the battalion managed to evacuate the town and head for Dunkirk – some twelve officers and 200 men eventually making it back to England – Viney and his men, after a superlative defensive effort, had no option other than to surrender.

Without room for manoeuvre, the Germans resorted to a grinding attritional method rather than concentrating their forces to create a local breakthrough at Gravelines. Indeed, this

First World War approach was reflected in Hitler's order to move within 'artillery firing range of Dunkirk', which was achieved that day by 1st Panzer Division. The fighting on the west flank of the pocket was particularly intense and bloody during the first two days of the renewed offensive as the Allied divisions recognized that, if they broke, the pocket would simply collapse. Between Bergues and Cassel, for example, 48th Division resisted bravely against SS Leibstandarte Adolf Hitler. The fighting at Wormhoudt was particularly vicious, but eventually a group from 4th Battalion Cheshire Regiment, 2nd Battalion Royal Warwickshire Regiment, and a group of gunners were overwhelmed and surrendered. The SS rounded up their prisoners, stripped them of their possessions – including their identification papers – and ordered them to a nearby barn. Those wounded that could not walk were shot on the spot. Around some 100 apprehensive British soldiers were eventually crammed inside the small, airless wooden building but when Captain James Lynn-Allen, the senior officer present, protested, he was told: 'Where you are going there will be a lot more room.'[23] Understanding their fate, the condemned were taking their first drags on what they expected to be their last cigarettes when hand grenades were thrown into the barn followed by sub-machine gun and rifle fire. Lynn-Allen was unhurt, but standing immediately behind him, nineteen-year-old Private Bert Evans had suffered a catastrophic injury to his right shoulder. The barn doors were then wrenched open and the forlorn survivors pulled out and executed. Rather than waiting for his turn, Lynn-Allen grabbed Evans and ran towards an open field, but only managed to reach the edge of a pond before Evans stumbled. Lynn-Allen stopped to help him, but as he did so a pursuer caught up with the pair and opened fire: Lynn-Allen was shot at point-blank range in the head and Evans in the neck. Meanwhile, the remaining prisoners were ordered out of the barn in groups of five and summarily shot by the SS troops waiting for them in the yard. Anti-tank gunner Lance-Bombardier Brian Fahey – who had already been shot in the leg during the fighting earlier in the day – also tried to escape. Dragging his wounded leg, Fahey did not get far before being shot in the back. As the young soldier lay unconscious, his lungs hissing and bubbling, the SS troops turned their attention to finishing off their captives by opening fire on them for a final time while they stood in the barn. They only left when there was no sign of movement in the mound of blood-drenched khaki which stood testament to their barbarity.*[24]

South of Wormhoudt, Major General Noel Irwin's 2nd Division continued to hold the west shoulder of the Lille salient on a fifteen-mile front either side of Béthune against several divisions which included SS Totenkopf and 7th Panzer Division. Rommel was determined to break through and trap several French divisions before they could withdraw, but standing in his way was 1st Battalion Queen's Own Cameron Highlanders in the Le Bassée sector. The unit held out for two days before being overrun, but not before one company had been reduced to just six men. Meanwhile, SS Totenkopf, having been thwarted at the village of Le Paradis by the Royal Norfolks, took revenge against a particularly stubborn company after it had surrendered. Signaller Bert Polley, already wounded when beaten by his guards, was forced to his feet and was marched with the other prisoners to a farm. Here, two machine guns opened fire on the British group and Polley, nicked by a bullet, acted dead. The SS troopers used pistols and bayonets to kill the wounded but they missed Polley and left.

Rumours of such atrocities as this and that at Wormhoudt against unarmed men had already washed across the Allied forces

---

* Just six men survived the Wormhoudt massacre, including Brian Fahey and Bert Evans. Fahey remained in the yard, where he was eventually found by a regular Wehrmacht unit. He recovered from his wounds and was sent to a PoW camp, where he worked on his musical skills. After the war, he worked as an arranger and composer for big bands, for the BBC and in film and theatre. Evans managed to crawl from the pond and across a field, where he lay for several hours. He was captured by a German ambulance unit. His arm was eventually amputated and he spent the rest of the war in a German PoW camp.

and while they undoubtedly had a negative effect on the fighting spirit of some, far more became determined to fight to the death. As 2nd Battalion Wiltshire Regiment passed through a nameless Belgian village during the evening of 28 May, Andrew Hardcastle later recalled, a 'loud-mouthed mechanic' informed them that the Germans were shooting prisoners and the wounded. 'I was furious,' Hardcastle says, 'and at that moment decided that I would not surrender. We all agreed. We would fight to the final man and save the last bullet for ourselves.'[25] In a similar vein later that same night, David McCullen wrote in his diary: 'Tales reach us of prisoners being badly handled by the enemy. Most agree that this will fortify our resolve to fight to the last round.'[26]

On 28 May, the shoulders of the salient began to fall in, having held the Germans just long enough for 1st, 3rd and 4th Divisions to withdraw. It was an organized and carefully co-ordinated process in which divisions were released at just the right time to either head for Dunkirk or establish a new defensive position in the rear. That evening, for example, 5th Division, which was holding the eastern shoulder, disengaged from the enemy and then, using the protection offered by 3rd and 4th Divisions between Ypres and Poperinghe, withdrew behind them. This 'leap-frogging' under the cover of darkness was extremely difficult to control but was successful enough to allow the British formations to fall back into the emerging perimeter around Dunkirk in good order. The withdrawal was assisted by some excellent work by rearguard units of French First Army deep in the diminishing bulge in the Allied line, the first bad weather of the campaign, which thwarted the Luftwaffe, and the lacklustre performance of some tired German formations which, unlike their Allied counterparts, were not 'fighting for their lives'.

Even so, there was no opportunity for the Allied divisions to lower their guard and General John Dill, the new Chief of the Imperial General Staff who had until April been a corps commander in France and subsequently become Ironside's deputy, brought all his knowledge and experience of the BEF to ensure that the force was extracted as quickly as the situation would allow. Reflecting on the events, John Colville wrote:

> Fortunately Ironside has gone and Dill, who inspires great confidence, has taken his place; but I do not envy him, confronted as he is with the problem of salvaging the wreckage of the BEF. I still feel convinced that we shall win, even if the French collapse; but we have reached all but the last ditch and a timely miracle would be acceptable.[27]

The replacement of Ironside as CIGS was not a surprise but, as Colville notes, took place at a very difficult time. Even as Dill was taking up the job on the evening of 27 May, the Belgian army's will was finally shattered and King Leopold, observing his troops' appalling situation, decided to capitulate. This was hardly a surprise either, and the British and French had made contingency plans for just such a decision, even though Churchill tried to dissuade Leopold by writing him a note stating that the Belgian surrender would have 'disastrous consequences to the Allies and to Belgium'.[28] Once again, Churchill was overstating the case, but the British were contemptuous of the Belgian decision as well as being, quite fairly considering their collapse, sneeringly dismissive of the nation's military performance since 10 May. Indeed, when Gort's Chief of Staff, Henry Pownall, was asked whether the Belgian troops in France might be evacuated from Dunkirk, the general replied: 'We don't care a bugger what happens to the Belgians.'[29] Nevertheless, when Leopold surrendered to the Germans on 28 May, the British were already in position behind them to protect the eastern half of the Dunkirk perimeter which was on Belgian soil.

In the meantime, Rommel managed to push through the BEF's 2nd Division holding the western shoulder of the Lille salient in a critical advance which carved out yet another opportunity for the

Germans. With the withdrawal of 4th, 3rd and 1st Divisions behind 5th Division at Wytschaete on the eastern shoulder producing a gap into which the two German infantry divisions could penetrate, the Wehrmacht's pincers were now in a position to pinch out the Allied bulge. Rommel had recognized the importance of a swift, short push into the enemy rear area and, still leading from the front in order to ensure that the enemy could not concentrate against him, was again nearly killed, this time by 150mm fire from his own guns. He was in the village of Lommel just to the west of Lille with the commander of the Reconnaissance Battalion, Major Erdmann, when the bombardment began. Both men ran back to the signals vehicle to send an urgent message to get the artillery to stop firing. Rommel later wrote of the incident:

> Erdmann [was] running a few yards in front, when a heavy shell landed close by the house door near which the vehicle was standing. When the smoke cleared, Major Erdmann … lay face to the ground, dead, with the back of his head shattered. He was bleeding from the head and from an enormous wound in his back. His left hand was still grasping his leather gloves. I had escaped unscathed, though the same shell had wounded several other officers and men.[30]

A shaken Rommel subsequently ensured that the Lille pocket was sealed and it was slowly reduced, despite continued attempts by French units to fight their way out of their incarceration. On 29 May, Halder wrote:

> The enemy pocket has again shrunk. It will indeed be interesting to see how much of the enemy did get caught in this pocket, 45 km [28 miles] in length and 30 km [18 miles] in width. Even now, with Lille, Roubaix, Tourcoing in our hands, the enemy is still fighting desperately against our troops pressing on his flanks.[31]

As it was, the remnants of five First Army divisions were trapped in the pocket and seven generals, 350 officers, 34,600 enlisted men, 300 guns and 100 armoured fighting vehicles were eventually captured when the French surrendered at midnight on 31 May-1 June.[32] Although their attempts to break out had been doomed to failure, they were of benefit to the Allied defences at the coast because they preoccupied seven German divisions for four vital days as the Dunkirk perimeter was completed. Von Brauchitsch was livid at the delay and told Halder that he believed not only that the Lille salient could have been eliminated far earlier had the panzer Halt Order not been in place but also that it could have been sealed at the coast, thereby ensnaring the entire Allied force.[33]

The final formation of the defensive line around Dunkirk and its beaches saw, at least from the operational perspective, the BEF and the French working in tandem as if blind to nationality. Although in the aftermath there was a plethora of accusations of selfishness as formations tumbled back towards a modicum of safety and the prospect of being taken off by boat, on the ground there was evidence of some solid teamwork. David Blundell, a Guardsman fighting near Furnes, has recalled that his company and a similarly sized French unit worked as one as they entered the perimeter. 'Our Major had a little Franglais,' Blundell recalled, 'but the officer with the French troops had not one word of English, but they both knew their jobs and with hand signals, pointing and diagrams on scraps of paper led us to our destination.'[34] The common bond felt by soldiers of different units, different arms and different nations drove them instinctively – and often unquestioningly – to assist others. Lance Corporal Tom Reed of 5th Battalion Green Howards recalls slumping down exhausted behind a wall in a small village while German machine-gun rounds crashed into the masonry above his head:

I was quite alone in my own world and had become inadvertently detached from my unit. I wondered whether I could go on but then, out of the shadows, a hand offered me a canteen of water. It was a sergeant from the East Yorks with half a dozen other men. He didn't smile, he didn't talk, but his small kindness probably saved my life. I joined that small band of men and fought with them all the way back to the beaches.[35]

The Allies fought on. Gefreiter Hans Liebler, an infantryman in 253rd Infantry Division, noted 'a distinct increase in resistance from 30 May onwards'. While he recognized that increasing numbers of Allied troops were being pushed into an ever-decreasing pocket, he also witnessed 'units and individuals fighting harder and longer than they had a few days before. This was frustrating for us because at the same time we were becoming very tired. I can only imagine that the enemy's survival instinct became extremely strong and so gave them an edge during this period.'[36] Indeed, Halder's diary contains a similar observation from an operational perspective:

> Disintegration of the bottled-up enemy forces is continuing. Some of the British units in there are still fighting stubbornly and with determination; others are streaming back to the coast and trying to get across the sea in anything that floats. *La Débâcle.*[37]

By 30 May, the Dunkirk perimeter had been formed. French regiments were clustered around the western end of the perimeter holding approximately one third of the line up to the town of Bergues while British divisions held the remainder from Bergues, through Furnes to Nieuport. 15/19 Hussars arrived in the perimeter 'weary and footsore' after a final twenty-five-mile movement, with Lieutenant Guy Courage writing:

This march was a most severe test, coming as it did after three weeks of fighting in the most exhausting and disheartening conditions of retreat. The roads were congested with traffic of all sorts and there was continual bombing … [I]t was a harrowing business, mile after mile in the dust and heat, with enemy planes circling overhead waiting to drop their bombs on any suitable target.[38]

Some of the British divisions arrived intact but others had been smashed beyond recognition: 3rd Division, for example, was still 13,000-strong, while 5th Division amounted to a mere 1,200 men and 2nd Division had ceased to exist.[39] It is estimated that some 300,000 Allied troops – although not all of them were fighting men – were crammed into the Dunkirk pocket. Exhausted, disorganized, stretched and lacking heavy weaponry, the defenders had to rely on their last reserves of energy and their advantageous defensive positions. They faced eight German divisions that included 9th Panzer and 20th Motorized Divisions, which were attacking the western defences barely three miles from Dunkirk. Well organized, with offensive momentum and with extremely strong reserves, the Germans had every reason to feel confident that the last flickering light of Allied hope could be extinguished quickly. Outside the perimeter, the roads were lined for miles with abandoned and disabled vehicles and heavy equipment which marked the end of the BEF's retreat.

By the time that the Dunkirk perimeter was fully formed, evacuations were entering their fourth day. Alan Brooke had written in his diary on 26 May that the withdrawal was 'going to be a very hazardous enterprise and we shall be lucky if we save 25 per cent of the BEF!'[40] but his prediction was eventually proved to be a very considerable underestimation. By 30 May, 77,000 troops had been lifted from the harbour and a further 48,000 from the beaches, and with every hour, embarkation techniques were further refined, to the point where 600 men were habitually loaded onto a destroyer in just twenty minutes. Although the Germans' attacks were undoubtedly weakened by their preparations for operations after the Dunkirk perimeter had been reduced, a combination of excellent defensive work, calm seas and first-class discipline and organization allowed for more men to be lifted from Dunkirk and its beaches than most thought possible. Eschewing rest until the job was done, Captain William Tennant, twelve officers and 160 men supervised the embarkation while Rear Admiral Wake-Walker commanded the shipping off the coast of Dunkirk. A collection of vessels were assembled for the task including a single cruiser, fifty-six destroyers and torpedo boats, minesweepers, coastal launches, yachts, fishing boats, barges, passenger ferries and a miscellany of other craft. In the end, the evacuation fleet, which included boats from the Netherlands, Belgium and France, grew to 861 vessels.[41] Small headquarters along the coast liaised with the fighting formations to ensure that units were released at the appropriate time and those troops then made their way to join the queues waiting patiently on the beaches or at the port for their turn to embark under the direction of Royal Navy teams. These men generally showed excellent discipline as they waited for the order to move forward and scramble aboard any craft that would take them away.

To Captain David Barlone, who led a column of French North Africans to the water's edge along roads 'strewn with dead and hundreds of wounded', the beaches were 'An impression of awful and irretrievable disaster ...'[42] Meanwhile, Guy Courage later wrote of the scene that greeted 15/19 Hussars:

> So to the beaches we came: it was an astounding spectacle, the like of which had not been seen before. Away to the left was Dunkirk itself, shrouded in a thick, black pall of smoke from its burning oil tanks and with the light of many fires kindled by the bombing. On the beaches were many thousands of troops waiting patiently to embark. Out to sea lay destroyers

and some little ships. Overhead the sky was filled with German bombers, diving low over Dunkirk and the beaches, wave after wave of Stukas, diving, dropping their bombs with a scream among the densely packed mass of soldiers, and circling away again, only to be replaced by more.*[43]

The Luftwaffe certainly remained active throughout the battle, even though Hitler and his commanders had given up hope of the ground forces being required to merely 'mop up'. Helmuth Mahlke had been flying missions against the port for one or two days before he wrote on 29 May:

Today, it seemed as if everybody who was anybody in the Luftwaffe was heading for Dunkirk. The airspace around us was crowded with German aircraft ... The target area [Dunkirk harbour] was already clearly visible in the far distance, marked by large fires and clouds of black smoke ... Shortly before 2000 hours we were over the target. Standing on our wings, we dived almost vertically into the attack. We saw our bombs explode close to the lock gates ... As we flew back to base I couldn't get the horrific spectacle that was Dunkirk out of my mind. An absolute inferno! Those poor beggars down there desperately fighting for survival. Just as well that at our height we were spared the gory details.[44]

Even so, the Luftwaffe's impact on the Dunkirk pocket was not as great as it might have been. There were many reasons for this, not least the fact that forward airfields in Belgium and France were still in the process of being constructed, which meant that aircraft enjoyed little time over their targets as they were at the limits of their effective range. It also proved difficult to concentrate

---

* The regiment was evacuated on 30 May, by which time, out of 455 officers and men, over 36 per cent had become casualties – and 80 per cent of the officers. (See Courage, p. 43.)

bombers and their escorts over the coast at a time when they were also needed elsewhere to confront the French in preparation for the next phase of German operations across the Somme and the Aisne to the south-west. Those that did manage to spend any time over Dunkirk and its beaches, however, were also often hampered in their targeting by low cloud and the black smoke from those burning oil storage tanks and tyres that veiled the embarkation.

In addition, the Luftwaffe was increasingly troubled by RAF fighters over Dunkirk as the battlefield was now relatively close to Air Chief Marshal Sir Keith Park's 11 Group airfields in southern England. In sanctioning the release of these precious assets from Air Chief Marshal Hugh Dowding's Fighter Command, which had been developed for home defence, Churchill was looking to the longer-term security of the British Isles and its need for manpower, rather than the short-term preservation of the valuable aircraft at all costs. To the French High Command, however, the withholding of British fighter squadrons until they appeared over Dunkirk to provide air cover for the evacuation smacked of betrayal. Weygand, who had shown little trust in the British since taking command from Gamelin, remarked: 'Apart from his distinguished qualities, the Englishman is motivated by instinctive selfishness.' For his part, Gort felt that the BEF had been so affected by French military incompetence that the British were merely doing what they could to extract themselves from 'a mess that was not of their own making'.[45] Even so, from the time of the Halt Order onwards, the Germans had noted a change in the skies above them, with the War Diary of von Kluge's Fourth Army recording:

> For two days, the enemy enjoys air superiority over the Group von Kleist and partially above Group Hoth. This is something completely new to us in this campaign and the reason is that the base of the English Air Force is in England and therefore now quite close, while our units on the whole are still based on German airfields.[46]

This new reality had been sustained over Dunkirk and, despite the commonly heard complaint from BEF troops that the RAF kept a very low profile during the withdrawal and evacuation, British aircraft played a significant part in the protection of the ground and naval forces. By flying intensively, RAF fighter squadrons were able to undertake 2,739 sorties during the evacuation,[47] with German pilots testifying that these Spitfire and Hurricane pilots were much better than those they had faced up to that point. There were, though, many who flew into action for the very first time during those heady days of late May and there was precious little time to learn vital lessons. Flying Sergeant Rab Riley piloted a Hurricane and watched two young officers make basic mistakes on their first sorties, for which they paid with their lives. Other 'green sticks', however, managed to survive and quickly gained knowledge and confidence. Riley later testified:

> It was never easy to leave the safety of an airfield, form a Vic – usually of three aircraft – and be in action all within thirty minutes. The speed at which one left safety and was hurtled into mortal danger was so quick that it took a pilot a little time to 'acclimatize' to his new condition, to ensure that his mind and body were ready for battle. A sluggish response or a loss of concentration could very easily lead to death. Air combat is a lonely business, but the more you do it, the better you get.[48]

The tenacity of the RAF pilots, as well as their flying ability, soon won the respect of their adversaries, but there were a variety of responses to the stress of battle. Squadron Leader J. E. McComb, who at the time was flying a Spitfire of 611 Squadron, later recalled:

> I saw above me a Spitfire [flown by Flight Sergeant Sadler] … dive into five circling Bf 110s [which were twin-engined and lacking in manoeuvrability] and then get trapped in the

circle. They could out-dive him but he could just turn inside them so that their shells and bullets went under his tail. Each time they fired and missed, Sadler leaned out of his cockpit and made a vulgar gesture with his two fingers.[49]

Stuka pilot Helmuth Mahlke, however, had a rather more genteel encounter with the RAF. He came wingtip to wingtip with a Spitfire, and its pilot 'looked across at us and raised his hand to his flying helmet in salute! Dumbfounded, I automatically returned the compliment. Then he banked away in a graceful arc and was quickly lost to sight … [T]here *was* such a thing as the brotherhood of the air … That unknown British pilot was a remarkable man.'[50] If there was indeed a 'brotherhood of the air', it was one built of the common experience of hard fighting – the Germans lost 132 aircraft over the coast.

In the end, although at certain times and in certain places German air power had significance at Dunkirk, just as the Luftwaffe had not been able to stop the withdrawal into the perimeter, it was unable to stop the evacuation. That defensive perimeter held firm, even as it shrank whenever units left the line for the port or the beaches, and Operation Dynamo continued – against all expectation – into the first days of June. The fighting was often fierce, with clashes in the shallow eastern sector of the perimeter having particular importance. Here German 256th Infantry Division had an opportunity to break through to the beaches and then roll the British line up towards Dunkirk. The defence offered by Montgomery's 3rd Division, however, was particularly intense and successful. Anchored at the small fortified town of Furnes, two battalions of Grenadier Guards rebuffed numerous assaults.

Guardsman Ernie Smith found himself alone overlooking the canal after the rest of his section had been blasted out of their position by German artillery. 'I shouted to them,' recalls Smith, 'but my ears were ringing so loudly from the explosions that I could not hear my own voice, let alone a response.'[51] Smith continued to fire on the approaching enemy until midnight on 31 May–1 June when his ammunition ran out and he went in search of his colleagues. Smith found two dead and three others wounded and was helping them to a first-aid point when a withdrawal was ordered. The non-walking wounded were to be left behind.

Smith's fellow Guardsman Douglas Rothery was part of the same action and later wrote:

> At a pre-arranged time, which was at about 2 or 3am [on 1 June], we were told that we were to tie blankets around our boots and creep away from our positions so as not to alert the enemy ... We were clambering over debris in pitch darkness, getting tangled up in telegraph wires, cursing as we tried to extricate ourselves, glass was being shattered and tin cans clattered as we fell over them and I would have thought that we could have been heard in Berlin ... The enemy shelling was getting worse, screaming in from all directions as we struggled on for about [three miles], past burning vehicles of all types including ambulances, trapped victims in demolished buildings were calling for help, some whimpering in the darkened rubble, whilst other wounded could be seen by the light of the burning vehicles crawling in the direction of the sea ... Eventually we arrived at the sand dunes of La Panne, where we (wait for it), were formed up and marched to attention down to the water's edge, Halted, Turned to the front, Ordered arms, Stood at ease, Stand easy. We were then informed it was every man for himself ...[52]

By this time, the evacuation was centred on the port at Dunkirk as the perimeter shrank further and an eleven-mile long inner line was formed to defend it. As a consequence, the Grenadiers were ushered along the beach towards the town but, pursued by Stukas and noting that their destination was also being bombed, a forty-man group, including Rothery, decided on a different course of action. Seeing that vessels were waiting offshore to receive evacuees, the men clambered aboard a large wooden boat they found in the dunes and paddled out to sea using their tin hats. After they had scrambled up the rope ladders of one of the ships and landed on the deck, Rothery recalls, a crew member greeted them. 'Welcome aboard *Little Audrey*,' he said, 'the last of the Minesweeper Flotilla.'*[53]

The inner perimeter was now occupied by units from the French 68th and 12th Infantry Divisions during the afternoon of 2 June and they defended the last evacuations selflessly and with great stoicism. That night, the final British troops embarked at Dunkirk and General Harold Alexander, the commander of 1st Division who had also been given responsibility for I Corps while he was still in France, searched the port and beaches with a megaphone, calling out into the darkness: 'Is anyone there? Is anyone there?'[54] Soon after, with Alexander safely on a waiting destroyer, Captain William Tennant signalled Ramsay a message that few thought conceivable ten days before: 'BEF EVACUATED'.[55]

The next morning, as the Germans sensed that Dunkirk would be in their hands by the end of the day, the French launched an unexpected counter-attack which temporarily rocked 254th Division. During the course of the day, the remnants of the French 68th Division were destroyed, but resistance throughout 3 June created the time and space required for one final embarkation of French troops that night. Two hundred and seventy-two vessels had been lost during Operation Dynamo, and the last ship departed from the East Mole on the morning of 4 June. It carried the final contingent of some 338,226 Allied troops to be evacuated from the Channel ports and Dunkirk beaches.[56] A few hours later, the Germans captured the port and took the surrender of the remaining 40,000 French troops who had formed the rearguard

---

* *Little Audrey* was a reference to an American cartoon character who laughed in the face of great adversity and catastrophe.

and had sacrificed themselves for the majority. Amidst the disaster that had befallen the Allies since 10 May, Dunkirk was a remarkable achievement, one appropriately described by Winston Churchill in a speech to the House of Commons on 4 June as a 'miracle of deliverance achieved by valour, by perseverance, by perfect discipline, by faultless service, by resource, by skill, by unconquerable fidelity ... '.[57]

The taking of Dunkirk and the capitulation of the remaining French forces there marked the end of *Fall Gelb*. Hitler was elated, calling the offensive 'the greatest battle in world history'[58] in his Order of the Day for 5 June, and directed that bells be rung across the Reich for three days in celebration. In just twenty-six days Germany had defeated the Netherlands and Belgium, seen off the BEF and destroyed thirty French divisions, including the most mobile and well-trained part of their army's order of battle. Yet the removal of formations from the battlefield, no matter how important, was just the most visible impact of the German offensive. The damage done to the Allied nations psychologically was immense, and while it may not have created a political collapse in Paris and London, it had led to the replacement of the head of the British army and, more significantly, a change in the French Supreme Commander and the sacking of dozens of field commanders. The Allies had been thoroughly humiliated and events had shamed those Frenchmen charged with the defence of their nation.

Even so, Hitler's 24 May direction 'to prevent the escape of English forces across the Channel'[59] had clearly miscarried in the wake of an unnecessary Halt Order that was itself the product of a power struggle – and breakdown in relations – in the upper echelons of the German command. Moreover, France was not defeated, and even though it had lost the vital north-eastern portion of its territory and suffered a catastrophic shock, it had not collapsed and was preparing to do its utmost to ensure that German attempts to attack into the main body of France were formidably resisted. It was a challenge to the invaders, therefore, to attack the rapidly forming Weygand Line running from the coast along the Somme and the Aisne before it reached optimum strength. This required the Battle of Dunkirk to be fought even as OKH's focus and vital fighting resources were being transferred to a new phase of operations. It was a process that was so demanding that von Rundstedt protested, 'You bring *one* operation *to a conclusion* before you can think of *the next one!*'[60] It was hardly an ideal situation, but Halder recognized that if a strategic victory was to be attained quickly, much depended on OKH's ability to produce a viable new plan and get what was needed where it was needed in both robust order and good time for that plan to be carried out. Although there was evidence for great optimism, Halder reminded the over-confident that even a severely weakened enemy could conceal a sting in his tail.

CHAPTER 11

5–8 June – *Fall Rot* and Resilience

O N 3 JUNE 1940, Paris experienced an event that it had feared for the past twenty years – a German bombing raid. The senses of the city's inhabitants had become heightened to the sound of aircraft engines and air-raid sirens during the previous autumn as they grappled with what it meant to be at war, but procedures were soon forgotten as the Luftwaffe kept its distance during the winter. The French authorities used every available means to remind the population how dangerous it was to become complacent in the face of the threat, but it was not until 10 May that Parisians really took notice. Since then, the capital's population had had their nerves tested by numerous false air-raid alarms which had led to some leaving the city for the safety offered by the country's more southern provinces. More had left when the enemy crossed the Meuse, and more still during the Dunkirk evacuation.

All the same, the period was marked by a lack of alarm and a confidence which was fortified by the old slogans: 'We shall win because we are the strongest', 'Remember the Marne' and 'From Verdun to victory!' Reynaud also took to the airwaves to reassure the nation, proclaiming, 'France has been invaded a hundred times and never beaten ... our belief in victory is intact'[1] – even though, as the British government well knew, this public confidence masked deep private concerns about the unfolding situation. By early June, a growing number of people in Paris began to share those concerns as an influx of refugees continued to arrive from the Netherlands, Belgium, Luxembourg and the borders. The air raid, though, was to make doubters of the majority.

With the next stage in the ground offensive looming and wishing to cause as much chaos as possible in the French capital, Göring's aircraft flew a terrorizing mission. Although their targets had been selected for their value to the military and included railway stations, warehouses, factories, bridges and communications centres, the German aircraft lacked any precision-bombing capability and their accuracy was further hampered by the capital's anti-aircraft guns, which would have forced them to fly at a greater altitude. As it was, the damage, although random, was considerable. Alexander Werth's journalistic instinct was triggered by the raid and he immediately took a taxi to become one of the first witnesses to the destruction done by German bombs near the Mirabeau Bridge over the Seine, where he found the Citroën factory ablaze and the Avenue de Versailles covered in broken glass. Over 1,000 bombs were dropped on Paris that day, killing 254 and injuring a further 652,[2] and coming as it did just as the Allied military disaster culminating at Dunkirk became clear, the raid unleashed a wave of panic through Paris.

Between the French interior and the burgeoning German forces, a dam of troops had been hastily cobbled together during the interlude offered by the Halt Order and the time it took to erode the Dunkirk pocket. The Weygand Line stretched 225 miles from the mouth of the Somme to the north end of the Maginot Line and sought to hold back the Germans in a positional battle that had previously been denied them as a consequence of Panzer Group Kleist's *Sichelschnitt* or scythe cut. The great problem for the French was not just the quantity and quality of resources available to them but, with the memory of their recent Plan D misdeployment so fresh, where to place them for the best effect. As Halder noted, while the French 'cannot but realize that we have considerable forces available for new operations ... he will not have a clear picture of our new offensive plans'.[3] The French High Command was confronted by three likely courses of German action: an attack on Paris, most likely through an encirclement, a push south behind the Maginot Line towards the Swiss border, or a combination of the two. Weygand remained pessimistic about the army's ability to defend for long against any of the options. Having taken over a situation that was already desperate, he quickly found that his ability to influence events in a positive manner was severely limited as France had long since relinquished the initiative. His Weygand Line was the physical manifestation of his need to react to the enemy, and the best that he could hope for was that the Germans would so dilute their attack as to provide the opportunity for a protracted attritional struggle. In such circumstances, there was the possibility, albeit faint, that France would be able to regain some of the strength that it had lost in the first phase of fighting, and that it might be further enhanced by British and, ideally, an American commitment to the Allied cause.

Weygand and senior French generals also drew a crumb of comfort from the fighting performance shown by various Allied formations at the beginning of the offensive, when the enemy had been forced to attack their prepared positions frontally. Thus, it was anticipated that the divisions of the Weygand Line might be able to hold out against an over-stretched enemy if he attacked, as expected, without delay. Indeed, even as the French defensive line began to take coherent form during the last week of May, senior officers encouraged their subordinates to take every opportunity to ensure that their charges understood their own, individual importance to the future of France. Gone were the days when a combination of the Maginot Line and the defence of Belgium was regarded as a guarantee of the nation's security, for now this rested on the fighting effectiveness, tenacity and courage of the divisions strung out from the Meuse to the Channel coast.

Artillery officer Lieutenant Michel Sigaut arrived at Bray on the Somme just as news arrived that Calais had fallen to the enemy, but was encouraged not to speak in negative terms about the military situation. On the evening of 1 June, Sigaut and around thirty fellow officers were ordered to attend a briefing held in a dark barn, where they were addressed by their regimental commander. He later recalled:

> We were told to ensure that our men understood the importance of the sector, to remind them of their duty and to emphasize how much everybody relied on each other. All along the front the line divisions were putting pressure on officers to encourage their men to stand and fight ... I was sent on a liaison task to another division and walked in on a regimental briefing to troops that was identical in tone to one that I had given just hours before: 'We can hold the Germans and it will lead to victory. Remember your history, remember your loved ones, do your duty. *Vive La France!*'[4]

The impact of motivational speeches on the troops is difficult to assess, but despite their forlorn position there is no evidence of the divisions in the Weygand Line suffering from a lack of morale and motivation during the first days of June. In fact, morale was resilient during this period: despite the undeniably poor strategic situation, the basic needs of the troops were met, assisted by shorter lines of communication and supply, and the majority of the formations along the Somme and Aisne had yet to encounter the Germans in battle.

A total of just sixty French and the equivalent of five other divisions from Poland, Czechoslovakia and Britain were available to Weygand, including a few – such as the incomplete and partially ravaged 1st British Armoured Division – that had been moved into the defensive line at the end of May during the formation of the Dunkirk perimeter. They included nine newly generated divisions and nineteen others that were formed from Maginot Line garrison fortress units which had been drawn north as the result of one of Gamelin's last acts as Supreme Commander. Although few, if any, could be said to have a first-class fighting capability, these formations went some way towards replacing those lost since 10 May and were bolstered by a further 30,000 men that had returned to France after their evacuation from Dunkirk.[5] Another three infantry divisions, two British and one Canadian, were due to be entered into battle through Cherbourg and St. Malo later in the month. The continued British involvement was partly a reaction to the French dismay at the recent evacuations, but was also regarded by Churchill as the vanguard of a new force that would be sent across the Channel if there was any healthy prospect of long-term French resistance against Germany. London realized, nonetheless, that the likelihood of any extended fighting depended on the ability of Weygand's defences to withstand the next enemy onslaught.

Although it is impossible to say what might have happened had *Fall Gelb* incorporated von Manstein's drive south behind the Maginot Line to stop the development of a Weygand Line, the Germans would have to face the consequences of not adopting this line of attack in their new offensive. Nevertheless, they had managed to take crossing points over the Somme at Péronne, Amiens, Picquigny and Abbeville during their advance to the coast which provided useful stepping stones for the offensive on the right. For their part, the French could only assume that these bridgeheads would be used for the German main effort, which would be followed by an attempt to encircle Paris with a strong punch from their right wing in the manner of von Schlieffen, and as a result they expended considerable effort in the last days of

May to eliminate the enemy's lodgements over the Somme. Their failure to do so was a considerable setback for the defenders, who used a combination of bombers, tanks and infantry to dislodge the Germans, but ran into opposition which reflected the importance that the enemy attached to the sites. Meanwhile, Weygand's formations continued to make their preparations. General Antoine-Marie-Benoît Besson's Third Army Group protected the Somme sector with its Tenth and Seventh Armies while Fourth Army Group, consisting of Second, Fourth and Sixth Armies and commanded by the recently promoted General Huntziger, was in position along the Aisne. The twenty divisions in these two army groups were spread more thinly: each held a frontage of around ten miles, double the figure on 10 May. They also had to take greater account of the Germans' 'new' methods.

The defences were developed in line with an order from Weygand promulgated on 24 May and the divisions worked frenetically to prepare aggressive, deep and forbidding defensive positions to receive the next German onslaught; every available pair of hands toiled in the task, often during German artillery bombardments and air attacks. A large number of lessons had been extracted from defending against the German spring offensives back in 1918, and these were augmented by conclusions drawn from the recent experience on the Meuse, then distilled into orders for implementation by commanders. The aim was to deny the enemy momentum by presenting him with obstacles in depth which slowed him, and then to confront the attackers with firepower which destroyed them. It was to be a chequerboard defence of interlocking positions with fire support from well-camouflaged anti-tank and machine-gun posts. Local populations were evacuated as a defensive zone of at least five miles in depth was rapidly constructed behind the Somme and the Aisne. Along the length of the front, hamlets and villages were militarized: some buildings were demolished for better observation, obstacles were positioned, trenches were dug, buildings had their windows knocked out, entrances were sand-bagged, and machine guns were sighted to create individual strongpoints that could fight on their own but also supported each other in a system of all-round defence that became known as 'Weygand's Hedgehogs'.[6] The whole region became a construction site, noisy and imbued with a sense of urgency.[7]

Commanded by General Paul-Henry Gérodias, the 29th Alpine Division had recently arrived in the Somme sector from Lorraine by rail and road and was greeted with orders to develop its defences. The formation was well-led, well-equipped and competent, but in common with many divisional commanders along the front, Gérodias was only too well aware that on his left flank was the less capable 19th Infantry Division, commanded by General Toussaint, which weakened his position. That division included 22nd Régiment de Marche de Volontaires Etrangers (RMVE or Foreign Volunteers Regiment), which was led by the languid reserve officer Lieutenant Colonel Pierre Villiers-Moriamé and was positioned on the flank adjoining Gérodias's sector. A mixture of anti-fascists from Spain, Italy, Czechoslovakia, Poland, Germany and Austria, the regiment was not easy to control and still lacked some basic training and equipment. On 31 May Toussaint reported to his corps commander, General Théodore Sciard, that his formation was 'absolutely incapable in its present state of fulfilling its mission in battle'.[8] Sciard was not impressed, and so with no reserves to play with, he shuffled his pack of commanders and replaced Toussaint with General Fernand Lenlud and replaced Villiers-Moriame with Major Paul Hermann, a regular officer from 41st Infantry Regiment. The timing was not ideal, but Sciard did what he could to revitalize the flagging division, believing the risk worth taking considering the impending challenge it faced.

In common with every division along the Somme and the Aisne, 29th Alpine and 19th Infantry Divisions made the best of their situation and made their preparations in order to fulfil Weygand's direction that each hedgehog 'must hold out at all costs while it awaits relief'. This was to be provided by a collection of infantry, half-mechanized 'light' divisions, DLMs and DCRs which were positioned to the rear of the static infantry division to strike back – as they had been earlier in the campaign – but were still vulnerable to communication breakdown, congested roads and resupply challenges. As a result, and as before, French counter-attacks would be a complicated race against time in order to get a strong force where it was needed when it was needed.[9] Once in position, the divisions were to drive into the over-extended German spearheads while the main defensive zone remained in position and continued to fight in order to isolate the anticipated German armoured penetration. The heavier divisions providing the 'relief' were best configured for this task and were in varying states of repair. 1st and 2nd DCRs had new, more capable commanders, although 4th DCR had lost the dynamic de Gaulle, who had taken up a position in government, and all armoured divisions had been re-equipped. Even so, the four DCRs still only had 150 tanks between them and, even when combined with the three remaining DLMs, could muster only 324 operational machines. Weygand hoped, however, that with the French aviation industry reaching full production in May, the air force might be in a stronger position to help suppress the German offensive than it had been less than a month before. Yet, although the service possessed 2,350 aircraft by early June, the number that were operational had declined from 879 on 10 May to a mere 600 on 5 June.[10] The army was not, however, alone in learning lessons from their recent experiences, and General Vuillemin had done what he could in a very short time to improve the reaction time of his ground-attack squadrons by concentrating them directly under a more centralized air force command, rather than parcelling them out in small numbers to provide local cover and placing them under army command.

The French tried to tackle some of the failings and frailties that had been shown up since the Meuse crossings, but there was only so much that could be done in the time available and with the resources at their disposal. Transforming the armed forces into the modern, mobile, free-thinking, initiative-taking force that was required to cope with German fighting methods was something that would have to wait. Moreover, commanders were continuing to work in desperate strategic and operational contexts in which the enemy retained the initiative while they had no meaningful sense of what they were facing or where the enemy's main effort might fall. Requests for aerial reconnaissance were more often than not refused because there were too few aircraft to meet the demand and those that took to the skies were quickly targeted either by German anti-aircraft fire or patrolling fighters.

As a consequence, the French High Command could give very little direction to the frustrated formation commanders, who sought to react as quickly as they could to whatever befell them, despite the systemic difficulties in doing so. It was a situation which led General Jules-Georges-Jacques Baudouin, the commander of 13th Infantry Division, to write, 'Personally, the absence of intelligence and firm orders from the high command caused me dreadful anguish.'[11] This made the positioning of the counter-attacking formations, particularly the valuable DCRs, little more than an educated guess. Units used raiding parties to obtain what information they could from the enemy's forward positions and used high ground to try and observe German movements, but the result was superficial, partial and generally highly inferior intelligence from which little of use was learned. In the circumstances, Baudouin believed that he and his fellow divisional commanders were in a 'covering and sacrificial role, to allow time to be won and a defence organized to the rear on the Oise, the Seine, the Loire perhaps'.[12] There was, in fact, a good deal of truth in this, for there were discussions between the government and the French High Command about what might be done if the Germans broke through. Various positions – usually rivers – had been identified as places where further resistance might be attempted, but the Weygand Line was always considered far more than a mere speed bump; it was the Line where the enemy really *had* to be caught and held.

— □ —

Weygand was under no illusion: the Germans could not be allowed to break through the new defensive line and yet he knew that their immense power made just such a breakthrough extremely likely. There were 104 German divisions available for *Fall Rot,* the new offensive, with another nineteen divisions in reserve. In this part of the campaign the panzer divisions served the infantry armies – albeit in different ways depending on circumstances and the commanders involved – for what the Germans recognized was a set-piece attack. The forty-seven divisions of Army Group B were pitted against the Somme and the western section of the Aisne, with three armies each led by a panzer corps. Fourth Army was in the coastal sector on the right with Hoth's 5th and 7th Panzer Divisions, Sixth Army in the central sector with 9th and 10th Panzer Divisions, while Ninth Army was on the left with 3rd and 4th Panzer Divisions. Eighteenth Army was in the second echelon. Other than Hoth's corps, the panzer divisions were part of Panzer Group Kleist and were to use the pre-existing crossings at Amiens and Péronne to launch their attacks and then surge forward against the Seine north-west of Paris followed by the infantry.

One of the infantry formations was XXXVIII Corps, commanded by Erich von Manstein, who had been promoted to General of Infantry on 1 June and, according to his biographer, was to see his experience 'hardly taxed by organizing what was essentially an administrative road movement exercise'.[13] To the east, Army Group A was to attack the remainder of the Aisne up to the end of the Maginot Line. Here von Rundstedt ordered that the infantry in the form of Second and Twelfth Army were to lead the attack around Rethel. Having crossed the river and broken the line, the infantry would then mop up while a new Panzer Group commanded by a promoted Heinz Guderian consisting of 1st, 2nd, 6th and 8th Panzer Divisions in two corps, was to conduct an exploitation across the Marne and then, at least in part, push to the rear of the Maginot Line. Once Guderian was making good progress, Army Group C was then to undertake an offensive which would see

First Army attacking in a southerly direction from east of Metz and Seventh Army crossing the Upper Rhine south of Strasbourg. Von Leeb's aim was to dislodge the Maginot Line defenders as Guderian, under his command, outflanked them in order to avoid the area becoming a last bastion of protracted French resistance. The neutralization of the 'Great Wall' was seen by OKH as an essential part of the wider offensive because, as Halder wrote, 'The Maginot Line represents everything that stands for security in the French people's mind. The line cannot be given up without risking the moral collapse of France.'[14] As a result, von Rundstedt's attack was made the main German effort.

The role of air power in the offensive revealed the change in the Luftwaffe's priorities during this stage of the campaign. Increasingly, despite the recent focus on operations over the Dunkirk perimeter, German aircraft – assisted by the relocation of airfields to sites in France and Belgium – became more concerned with conducting operations deeper into the French interior. Although some Stukas remained available for ground support, bombers and their escorting fighters were used to target ports, hamper road and rail communications and generally undermine the enemy's ability and desire to pursue the war. As part of this, on 3 June the Luftwaffe launched Operation Paula, which sought not only to undermine enemy morale and destroy factories around Paris – as noted by Alexander Werth by the Seine – but also destroy airfields and the remaining French air force. That day, the Germans not only insisted that their attack had produced panic in Paris but also claimed 400 enemy aircraft destroyed on the ground and a further seventy-five in the air for minimal losses themselves. Indeed, the Luftwaffe was so sure that it had succeeded in many of its aims on that single day that thereafter it moved back to its operational targets. In reality, however, it had destroyed a mere twenty operational aircraft on the ground and fifteen in the air and the damaged French airfields were all returned to action within forty-eight hours.[15]

Where Paula had succeeded, however, was, as we have seen, in taking the campaign to Paris, where it had caused damage to the capital's fabric and significant casualties as well as panic. Thus, although the operation had failed to significantly damage the French air force, this was not of any great importance for it had dented French morale and the Luftwaffe remained dominant as Germany sought to bring France to her knees.

Halder's plan for *Fall Rot* was relatively simple, sensible and achievable: an attempt through three co-ordinated offensives to strip France of its last defenders, isolate Paris and, through the widening of the fissures created since 10 May in France's ability to resist, bring about collapse. Coming so soon after *Fall Gelb*, however, and requiring rapid planning and movement of assets, the offensive posed a considerable challenge to the General Staff and the staffs of von Bock and von Rundstedt. As a result, Halder focused on detail and paid due respect to the enemy, an attitude he believed to be more in keeping with what the situation required and stood in stark contrast to the blasé over-confidence displayed by some members of OKW. He was also anxious that Hitler's headquarters remained one step removed from a true understanding of how the campaign was being fought for, while the General Staff was concerned only with those objectives that would lead to the military collapse of the enemy, Hitler wanted to grasp as much territory as possible before the French capitulation for reasons of prestige, the longer-term subjugation of the country and protection of his new Continental acquisitions. This difference in priority was something that Halder recognized he would have to face once the Weygand Line had been broken, for while OKH sought for elements of Army Group A and B to encircle French troops in north-eastern France – including Paris – behind the Somme and Aisne, OKW was much more set on the full weight of Army Group A plunging south to contain any threat of a counter-attack from the region and to seize the rich resources of the Lorraine ore basin before considering a drive south-west. The difference of opinion was relatively minor and lay in emphasis rather than main focus, but it was another example of the growing friction between the two headquarters and was a frustration for OKH, whose *raison d'être* was, after all, the facilitation of military victory through its direction of operations.

As the Dunkirk evacuations came to an end, it was decided that *Fall Rot* would commence on 5 June with Army Group B, which was already in position, while Army Group A would attack several days later on the completion of its relocation and preparations. Both Army Groups did what they could to maintain as much operational and tactical surprise as they could and, in the immediate prelude to the attack, sought to add to the thickness of the fog that was already enveloping the Allies. Shooting down French reconnaissance aircraft was merely the most obvious sign of an attempt to deny the enemy any useful information, but the Germans also went to great lengths to ensure that only disinformation was transmitted by radio and that anything of importance was communicated by field telephone. The change of Enigma codes, coincidentally, denied the enemy valuable intelligence at a vital time, and the German divisions also put considerable effort into making the French think that troops and vehicles were on the move at night when in fact they remained in place and under camouflage. Daniel Le Roy, a young French officer in the line near Rethel, recalls the confusion caused by such methods:

> I was kept awake night after night listening to the sound of German vehicle movements and could even hear the shouts of the enemy who goaded us. The comings and goings were very confusing because they did not follow any pattern ... We sent a raiding party across to try and capture a prisoner, but they returned only with a fresh corpse. We stripped him of any information that we thought important and passed it on to the Intelligence section. We thought that we had

found out a great deal of information from the body. Later we learned that it had probably been planted there and contained false unit badges and papers.[16]

The Germans, meanwhile, continued to take advantage of poor French security and managed to capture prisoners, written orders and marked maps all along the line. This intelligence, when added to aerial reconnaissance photographs, provided a relatively detailed picture of French strength and deployments and led one German staff officer to boast later that he knew the names of every French officer in the regiment facing his division as well as 'a full inventory of their weaponry, equipment, ammunition supplies and stores'.[17] With the information supplied to him, on 4 June Halder surmised that the French had some sixty divisions in France, 'enough for a weakly held front and some reserve groups'[18] and correctly identified that Weygand believed that his main effort would come across the Somme. Even so, OKH believed it vital to remain flexible in the face of the enemy's response to its opening moves but hoped that by drawing Third Army Group into battle first, the task of Army Group A's main effort across the Aisne would become that much easier when it was launched a few days later. Rommel, personally decorated by Hitler just days before, wrote to his wife hours before the start of the new offensive:

> We're off again today. The six days' rest has done a lot of good and helped us to get our equipment more or less back into shape. The new move won't be so very difficult. The sooner it comes, the better for us. The country here is practically untouched by war. It all went too fast. Would you cut out all the newspaper articles about me, please? I've no time to read at the moment, but it will be fun to look at them later.[19]

Fall Rot began with von Bock's attack at first light on 5 June accompanied by a huge air and artillery bombardment along the length of Tenth and Seventh Army's front.[20] It was an event more reminiscent of the loud and brutal preliminary to the Meuse crossing on 13 May than the insertion of airborne troops and the deception that had accompanied the opening of *Fall Gelb*. As at Sedan, the French were waiting and cowered within defences which, when they emerged through the smoke and dust, they discovered had only suffered minimal damage from the enemy bombs and shells. This time, however, the Germans did not have to wait for bridges to be constructed and the panzers, anti-tank guns and artillery were hard on the heels of the leading infantry and engineers. Nevertheless, this was more in keeping with the sort of warfare for which the French had prepared and the troops were not so traumatized by the onslaught. Rommel himself was supremely confident in his own abilities and those of his division and, despite the challenges facing both, had no doubt that 7th Panzer Division would prevail and, moreover, that the campaign would be won within a fortnight. With a bridgehead already established across the Somme, the formation fell on the French defences and set to work as it had done during the break-in and breakthrough of the extended Maginot Line at Soire-le Château, but without the benefit of surprise. The division displayed well-practised all-arms co-operation, benefited from superb leadership and drew heavily on its recent experiences to avoid the French hedgehogs by keeping off major roads and ignoring important features of the terrain. In this way, units identified and opened weaknesses in the French defences so that the division could advance and not become sucked into the static, positional battle that was their enemy's preference.

Watching from his command vehicle just behind the leading panzers, Rommel later wrote that 'The various arms worked in such perfect co-ordination that it might have been a peacetime exercise'[21] although more objective participants said that the defences were the most troublesome they had faced since the beginning of the invasion.[22] Even so, 7th Panzer Division had advanced eight miles by the evening of the first day and in doing so had carved its way through the Weygand Line far more quickly than Besson would have liked. It was now up to the French counter-attacking forces to stop the fast-moving division before it caused chaos in the rear while the defenders on the Somme attempted to close the breaches made by Rommel and hold the infantry regiments that were following in his wake to mop up. These German troops, less well-trained, with limited experience and with fewer resources, were made to fight hard for every yard of ground. As a result the French defences did not burst open on 5 June, and Besson's divisions generally did a good job of soaking up the initial momentum of von Bock's attack along the majority of the Line. The commander of Army Group B wrote at the end of the day:

> The French are defending themselves stubbornly. Their tactics in the face of our panzer attacks is to establish themselves in towns and forests, placing the main weight of their defence in 'tank-proof' terrain. This has caused some local discomfort, however; since they are leaving the intervening spaces between strongpoints free, this tactic will do them little good in the long run. For the moment, however, it provides them with an advantage, for while near Amiens and Péronne the panzer divisions can advance between the occupied towns, their riflemen are unable to follow under the effects of flanking fire from the towns. Consequently, moving motorized divisions forward today was not yet possible.[23]

Von Bock was correct in his analysis. The French could not resist the Germans indefinitely and in the days that followed the infantry divisions continued to fight among the French defences while 7th Panzer Division struck out alone. Rommel's intention was to drive deep into the French rear, undermining the enemy's cohesion and breaking any subsequent French defensive lines while the infantry completed their breakthrough. Thus, while the fighting on the Somme remained intense and congested, Rommel advanced through more open countryside towards the Lower Seine. On 6 June, 7th Panzer Division advanced a further thirteen miles and on the next day another sixteen miles. To achieve this, Rommel put into practice a method he had rehearsed before 10 May for just such a scenario. For a *Flachenmarsch* (area march) the division formed up on a 2,000-yard front and twelve miles in depth to advance as one block which avoided villages and main roads and fired on the move into places that concealed the enemy. Clearly impressed by what his formation had achieved during this period, Rommel later wrote:

> The advance went straight across country, over roadless and trackless fields, uphill, downhill, through hedges, fences and high cornfields … We met no enemy troops, apart from a few stragglers … Fleeing civilians, and also troops, were on all roads. Sometimes we even surprised refugee lorries in open country, their occupants, men, women and children, underneath the vehicles, where they had crawled in mortal fear. We shouted to them, as we passed, to go back home.[24]

Rommel's thrust was so rapid and concentrated that it undid French attempts to counter-attack it. Those valuable forces that might have mounted such an attack were just too widely spread and slow to respond in the face of his speed and aggression. The timely and accurate application of German air power also managed to stifle the enemy's reaction and generally undermined its ability to reinforce the fighting front and supply it with vital resources. In such circumstances, movement by train or road during daylight hours was extremely dangerous and so mobile units either split up and tried to keep off major roads to make themselves more difficult targets or were forced to move at night. Thus, 1st and 2nd DCR, which had been positioned around thirty miles south of the Somme, found themselves in fragmented, un-coordinated groups lacking clear orders and in no position to engage Rommel's advance. As a consequence, by 8 June 7th Panzer Division was moving rapidly towards Rouen on the Seine. The river was the last major barrier that could thwart either the encirclement of Paris or a push towards Normandy and Brittany. An attempt was made by the division to cross the river that night but having been rebuffed – much to Rommel's anger at his motorcycle infantry – an operational pause was made to allow for von Manstein's infantry divisions to catch up.

As it was, after managing to reduce the enemy's defences on the Somme, von Manstein sent his corps forward with remarkable speed. Although it did indeed include the motorized 1st Cavalry Division, he treated his three infantry divisions as if they were all motorized and drove them hard towards the Seine. It was a move which was to have major implications for the integrity of the Weygand Line because its breakthrough forced the French Seventh Army into withdrawal but at a slower speed than the advancing German formations. As a result, 7th Panzer Division on the Seine found that a corps-sized group of French and British troops came tumbling back towards it, looking, perhaps, to reinforce the river line or for evacuation from Le Havre, and Rommel was sent to stem the flow on 10 June. In the meantime, 5th Panzer Division was designated to take Rouen and von Manstein's 6th and 46th Infantry Divisions to forge a crossing of the Seine. By the time that this had been successfully achieved, 7th Panzer Division had made another huge contribution to the campaign. The Armoured Reconnaissance Regiment followed by the Panzer Regiment first made for the seaside town of Fécamp with the division commander, as usual, in the lead group. Reaching the coast, Rommel later wrote, 'thrilled and stirred every man of us'[25] but although there was a temptation to feel that a culminating point had been reached in the formation's offensive, officers were quick to remind the men of the important task that was before them.

The appearance of elements of 7th Panzer Division at Fécamp had scuppered the plans of the Allied divisions withdrawing along the coast and forced them to try and expedite a rapid evacuation from St. Valéry on 11 June. Recognizing what was happening, Rommel stalked his enemy and, when it was bottled up in and around the town, went for the kill. Within one or two hours of his guns starting to bombard the concentrated Allied group, around 1,000 French troops surrendered but the vast majority continued fighting as they sought to avoid being encircled. Caught in an unedifying situation without heavy weaponry, the ability to manoeuvre or any chance of relief, the Allied divisions fought bravely throughout 11 June but as 7th Panzer Division arrived in increasing strength, the encirclement was complete and its firepower took a heavy toll. By 12 June, the commanders in the pocket recognized that they could ask their men to engage in a futile defence of a militarily unimportant French town, or they could surrender. Gradually, groups of Allied troops began to capitulate – most often when they had expended all their available ammunition – and the position collapsed. One German section was surprised to find that a large French group that surrendered to it included General Marcel Ihler, the commander of French Ninth Corps. Ihler, however, was just one of twelve generals taken prisoner that day and Rommel was delighted to hear one remark, 'You are too fast, much too fast for us. That's all there is to it!'[26] The 46,000 prisoners 7th Panzer eventually took at St. Valéry included the remnants of five divisions and 8,000 men of the BEF's 51st (Highland) Division. Having ensured that photographers were on the spot to capture his latest triumph, that evening Rommel wrote to his wife: 'The battle is over here. Today one corps commander and four division commanders presented themselves before me in the market square of St. Valéry, having been forced by my division to surrender. Wonderful moments.'[27]

Although held back by its brief siege of the St Valéry pocket on the Channel coast, Rommel's division had carved a deep wedge in the enemy's defences, one which allowed 5th Panzer Division and von Manstein's divisions a freedom of movement that unlocked the coastal sector of the French defences. No formation enjoyed similar success on the remainder of von Bock's front where, despite the best efforts of von Kleist's two panzer corps at Amiens and Péronne, the French held firm. Progress was made, but although highlighting both solid French defence and impressive German all-arms co-operation, it was grinding and relied on what limited Luftwaffe support was made available. At Péronne, for example, Hoepner's XVI Panzer Corps found that, despite pre-battle concerns about their adjoining flanks, 29th Alpine Division and 19th Infantry Division withstood the pounding meted out by the artillery and the Stukas and fought the ensuing ground attack with considerable composure. At the fortified hamlets of St. Christ and Miséry, Lieutenant Albert Besson, a company commander in 112th Alpine Regiment, recorded 'six wave assaults' on 5 June alone. Another defender ensconced in St. Christ, eighteen-year-old Serge Winter, later wrote:

> My team had made a strong position for our machine gun in a farm building. There was another [500 yards] to our right and together we covered an obvious approach route up a small valley to our piece of higher ground ... The enemy probed us to try and get us to give our positions away. We resisted the temptation to open fire, and some men in trenches [200 yards] in front of our building dealt with them ... Twenty minutes later, those trenches were hit by a mortar bombardment and the enemy immediately followed up screaming. There were hundreds of them and we opened fire. We cut the enemy down, but more took their place and there were too few of our machine guns to stop them. We desperately called for artillery support, but none came ... We were overrun after about an hour, our lives saved by an NCO who ordered one of his men not to shoot but to take us for interrogation.[28]

Winter could not have known at the time, but elsewhere in the sector some captured French troops were used at the head of a German attack as a human shield. Some were shot by their capturers when they refused to advance, while others threw themselves to the ground when a fire-fight began. Meanwhile, 19th Division's 22nd RMVE also fought bravely and with some skill at Fresnes-Mazancourt, Marchélepot and Miséry on 5 and 6 June, and used its 3rd battalion to co-operate closely with 112th Alpine Regiment's 2nd Battalion to ensure a strong seam between the two divisions. Attempts to infiltrate the French line were consistently rebuffed with excellent artillery support, all of which led to eighty German armoured fighting vehicles being lost on the first day alone.

Similar difficulties were faced by XIV Panzer Corps and it was only when the Stukas, having been forced to wait for a fighter escort due to a stronger than expected French air presence, turned their attention to the destruction of the French guns that any forward momentum could be made. By the end of 5 June, a six-mile-deep bridgehead had been won at Amiens and Péronne which, although insignificant considering what the Germans had achieved for much of *Fall Gelb*, was more in line with the amount of ground taken immediately after the Meuse crossing – albeit that there were bridges already in place across the Somme. As the Germans later admitted, the battles in this area were 'hard and costly in lives, the enemy putting up severe resistance, particularly in the woods and tree lines continuing the fight when our troops had pushed past the point of resistance'.[29] As a consequence, von Kleist's divisions managed to break into the French defences, where they had to fight hard ground, rather than break through them and over the next couple of days struggled in a defensive web while Rommel raced towards the Seine.

It was not uncommon for French units to fight until they could fight no more. Indeed, the remnants of 112th Alpine Regiment – 100 men, of whom half were wounded – only surrendered after three days when their ammunition ran out. The Germans found this difficult to cope with, for the situation allowed the French to commit their limited reserves to plug gaps in the line while the attackers were forced to commit poorly trained second-rate troops who had not been intended to fight in such conditions. To the east of 19th and 29th Alpine Divisions, for example, General Louis-Émile Noiret's 7th Colonial Division reported that, by the fourth day of the offensive, the enemy was 'starting to show undeniable signs of fatigue'.[30] To support this assertion, Noiret quoted a German infantryman from a regiment in reserve which had been sent into battle on the afternoon of 7 June and by daylight the next morning had already lost its cohesion. The German soldier was brought into division headquarters after his capture on 8 June and Noiret reported that he 'was sobbing with fatigue and dead on his feet' as he told French officers:

> We haven't slept more than three hours a night for three weeks and we've marched on foot over 260 kilometres (162 miles) in a week … My comrades are keeling over, they're so tired, our regiment could only defend itself now not attack any more … and the regiment has had three commanding officers in the past twelve hours. Your artillery has caused us some losses, but what's really stopping us is your dug-in entrenched infantry.[31]

In fact, the French defences so impeded the advance of XIV and XVI Panzer Corps that on 8 June a decision was taken for both to disengage and shift further east to exploit Ninth Army's crossing of the Aisne towards the Oise against the French Sixth Army. In itself, this was a clear success for the divisions facing the power of Panzer Group Kleist and was one of just two occasions during the entire campaign – the defence of the Dunkirk perimeter being the other – when operational initiative was wrested from the Germans and they were forced to deviate from their preferred course of action. However, just like at Dunkirk, the attackers were only temporarily inconvenienced. In the case of von Kleist's panzer divisions, the disruption was considerable as the moving of such a force could not be done without the requisite planning and preparation, but the fact that the Germans managed it was further evidence of the benefits that can be reaped from slick staff work and decisive action. Yet even as the two corps were redeploying, leaving Eighteenth and Sixth Army to reduce the defences south of Amiens and Péronne, the French front began to crumble. Assisted by Rommel's success to the east, which had forced Seventh Army to withdraw, Tenth Army also began to give ground as its left flank became exposed. Thus, even as von Kleist's panzers began to reach the Aisne, Weygand gave the order for a general withdrawal from the Somme.

During the opening days of *Fall Rot*, the French had shown a great deal of fighting spirit, not to say impressive tactical competence, and made good use of the benefits of a defensive system which was much more conducive to upsetting German ambitions. There were enough weaknesses in Weygand's operational circumstances, however, to render his line little more than the fleeting encumbrance to the enemy that General Baudouin believed it to be. To some, therefore, the fighting that cost the Allies so dear in lives and resources during the first three days of the new German offensive was a futile gesture. This line of reasoning is understandable considering the outcome, but one has to recognize the impact that *Fall Gelb* had had on the decision-making system of the French and their ability to move troops and equipment where they might do the most damage. Considering the recent change in Supreme Command and the fact that French formations were already forming up on the Somme and the Aisne as von Kleist swept towards the Channel, the Weygand Line was a natural and logical defensive option. In such circumstances, alternatives to it were not readily available and, incidentally, the fighting on the

Somme eventually offered a good insight into what might have befallen the Germans had they not taken up the essence of von Manstein's scheme. As it was, a lack of time, too few resources, poor command and control and a severely limited counter-attacking ability, undid the defenders. Despite their courage, the bridgeheads over the Somme and the power of the Germans when married with another remarkable advance by Rommel led to the need for a withdrawal from the Somme after a mere four days. As one French staff officer in 47th Infantry Division's headquarters later said:

> The situation had not changed fundamentally. We had managed to hold the line for a while, which gave us some renewed sense of worth, but ultimately we were forced back by a superior enemy ... We were like that little Dutch boy trying to plug holes in the Dyke. The Germans were a force of nature and we soon recognized that we were going to be washed away. It was a matter of *when* the dam burst, not *if*.[32]

As von Bock's troops occupied the enemy's former positions, Army Group A completed its final preparations for the launching of the German main effort. It was an attack that sought to sweep away the last foundations of French resilience and, in co-operation with von Bock's own continued operations, to bring the nation to its knees.

CHAPTER 12

9–22 June – Driving South, Paris and Armistice

Taken prisoner by the Germans at St. Christ on the first day of *Fall Rot,* a nervous Serge Winter joined other members of his 112th Alpine Regiment who were herded across a devastated landscape which was still under artillery fire, across the River Somme and into the enemy's rear area. The group of approximately forty prisoners were escorted by four German infantrymen who, Winter later said, 'looked even more exhausted than we did, but were friendly enough even if they did keep saying, "France is finished".'[1] After being handed over to the military police and marched for another hour, each man waited in a queue by a church in a hamlet where they were searched for a second time and their papers and personal effects were placed in a large box. On reaching a small table manned by an enormous German officer, Winter was asked his name and service number, an attendant NCO checked the remaining papers that were laid out on a larger table before him and mumbled a few words to his colleague. 'The officer barely looked up,' Winter recalled, 'and when the sergeant confirmed that the information that I had given matched those on my papers, the officer scribbled a few notes on some official-looking papers and I was waved through.'[2]

There was little opportunity to escape, although the thought barely crossed the minds of Winter and his colleagues: they hardly wished to run the gauntlet through so many German troops to rejoin a battle that they were glad to have left behind them. After being ushered into a large *salle de fêtes* and offered 'water and some vile German sausage', Winter and his comrades felt safe and even managed to crack a joke or two among themselves to help raise their spirits and pass the time. 'We had heard of prisoners being roughed up by the enemy and even stories of them being murdered, but we experienced good treatment,' Winter explained, 'and within a couple of hours we were in a truck heading east.' Four days later, Winter and his colleagues had crossed the Rhine and had entered a former army barracks that was to act as their temporary prisoner of war camp. Having been shown to a hut and to his bunk by a Belgian prisoner who had already been at the camp for ten days, Winter wrote the only entry he was to make in his little diary, 'I am alive, but there is little hope for France.'[3]

Winter's solitary diary entry was made after he had seen a little of the immense German military machine in action and its workings behind the lines. Although he had no more knowledge about the unfolding situation than he was able to glean on his journey into captivity, it was enough to convince him that France was doomed. Although *Fall Rot* suffered some early operational setbacks, they were significant only in relation to the speed with which the Allies had been defeated in previous battles and were quickly overcome. During the opening days of the offensive, Halder and von Brauchitsch revealed no great concern about how it was progressing and instead immersed themselves in the area of higher operations on the assumption that the Weygand Line would be broken within a matter of days. As they contemplated how best to bring about the military collapse of the French, they were more convinced than ever that OKW should approve the

---

* Winter remained a German prisoner until the end of the war.

opportunity that existed to encircle the vast bulk of the French force that remained in north-eastern France. Halder continued to argue that sending just *part* of Army Group A behind the Maginot Line would be enough to contain and encircle any latent threat from the region, and would also allow the inner wing of von Rundstedt's formation to swing westwards to assist in a wider encirclement somewhere south of Paris. Hitler, however, would not agree to the change as he demanded the containment of the Maginot Line forces – his flank psychosis had not abated – before developing operations. It was a position that led Halder to write on 6 June:

> The Führer thinks that changing the direction of the offensive, as proposed by me, is still too hazardous at this time. He wants to play absolutely safe. First, he would like to have a sure hold on the Lorraine iron ore basin ... After that he believes it would be the time to consider a drive in a westerly direction ... There we have the same old story again. On top there just isn't a spark of the spirit that would dare put high stakes on a single throw. Instead, everything is done in cheap piecemeal fashion, but with the air that we don't have to rush at all.[4]

As it was, on the morning of 9 June, the fourth day of *Fall Rot*, Army Group A began its offensive. Attacking either side of Rethel, Second and Twelfth Armies sought to cross the Aisne and prepare a way for Guderian's two panzer corps to crack the enemy's defences open and exploit to the south. Here the French Fourth Army fought as tenaciously as their colleagues had done on the Somme and with the advantage gained from the fact that the Germans had to make assault crossings of the river. They were met with considerable French firepower, which led to some heavy casualties, but the attackers threw increasing numbers of infantry and engineers across the river and eventually some made a lodgement on the opposite bank and bludgeoned their way forward. This unsophisticated technique stood in stark contrast to the careful preparation, planning and all-arms fighting that had marked out Guderian's crossing of the Meuse at Sedan, yet the attack across the Aisne suffered not only from a rushed prelude and a lack of surprise but also from troops of lower quality and less intensive air support. Guderian's attitude to the struggle gave every impression of a gloating general who felt that his own troops could have done better, and reflected a brashness that was not missed when List visited him during that tumultuous day and found his troops relaxing in the sun and some even bathing in a stream. When List asked Guderian why his troops were not ready for action, the panzer commander replied that it was the infantry's job to establish a bridgehead. Under the cover of darkness that night, however, Guderian did begin to filter 1st and then 2nd Panzer Divisions across the Aisne as soon as pontoon bridges had been constructed and their infantry immediately reinforced the small force that were found to be rebuffing local French counter-attacks.

The building of military bridges and the subsequent enlargement of the German bridgeheads by armour on 10 June was an important step for Army Group A but there was no dissolution of the French defences. List read numerous reports that left him in no doubt that the opposition was stronger than had been expected and he developed a grudging respect for the enemy's resolve, concluding: 'The French are putting up strong opposition. No signs of demoralization are evident anywhere. We are seeing a new French way of fighting.'[5] General Lattre de Tassigny's 14th Division even managed to produce a counter-attack which took 800 prisoners. The French also threw their armour against Guderian's massing panzers in an attempt to stop them from gaining an irresistible mass. While 3rd DCR hit the flank of General Rudolf Schmidt's 1st and 2nd Panzer Divisions with eighty-six tanks from Juniville on the afternoon of 10 June and a further attack was mounted by 7th DLM on the following day, Reinhardt's 6th and 8th Panzer

Divisions were forced to 'beat off several counter-attacks by French armoured and mechanized brigades'.[6] Yet despite valiant attempts, French Fourth Army could not hold Guderian's Panzer Group indefinitely. By 10 June, the forward elements of 2nd Panzer Division had already reached the outskirts of Rheims as Schmidt, encouraged by Guderian, sought to complete the breakthrough and by 12 June all four panzer divisions were flooding south through the Champagne region's open countryside, leaving the infantry to mop up in their wake. Halder could not help but see huge possibilities now that a breakthrough had been achieved and, anticipating a battle of encirclement and annihilation, he wrote: 'A "Battle of Cannae" is in the making.'[7]

OKH simply would not let go of its desire to complete a victory in the shortest possible time. Halder was in no mood for protracted fighting and revealed his concern at the cumulative, grinding effect on the army of operations that were now in their second month by writing on 11 June: 'The troops are said to have reached the limits of their physical endurance. They are fit now for pursuit fighting, but not for heavy attacks (battle fatigue). Striking power of the rifle units of the divisions is down to 50 per cent ...' [8] In this context, the question of how the campaign was to develop was a critical one now that the Weygand Line had been broken. Indeed, the decision taken by OKW on 13 June not only to occupy Paris but to authorize a giant encirclement north of the Loire to match the attempt to encircle the troops of the Maginot Line represented a considerable shift towards defeating the enemy through movement rather than physical fighting. Although Paris had little military importance, its loss would very likely undermine the morale of the French and weaken their will. As a consequence, Halder gave verbal orders to the headquarters of Army Group B that evening: 'Order Fourth Army to start offensive tomorrow. Secure Paris with strong forces (five divisions) ...'[9] On the following day, 14 June, a Directive from Hitler gave further clarity to the aims of von Bock's army group by stating:

> Enemy forces on the lower Seine and in the Paris area will be vigorously pursued by the advance of the right flank of the Army [Group B] along the coast towards the Loire estuary and by a turning movement from the Château-Thierry area towards the Loire above Orléans. Paris will be occupied in force as soon as possible.[10]

A pincer comprised of the two wings of von Bock's army was, therefore, to use its crossings of the Marne east of Paris at Chateau-Thierry and the Lower Seine west of Paris near Rouen to launch a massive encirclement aiming at the Loire while Guderian continued towards Switzerland. To Halder and von Brauchitsch, the decisions were a victory for common sense, but they were also aware that the enemy would still be likely to have plenty of time to withdraw behind the Loire while Army Group B advanced and so felt that an opportunity had been missed to force an earlier French capitulation by means of a less deep envelopment.

As it was, the prompt withdrawal of the French armies to the south by Weygand ensured that as far as possible, the formations did not collapse and retained the ability to resist. It was a fighting withdrawal which was designed not only to cover those troops moving away from the front but also to significantly delay the enemy. As one German soldier later explained: 'There were pockets of resistance where they held out when our infantry were already thirty kilometres [eighteen miles] to the rear ... the French regiments fought as if they felt they were defending the last street in France in a battle that would decide the very existence of their country.'[11] The problem for the French, however, was their ability to retain a defensive coherence against an enemy attacking on such a broad front. As a result, they withdrew into the interior of France in an attempt to hold a line from the Atlantic coast, along the Loire and then along the Rhône to the Swiss border with Third Army Group in the west, Fourth Army Group in the centre and Second Army Group in the east. Their ability to get into position depended as much on the speed of the enemy as it did on their own ability to disengage and redeploy quickly and, as Halder had said, the German forces were still capable of 'pursuit fighting'. In such circumstances, the question of whether France could and should continue to fight was one that became increasingly difficult for the country's decision-makers to ignore.

Since the end of the First World War, the defence of Paris had never been considered as something that would be undertaken in its suburbs or along its avenues. The development of the Maginot Line and a force that *would* stop the Germans in Belgium was part of a strategy designed to allow the capital city to continue to function while its rich heritage and cultural significance was protected. So the threat that emerged to the city as the result of *Fall Gelb* and then, more specifically, the success of *Fall Rot*, did not lead to a decision to fight amongst the ruins of the Arc de Triomphe while the government struggled on in the capital – quite the opposite. After the destruction of non-essential documents that might assist the Germans and the transport of others out of the city, arrangements were made for the critical working parts of the national decision-making machinery to be evacuated to a temporary administrative centre on the Loire. Meanwhile, Parisians watched and waited. Over the previous week, the bombing of Paris, defeat at Dunkirk, the opening of the new German offensive, the withdrawal of the Weygand Line and then the appearance of French troops from the front in the city had encouraged increasing numbers to quit the city and head south. Few retained confidence in official sources of information in a country that was increasingly befuddled and led by a government which seemed to be saying that the population should do nothing but await further announcements. The capital began to disassemble while smoke continued to rise from the government quarter as officials incinerated official papers.

On 9 June, Alexander Werth wrote a cable to his newspaper:

Paris in its anguish strangely calm and beautiful these days. [Stop] During day numerous luggage-laden cars seen leaving town with passengers having tears in eyes. [Stop] At night streets almost deserted excepting rifled guards outside Government buildings and underground stations. [Stop] … At night distant gunfire hearable also occasional bombs dropping closer by and in night air there's faint sweet scent of resin and burning trees. [Stop] It may be wood burning somewhere near front. [Stop] Government's decision in case Paris immediately threatened being awaited. [Stop] But it's still too early to dwell on darker possibilities of coming week.[12]

That same day, the government left the capital for Tours on the Loire. An official announcement was made in their wake: 'The government has been obliged to leave the capital for compelling military reasons.'[13] Writer André Maurois took this as a statement of defeat, noting: 'At that moment I knew everything was over. France, deprived of Paris, would become a body without a head. The war had been lost.'[14] Marie-Madeleine Fourcade, who would become a prominent Resistance leader, said that 'Paris was a city in mourning', clinging to the past but recognizing that the future had changed for ever. She added that there was a 'sad frenzy of departure'[15] but despite the government's evacuation, no official arrangements had been made for that of the wider population and this caused suffering, chaos and despair.

Eugène Dépigny, who worked in the *mairie* of Paris, later recalled:

Population movements increased hourly. The objectiveness of the exodus developed and a sort of pathological panic-filled nervous anxiety overtook the crowds. People left, abandoning everything, more concerned to escape their fear of war than to escape the war itself.[16]

Railway stations were overwhelmed by the numbers arriving and the demand for trains massively outstripped supply. On 10 June, Aren Arnstraum arrived at Montparnasse in the hope of boarding a train to Bordeaux and noted in his diary: 'About 20,000 people are massed in front of the station, most of them seated on their belongings. It is impossible to move and the heat is unbearable.'[17] For most, the only route out of the city was on roads clogged with cars, trucks, carts, bicycles and all manner of improvised wheeled devices carrying the possessions of thousands as they trudged away from the advancing Germans. Most were under-prepared both mentally and physically for what they encountered on their hot, dusty journeys. Alexander Werth was one of those who left Paris in a car with four others and wrote: 'Evacuation is like a funeral. All the bother of the practical arrangements blunts you during a large part of the time to the tragedy, to the loss of something you loved.'[18]

Having arrived in Tours, the government was faced with having to make a number of hugely important decisions, but in conditions that were hardly conducive to the task. Its various ministries were scattered across the town and wider district due to the lack of suitable accommodation, which meant that all manner of buildings had to be utilized. Some did not even have a telephone and so messages had to be relayed by runners and despatch riders who had to try and negotiate their way through the congested streets. Weygand himself, who left Vincennes on 9 June for the Château du Muguet near Briare on the Loire, had access to just one telephone which could not be used for two hours in the afternoon when the lady manning the switchboard at the local exchange went on her lunch break.[19]

In spite of all this, a decision still had to be made about France's continued resistance against Germany. Strategy was reviewed at a Supreme Allied War Council meeting held on 11 June at Weygand's headquarters. Reynaud, Pétain, Weygand and de Gaulle, the new under secretary of state for national defence, were joined by Churchill, British foreign secretary Anthony Eden, General Ismay and General Edward Spears, who was liaison officer with the French government. The atmosphere was tense. Recent German advances and the government's relocation had deepened France's humiliation while the British contingent recognized that the evacuations from Boulogne and Dunkirk had been regarded as an act of selfish betrayal by many around the table. Weygand lost no time in making his position clear, saying: 'I am helpless, I cannot intervene as I have no reserves.'[20]

Churchill was deeply concerned by the negativity that exuded from the French at the meeting, one which left him in little doubt that a strong faction wished for an armistice. He had tried to encourage France to try and save herself and had travelled back and forth across the English Channel to France six exhausting times – and at the risk of being shot down – to build some fighting spirit. As one commentator has said: 'At the cost of an enormous injection of energy – physical and emotional – he did all he could for France, the country he loved so much and whose history he knew so well, and in which he chose to spend so much of his time ...'[21] As a result, the British prime minister, who was happy to converse in either English or French, suggested that there was hope if they continued to resist the German advance and created the time for more resources to be brought to bear against Nazi Germany. Pétain dismissed the idea, but Churchill was not put off his stride and argued for a withdrawal into the north-west of the country in preparation to fight from a 'Breton Redoubt'. The conference was well aware that it was to Britain's advantage for the French to prolong their struggle but Weygand – supported by Pétain – believed that this should not be at the expense of the best possible terms which could be negotiated from the conclusion of an early armistice. Nevertheless, Reynaud was interested enough in Churchill's idea to direct de Gaulle to look into its prospects without delay.

After spending the night at the Château de Muguet, Churchill flew back to England on the morning of 12 June and saw Le Havre in flames. He was in a gloomy mood on returning to London and, having received a briefing from him on the situation, Colville wrote:

> Apparently the Generals have no reserves left. Their divisions are decimated and every man and weapon has been thrown into the line; but nothing can stop the German steamroller. Weygand and Georges talk about the impossibility of carrying on the struggle, at any rate on co-ordinated lines, but Reynaud is as indomitable as Pétain is defeatist.[22]

The meeting had not come to a definite conclusion about whether the French should continue their fight, but it did prepare the ground for the official declaration on 13 June that Paris was now an 'open city' in an attempt to avoid it becoming a battleground. That morning, posters appeared on the walls of official buildings:

> Paris having been declared an open city, the military government asks the population to abstain from all hostile acts and hopes that the people will remain calm and dignified in a manner which appears appropriate in the circumstances.[23]

The announcement was a relief for those who remained in the capital but angered those who had recently left the city in fear of it becoming another Warsaw. The defence of the city was abandoned, leaving the Armée de Paris to fall back on the Loire east of Nantes. It was a decision that also angered some of the military in the capital, including Colonel G. A. Groussard, who immediately demanded to be relieved of his duties. He fell into line, however, after being told by General Henri Dentz, the commander of the Paris military region, that he could be shot for desertion if he did not carry out his orders. Even so, Groussard later wrote: 'I have never felt so humiliated and full of anger. The military should fight not to hand itself over. I sincerely believe that I would have given my life to save myself from having to obey these orders.'[24]

Churchill returned to France for another session of the Supreme War Council on 13 June. He travelled to Hendon airport with his defence secretariat, Colonel Leslie Hollis, who later recalled: 'I remember the morning well. It was a warm day with the sun shining. I marvelled at the calmness and serenity everywhere, and then realized with a shock that hardly anyone in the crowds of people out in the sunshine – the clerks, the typists in their summer frocks, the shoppers – realized what fearful danger faced Britain.'[25] As bad weather was forecast later in the day, Churchill was advised not to fly when he reached Hendon, where he was met by other members of the British delegation, but he ignored the suggestion with a 'To hell with that … ' and boarded the aircraft – which raised the eyebrows of some in the party. The two aircraft landed in thunderstorms and heavy rain and then taxied between bomb craters made during a raid the previous night. There was nobody at the airfield to meet them, but Churchill personally managed to secure a car from two French airmen, and headed to Tours.

It was another upsetting day for the British prime minister who, by the end of it, was convinced that 'the possibility of France remaining in the war had almost disappeared'.[26] At the meeting he was told by Reynaud that the High Command believed that it was too late for the Breton Redoubt idea to work and that Weygand believed that France's military was a spent force. Churchill's tone, full of encouragement and conciliation at the previous meeting in Briare, became stern. He made a point of saying that he would hold the French to an agreement which had been made in March and forbade either side to engage in unilateral armistice negotiations, and that the French government should immediately appeal to Washington to establish whether the United States would enter the war on the Allied side. Churchill's apprehensions were somewhat alleviated, however, by his impression that, despite the High Command's nihilism, Reynaud was not ready to enter into armistice negotiations until he had exhausted all other options. The British prime minister was nonetheless aware that those other options were on the verge of being exhausted. As it was, at a cabinet meeting held after the British delegation had left, Reynaud found that only six out of twenty-seven colleagues agreed with Pétain and Weygand that France should seek an early armistice agreement and so, bolstered by this fact, he made his approach to Washington. He did so knowing that if the Americans rejected his entreaties, Paris fell and the Germans continued to exploit their advantage, Pétain and Weygand would win over a majority of the cabinet. As if to underline the urgency of the situation, the government vacated Tours and headed further south to the Atlantic coastal town of Bordeaux. Here Reynaud would wait for President Roosevelt's response and the cabinet would continue to discuss the nation's rapidly diminishing options.

Although the majority of France was as yet physically untouched by the German invasion and those living in the rural south and west would have felt quite removed from the war, it should be remembered that French troops were drawn from all corners of the nation – the French colonies too – and that the outcome of the conflict would affect everyone living under the Tricolour, whether in metropolitan France or elsewhere. In such circumstances, what was best for France was immensely complicated, but while Reynaud was sympathetic to the need to embrace attempts to defeat Nazism over several years with the government decamping to North Africa, the influential Pétain opined: 'I personally refuse to leave French soil: I will stay among the French people and share its pains and its miseries.'[27] The old soldier, whose mind had been made up around the time of Dunkirk, had consistently argued that French suffering should be ended as soon as possible by reaching terms with the Germans. In Paris, on their journey to Tours and then as they moved to Bordeaux, Pétain and his colleagues would have seen the refugees struggling along the roads or clamouring for space on trains, and would have heard the stories of them being machine-gunned by the Luftwaffe. The politicians were not left unaffected by the experience nor by the reports that they were reading about the unsettling effect of events from Normandy to the Côte d'Azur.

Georgette Guillot, a secretary in the ministry of the interior, noted the 'terrible spectacle of anxious faces, nervously apprehensive about what future calamities they may face'.[28] After leaving a roof and hearth far behind them, the refugees that Guillot observed had found hunger, thirst and uncertainty but precious little safety and many began to regret their decision to flee. One Parisian, Julianne Deros, who was sixteen years old in 1940, later recalled:

> On hearing that the city would not be destroyed, my mother began to cry. I asked her why and she said, 'I have made a terrible mistake.' With my only pair of shoes long since disintegrated with all the walking we had done, an empty stomach and many more miles to some other place to be covered, I felt inclined to agree. But we were very frightened living in the middle of Paris, very frightened. The road was a hard place to be, but at least we were doing something. I just wish I had understood that at the time, and told my poor mother.[29]

The Deros family had been machine-gunned on the road out of Chartres, having walked nearly sixty miles in four days. It was 'a brief affair that left no casualties'[30] according to Julianne, but the fear that it engendered in those stuck on the roads or in railway carriages without protection was hugely disturbing. Indeed, in their continued attempt to cause congestion and undermine the Allied armies' ability to move while causing panic among the population, the Germans bombed and strafed anything that moved. Metal worker Georges Adrey wrote that, even as he left Paris, he and those with him were on several occasions obliged to 'lie flat on our stomachs in the ditch or on the grass or even hide in the woods in order to escape death'.[31] Parents would throw themselves on their children to protect them, screaming at the aircraft as they swooped down on the hapless refugees. Those in vehicles often struggled to extract themselves in time. André Morize later recalled:

> I saw and touched the lacerated cars. I saw blood on the cushions of the seats … I saw a ten-year-old boy whose shoulder was fractured by a bullet. I saw a woman who hardly knew how to drive at the wheel of an old Renault taking her three children away with her because her husband was killed on the road in the Pas-de-Calais.[32]

The Luftwaffe's murderous marauding gave many refugees the impression that their quest for safety was futile. To make matters worse, large numbers were overtaken by German ground units, and even those that made it to the Loire Valley – which many believed to be far enough from the front to keep them out of harm's way – found the 'Boche' on their heels and aircraft bombing the bridges over the river to hamper the army's withdrawal.[33]

During the afternoon of 13 June, Paris lay quiet, its streets largely deserted, an anxious city awaiting its fate. Four million people had left the city, 80 per cent of its population. The last trains had departed, the last troops had withdrawn. Journalist and soldier Georges Sadoul wrote in his diary on that day after he had participated in the army's extraction from the capital: 'The Eiffel Tower passes by my left shoulder little by little … We are abandoning Paris, where, from the Eiffel Tower, tomorrow the swastika will fly.'[34] Parisians stayed at home, since factories, shops and offices were shut. There was no information, but the sound of gunfire could be heard in the far distance, which made the city's inhabitants wonder whether the invader, who they had grown up learning was untrustworthy, would honour the open status of Paris or endeavour to subjugate the population by terror and destruction.

Von Bock had ensured that his commanders were in no doubt about what was to be done and wrote:

> The most vital parts of Paris are to be occupied by just one division at first. I called special attention to the rigorous sealing off and monitoring of through roads, so that no man lags behind in Paris and the march through the city results in no delaying of the general movement ... Now even those 'up above' are thinking of turning south-west.[35]

As it happened, the troops of 87th Infantry Division merely walked into the city and occupied it without fuss or ceremony on 14 June. Lieutenant Colonel Dr Hans Speidel took the surrender of the French capital. Ralf Buckholtz, a nineteen-year-old Schütze whose father had died from wounds received at Verdun before he was born, recalled:

> I was barely trained and fresh into uniform and yet here I was, craning my neck at the famous buildings I had only dreamed of seeing. I had never left Cologne before September 1939 and here I was, in Paris, making history ... I felt emotional knowing how proud my mother would be had she known where I was that day.[36]

Von Bock himself arrived in Paris to review troops marching past the Arc de Triomphe, and it must have been a proud moment indeed for the fifty-nine-year-old general. 'Afterward,' he wrote, 'I then drove to see Napoleon's tomb in the Invalides Church, then had a very good breakfast at the Ritz.' He found the city quiet and numbed by the experience, noting: 'Paris is rather empty; apparently only the poorer elements of the population stayed there. They stand around curiously by the roads leading into the city and voluntarily provide information when asked. The reception from and behaviour of the police is also courteous.'[37] Meanwhile, Halder recognized that the taking of Paris was a turning point in the campaign, calling it 'A great day in the history of the German army'.[38] With the arrival of the enemy, the city of lights drifted into darkness.

The fall of Paris was a significant step towards German victory. Although the city had ceased to be of any great military significance, its occupation – as the Germans had intended – was a deep wound to French pride, morale and fighting spirit. It was now left for the army to apply the *coup de grâce* by occupying great swathes of territory, encircling the remaining troops heading to the Loire and out of the Maginot Line, forestalling evacuations and forcing the capitulation of as many French formations as possible. One last effort was required by the Wehrmacht to remove the final vestiges of the enemy's military capability and in so doing leave the French without any room for negotiation when Reynaud finally requested armistice talks.

The final flush of military activity across France therefore saw the mobile German formations drive hard and deep into the interior. By 14 June, von Kleist's panzers were across the Seine south-east of Paris and plunging south with their right heading towards the Loire south of Nevers and their left to Dijon. Five days later, they were at Vichy west of the Loire and Lyon on the Rhône. Hoth's Corps, meanwhile, swept westwards with 7th Panzer Division advancing towards Cherbourg on the Normandy coast and 5th

Panzer Division moving towards ports on the Brittany coast, while Manstein's corps pushed down to the Loire to complete the encirclement. Resistance occurred in a few pockets but was quickly overcome and had little or no bearing on the forward momentum of the German divisions. Rommel's 150-mile advance from the Seine to the Cotentin peninsula was achieved in a single day. As a driver of one of 7th Panzer Division's PzKpfw Mk IIIs commented about his advance: 'The only real constraints on our advance were the wear and tear on our vehicles. The mobile workshops were kept extremely busy, but the weather was good and we knew that the end of the campaign was in sight. I personally felt that we had just won the war.'[39]

Hoth's aim was to stop more Allied troops leaving French shores for England. Alan Brooke had been unwillingly ordered back to England by CIGS during the Battle of Dunkirk, as he noted in his diary, 'to form a new BEF!'[40] and returned through Cherbourg on 12 June to command it from Brittany. This 'second BEF' consisted of those troops that had not been evacuated and included part of 1st Armoured Division, an ad hoc collection of BEF units known as Beauman Division, 150,000 line of communication troops together with the newly arrived 52nd (Lowland) and 1st Canadian Divisions. On Brooke's arrival, however, he was told that the French had rejected the idea of a Breton Redoubt and, recognizing the hopelessness of the Allied situation, he asked for Churchill's permission to evacuate the force. The prime minister responded by reminding the general that he been sent back to France to make the French feel that Britain was supporting them, but as Brooke later wrote, 'I replied that it was impossible to make a corpse feel.'[41] In the end, the prime minister conceded that the needless sacrifice of Brooke's force ran contrary to all logic considering the threat that Germany would soon pose to Britain, and so evacuation commenced on 15 June – Operation Ariel – and took place from increasingly southerly ports as the Germans drew forward. Embarkations from Cherbourg were completed on the afternoon of 18 June, just as Rommel's men began to enter the city and 5th Panzer Division reached Brest. Thousands were also evacuated from the Brittany port of St. Malo and the Atlantic coast ports. At St. Nazaire, the sinking of the liner RMS *Lancastria* in a Luftwaffe raid led to the loss of around 4,000 lives, nearly twice the number of BEF troops killed in the campaign to that date and the largest loss of life in British maritime history. Further evacuations took place at La Pallice, Bordeaux, Le Verdon, Bayonne and St. Jean de Luz and only ended on 25 June. When all Allied troops evacuated during this period are taken into account – British, Canadian, French, Polish, Czech and Belgian – the total number was nearly 192,000 men, over 300 guns, 2,300 vehicles and a paltry twenty-four tanks.[42]

Two panzer divisions were never likely to have much of an impact on the broadly based Operation Ariel, but when combined with the failure to prevent the earlier evacuations during Operation Dynamo, their inability to disrupt Allied arrangements had longer-term strategic implications. These, though, were lost in the dust and euphoria of Germany's budding triumph. More emphasis was placed by OKW on the encirclement of General Gaston Prételat's second-rate Second Army Group formations still holding the Maginot Line. There had been a limited German attack against the French fortress at Le Ferté in the Maginot Line extension twelve miles south-east of Sedan by Army Group A on 16 May. Its success not only opened a route round the main Maginot positions, but also protected von Rundstedt's flank as his divisions surged towards the Channel coast.[43] Yet the Germans were mindful that Le Ferté had only fallen after three days' hard fighting which revealed that Prételat's forces could well prove difficult to dislodge from their strong, well-protected forts. Yet as General Wilhelm von Leeb's Army Group C prepared itself for a major attack against the Maginot Line, its senior commanders drew confidence from the fact that French formations seemed to be leaving their positions. Indeed, of the fifty infantry divisions that had supported Prételat's static defences a month earlier, the requirements of the Weygand Line meant that just seventeen now remained. These same officers were further encouraged by the intelligence gleaned from a captured messenger that the French High Command, recognizing that Guderian's thrust had left those manning the Maginot defences increasingly isolated and vulnerable, had on 12 June ordered Prételat to withdraw them. The first troops that pulled back during the night of 13–14 June were the Second Army Group's immobile infantry and artillery formations which had been tasked with supporting the main defensive positions. The plan demanded that the fort garrisons would be the last Maginot Line troops to leave, and that their withdrawal would take place on 18 June.[44]

Von Leeb's offensive, its start date advanced in order to take advantage of the turmoil caused by Prételat's withdrawal and the increasing speed of Guderian's advance, was to concentrate its attack against the Maginot Line in two areas. In the Lorraine, Operation Tiger required First Army to attack the Sarre Gap – a thirty-one-mile sector with lesser defences due to its proximity to the Saarland, which was in French hands during the construction of the defences. This area had first been attacked by the Germans between 12 and 15 May to divert French attention away from the Ardennes and during this time they had gathered valuable information which a month later was to shape First Army's plan. The second attack would take place simultaneously in the Alsace sector; it would see Seventh Army launch Operation Kleiner Bär and required its divisions to cross the Upper Rhine before grappling with the French defences. Even so, von Leeb was confident that in the circumstances the offensive spirit of his troops would overcome an isolated and apprehensive enemy and looked forward to the creation of two pincers which would snap shut behind the French as Guderian's Panzer Group raced south to the Swiss border to seal the region from the French interior.

Guderian's advance had, in fact, picked up considerable momentum since its initial breakthrough and his troops were soon dashing through the Champagne region. Little resistance was encountered during this period, as the commander of an armoured reconnaissance unit, Leutnant Wolf-Max Ostwald, noted: 'There is no sign of life anywhere; the Frenchies have decamped en masse once again. Fine, we'll just go on keeping them moving!'[45] During this stage of the offensive, despite having access only to poorly copied 1:300,000 scale maps, Guderian's leading formations were advancing sixty miles a day and jostling each other for the limited road space. Ostwald wrote:

> ... Sweat is running down the faces of the wireless operators. The dispatch riders, roaring along to find the commander, the fluttering report pads in their mouths making them look like hunting hounds, are hardly recognizable with their swollen eyes in faces furrowed by dust, heat and sweat beneath the dust-white helmets.[46]

Indeed, such was the speed at which the Germans were moving south across the front that Helmuth Mahlke, the Stuka pilot who was now flying in support of von Kleist's drive, said that he nearly bombed German troops at Châtillon-sur-Seine, where a pocket of resistance was being mopped up. He later wrote: 'I was already committed to the dive when I saw German troops feverishly laying out air recognition panels and German flags on the edge of the town.'[47] Mahlke just managed to pull out in time and flew over Châtillon to see that German troops had already occupied the town and were waving up at the dive-bombers in relief.

With German formations rolling forward towards central France as energetically as their lines of communication would allow, von Leeb began his offensive against the Maginot Line. Although a supporting manoeuvre by Army Group A divisions around the end of the Maginot Line at Longuyon quickly began to outflank the French defences, the seven-division-strong Operation Tiger was rebuffed on 14 June. Yet although the strong resistance offered by the defenders on the first day stalled the Germans' attack, on the second von Leeb's divisions exploited the diminishing strength of the French defences between the fortifications caused by Prételat's withdrawal order and made vital penetrations which led to the encirclement of French strongpoints. Even so, despite the advance and concentrated artillery bombardments, the much anticipated collapse did not occur and the forts continued to fight back.

Eventually, the static French defences could not stop the German outflanking formations from making progress and on 16 June two Operation Tiger divisions, which had worked their way behind the Maginot Line heading west, managed to link up with formations from Army Group A coming in the other direction. In Operation Kleiner Bär, however, Seventh Army could not benefit from any such outflanking manoeuvre and was further disadvantaged by having to cross the Rhine. This, together with the dispersed nature of the attack and some resilient French defence, which included dogged resistance by the Marckolsheim casemate, meant that by nightfall on 15 June the Germans held only a shallow bridgehead. Even so, they persisted and, having constructed two pontoon bridges over the river and narrowed their attacking front to increase their concentration, managed to crack the sector open on the next day with the support of Stuka raids and the power of some 88mm guns. As Dominic Royer, a young engineer in the defending 42nd Fortress Infantry Regiment, later confided:

> There is only so much pressure any one position can take ... By 16 June we were finding it impossible to stop the infiltration of German units between our positions and we were isolated by incessant bombing raids and heavy bombardment. My blockhouse was about [1.5 miles] from the river and our

communications had been cut with neighbouring units and
battalion. Then we ran out of ammunition. We surrendered
when a German grenade was pushed through an embrasure
– but we only capitulated when there was no other option.
That was important to us.[48]

As the fighting in Alsace and Lorraine began to gain some
momentum, on 17 June Guderian's 29th Motorized Division
reached the Swiss frontier in an advance so swift that OKW failed
initially to believe a signal informing it of this success. It was a
critical event in the later phase of the campaign for in reaching
the border the Germans had once again blocked their enemy's
escape route and this time they had trapped half a million French
troops. That evening, the division was ordered to turn north-east
and advance forty miles to take the fortress town of Épinal.

Épinal is situated on the Moselle forty-two miles west of Colmar
and sixty miles south of Metz, and since German intelligence
had identified French troops withdrawing to the town, Guderian
sought to seize it before the area became a rallying point for a last
stand. 6th Panzer Division's Pursuit Detachment von Esebeck was
given a similar role to the one that it had enjoyed on the west bank
of the Meuse and sped to Épinal in order to catch its defenders by
surprise. The town capitulated quickly, but the fortress held out
despite the pounding it took from the German guns. In the end,
a team from 65th Panzer Battalion was sent to parley with the
enemy, but it was only when the fortress's commander recognized
the hopelessness of the strategic situation and was reassured by the
German contingent that honour had been served that the garrison
lay down their weapons on 22 June.

The bravery shown by the French troops at Épinal was mirrored
in a host of forts along the Maginot Line – the last hurrah of the
French Army protected by the concrete in which they had placed
so much faith. Fort Fermont's 500-man garrison at the end of
the line in Lorraine, for example, stood firm despite a series of

attacks. First the Germans cut the fort's electricity supply as they encircled their objective, which forced its occupants to rely on a diesel generator for power while the position was smashed by heavy artillery, then Stukas and finally 88mm guns which fixed on a single point in the gun casemate before firing a shell at it every three minutes for several hours. When the generator caught fire and belched out toxic fumes which engulfed the interior and lingered because the bombardment had blocked the ventilation system, the fort's commander, Captain Aubert, ordered his men to fight on in their respirators. The conflagration was gradually brought under control, only for the French to find that the Germans had succeeded in piercing the gun casemate. Just one more round fired at this juncture might well have entered and exploded in the French magazine, but the 88mm guns instead stopped firing because their teams were unaware of their success. That night – 17/18 June – the French manoeuvred steel and iron sections into the breach and poured concrete over them to make a seal to deceive the enemy. The ruse worked, for the next German assault did not take place until 21 June and came in the form of a regiment of 183rd Division. It was resolutely rebuffed, however, and cost the formation so many casualties that its corps commander decided to cancel all further attacks on this section of the Maginot Line.

Meanwhile, at the 'elbow' of the Line, in between the two main operations, a lesser German advance sought to penetrate the Fortified Sector of Haguenau and encircle several forts including that at Schoenenbourg. According to Colonel Pierre Stroh, the Commander of Engineers at the fort, on the day that von Leeb began his attack on the Maginot Line on 14 June, Schoenenbourg was visited by the sector commander, the impressively moustachioed Lieutenant Colonel Schwartz.[49] A Great War veteran who had been wounded in action and relied on a stick to walk, Schwartz toured the fort, partly to give encouragement to the garrison by his presence and partly to check on its fighting spirit. He need not have worried for during a brief 'Council of War' held with the fort's officers it became clear that they were not interested in withdrawing at any time and in keeping with the role, traditions and honour of the fortress infantry, wanted to fight to the last man. When, therefore, the fort came under direct attack five days later by a massive bombardment from the artillery and then from the air – an attack which eventually cracked the walls of the fort just as the garrison heard word of Pétain's peace overtures to the Germans – the position continued to fight and was eventually hit by approximately 3,000 shells and 160 bombs.[50] Reflecting on these events after the war, Stroh wrote:

> [W]e had a universally high level of esprit to prevail over our attackers ... The six thousand men of the Fortified Sector of Haguenau tied up two German divisions with a strength five or six times greater than their own, supported by a squadron of dive-bombers, and by the largest artillery of the Wehrmacht. These means of attack gave Schoenenbourg the sad privilege of becoming the most heavily bombarded fort on the Maginot Line.[51]

The tenacity of the French troops in the Maginot Line was revealed in the fact that most forts held out until the cessation of hostilities and, along with several others, Schoenenbourg continued to do so for a week beyond that. In the end, just ten out of the fifty-eight fortresses fell in German assaults.[52] Indeed, it is entirely possible that had Prételat's troops not undertaken a withdrawal, Second Army Group could have beaten off von Leeb's offensive on the Maginot Line. It is very unlikely, however, that any such event would have dramatically altered the strategic landscape for on 19 June, the day that Metz fell, Halder wrote triumphantly:

> The German flag is flying from the cathedral of Strasbourg. Toul is in our hands. Belfort was taken yesterday. On

the Channel coast we have reached Cherbourg. Almost everywhere the front of our armies has reached the Loire and in some places even crossed it.[53]

The successes of the German forces as they poured irresistibly south and west was set against the tragic backdrop of the Third Republic in its death throes. In a Bordeaux crammed with refugees, staff officers from the services mixed with a mass of civil servants as the government tried once more to co-ordinate its activities and make some difficult choices. Clustered around the centre of the town, ministers again found communications difficult and accommodation cramped while parliament was reduced to 100 members and had to meet on the benches of a school classroom. Here the nation's representatives wanted answers to two questions: Was France going to seek an armistice and who was responsible for the catastrophe? Although the subject of blame was natural in the circumstances, such debate would have to wait because a decision needed to be taken about the opening of negotiations with Germany and, as a consequence, how to handle the British. A cabinet meeting on 15 June was torrid. Half of its members believed that the war should be continued from abroad and the remainder that an armistice should be sought. Discussion centred on the prerequisites of any prolonging of the war. Prime among these was the ability of Britain to hold out against Germany, which, it was thought, depended on the United States joining the war effort. It was agreed, however, that the practical difficulties posed by the government and remnants of the armed forces decamping to North Africa would be immense and that their departure was hardly likely to garner the support of a population that might suffer the bombing of its towns and cities as the enemy rolled towards southern France. Even so, it was agreed that the positions of the United States and Britain had to be confirmed before a decision could be made. Indeed, Reynaud continued to hang on to a slim hope that a positive message from Washington and a hard line by the British would be enough to ensure that France would continue to fight.

The French prime minister was to be disappointed. The next day – 16 June – the United States officially refused to intervene in the war and the cabinet also voted against a bizarre proposal that France and Britain should join together to become a single nation in the face of the German Reich. This deal, brokered by de Gaulle in London, would have seen France and Britain develop 'joint organs of defence, foreign, financial and economic policies' while 'Every citizen of France will enjoy immediately citizenship of Great Britain, every British subject will become a citizen of France'.[54] Most cabinet ministers – who had met four times over the previous twenty-four hours and were now impatient – thought the idea smacked of desperation and could not suppress their belief that it would lead to Britain taking French colonies while reducing France herself to dominion status. Alexander Werth saw Weygand at this time and wrote: 'He looked extraordinarily unperturbed – almost pleased with himself … Paul Reynaud looked badly harassed.'[55]

Reynaud's last hopes of continuing the war hung on the Declaration of Union and so, when the idea failed to gain support, he resigned as prime minister in the belief that the cabinet wished for an armistice. His assumption was incorrect – nine were for an armistice and fourteen against – for he had misinterpreted the desires of those who wanted to propose what were in reality impossible armistice terms to the Germans and favoured fighting on until this could be achieved. Nevertheless, Reynaud recommended that Pétain should be appointed as prime minister. The diminutive, wheezing, skeletal figure, once the victor of Verdun but now devoid of fight and fit only for capitulation, readily agreed to take the appointment. He immediately established a new cabinet which included Weygand, who replaced de Gaulle as minister for national defence. A day or two earlier, Alan Brooke had met with Weygand and was unimpressed when the Frenchman had confided that he felt that the situation was a blot on what had been an otherwise unblemished service record. Brooke later wrote: 'I remained dumb and unable to make any adequate remark; it seemed impossible that the man destined to minister to France in her death agonies should be thinking of his military career.'[56]

Pétain also approached the Spanish government to act as an intermediary between the French and Germans with a view to opening negotiations about the cessation of hostilities between the two countries. In the meantime, Churchill, recognizing that trying to hold the French to their unilateral armistice agreement was futile in the circumstances, released Pétain from it, although he did so on the somewhat optimistic condition that the French navy sailed to British harbours. Watching events develop from Führerhauptquartier *Wolfsschlucht* at Brûly-de-Pesche in southern Belgium, an exultant Hitler slapped his thigh and even laughed on being told that Pétain had sued for peace. That evening, the German forces heard the momentous news and it led to instinctive celebrations. Oberleutnant Dr Hans Berenbrock, fighting with Kempf's 6th Panzer Division, later wrote: 'We stood and sang, sang the songs of our homeland.'[57]

As it was, the new French prime minister did not wait for a response from the Germans before announcing to the French people on 17 June that, despite the 'magnificent resistance'[58] offered by the military, such was the suffering of the country that his aim was to bring the fighting to an end. It was a speech that sought to reassure the French people and its armed forces, but it also caused confusion. Although Pétain was making the case for an armistice request, the population was unsure what he meant: was he saying that France had lost the war and that the military would lay down their arms, or was he informing them that France had requested a ceasefire in order to enter negotiations with a view to striking a political deal with Germany?

However it was interpreted, Pétain's broadcast stunned France. After decades of preparation and years of being told that 'France was strongest', the government seemed to be set on capitulation after just five weeks of fighting. 'It was unfathomable,' recalled Lieutenant Daniel Le Roy, who had escaped death by inches fighting south of Rethel when a shard of shell casing passed through his torso but missed his vital organs. Languishing in a German-occupied field hospital when he was told about Pétain's speech, Le Roy later said: 'I cried. I cried for me, I cried for my men and I cried for France. We had sacrificed so much and yet someone, somewhere had let us down.'[59] Julianne Deros, meanwhile, was approaching the Loire with her family at the time of the broadcast. She later recalled:

> We heard the news on a radio that had been brought out onto a small table in a village square … There were hundreds of people listening, all crammed into a tiny space, but there was complete silence for Pétain's words. It was not a long speech, but it was greeted with shock, not joy. For a few seconds after he had finished speaking, the silence continued – but then everybody erupted into animated conversation. Some sobbed while others wandered off to sit on the grass, lost in their own thoughts.[60]

For a number of Deros's fellow refugees, Pétain's words made the continuation of their uncomfortable and often terrifying quest for security unnecessary. Some immediately turned back north and headed for home, others sat on sun-scorched verges to weigh up their options, and a few continued their journey, saying that the way had not yet ended and that 'Safety meant south'. Indeed, the bombing and strafing of refugees on the roads did not stop and raids continued, even on towns and cities such as Le Mans, Rennes, Nantes, Tours and Bordeaux, despite the fact that conurbations of more than 20,000 inhabitants had been declared open cities. The military, meanwhile, were largely relieved that an armistice was being sought but continued to fight, although their spirit was broken and few felt moved to die for France at a time when, in the words of one soldier, 'the nation was in discussions about its own funeral'.[61] As a result, the Germans took huge numbers of prisoners from 17 June onwards while French officers tried to maintain control of their men and implored them to 'stand firm, do their duty, remain honourable and await events'.[62]

There were, though, numerous valiant stands made by disparate troops as the Germans sought to cross the Loire. Some of these actions lasted hours, but one led by Colonel Daniel Michon, the commandant of the Cavalry School at Saumur, in the defence of a cluster of bridges around Saumur and Gennes was particularly noteworthy. In a briefing to his 780 cadets and their instructors, Michon sought to motivate them despite the pitiful situation and said, 'Gentlemen, for the school it is a mission of sacrifice. France is depending on you.'[63] Not all were convinced but, reinforced by some mixed units of withdrawing troops, a few hundred Algerian Regiment trainees and a handful of tanks, Michon's men took up defensive positions ready to fight for their lives. They first came under fire at midnight on 18 June from the advance guard of General Kurt Feldt's 1st Cavalry Division, and after unsuccessful attempts to obtain a French surrender through parley, the Germans attempted a breakthrough. Their artillery had already ascertained that the bridges had been destroyed and so Feldt's men were forced into an assault river crossing in small boats, only to be repelled on 19 June and then again on the following day. In such circumstances, 1st Cavalry Division was forced to rely on other formations on their flanks making crossings of the Loire to encircle the defenders, but even then Michon's men continued to fight until they were overrun. This stoicism cost the French nearly 130 casualties and the Germans almost double that number.[64]

Across the Channel, de Gaulle was frantic about the way in which France seemed to be haemorrhaging its spirit and will and slipping into oblivion. He had made his base in London since he feared being arrested as a strong advocate for France's continued participation in the war against Germany without the government's approval. Churchill had been impressed with the young officer, recently promoted to general, since their first meeting, and on 18 June provided him with a platform at the BBC from which to broadcast a message to the French people. Although few in France would hear his words, a passionate de Gaulle said:

> The leaders who, for many years, have been at the head of the French armies have formed a government. This government, alleging the defeat of our armies, has made contact with the enemy in order to stop the fighting. It is true, we were, we are, overwhelmed by the mechanical, ground and air forces of the enemy ... It was the tanks, the aeroplanes, the tactics of the Germans that surprised our leaders to the point of bringing them to where they are today. But has the last word been said? Must hope disappear? Is defeat final? No! Believe me, I speak to you with full knowledge of the facts, and tell you that nothing is lost for France. The same means that overcame us can bring us victory one day. For France is not alone! She is not alone! She is not alone! She has a vast Empire behind her. She can align with the British Empire that holds the sea and continues the fight. She can, like England, use without limit the immense industry of the United States ... Whatever happens, the flame of the French resistance must not be extinguished and will not be extinguished.[65]

It was an announcement which argued that, although Pétain was prime minister and his government retained sovereign power, their decisions did not represent the best course of action for France and there was indeed another way. De Gaulle's words were transcribed and re-broadcast several times in the days that followed, as well as being published in the press. The general's aim was undoubtedly to encourage and give some form to what he believed to be the latent French desire to resist the Germans, and his broadcast was also designed to bolster British hopes in the face of a German menace that was now prowling just twenty-two miles from Dover. But although his broadcast may well have given his host country an indirect boost, there was no doubting that, despite its desolate courage, de Gaulle's rallying cry hardly registered in a defeated France that seemed to accept its fate with a sense of angry relief.

Meanwhile, Pétain waited for a response from Germany. As he did so, the enemy overran more departments, took more prisoners and pushed harder on the nation's windpipe. Although a contingent of largely Jewish deputies and ex-ministers left for North Africa, the prime minister refused to authorize parliament and the government to leave France. Along with Pétain, the nation's political leaders would face the Germans and share the consequences of any armistice with the French people. The Führer, meanwhile, was enjoying France's excruciating predicament and orchestrated the armistice negotiations with a heavy nod to history. The timing of the talks allowed for the Wehrmacht to reach the end of their lines of communications, but not for France to recover its poise.

The site that Hitler chose to meet the French armistice negotiation delegation was the Forest of Compiègne in Picardy, just forty miles north of Paris. It was here, in Napoleon III's railway carriage, that in November 1918 the Germans had signed the armistice agreement that led to the end of the First World War. In the 1920s, the place had become a memorial to the French fallen of the conflict which, in the great tradition of Franco-German enmity, embraced the concepts of victory and revenge. Now, in June 1940, the woods would once again host armistice talks and the old railway carriage would be retrieved from a museum and placed exactly where it had stood a generation before.

The terms that were to be offered by the Germans had been carefully drafted to ensure that, although leaving the French in no two minds about the nature of their defeat, they were not overtly humiliating. Hitler was already thinking about his next step in Europe and did not want to encourage any French desire to reject the package and continue the fight from overseas. As a result, the terms did not refer to the annexation of large areas of territory, colonies were not to be seized and the French fleet was merely to be disarmed. France was to be divided into two parts: the occupied north, which included a corridor down to the Spanish border and gave Germany access to all Channel and Atlantic ports, and the south, which comprised three fifths of the country and would become a *Zone Libre* (Free Zone) that retained a government to administer all of metropolitan France except Alsace-Lorraine, which was to be placed under German administration but not formally annexed.

It was at this point that Italy launched an offensive after the opportunistic Italian prime minister Benito Mussolini had declared war on France and Britain on 10 June. Mussolini had told his Army Chief of Staff, Marshal Pietro Badoglio, that he needed several thousand dead Italian troops to strengthen his hand with the Germans in peace negotiations and also remarked to General Rodolfo Graziani, the Commander-in-Chief of the General Staff, that 'It would be a grave blow to our prestige to receive territory from the hands of our ally without having occupied it.'[66] While the obsequious Graziani said that 'the morale of the troops was of the highest' and they 'yearned' to cross the French border,[67] senior officers were relying more on a French collapse than the preparedness of their 450,000 troops for a successful attack in difficult conditions against strong pre-prepared defences through complicated terrain and along routes known to be protected by fortresses and other obstacles. But General René Olry, the commander of the 190,000-strong French Army of the Alps, was in no mood to give ground to either the Germans advancing to his rear along the Rhône Valley to Grenoble and Chambéry to assist Mussolini's attack or to the Italians facing him: he would fight to the last man.

The pitiful attack launched by the Italians on the Alpine front by their Army Group West had one thrust in the north near the Swiss border conducted by Fourth Army, but its main effort was carried out by First Army along the Mediterranean coast to capture Marseilles. At 0300 hours on 21 June, both Italian Armies crossed the French border but immediately found that their ability to manoeuvre was extremely limited and so their momentum was severely compromised in ground that one German officer called 'perhaps the most unsuitable of all conceivable theatres of operation.'[68] In one sector of General Alfredo Guzzoni's Fourth Army attack, the Italian Alpine Corps advanced on a twenty-five-mile front with the aim of taking Albertville, which was itself twenty-five miles into French territory. They advanced a mere five miles before the offensive ground to a halt. In another sector, First Corps struggled on a similar frontage but, despite enjoying local success in outflanking some French positions, the attack was stopped just ten miles from the border. To the south, the main effort by First Army fared even worse and failed even to get as far as the French main line of resistance and only managed penetrations of one mile or two along the coast itself.[69]

In the Alps, seven French divisions halted more than 30 Italian divisions while also temporarily stalling the Germans approaching from the rear along the Rhône Valley. The offensive enterprise cost Olry's Army around 500 men, over half of whom were prisoners, but cost the Italians around 900 casualties with another 616 missing in the snow, a further 2,151 suffering frostbite and some 1,100 taken prisoner.[70] Despite Mussolini's bravado in public, his alpine fiasco left the Italian prime minister humiliated in the face of Germany's military prowess for he had contributed precious little to the defeat of France and taken a trifling amount of enemy territory. On the evening of 24 June – the day Halder noted that Mussolini wanted to send several battalions by air to the vicinity of Lyon so they could negotiate for rights to occupied French territory, a move he described as '... the cheapest kind of fraud' – an armistice was signed in Rome by the Italians and the French.

In the meantime, Germany had signed a separate agreement. On 21 June Hitler had greeted the French delegation at the Compiègne armistice negotiations in silence and then sat in the same seat that had been occupied by Ferdinand Foch, the Allied generalissimo, in 1918 and listened – again in silence – to the preamble of the armistice terms. Upon its completion, Hitler and his entourage left the railway carriage to make the point that there was nothing to discuss, that French agreement was a foregone conclusion and that the German leader had already moved on to more important things. The head of the French delegation, General Huntziger, was left to discuss the terms with General Wilhelm Keitel, the chief of OKW. Von Brauchitsch watched proceedings carefully and returned from the historic event to brief Halder, who wrote that evening:

> The French ... had no warning that they would be handed the terms at the very site of the negotiations in 1918. They were apparently shaken by this arrangement and at first inclined to be sullen... [In the] negotiations, presided over by Keitel, there seems to have been a great deal of wrangling, and [von Brauchitsch] is worried that the French might not accept. I don't understand his apprehension. The French must accept and, with Pétain at the helm, will do so. Moreover, our terms are so moderate that sheer common sense ought to make them accept.[71]

The discussions lasted for just one day before, on the evening of 22 June, Huntziger, having failed to soften the terms, was given authority by the government in Bordeaux to sign the armistice document on its behalf. The agreement was to come into effect on 25 June 1940 at 0135 hours – the same day and time as the French armistice with the Italians would be scheduled to begin. On the announcement that the armistice had been signed, von Bock issued the following order to his armies:

The war with France is over!

In forty-four days the Army Group has overrun the Dutch and Belgian land fortifications, forced the armies of both states to surrender after a tough struggle, and in a bloody battle inflicted a destructive defeat on the Anglo-French armies hastening to the scene. Paris and the coasts of France are in our hands.

The number of prisoners taken on the army group's front has exceeded 1½ million men. The booty in tanks, guns and weapons of all kinds is huge.

Shoulder to shoulder with the Luftwaffe, we have won a victory whose beauty and scope is unsurpassed in history.

The young German Army has passed its severest test before the whole world, before history and before itself. The distress and disgrace that descended over our people after the World War has been blotted out by your loyalty and bravery!

The main burden of bloody sacrifice was borne by the German Army. We will bear it proudly and willingly in firm belief in ultimate and total victory! Long live the Führer.[72]

With the armistice signed, an historical disgrace extinguished and Germany reborn, Hitler ordered the Compiègne site to be destroyed.

Epilogue

O N 28 JUNE 1940, Hitler became a tourist in Paris. He had wished to visit the city ever since his youthful blossoming into an aesthete. He was an untalented artist, yet he had a great interest in architecture and later said that he would have liked to have become an architect. His early years had shaped his taste in art and design as much as his political and ideological preferences and they had barely developed since. The relationship between art and power was not lost on him for, as Robert Hughes argues, 'Architecture is the only art that moulds the world directly. Of all the arts, it is the supreme expression of politics and ideology. It marshals resources and organizes substance in a way that music, painting and literature cannot. It is an art that lives from power.'[1] Hitler had grand designs and saw architecture as a way of embodying and reflecting them. He sought to create buildings that would stand for endless generations as a physical manifestation of the indomitable strength and influence of the German Reich just as ancient buildings provided a touchstone for the empires of antiquity. 'His vision of the world he wanted to make to commemorate himself and his ideology,' Hughes says of Hitler, 'was complete, overwhelming and Pharaonic.'[2]

The Führer's entourage on his tour of Paris included his two favoured architects, the middle-aged, experienced and accomplished Hermann Giesler and the twenty-five-year-old Albert Speer, who, although having built nothing of note, was already trusted to give some shape to Hitler's more megalomanic architectural fantasies. Having just completed a sentimental tour of his old First World War battlefields, Hitler entered Paris in a convoy of three black Mercedes sedans with his mind as much on the future as the past. The city shimmered in the early morning sun, beguiling but still grieving. The first stop was at L'Opéra, the one place above all others that Hitler wished to visit since he had studied the building's plans. A deferential white-haired attendant accompanied the group and confirmed that Hitler's assertions about the building's renovations were correct. At the end of their visit, the Frenchman refused a fifty-mark tip. Minutes later, the party of field grey-clad sightseers drove past the neo-classical La Madeleine, a church whose modern incarnation was as a memorial to the successes of Napoleon's army and which had been built on ground initially seized from Parisian Jews in the twelfth century. The building pleased Hitler, who nodded his approval.

The next stop was at the Eiffel Tower, a photo opportunity for the Führer that was simply too good to miss, before a brief pause at the Tomb of the Unknown Soldier beneath the Arc de Triomphe and a longer one at Les Invalides. After cogitating in silence before the tomb of Napoleon, Hitler ordered the remains of Napoleon's son to be moved from Vienna to be placed by the side of his father. Shortly after, he also directed that two First World War monuments in Paris be destroyed: that erected in memory of General Charles Mangin, the leader of France's sizeable contingent of colonial troops, and included the images of four black soldiers, and the monument to the British nurse Edith Cavell, who had been executed by the Germans in 1915.

The group pressed on, visiting the Panthéon, which boasted a neoclassical façade that impressed Hitler but an interior that was 'a terrible disappointment'. The last stop was at the Sacré Coeur on Montmartre, the highest point in Paris. A working church with Romano-Byzantine features and nationalist themes, it had been built to remind the nation of the French defeat by Prussia in 1871 in the wake of a speech by Bishop Félix Fournier which had stated that its cause had been the moral decline of France. The construction of Sacré Coeur's basilica had been completed in 1914 as Germany gripped France and consecrated in 1919 as France gripped Germany. The building was not to Speer's taste, but Hitler took considerable interest in its motifs and stood for a while pointing at various parts of the edifice, recognized but ignored by local churchgoers. Before heading back to the airport, Hitler took one last look at Paris from his magnificent viewpoint and nodded in silent appreciation.

The tour had lasted barely three hours but had thrilled Hitler. That evening, he summoned Speer, one of those men of education and training who were necessary to fulfil his ambitions. His interview with the architect was short: 'Wasn't Paris beautiful? But Berlin must be made far more beautiful. In the past I often considered whether we would not have to destroy Paris, but when we are finished in Berlin, Paris will be only a shadow. So why should we destroy it?' Hitler had seriously considered razing to the ground what he saw as a prodigious symbol of German humiliation, but now it had been conquered, he no longer felt the need. By the end of 28 June, France was already a fading memory, the idea of a formal ceremony in Paris dismissed as irrelevant. 'I am not in the mood for a victory parade,' Hitler declared. 'We aren't at the end yet.'[3]

Conclusion

The Germans make everything difficult, both for themselves
and for everyone else.

Johann Wolfgang von Goethe[1]

WILSON: The Germans have reached Holland.

MAINWARING: Good lord! How on earth did they manage
to do that? I could've sworn that they'd never break
through the Maginot Line.

WILSON: Quite right, sir – they didn't.

MAINWARING: Ah-ha! I thought not. I'm a pretty good
judge of these matters, you know, Wilson.

WILSON: They went round the side.

MAINWARING: I see. (*He does a double take*) They *what*?

WILSON: They went round the side.

MAINWARING: That's a shabby Nazi trick! You see the sort
of people we're up against, Wilson?

WILSON: Most unreliable, sir.[2]

Dad's Army: The Movie, screenplay by Jimmy Perry & David Croft

The Fall of France and the Low Countries in 1940 is a staple on
military history courses in universities and military academies

around the world. Its size, scope, audacity and clinical outcome beg obvious questions, not least how it was possible for a powerful nation such as France to be defeated so quickly. It is an event that writers, commentators and historians have grappled with ever since, producing a wide range of conclusions. Yet among all the excellent and insightful work that has added a depth and richness to our understanding of the campaign, there are the inevitable, misleadingly simplistic offerings which have gained popularity precisely because they explain events in an easily digestible fashion. At their heart is the argument – one promulgated by Hitler and his cronies during the summer of 1940 in an effort to alarm enemies and promote the perception of German invincibility – that the victory over France and the Low Countries had come about through the application of a radically new and all-conquering fighting method based on an irresistible panzer army closely supported by the Luftwaffe. The truth, of course, is more complex – and considerably more interesting. As with many myths and over-simplifications, there is a kernel of truth in the idea that German armour and air power in the guise of something commonly known as *Blitzkrieg* steamrollered an inept enemy, but it needs to be put in its correct context with important corrections made and nuances identified.

German operational methods and the war-fighting machine that applied them were the product of careful and often secret work done to keep the armed forces healthy, despite their diminished size and capability, by a general staff that was not supposed to exist in the wake of the Versailles settlement. Through the years of trauma in the deep, dark shadow of the 1914–18 war and the humiliation of a defeat wrapped in a toxic peace treaty, the German state, its people and generals looked to a brighter future. The wish for revenge was an understandable, if unsavoury, reaction to events and circumstances. Its voracity also meant that for two decades before Hitler's offensive in the West, although the German people may not have *wanted* another war, they were sympathetic to the development of a military that might help lead the nation to what Germany was 'meant to be'.

By the early 1930s, the German armed forces were a small, well-trained, thinking elite. Although severely limited in its capabilities by a lack of physical and mechanical muscle, that elite's moral and conceptual requirements had been carefully nurtured by General Hans von Seeckt and his successors and made it ripe for expansion and employment by Hitler. Under the Nazis, the army developed strength while continuing to evolve its doctrine and looked to harness the potential of new technology and give old German army battlefield ambitions – encirclement and the battle of annihilation – the mobility, speed and co-ordination that could provide significant operational impact and, possibly, a decisive strategic result. Thus, along with the bulking out of the army with conscripts who were largely sent to the foot infantry divisions came the advance of a refined cutting edge in the shape of panzer divisions. In this way, Germany developed armed forces that could, given the correct circumstances, resources and planning, avoid an attritional war which Germany had neither the resources to win nor the inclination to fight.

By 1939, the French had been preparing for and were content to fight a total, defensive, attritional war. They could see no other way to defeat a German offensive; this was, after all, how they had emerged victorious from that terrible conflict twenty years earlier. While there was no public appetite for war, having lanced the German boil once but then failed to successfully treat the subsequent infection, the population would not hesitate in protecting French soil again. Its ability to do so was, nevertheless, shaped by a political, social and economic turbulence which was itself rooted in those same bloody and costly five years of fighting and had consequences that fragmented France. Although Germany remained a threat, albeit a muzzled one, to the country's eastern border, France had little desire to see a large, powerful and expensive military soak up valuable resources that were so desperately needed elsewhere. In any case, there was neither the strength of leadership nor the political stability to indulge in the sort of long-term thinking that was required for a bespoke, flexible military machine that perfectly fitted the country's strategic requirements. As a result, by the early 1930s France leant heavily on the construction of the Maginot Line, its preparations for total mobilization and a relatively small professional military cadre which was limited to defensive action to protect the nation's security. There were consequences, however, for this meant that France was rendered impotent in the face of the challenge posed by Germany from the mid-1930s onwards, and the subsequent collapse was the direct consequence of its military failure.[3]

After the Second World War, a French parliamentary committee which was investigating the French defeat in 1940 concluded that the army had 'retired to its Mount Sinai [after World War I] and sat among its revealed truths and remnants of past glories ... '.[4] Yet such words unhelpfully implicate the French army as an organization which actively sought to be manacled to a limited capability and revelled in the recent past, whereas the truth of the matter was that circumstances dictated that the politicians ushered the army into a trench where it all too readily settled and atrophied. With the Maginot Line in place and an alliance with Belgium, the French leadership felt confident that they had sufficiently limited Germany's attacking option to something that approximated a mechanized rerun of the 1914 Schlieffen Plan which could be stopped and drawn into positional warfare.

Had the Germans followed through with a broadly similar plan and in so doing given the initiative to the French and let them fight the type of campaign they wanted to fight and on ground dictated by Gamelin, they may very well have found success – and victory – exponentially more difficult to achieve than they did. Indeed, it was just such potentially terminal complications that senior German generals recognized but felt that Hitler might have overlooked in his desire to attack the West. Von Manstein's plan came, therefore, at a juncture when few were inspired by OKH's schemes for the invasion of France, although at the same time its radical character caused some of those generals to feel that it could lead to disaster. Halder, however, was quickly seduced by the possibility of placing concentrated German strength against known French weakness. OKH became convinced that it would make best use of the light mobile forces that Germany possessed and that there was far more value in avoiding the enemy than in deliberately initiating a clash with his best formations. Halder's ambition was to use surprise to start a sequence of events that would be psychologically damaging to the enemy's ability and will to resist, with breakthroughs aggressively and ruthlessly exploited by mobile troops to create operational success that could be converted into strategic victory. It was the antithesis of the French outlook and, as Allan Doughty has argued, 'German strategy was riskier than French strategy. Yet, it sought swift victory, while French strategy initially sought only to avoid defeat.'[5]

The plan that became *Fall Gelb* would not have been possible without the careful nurturing of the German armed forces before 1940 and that included the vital role of the general staff, who kept fighting traditions alive and allowed for them to be updated to make best use of new technology. The fact that this process had not been completed and the Wehrmacht and Luftwaffe were still flexible, allowed tactical doctrine, when added to that new technology, strong leadership, spirit and aggression to become the basis for a new operational fighting method. In this respect, and as the thinking which led to the formation of the mighty panzer groups bore fruit, the German military machine was not so much intentionally unleashing a doctrine of *Blitzkrieg* upon France and the Low Countries in 1940 as 'doing little more than following its own nose'.[6] It was a situation which both before and during the campaign understandably worried some conservative generals who were worried that German armed forces were not yet the finished article despite their success in Poland. This created a tension within the German High Command that was never fully resolved, although the proponents of the more radical aspects of the plan had faith that its speed and momentum would render detractors as helpless as they expected the enemy to be as the panzers raced across northern France.

This German improvisation was remarkable considering the scale of the military challenges posed not only by their enemies in the West, but also by the growing frictions within the High Command and the nation's unfinished preparations for war. Yet it was these very impediments that led directly to the inception of one of the most famous plans in military history and powered what was a barely formed fighting method because they forced the Germans to think and act radically if the episode was not to end in disaster. With Halder providing the foundation for success with his offensive scheme and officers such as Guderian, Rommel and Balck seeking to exploit the opportunity afforded to them with high-risk, high-gain actions on the ground, Army Group A in particular provided just the momentum and initiative that was required to pull the otherwise conservative German army and air force forward while befuddling its adversaries. The achievement of these same officers was nonetheless rooted in all the advantages provided by a thinking military that had a strong tradition and benefited from relevant training, a sound doctrine, robust leadership and a formidable fighting spirit. It was a virtuous circle. Eventual German success, of course, was not due to either the quality or quantity of their military hardware – and certainly not their armour – but where and how their resources were used.

Although it was understandable that potential enemy threats to the plan were aired and one has to sympathize with those who were startled by the audacity of what *Fall Gelb* sought to achieve and how it sought to achieve it, the plan was designed to uncover and then ruthlessly exploit French weaknesses. In the words of historian André Beaufre, 'The French Army was nothing more than a vast, inefficient tool, incapable of quick reaction or adaptation, quite incapable of taking the offensive or of any mobility.'[7] French strategic decision-making had so limited the armed forces' abilities to coping with a rerun of the Schlieffen Plan but not with anything else. As things stood, there was little wrong with French doctrine, which was well suited to the nation's strategy. Unfortunately, however, it was not so well suited to what the Germans had in mind.[8] For the war that the French expected, where they expected it and with the resources they had available, the Methodical Battle was a good fit. In the years following the First World War, the now small, poorly equipped and under-resourced French army did not need to look further than Verdun for inspiration about how it might fight a great defensive battle. Its conclusions were necessarily reflected in training, procurement, promotion and other preparations and they led to the creation of an army physically unprepared to cope with *Fall Gelb* and also ensured that its troops, leaders and commanders were psychologically and intellectually ill-equipped for anything other than the slow tempo of positional warfare.[9] In short, the High Command rejected the need for flexibility and diligently prepared the French armed forces for a type of warfare in which they were undoubtedly competent.[10] But the Germans had rather different ideas, and in this light charges of French incompetence need to be qualified. As Faris Kirkland has submitted, 'French military leaders were neither traitors, pacifists nor fools.'[11]

Halder's plan recognized French frailties and used manoeuvre as the means by which to expose them. Indeed, as von Manstein's biographer Mungo Melvin has written: 'The plan worked *because* it was so daringly unconventional, exploiting inherent systematic weaknesses in French force structures, command and control, and above all, in will and morale.'[12] But while it is easy to see the role played by the panzer corps in the success, one should not forget the vital role played by Army Group B pinning and fixing the

Allied Dyle force, the airborne forces' novel operations, the foot infantry divisions' disconcerting mass, the non-tactical endeavours of the Luftwaffe, and all the supporting troops and personnel that allowed operations to unfold as they did.

Far from being a mere panzer and Stuka victory, *Fall Gelb* was a sophisticated inter-service, all-arms team effort in which the infantry played a central role. With excellent communications enabling first-class co-ordination and the application of *Auftragstaktik*, the Germans could react quickly and effectively to most of the situations with which the spearhead divisions were confronted and could exploit fleeting opportunities quickly and without fuss. The great combined arms success of the Meuse crossing, the breaking of the French defences and the establishment of a bridgehead was also a triumph for German leadership and mission command with the likes of men such as Rubarth and Balck making vital contributions which had a significant operational impact. The Germans' methods, along with their ability to apply them consistently and professionally, constantly gave them the edge, enabled them to get inside the Allied decision-making loop, maintain tempo and retain the initiative. In such circumstances, the panzer divisions – sometimes enhanced by tactical air support – became irresistible and remained so as their excellent logistical support meant that there was no need for them to pause in order to be resupplied. Indeed, an after-action report for Group von Kleist stated: 'Between 10 May and the capture of Calais, there was not one single supply crisis that could not be resolved with the resources of the Group von Kleist, without in any way interfering with command functions.'[13] Although the ability to sustain independent operations of considerable distance was open to abuse – as exemplified by the actions of the ambitious and headstrong Rommel and Guderian – these same operations were also central to the campaign developing in a certain way and, although they exacerbated the worries of the more risk-averse naysayers who sought to slow the tempo down, they also revealed what could be achieved by the well-timed faits accomplis achieved by the panzer commanders. To the leaders in the spearhead formations, chaos was something to be created and embraced because it was so potent with possibilities, while to the French chaos was to be avoided at all costs because it was incompatible with their mindset and fighting methods.

The success that was eventually created by the panzer corps led to the largest encirclement in military history, one of 1.7 million men, and the capture of the best of the Allied forces and much of their equipment. But the fact that so many escaped south between the advancing panzer divisions and the following foot infantry and that this was then followed by the evacuation of 370,000 Allied troops from the Channel coast reveals that the operation was not unblemished nor unfettered by flaws and errors. Some of these had their basis in factors common to all complex human endeavours and included personality clashes, resource challenges and over-ambition. But others were specific to the German plan and included serious disagreements about independent panzer operations which led to echeloning issues, flank psychosis, Halt Orders and further encouraged OKW's smothering of OKH as some senior officers became extremely worried about those same vulnerable flanks, the gaps between panzers and foot infantry and undefended lines of communication. The inability of the Allies to exploit these frailties was indicative of their own wider capability issues and their failure to regain the initiative. As a result, the most senior French generals could not impose their will on events, partly because they remained fixated on the attack by Army Group B with its mesmeric air support and airborne operations as von Rundstedt got into position and then began to rip into Georges's formations. Despite the opportunity, there was no timely intervention by a significant Allied counter-attacking force either before or after the Meuse crossing, or against the Somme corridor or after the Germans had broken the Weygand Line.

Gamelin's fundamental role in the disaster can hardly be ignored. Although he was not personally responsible for French strategy and the limitations put on the military, he signally failed to challenge them and allowed politics to affect his military judgement. Balanced against this, however, it should be remembered that the head of the French army was a political appointment and that Gamelin had achieved his position because he would be a light hand at the tiller. The 'Grey General' was rather the product of a system that encouraged mediocrity and rejected the mavericks and free-thinkers who might have shaken France out of her self-enforced malaise. Like the Maginot Line and Methodical Battle, Gamelin and the wider High Command were the symptom of the French approach to defence and not the cause of it. As it was, the Supreme Commander's lack of grip, his presiding over a sluggish army, his faith in the Maginot Line, his decision not to sack Georges, his ill-advised Breda Variant to Plan D, the lack of an alternative to defensive operations along the Franco-Belgian border or central Belgium, and the failure to see the possibility of a threat emerging from the Ardennes, were all, to a large extent, the consequence of poor strategic choices.

It should also perhaps be remembered that while Gamelin is judged, quite understandably and correctly, by what the Germans did, it is difficult to think of anybody who could have avoided what befell France in the circumstances. To call Gamelin incompetent is fair only in the context of wider criticisms of French political and military leadership, and it is possible that had the Germans attacked with a rerun of the Schlieffen Plan, as they might have done, history and events may well have been kinder to a 'new Foch'. After all, the sort of French defensive capabilities which Gamelin had developed and overseen were on show in the Weygand Line.[14] Although it was Weygand who was responsible for the more appropriate and specific measures adopted in early June, their basis was fully Gamelin's and was far more in line with what he expected on the Dyle. As Martin Alexander has argued: 'Extending analysis of the fighting in 1940 beyond the usual preoccupations – the combats along the Meuse and around the Dunkirk perimeter – provides a more complex, richly textured canvas of France's military performance.'[15] It challenges the view that *Fall Rot* was a mere 'epilogue'[16] and that for the French the campaign was without 'even the smallest redeeming feature'.[17] Indeed, on the few occasions that the French were given the opportunity to fight as they had planned to, they often did so with great courage and tenacity. For the Allies, however, the defence of the Weygand Line was too brief, was not decisive and is merely instructive: it was too little, too late.

The ability of the Germans to achieve in some six weeks what they had failed to achieve in the four years and a few months of the First World War was reflected in their casualties, just 49,000 killed and missing and 111,000 wounded.[18] The character of the German campaign contrasted with an attritional grind which meant that even those formations charged with making the breakthrough took relatively light losses: Grossdeutschland Regiment, for example, suffered 221 men killed out of 3,900, 1st Panzer Division accumulated only 267 deaths, and 7th Panzer Division lost 682 men killed. The Luftwaffe, however, lost over a quarter of its operational strength, with around 1,284 aircraft destroyed and some 6,653 personnel killed or wounded. French casualties were around 85,000 dead, 120,000 wounded, 12,000 missing and another 1.54 million becoming prisoners of war. The French air force lost 1,274 aircraft destroyed. The British lost around 10,000 dead – including those killed in the *Lancastria* – with another 58,000 becoming casualties. The RAF lost 931 aircraft, of which 477 were valuable fighters. Belgian casualties were around 23,000 and Dutch 9,779.[19]

What had been achieved for such small cost was immediately apparent to Hitler, who by mid-June had taken the victory as his own and refused to share it with von Brauchitsch, Halder and OKH. During the summer of 1940, the German Supreme Commander explored what the operational methods that had been used by his armed forces to such acclaim in France and the Low Countries might achieve elsewhere and as he did so, those methods began to gain the standing of doctrine. It was a mistake, for the transplanting of *Blitzkrieg* elsewhere took little account of the achievability of objectives, proper resourcing, and the uniqueness of different enemies, terrains, weather and a host of other factors that affect the application of force. As Hew Strachan has written: 'Germany lost the Second World War in part because ... it made operational thought do duty for strategy, while tactical and operational success were never given the shape which strategy could have bestowed.'[20] Nevertheless, the German victory over France and her allies had a huge influence not just on the form and future conduct of the developing Second World War, but on warfare more generally. The way in which the Germans took some of the timeless principles of war-fighting and remodelled them so successfully in a modern context to achieve strategic results so efficiently, effectively and swiftly with such minimal losses has consistently caught the attention of politicians and the military since 1940. The influence of the German *Blitzkrieg* on doctrine and military thinking can still be seen around the world to this day: it changed warfare for ever.

Order of Battle (ORBAT) – Ground Forces (10 May 1940)

Germany
Chief of OKW – Generaloberst Wilhelm Keitel
Commander in Chief OKH – Generaloberst Walter von Brauchitsch
Chief of the General Staff – General der Artillerie Franz Halder

German Army Group A – Generaloberst Gerd von Rundstedt
Chief of Staff – Generalleutnant Georg von Sodenstern
Fourth Army – Generaloberst Günther von Kluge
II Corps – General der Infanterie Infantry Adolf Strauß
12th Infantry Division
32nd Infantry Division
V Corps – General der Infanterie Richard Ruoff
28th Infantry Division
251st Infantry Division
VIII Corps – General der Artillerie Walter Heitz
8th Infantry Division
XV (Motorized) Corps – General der Infanterie Hermann Hoth
5th Panzer Division
7th Panzer Division
62nd Infantry Division
Reserves
87th Infantry Division
211st Infantry Division
263rd Infantry Division
Twelfth Army – Generaloberst Wilhelm List
III Corps – General der Artillerie Curt Haase
3rd Infantry Division
23rd Infantry Division
VI Corps – General der Pioniere Otto-Wilhelm Förster

16th Infantry Division
24th Infantry Division
XVIII Corps – General der
Infanterie Eugen Beyer
5th Infantry Division
21st Infantry Division
25th Infantry Division
1st Mountain Division
Reserves
9th Infantry Division
27th Infantry Division
Sixteenth Army – General der
Infanterie Ernst Busch
VII Corps – General der Infanterie
Eugen von Schobert
36th Infantry Division
68th Infantry Division
XIII Corps – Generalleutnant Heinrich
von Vietinghoff
17th Infantry Division
34th Infantry Division
XXIII Corps – Generalleutnant Albrecht
Schubert
58th Infantry Division
76th Infantry Division
Reserves
6th Infantry Division
15th Infantry Division
26th Infantry Division
33rd Infantry Division
52nd Infantry Division
71st Infantry Division
73rd Infantry Division
197th Infantry Division
Panzer Group Kleist – General der
Kavallerie Paul Ludwig Ewald von
Kleist
Under direct command
Infantry Regiment (Motorized)
Grossdeutschland
XIV Corps – General der Infanterie
Gustav von Wietersheim
13th (Motorized) Infantry Division
29th (Motorized) Infantry Division
2nd (Motorized) Infantry Division

XIX Corps – General der Panzertruppen
Heinz Guderian
1st Panzer Division
2nd Panzer Division
10th Panzer Division
XXXXI Corps – Generalleutnant Georg-
Hans Reinhardt
6th Panzer Division
8th Panzer Division
Army Group A Reserves
4th Infantry Division
267th Infantry Division

German Army Group B –
Generaloberst Fedor von Bock
Chief of Staff – Generalleutnant Hans
von Salmuth
Sixth Army – Generaloberst Walter von
Reichenau
IV Corps – General der Infanterie Viktor
von Schwedler
18th Infantry Division
35th Infantry Division
IX Corps – General der Infanterie
Hermann Geyer
19th Infantry Division
30th Infantry Division
56th Infantry Division
XI Corps – Generalleutnant Joachim
von Kortzfleisch
7th Infantry Division
14th Infantry Division
31st Infantry Division
XXVII Corps – General der Infanterie
Alfred Wägner
4th Panzer Division
253rd Infantry Division
269th Infantry Division
Reserve
3rd Panzer Division
20th (Motorized) Infantry Division
61st Infantry Division
216th Infantry Division
I Corps – Generalleutnant Kuno-Hans
von Both

1st Infantry Division
11th Infantry Division
223rd Infantry Division
Eighteenth Army – General der
  Artillerie Georg von Küchler
Under Direct Army Command
9th Panzer Division
1st Cavalry Division
X Corps – Generalleutnant Christian
  Hansen
207th Infantry Division
227th Infantry Division
SS 'Verfügungstruppe' (Motorized)
  Division
XXVI Corps – General der Artillerie
  Albert Wodrig
254th Infantry Division
Reserves
208th Infantry Division
225th Infantry Division
256th Infantry Division
Army Group B Reserve
XVI Corps – General der Kavallerie
  Erich Hoepner
XXXIX Corps – Generalleutnant Rudolf
  Schmidt

German Army Group C –
  Generaloberst Wilhelm von Leeb
Chief of Staff – Generalleutnant Hans
  Felber
First Army – Generaloberst Erwin von
  Witzleben
XII Corps – General der Infanterie
  Gotthard Heinrici
75th Infantry Division
93rd Infantry Division
258th Infantry Division
XXIV Corps – General der Kavallerie
  Leo Geyr von Schweppenburg
252nd Infantry Division
257th Infantry Division
262nd Infantry Division
268th Infantry Division

XXX Corps – General der Artillerie Otto
  Hartmann
79th Infantry Division
95th Infantry Division
XXXVII Corps – Generalleutnant
  Alfred Boehm-Tettelbach
215th Infantry Division
246th Infantry Division
Reserves
94th Infantry Division
98th Infantry Division
Seventh Army – General der Artillerie
  Friedrich Dollmann
XXV Corps – General der Infanterie
  Karl von Prager
555th Infantry Division
557th Infantry Division
XXXIII Corps – Generalleutnant Georg
  Brandt
554th Infantry Division
556th Infantry Division
Reserves
96th Infantry Division
22nd Airlanding Division

France
Supreme Commander – Général
  Maurice Gamelin
Chief of Staff – Général Joseph
  Doumenc
Supreme Headquarters Reserve
3rd Division d'infanterie motorisée
  (DIM)
10th Infantry Division
14th Infantry Division
23rd Infantry Division
28th Infantry Division
29th Infantry Division
36th Infantry Division
43rd Infantry Division
5th Colonial Infantry Division
7th Colonial Infantry Division
1st North African Infantry Division
2nd Polish Infantry Division Division

XXI Corps – Général de Corps d'Armée Jean Flavigny [No organic divisions, supporting corps units only]

XXIII Corps – Général de Division Maxime Germain [No organic divisions, supporting corps units only]

1st Armoured Group – Général de Division Louis Keller

2nd Division Cuirassée de Réserve (DCR)

3rd Division Cuirassée de Réserve (DCR)

North East Front – Général Alphonse Georges

Chief of Staff – Général Gaston Roton

First Army Group – Général Gaston Billotte

Chief of Staff – Général Jacques Humbert

First Army – Général Georges Blanchard

III Corps – Général de Fornel de la Laurencie

1st Division d'infanterie motorisée (DIM)

2nd North African Infantry Division

IV Corps – Général de Corps d'Armée Boris

15th Division d'infanterie motorisée (DIM)

1st Moroccan Division

V Corps – Général de Corps d'Armée Bloch

12th Division d'infanterie motorisée (12 DIM)

5th North African Division

101st Fortress Infantry Division

Cavalry Corps – Général de Corps d'Armée René Prioux

2nd Divisions Légères Mécanisées (DLM)

3rd Divisions Légères Mécanisées (DLM)

First Army Reserves

1st Division Cuirassée de Réserve (1 DCR)

32nd Infantry Division

Second Army – Général Charles Huntziger

Chief of Staff – Général Jean Langlois

X Corps – Général de Corps d'Armée Pierre Grandsard

3rd North African Division

55th Infantry Division

XVIII Corps – Général de Corps d'Armée Eugene Rochard

1st Colonial Infantry Division

3rd Colonial Infantry Division

41st Infantry Division

Second Army Reserve

2nd Light Cavalry Division

5th Light Cavalry Division

71st Infantry Division

Seventh Army – Général Henri Giraud

Chief of Staff – Général Jean Baurès

I Corps – Général Théodore Sciard

25th Division d'infanterie motorisée (DIM)

XVI Corps – Général Alfred Fagalde

9th Division d'infanterie motorisée (DIM)

Seventh Army Reserve

4th Infantry Division

21st Infantry Division

60th Infantry Division

1st Division légère mécanisée (DLM)

Ninth Army – Général André Corap

Chief of Staff – Général Olivier Thierry d'Argenlieu

II Corps – Général Jean Bouffet

5th Division d'infanterie motorisée (DIM)

XIth Corps – Général de Corps d'Armée Julien Martin

18th Infantry Division

22nd Infantry Division

XLI Corps – Général Emmanuel Libaud

61st Infantry Division

102nd Fortress Infantry Division

Ninth Army Reserve

1st Light Cavalry Division

4th Light Cavalry Division

4th North African Division
53rd Infantry Division
3rd Spahis Brigade

Second Army Group – Général André
  Prételat
Chief of Staff – Général Louis Bérard
Third Army – Général Charles Condé
Colonial Corps – Général Henry
  Freydenberg
2nd Infantry Division
56th Infantry Division
51st (British) Division
VI Corps – Général Georges Loizeau
26th Infantry Division
42nd Infantry Division
XXIV Corps – Général Loiseau
36th Infantry Division
51st Infantry Division
XLII Corps – Général Désiré Sivot
20th Infantry Division
58th Infantry Division
Third Army Reserve
6th North African Infantry Division
3rd Light Cavalry Division
6th Infantry Division
7th Infantry Division
8th Infantry Division
1st Spahis Brigade
Fourth Army – Général Pierre Requin
Chief of Staff – Général Pierre Dame
IX Corps – Général Émile Laure
11th Infantry Divison
47th Infantry Division
XX Corps – Général de Corps d'Armée
  Louis Hubert
52nd Infantry Division
82nd African Infantry Division
Fourth Army Reserve
45th Infantry Divisions
1st Polish Infantry Division
Fifth Army – Général Victor Bourret
Chief of Staff – Général Jean de Lattre
  de Tassigny
VIII Corps – Général Aubert Frère

24th Infantry Division
31st Infantry Division
XII Corps – Général Henri Dentz
16th Infantry Division
35th Infantry Division
70th Infantry Division
XVII Corps – Général de Corps d'Armée
  Onésime-Paul Noël
62nd Infantry Division
103rd Fortress Infantry Division
XLIII Corps – Général Fernand
  Lescanne
30th African Infantry Division
Fifth Army Reserve
44th Infantry Division
Second Army Group Reserve
4th Colonial Infantry Division
87th African Infantry Division

Third Army Group – Général Antoine
  Besson
Eighth Army – Général Marcel
  Garchery
Chief of Staff – Général Louis Koeltz
VII Corps – Général Pierre Champon
13th Infantry Division
27th Infantry Division
2nd Spahis Brigade
XIII Corps – Général de Corps d'Armée
  George Misserey
19th Infantry Division
54th Infantry Division
XLIV Corps – Général de Brigade Julien
  Tencé
67th Infantry Division
Third Army Group Reserve
XLV Corps – Général Daille
57th Infantry Division
63rd Infantry Division
North East Front Reserve
68th Infantry Division

British Expeditionary Force

Commander-in-Chief – General John Vereker, 6th Viscount Gort

Chief of the General Staff – Lieutenant General Henry Pownall

GHQ Troops

Under command:

First Army Tank Brigade

1st Light Armoured Reconnaissance Brigade

5th Infantry Division

I Corps – Lieutenant General M. G. H. Barker

1st Infantry Division

2nd Infantry Division

48th Infantry Division

II Corps – Lieutenant General A. F. Brooke

3rd Infantry Division

4th Infantry Division

50thInfantry Division

III Corps – Lieutenant General Sir R. F. Adam, Bt.

42nd Infantry Division

44th Infantry Division

Divisions undertaking training and carrying out labour duties:

12th Infantry Division

23rd Infantry Division

46th Infantry Division

N.B. the BEF's 51st Division was attached to French Third Army's Colonial Corps (see French Order of Battle above).

Belgian Army

Commander-in-Chief – King Lieutenant

Chief of the General Staff – General Édouard van den Bergen

Belgian I Corps

1st Infantry Division

4th Infantry Division

7th Infantry Division

Belgian II Corps

6th Infantry Division

11th Infantry Division

14th Infantry Division

Belgian III Corps

1st Chasseurs Ardennais

2nd Infantry Division

3rd Infantry Division

Belgian IV Corps

9th Infantry Division

15th Infantry Division

18th Infantry Division

Belgian V Corps

12th Infantry Division

13th Infantry Division

17th Infantry Division

Belgian VI Corps

5th Infantry Division

10th Infantry Division

16th Infantry Division

Belgian Cavalry Corps

1st Cavalry Division

2nd Cavalry Division

Dutch Army

Commander-in-Chief – General Henri Winkelman

Chief of Staff – Major General H. F. M. Van Voorst tot Voorst

II Corps

2nd Infantry Division

4th Infantry Division

III Corps

5th Infantry Division

6th Infantry Division

Dutch Light Division

Dutch IV Corps

7th Infantry Division

8th Infantry Division

Formations not in a corps:

Independent Brigade Group A

Independent Brigade Group B

Reserve – I Corps

1st Infantry Division

3rd Infantry Division

Endnotes

Prologue

1   Written with reference to Marguerite Joseph-Maginot *He Might Have Saved France – The Biography of André Maginot* Doubleday, Doran & Co. Inc. New York 1941 and *Time: France: Death & Crisis* Monday, Jan. 18, 1932.

Introduction

1   Quoted in G. Germond and H. Türk (eds.) *A History of Franco-German Relations in Europe: from 'Hereditary Enemies' to Partners* Palgrave Macmillan, New York 2008, unpaginated.

2   Michael Howard 'The Use and Abuse of Military History' in *Royal United Services Institute Journal*, No. 107 February 1962 p. 8.

3   Quoted in Allan R. Millett and Williamson Murray *Military Effectiveness Volume 3: The Second World War* Cambridge University Press, New York, 2010 p. xi.

4   See Howard RUSI p. 6.

Chapter 1

1   Quoted in Eugen Weber *The Hollow Years – France in the 1930s* Sinclair-Stevenson, 1995 p. 9.

2   *The War Illustrated* 21 October 1939 Vol.1 No. 6 pp. 162–63.

3   General Franz Halder *The Halder War Diary 1939–1942* Burdick, Charles and Jacobsen, Hans-Alfred (eds.) Greenhill Books, 1988 pp. 64–65. The Private War Journal of General Oberst Franz Halder, Chief of the General Staff of the Supreme Command of the German Army (OKH) has also been used in the preparation of this book. The journal runs from 14 August 1939

to 10 September 1942, when Halder was dismissed by Hitler. Sections cited include: Vol. I The Polish Campaign Part I (N-16845-A); Vol. II The Polish Campaign Part II (N-16845-B); Vol. III The First Winter 7 December 1939 to 9 May 1940 (N-16845-C); and Vol. IV The Campaign in France 10 May 1940 to 30 October 1940 (N-16845-D), all Combined Arms Research Library, Digital Library, Fort Leavenworth, Kansas, USA. On occasion the typescript translation of Halder's original lacks the detail of the later published version. Where this extra information has been used, the published version of the diary is referenced rather than the original typescript version.

4   *The Halder War Diary 1939–1942* p. 63.

5   Führer Directives were instructions and outline strategic plans that were legally binding for all Germans and overruled all other instructions and laws. The German army leadership was very uneasy with these promulgations as they were sufficiently detailed to bind them to certain military strategies, no matter how impractical they were. There were several relating to the campaign in France and the Low Countries.

6   Führer Directive No. 6 dated 9 October 1939 Author's Archive.

7   *The Halder War Diary 1939–1942* pp. 65–66. At a Führer Conference on 22 August 1939, Hitler had stated: 'Germany can be counted on to make a better showing of herself in a long war than she did in 1914.' 22 August 1939 The Private War Journal of General

Oberst Franz Halder, Chief of the General Staff of the Supreme Command of the German Army (OKH): 14 August 1939 to 10 September 1942 Vol. I: The Polish Campaign Part I (N-16845-A) p. 21.

8   Samuel W. Mitcham, Jnr *Hitler's Field Marshals and their Battles* Grafton Books, 1989 p.167.

9   Quoted in Samuel W. Mitcham, Jnr *Hitler's Field Marshals and their Battles* Grafton Books, 1989 p.125.

10   Karl-Heinz Frieser *The Blitzkrieg Legend – The 1940 campaign in the West* Naval Institute Press, Annapolis, 2005 p. 55 and p. 57.

11   Quoted in Frieser *The Blitzkrieg Legend* p. 55.

12   See Messerschmidt chapter in Allan R. Millett and Williamson Murray *Military Effectiveness Volume 2: The Interwar Years* Cambridge University Press, New York, 2010 pp. 220-21.

13   Quoted in Richard Overy with Andrew Wheatcroft *The Road to War* Vintage, 2009 p. 53.

14   Figures from Overy *The Road to War* p. 67.

15   Quoted in Messerschmidt chapter Allan R. Millett and Williamson Murray *Military Effectiveness Volume 2: The Interwar Years* p. 236.

16   For all these figures see Frieser *The Blitzkrieg Legend* p. 23, James S. Corum, *The Roots of Blitzkrieg: Hans von Seeckt and German Military Reform* University of Kansas Press, Lawrence, Kansas 1994 p. 200 and Förster chapter in Millett and Murray Vol. 3 pp. 187–88.

17   See Förster chapter in Millett and Murray Vol. 3 pp. 187–88.

18   Quoted by Messerschmidt in Millett and Murray Vol. 2 p. 227.

19 Figures from Messerschmidt chapter in Millett and Murray Vol. 2 p. 232 and pp. 247–48.

20 See Messerschmidt in Millett and Murray Vol. 2 p. 235.

21 See John Andreas Olsen and Martin van Creveld (eds.) *The Evolution of Operational Art: From Napoleon to the Present* Oxford University Press, Oxford 2010.

22 For all this see João Resende-Santos *Neorealism, States, and the Modern Mass Army* Cambridge University Press, Cambridge, 2007 pp. 97–99.

23 Hans von Seeckt 'Grundsätzemoderner Landesverteidigung' in *Gedankeneines Soldaten* K.F. Koehler, Leipzig 1935 p. 77.

24 Quoted in Frieser *The Blitzkrieg Legend* p. 330.

25 For more on this see Corum *Roots of Blitzkrieg*.

26 Translation of taped conversation with General Hermann Balck, 12 January 1979 p. 19.

27 General Ludwig von Eimannsberger was Germany's best-known armoured warfare writer in the 1930s, but of all armoured warfare theorists, Heinz Guderian is most remembered as the 'father of German armoured forces'. This is due largely to Guderian's later success as a practitioner of panzer warfare and his gift for self-publicity rather than his originality of thinking.

28 Most panzer divisions taking part in the invasion of Poland had under 350 tanks, and some considerably fewer.

29 For all this see Buckley chapter in B. Bond and M. Taylor *Battle for France*

and Flanders Sixty Years On Leo Cooper, Barnsley, 2001.

30 Westerners first became aware of the word after it appeared in a 1939 issue of *Time* magazine to describe the lightning speed of the German army in Poland: 'This was no war of occupation, but a war of quick penetration and obliteration – *Blitzkrieg*, lightning war.' *Time* 25 September 1939. For more on this see Frieser *The Blitzkrieg Legend* and Robert M. Citino *Quest for Decisive Victory – From Stalemate to Blitzkrieg in Europe, 1899–1940* University Press of Kansas, Lawrence, Kansas, 2002 p. 181.

31 See Halder Diary various entries during autumn 1939 and winter 1939/40.

32 Marc Bloch *Strange Defeat – A Statement of Evidence Written in 1940* W. W. Norton, New York, 1968 p. 126 Emphasis in the original. This book was not published until 1946, two years after Bloch had been executed by firing squad along with twenty-seven other members of the Resistance.

33 Weber *The Hollow Years* p. 11. See also Thomas R. Christofferson with Michael S. Christofferson *France During World War II: From Defeat to Liberation* Fordham University Press, New York, 2006 p. 2.

34 Omer Bartov's chapter in Joel Blatt (ed.) *The French Defeat of 1940 – Reassessments* Berghan Books, New York, 2006 pp. 56–57.

35 See George Q. Flynn *Conscription and Democracy: The Draft in France, Great Britain and the United States* Contributions to Military Studies, Nos 210, Westport, Conn. Greenwood, 2002.

36 See Millett and Murray *Military Effectiveness* Vol. 2 p. 52.

37 Doughty chapter in Millett and Murray Vol. 2 pp. 42–43.

38 The Dunkirk-Strasbourg-Paris triangle contained 75 per cent of the country's coal and 95 per cent of its iron ore production, and nearly all of its heavy industry. The Paris-Lille-Rouen triangle contained 90 per cent of its factories producing French cloth and 80 per cent of its woollen goods, the majority of its chemical products and a good deal of its vehicle and aircraft production.

39 See Col. J. J. O'Connell *The Maginot Line: Dream or Reality?* in *Studies: An Irish Quarterly Review*, Vol. 29, No.116, Dec. 1940 p. 607.

40 For more on this see Judith M. Hughes *To The Maginot Line – The Politics of the French Military Preparation in the 1920s* Harvard University Press, Cambridge, Masschusetts, 2006 pp. 199–219.

41 Quoted in Robert Allan Doughty *The Breaking Point – Sedan and the Fall of France, 1940* Archon Books, Hampden, Connecticut, 1990 p. 11. See also General Maurice Gamelin *Servir* Vol. 2 Librairie Plon, Paris, 1946 p. 128.

42 Quoted in Alistair Horne, *To Lose a Battle – France 1940* Penguin Books, 1990 p. 80.

43 Eugenia C. Kiesling *Arming Against Hitler – France and the Limits of Military Planning* University of Kansas, Lawrence, Kansas, 1996 p. 174.

44 Figures from Overy *The Road to War* p. 164. See also Martin Thomas *French Economic Affairs and Rearmament: The First Crucial Months, June-September 1936* Journal of Contemporary History Vol. 27, No. 4 (Oct. 1992).

45 The French referred to the building of the Maginot Line up to 1935 as the First Phase, and these lighter defences as the Second Phase. It should be noted that this Second Phase had been discussed and anticipated, but not been built earlier due to the cost and importance of finishing the fortifications along the common border with Germany first.

46 A. Danchev and D. Todman (eds.), *War Diaries of Field Marshal Lord Alanbrooke* Weidenfeld and Nicolson, 2001. Entry dated 20 December 1939 p. 26.

47 For more on Alan Brooke see David Fraser's chapter in Keegan, J. (ed.) *Churchill's Generals* Weidenfeld and Nicolson, 1991.

48 Quoted in Doughty chapter in Millett and Murray Vol. 2 p. 48.

49 Figures from Overy *The Road To War* Appendices Table 1 Government Expenditure for Defence in the Major Powers, 1931–40 p. 429.

50 See Weber *The Hollow Years* pp. 23–24.

51 Overy *The Road to War* p. 180

52 See Colonel Igors Rajevs *The French Army in the Interwar Period* in Baltic Security & Defence Review, Vol. 11, Issue 2, 2009 p. 186 and Robert Allan Doughty, *The Evolution of French Army Doctrine 1919–1939* University of Kansas PhD, 1979.

53 *Instruction provisoire de 6 Octobre 1921 sur l'emploi tactique des grandes unités* Charles-Lavauzelle et Cie, impr.-éditeurs, 1928 p. 16.

54 Doughty *The Breaking Point* p. 27.

55 For more on all this see Buckley chapter in B. Bond and Michael D. Taylor (eds.) *Battle for France and Flanders Sixty Years On* Leo Cooper, Barnsley, 2001.

56 For a description of military education in this period see General André Beaufre, *1940: The Fall of France* Cassell, London, 1967, transl. by Desmond Flower, pp. 36–59 and Faris Russell Kirkland, *The French Officer Corps and the Fall of France: 1920-1940* University of Pennsylvania, PhD 1982, pp. 276–88.

57 See Elizabeth Kier *Imagining War: French and British Military Doctrine between the Wars* Princeton, N. J., Princeton University Press, 1997.

58 See Douglas Porch *Military 'Culture' and the Fall of France in 1940: A Review Essay* in *International Security*, Vol. 24 No. 4 Spring 2000 p. 179,

59 Doughty's chapter in Millett and Murray Vol. 2 p. 46 and Martin S. Alexander 'The Fall of France' in *Journal of Strategic Studies* Vol. 13 No. 1 1990 p. 16.

59 Quoted in Karl-Heinz Frieser *The Blitzkrieg Legend* p. 1.

60 France: The Good Grey General *Time* Monday, August 14, 1939 p. 31.

61 Quoted in Horne p. 25.

62 Quoted in Kiesling *Arming Against Hitler* p. 186.

63 Kiesling *Arming Against Hitler* p. 175.

64 The Private War Journal of General Oberst Franz Halder Vol. I: The Polish Campaign Part I (N-16845-A). Entry dated 14 August 1939. p. 8.

65 Quoted in Kiesling *Arming Against Hitler* p. 186.

Chapter 2

1 Albert Winkler Interview 16 March 2013 and Email 20 December 2014.

2 Quoted by Richard Overy in *The Origins of the Second World War* Routledge, 2008 p. 122.

3 The Private War Journal of General Oberst Franz Halder Vol. I: The Polish Campaign Part I (N-16845-A). Entry dated 28 August 1939. p. 37.

4 Quoted in Overy *The Road to War* p. 81.

5 Quoted in Overy *The Road to War* p. 82.

6 Daniel Barlone *A French Officer's Diary 23 August 1939 To 1 October 1940* Cambridge: At the University Press New York: The Macmillan Company, 1943 p. 1.

7 The Private War Journal of General Oberst Franz Halder Vol. I: The Polish Campaign Part I (N-16845-A). Entry dated 14 August 1939. p. 14.

8 The Private War Journal of General Oberst Franz Halder Vol. I: The Polish Campaign Part I (N-16845-A) p. 13 and Citino *Quest for Decisive Victory*. Entry dated 14 August 1939. p. 258.

9 Samuel W. Mitcham Jnr *Panzer Legions – A Guide to the German Army Tank Divisions and their Commanders* Stackpole Books, Mechanicsburg, PA, 2007 pp. 14–15.

10 Barlone p. 13.

11 Figures from Citino *Quest for Decisive Victory* p. 257.

12 Citino *Quest for Decisive Victory* p. 257

13 J. E. Kaufmann and H. W. Kaufmann *Hitler's Blitzkrieg Campaigns – The Invasion and Defense of Western Europe, 1939–1940* Da Capo Press, Cambridge, MA, 1993 p. 9.

14 *The Memoirs of Field Marshal Wilhelm Keitel* Walter Gorlitz (ed.) First Cooper Square Press, New York, 2000 p. 102.

15 The Private War Journal of General Oberst Franz Halder Vol. II The Polish Campaign Part II (N-16845-B). Entry dated 22 October 1939. p. 36.

16 Quoted in I. Kershaw *Hitler 1936–1945 Nemesis* Allen Lane, 2000 p. 291.

17 See Doughty *Breaking Point* p. 17.

18 The Private War Journal of General Oberst Franz Halder Vol. II The Polish Campaign Part II (N-16845-B). Entry dated 3 November 1939. p. 43.

19 Generalfeldmarschall Fedor von Bock *The War Diary 1939–1945.* Schiffer Publishing Ltd, Atglen, PA, 1996 Entry dated 23 November. p. 88.

20 Quoted in Samuel W. Mitcham Jnr *Hitler's Field Marshals and their Battles* Grafton Books, 1989 p. 64.

21 Von Bock *The War Diary 1939–1945.* Entry dated 30 October. p. 78.

22 Von Bock *The War Diary 1939–1945.* Entry dated 3 November. p. 80.

23 Von Bock *The War Diary 1939–1945.* Entry dated 12 November. p. 84.

24 Von Bock *The War Diary 1939–1945.* Entry dated 18 November. p. 86.

25 The Private War Journal of General Oberst Franz Halder Vol. II The Polish Campaign Part II (N-16845-B) Halder. Entry dated 26 October p. 39.

26 Quoted in Citino *Quest for Decisive Victory* p. 260.

27 Quoted in Alexander chapter in Brian Bond (ed.) *Fallen Stars: Eleven Studies of Twentieth Century Military Disasters* Brassey's, 1991 p. 119.

28 France: 'The Good Grey General' *Time* Monday, August 14, 1939 p. 22.

29 For more on all this see Alexander chapter in Bond (ed.) *Fallen Stars.*

30 See David French *Raising Churchill's Army – The British Army and the War against Germany 1919–1945* Oxford University Press, Oxford, 2000.

31 Figures from Overy *The Road to War* p. 111.

32 See Murray chapter in Millett and Murray vol. 3 p. 94 and Overy *The Road to War* p. 132.

33 See Barry R. Posen *The Sources of Military Doctrine: France, Britain and Germany Between the Wars* Cornell University Press, New York, 1984 and Elizabeth Kier *Imagining War: French and British Military Doctrine between the Wars* Princeton, N.J., Princeton University Press, 1997.

34 Gavin J. Bailey *The Arsenal of Democracy: Aircraft Supply and the Evolution of the Anglo-American Alliance, 1938–1942* Edinburgh University Press, Edinburgh, 2013 pp. 278–80.

35 Murray chapter in Millett and Murray Vol. 2 p. 120.

36 See Buckley chapter in Bond, B. and Taylor, Michael D. (eds.) *Battle for France and Flanders Sixty Years On* p. 122.

37   A. Danchev and D. Todman (eds.)
     Lord Alanbrooke *War Diaries of
     Field Marshal Lord Alanbrooke*. Entry
     dated 28 January 1940. pp. 34–35.

38   See French *Churchill's Army* and also
     his *Doctrine and Organisation in the
     British Army, 1919–32* The Historical
     Journal Vol. 44, No. 52 (June 2001)
     p. 504. See also J. P. Harris *Men,
     Ideas and Tanks – British Military
     Thought and Armoured Forces,
     1903–1939* Manchester University
     Press 1995.

39   French *Churchill's Army* pp. 15–16.

40   See French *Raising Churchill's Army*
     p. 25.

41   See Kiesling *Arming Against Hitler*
     p. 178.

42   *Kriegsspiel* (war game) had been
     used since the Napoleonic Wars to
     train Prussian officers. It simulated
     operations on a specially designed
     table marked with a grid system
     with specifically made terrain
     types laid on top. The 'game' used
     special gaming pieces and a dice
     to add an element of controlled
     randomness. There was also the
     ability to simulate the fog of war
     and communication difficulties
     (friction), and for an impartial
     umpire to calculate and assess
     the moves. Rules developed over
     the years to provide various
     conventions which continue to be
     used to the present day.

43   For all this see Sebag-Montefiore,
     Hugh *Dunkirk – Fight To The Last
     Man* Viking, 2006 Chapter 3 'The
     Mechelen Affair'.

44   General Jodl's Diary (Armed Forces
     Operational Staff) from 1 February
     to 26 May 1940 Document 1809-PS.
     Entry dated 12 January 1940.

45   Mungo Melvin *Manstein – Hitler's
     Greatest General* Weidenfeld &
     Nicolson, London, 2010 p. 143.

46   See Russell A. Hart *Guderian: Panzer
     Pioneer or Myth Maker?* Pentagon
     Press, New Delhi, 2010 p. 60.

47   General Jodl's Diary (Armed Forces
     Operational Staff) from 1 February
     to 26 May 1940 Document 1809-PS.
     Entry dated 13 February 1940.

48   Quoted in Melvin p. 135.

49   Melvin p. 135.

50   Heeresgruppenkommandos:
     Heeresgruppe A: RH 19I/38
     Bundesarchiv-Militärarchiv
     Freiburg, Germany.

51   Heeresgruppenkommandos:
     Heeresgruppe A: RH 19I/38
     Bundesarchiv-Militärarchiv
     Freiburg, Germany.

52   Quoted in Frieser *Blitzkrieg Legend*
     p. 95.

53   Von Bock *The War Diary 1939–
     1945*. Entry dated 24 February
     1940. p. 114.

54   Quoted in Horne p. 153.

55   The Private War Journal of General
     Oberst Franz Halder Vol. III The
     First Winter 7 December 1939 to 9
     May 1940 (N-16845-C). Entry dated
     24 February 1940. p. 103.

56   Quoted in Melvin p. 159.

57   Samuel W. Mitcham, Jnr *Hitler's
     Field Marshals and their Battles*
     Grafton Books, 1989 p.75.

58   See Doughty *Breaking Point* p. 34.

59   Quoted in Frieser *Blitzkrieg Legend*
     p. 97.

60   The Private War Journal of General
     Oberst Franz Halder Vol. III The
     First Winter 7 December 1939 to 9
     May 1940 (N-16845-C) Entry dated
     17 March 1939. p. 106.

61   Quoted in Frieser *Blitzkrieg Legend*
     p. 114.

62 See Doughty *Breaking Point* p. 15 and also Don W. Alexander 'Repercussions of the Breda Variant' in *French Historical Studies*, Vol. 8 No. 3 Spring 1974.

63 Quoted in A. Goutard *The Battle for France 1940* Washburn Inc., New York, 1959 p. 147.

64 See Alexander chapter in Bond (ed.) *Fallen Stars* p. 121.

65 TNA Col. W Fraser Despatches, 16–30 June 1939 FO 371, 22917, C8681/130/17 and C9363/130/17.

66 General Sir Edmund Ironside *Time Unguarded: The Ironside Diaries, 1937–1940* ed. Col Roderick Macleod and Denis Kelly Constable, New York, 1962. Entry dated 10 January 1940. p. 204.

Chapter 3

1 Barlone p. 21.

2 Hanna Diamond *Fleeing Hitler – France 1940* Oxford University Press, Oxford, 2007 p. 24.

3 See Alexander chapter in Bond (ed.) *Fallen Stars* p. 117.

4 Alexander Werth *The Last Days of Paris: A Journalist's Diary* Hamish Hamilton, 1940 p. 15.

5 Barlone pp. 34–35.

6 Barlone p. 1.

7 Barlone p. 4.

8 Pierre Roussel diary 1939. Entry dated 20 December 1939. Roussel family archive.

9 George Aris *The British Fifth Division 1939 to 1945* The Fifth Division Benevolent Fund, 1959 p. 3.

10 Quoted in Kiesling *Arming Against Hitler* p. 183.

11 Quoted in Frieser *Blitzkrieg Legend* p. 145.

12 See Doughty *Breaking Point* p. 105.

13 30 N 92 10ème Corps d' Armée, 3ème bureau, Service Historique de la Défense, Vincennes, Paris.

14 30 N 92 10ème Corps d' Armée, 3ème bureau and 32 N 251 55ème Division d'Infanterie, de l'Armée de Terre, Vincennes, Paris.

15 Quoted in Doughty *Breaking Point* p. 111.

16 See Alexander chapter in Bond (ed.) *Fallen Stars* pp. 114–15.

17 Quoted by Alexander in Bond (ed.) *Fallen Stars* p. 117.

18 18 September 1939 1K 224, 9 Cabinet du Général Gamelin – Journal de marche Fonds Gamelin, SHAT.

19 General Sir Edmund Ironside *Time Unguarded: The Ironside Diaries, 1937–1940*. Entry dated 10 February 1940. pp. 203–4.

20 *War Diaries of Field Marshal Lord Alanbrooke*. Entry dated 16 October 1939. pp. 7–8.

21 *War Diaries of Field Marshal Lord Alanbrooke*. Entry dated 9 October 1939. pp. 5–6.

22 The founder of the Taittinger champagne house who later collaborated with the Germans as chairman of the municipal council of Paris.

23 29 N 27 2ème Armée Historique des operations. Service Historique de la Défense, Vincennes, Paris.

24 29 N 27 2ème Armée Historique des operations. Service Historique de la Défense, Vincennes, Paris.

25 Quoted in Doughty *Breaking Point* p. 148.

26 For all this see Wesley chapter in Bond (ed.) *Fallen Stars* p. 144.

27 See Brian Bond's chapter on Gort in John Keegan (ed.) *Churchill's Generals* Weidenfeld and Nicolson, 1991.

28 *War Diaries of Field Marshal Lord Alanbrooke*. Entry dated 22 September 1939. p. 18.

29 Major G. Courage *The History of the 15/19 The King's Royal Hussars 1939–1945* Gale & Polden Ltd, Aldershot, 1949 pp. 7–8.

30 Courage p. 6.

31 See Spencer Tucker (ed.) *Encyclopedia of World War II – A Political, Social and Military History* Santa Barbara, California, 2005 Vol. I p. 200.

32 For all this see M.B. 'The Strategic Position of Holland and Belgium' *Bulletin of International News* Vol. 16 No. 24 (Dec 2 1939) pp. 1304–6.

33 Figures from P. L. G. Doorman *Military Operations of the Dutch Army 10-17th May 1940* Helion, Solihull, 2005 p. 10 and Spencer Tucker (ed.) *Encyclopedia of World War II – A Political, Social and Military History* p. 1063.

34 Figure from Walter B. Maass *The Netherlands at War: 1940–1945* Abelard–Schuman, Amsterdam, 1970 p. 16.

35 L. De Jong *Holland Fights the Nazis* The Right Book Club, 1941 pp. 5–6.

36 The Private War Journal of General Oberst Franz Halder Vol. III The First Winter 7 December 1939 to 9 May 1940 (N-16845-C). Entry dated 26 March 1940. p. 131.

37 See Williamson Murray's article 'The German Response to Victory in Poland: A Case Study in Professionalism' in *Armed Forces and Society*, Vol. 7 1981.

38 Frieser *Blitzkrieg Legend* p. 22.

39 Figure from Frieser *Blitzkrieg Legend* p. 29.

40 Frieser *Blitzkrieg Legend* p. 32.

41 Von Bock Diary *1939–1945*. Entry dated 13 March 1940. p. 118.

42 Von Bock Diary 1939–1945. Entry dated 26 April 1940. p. 131.

43 Email from Peter Gerber (1 May 2014) whose father worked in von Bock's headquarters during this period.

44 See Niall Cherry *Doomed from the Start: The Allied Intervention in Norway 1940* Helion & Co., Solihull, 2016 and Anthony Dix *The Norway Campaign and the Rise of Churchill 1940* Pen and Sword, Barnsley, 2014.

45 Gruppe XXI, Notiz fuer das Kriegstagebuch, 1.4.40, in Anlagenband 1 zum K.T.B. Nr. k, Anlagen 1-52, AOK 20 E 180/7.

46 Ian Kershaw, *Hitler 1936–1945 Nemesis* p. 289.

47 David Fraser *Knight's Cross – A Life of Field Marshal Erwin Rommel* HarperCollins, 1993 pp. 160–61.

48 Fraser *Rommel* p. 159.

49 Taped Conversation with Balck, 12 January 1979 p. 19.

50 Hermann Balck *Ordnung im Chaos. Erinnerungen 1893–1948* Osnabrück Biblio Verlag, 1980 p. 267.

51 All figures from Frieser *Blitzkrieg Legend* pp. 35–48.

52 Carl Clausewitz *On War* (Translated and edited by Michael Howard and Peter Paret) Princeton, N.J., Princeton University Press, 1976 p. 86.

53 Barlone p. 26.

54 See Doughty *Breaking Point* p. 74; Ernest R. May *The Intelligence Process: The Fall of France, 1940* Unpublished paper Kennedy School

of Government n.d.; Robert J. Young chapter in Ernest R. May (ed.) *Knowing One's Enemies* Princeton, N.J., Princeton University Press, 2014 and Douglas Porch *French Intelligence and the Fall of France 1930-40 in* Intelligence and National Security 4, No. 1 Jan 1989.

55 Ian Kershaw *Hitler 1936–1945 Nemesis* pp. 290-91.

56 Doughty *Breaking Point* pp. 74–76.

57 Quoted in Frieser *Blitzkrieg Legend* p. 142.

58 See The Private War Journal of General Oberst Franz Halder Vol. III The First Winter 7 December 1939

– 9 May 1940 (N-16845-C). Entry dated 5 May 1940. p. 190.

59 Quoted in Alexander chapter in Bond (ed.) *Fallen Stars* p. 127.

60 See Julian Jackson *The Fall of France: The Nazi Invasion of 1940* Oxford University Press, Oxford, 2003 pp. 128–29.

61 B. H. Liddell Hart (ed.) *The Rommel Papers* Collins, 1953 p. 6.

62 Quoted in Doughty *Breaking Point* p. 43.

63 Helmut Mahlke *Memoirs of a Stuka Pilot* Frontline Books, Barnsley, 2013 p. 81.

64 Quoted in Ian Kershaw, *Hitler 1936– 1945 Nemesis* p. 294.

Chapter 4

1 Gilberto Villahermosa *Hitler's Paratrooper – The Life and Battles of Rudolf Witzig* Frontline Books, 2010 p. 51.

2 Otto Gull Interview 18 July 2011.

3 Otto Gull Interview 18 July 2011.

4 VIII. Fliegerkorps: RL 8/43, 45.

5 See Chapter 3 Lloyd Clark *Arnhem – Jumping the Rhine 1944 and 1945 – The Greatest Airborne Battle in History* Headline 2008.

6 Quoted in Villahermosa p. 41.

7 Mahlke p. 82.

8 Mahlke p. 84.

9 E. R. Hooton *Luftwaffe at War: Blitzkrieg in the West 1939–1940* Ian Allan, Hersham, Surrey, 2007 p. 15.

10 Letter from Conrad Houtkooper 21 May 2013.

11 See James J. Weingartner *Hitler's Guard: The Story of the Leibstandarte SS Adolf Hitler 1933–1945* Southern Illinois University Press, Carbondale and Edwardsville, 1968 pp. 38–39.

12 Quoted in Villahermosa p. 43.

13 Quoted in Villahermosa p. 46.

14 Von Bock *The War Diary 1939– 1945*. Entry dated 30 October 1939 p. 135.

15 Aris p. 27.

16 Philip Gribble *The Diary of a Staff Officer, Air Intelligence Liaison Officer, at Advanced Headquarters North B.A.F.F., 1940* Methuen & Co., 1941 p. 3.

17 10 May 1940 *War Diaries of Field Marshal Lord Alanbrooke* p. 60.

18 Major G. Courage *The History of the 15/19 The King's Royal Hussars 1939–1945* Gale & Polden Ltd, Aldershot, 1949 p. 16.

19 Courage p. 16.

20 See Doughty *Breaking Point* p. 81.

21 Translation of Taped Conversation with General Hermann Balck p. 28.

22 Quoted in Doughty *Breaking Point* p. 48.

23 1.PzDiv: RH 27-1 Bundesarchiv-Militärarchiv Freiburg, Germany.

24 Robert Kershaw *Tank Men – The Human Story of Tanks at War* Hodder and Stoughton, 2008 p. 102.
25 Quoted in Frieser *Blitzkrieg Legend* p. 118.
26 Gull Interview 2011.
27 Horne p. 215.
28 Frieser *Blitzkrieg Legend* p. 142.
29 Quoted in Doughty *Breaking Point* p. 95.

Chapter 5

1 Arnaud Bauwens Interview 21 November 2014.
2 Courage p. 20.
3 Courage p. 20.
4 Diamond p. 32.
5 Courage p. 20.
6 Gerd Ritter Interview 16 April 2013.
7 Peter Meier Interview 21 April 2013.
8 Peter Meier Interview 21 April 2013.
9 See Weingartner p. 40.
10 Email from Lisa Hanson 8 April 2013.
11 Adolf Galland *The First and Last* Methuen and Co., 1955 pp. 12–13.
12 Michael J. F. Bowyer *2 Group RAF – A Complete History 1936–1945* Faber and Faber, 1974 p. 85.
13 Quoted in Robert Kershaw *Tank Men* p. 102.
14 Quoted in Robert Kershaw *Tank Men* p. 103.
15 Quoted in Robert Kershaw *Tank Men* p. 103.
16 Charles-Michel Lépée Interview 16 November 2014.
17 See Preface to Emile Cammaerts *The Prisoner at Laeken: King Leopold – Legend and Fact* Cresset Press, 1941.
18 Quoted in Doughty *Breaking Point* p. 68.
19 Doughty *Breaking Point* p. 286.
20 Quoted in Frieser *Blitzkrieg Legend* p. 118.
21 Quoted in Doughty *Breaking Point* p. 96.
22 Belgium Ministry of Foreign Affairs *Belgium: The Official Account of What Happened 1939–40* Evans Brothers Ltd, London, 1941 p. 38.
23 Figures from Frieser *Blitzkrieg Legend* p. 241.
24 Robert Kershaw *Tank Men* pp. 108–9.
25 Robert Kershaw *Tank Men* pp. 110–11.
26 4.PzDiv: RH 27-4 Bundesarchiv-Militärarchiv Freiburg, Germany.
27 Geoffrey Stewart *Dunkirk and the Fall of France* Pen and Sword, Barnsley, 2008 p. 35.
28 B. H. Liddell Hart (ed.) *The Rommel Papers* p. 7
29 6.PzDiv: RH 27-6/1D Bundesarchiv-Militärarchiv Freiburg, Germany.
30 Quoted in Doughty *Breaking Point* p. 99.
31 David Boyer Email 18 February 2015.

Chapter 6

1 David Boyer Email 18 February 2015.
2 For more see Frieser *Blitzkrieg Legend* p. 156.
3 John Williams *The Ides of May: The Defeat of France May-June 1940* Constable, 1968 p. 130.
4 Otto Gull Interview 18 July 2011.

5   29 N 27 2ème Armée Historique des Operations, Service Historique de la Défense, Vincennes, Paris.
6   Quoted in Doughty *Breaking Point* p. 99.
7   Max Meers Email 20 June 2012.
8   Peter Meier Interview 28 July 2013.
9   Joop van Praag Email 1 August 2013.
10 Quoted in Frieser *Blitzkrieg Legend* p. 230.
11 See Telp chapter in Ian Beckett (ed.) *Rommel – A Reappraisal* Pen and Sword, Barnsley, 2013 p. 48.
12 Quoted in Frieser *Blitzkrieg Legend* p. 233.
13 Quoted in Frieser *Blitzkrieg Legend* pp. 219–20.
14 See Frieser *Blitzkrieg Legends* p. 219.
15 32 N 251 55ème Division d'Infanterie, Service Historique de la Défense, Vincennes, Paris.
16 The Private War Journal of General Oberst Franz Halder Vol. IV The Campaign in France 10 May 1940 to 30 October 1940 (N-16845-D). Entry dated 13 May 1940 p. 9.
17 Heinz Guderian *Panzer Leader* Penguin, 2000 p. 101.
18 34 N 145 147ème Régiment d'Infanterie de Fortresse Service Historique de la Défense, Vincennes, Paris.
19 Robert Kershaw *Tank Men* pp. 103–104.
20 David Boyer Interview 18 February 2015.
21 Quoted in Citino *Quest for Decisive Victory* p. 269.
22 Quoted in Frieser *Blitzkrieg Legend* p. 159.
23 David Boyer Interview 18 February 2015.
24 See Frieser *Blitzkrieg Legend* p. 161.
25 Quoted in Doughty *Breaking Point* p. 143.
26 See Doughty *Breaking Point* pp. 149–150.
27 10.PzDiv: RH 27-10/9 Bundesarchiv-Militärarchiv Freiburg, Germany.
28 Quoted in Doughty *Breaking Point* p. 155.
29 Quoted in Doughty *Breaking Point* pp. 156–57.
30 Quoted in Doughty *Breaking Point* p. 190.
31 Quoted in Doughty *Breaking Point* p. 190.
32 1.PzDiv: RH 27-1/5 Bundesarchiv-Militärarchiv Freiburg, Germany.
33 1.PzDiv: RH 27-1/4 Bundesarchiv-Militärarchiv Freiburg, Germany.
34 32 N 251 Rapport de Général Lafontaine Service Historique de la Défense, Vincennes, Paris.
35 Quoted in Doughty *Breaking Point* p. 100.
36 Quoted in Horne p. 273.
37 Von Bock *The War Diary 1939–1945*. Entry dated 13 May 1940. p. 140.

Chapter 7

1   Otto Gull Interview 19 July 2011.
2   Jackson *The Fall of France 1940* p. 47.
3   Quoted in Alexander chapter in Bond (ed.) *Fallen Stars* p. 127.
4   Otto Gull Interview 19 July 2011.
5   Quoted in Doughty *Breaking Point* p. 255.
6   Krajewski in Guderian, H. (ed.) *Mit den Panzern in Ost und West* Volk

und Reich Verlag, Berlin, Prague and Vienna, 1942 p. 137.

7   Rapport de l'Aspirant Penissou S.H.A.T. 34N165.

8   Rapport de l'Aspirant Penissou S.H.A.T. 34N165.

9   Rapport de l'Aspirant Penissou S.H.A.T. 34N165.

10   See Rapport de Lieutenant Colonel P. Labarthe S.H.A.T. 34N165.

11   Heinz Guderian *Panzer Leader* Penguin, 2000 p. 84.

12   De la Vigerie, General François d'Astier *Le ciel n'était pas vide 1940* René Julliard, Paris, 1952 p. 107.

13   Figures from Frieser *Blitzkrieg Legend* p. 180.

14   Figures from Frieser *Blitzkrieg Legend* p. 180.

15   Quoted in Stewart p. 54.

16   Denis Richards, *Royal Air Force Vol. I, The Fight At Odds* HMSO, 1953 p. 120.

17   Quoted in Michael J. F. Bowyer *2 Group RAF – A Complete History 1936–1945* Faber and Faber, 1974 p. 89.

18   Quoted in Stewart p. 54.

19   Gerd Brausch 'Sedan 1940. Deuxième Bureau and Strategische Überraschung' *Militärgeschichtliche Zeitschrift* Vol. 2. No. 2 1967 p. 84.

20   Marc Bloch *Strange Defeat – A Statement of Evidence Written in 1940* W. W. Norton, New York, 1968 p. 43.

21   7.PzDiv: RH 27-7/2; 7/9; 7/11 Bundesarchiv-Militärarchiv Freiburg, Germany.

22   B. H. Liddell Hart (ed.) *The Rommel Papers* p. 13.

23   7.PzDiv: RH 27-7/2; 7/9; 7/11 Bundesarchiv-Militärarchiv Freiburg, Germany.

24   Quoted in Frieser *Blitzkrieg Legend* p. 235.

25   Quoted in Nick Shepley *Darkest Hour, Finest Hour: Norway, Dunkirk and the Battle of Britain – Britain at War: Part One* Andrews UK, Luton 2013 p. 134.

26   Führer Directive No.11 dated 14 May 1940 Author's Archive.

27   Figures from Stewart p. 38.

28   Barlone p. 47.

29   Werth p. 34.

30   Gribble p. 10.

31   Quoted in William L. Shirer *The Collapse of The Third Republic: An Inquiry into the Fall of France in 1940* Simon and Schuster, New York 1960 p. 679.

32   Winston S. Churchill *The Second World War – Volume II: Their Finest Hour* Cassell, 1949 pp. 38–39.

33   Quoted in Stewart p. 56.

34   Hermann Balck *Ordnung im Chaos. Erinnerungen 1893–1948* Osnabrück Biblio Verlag, 1980 p. 276.

35   Balck *Ordnung im Chaos. Erinnerungen* p. 276.

36   Balck *Ordnung im Chaos. Erinnerungen* p. 276.

37   Quoted in Robert Kershaw *Tank Men* p. 113.

38   Bruno Cantel Letter dated 12 June 1995.

39   Figures from Frieser p. 239.

40   B. H. Liddell Hart (ed.) *The Rommel Papers* p. 13.

41   B. H. Liddell Hart (ed.) *The Rommel Papers* p. 16.

42   B. H. Liddell Hart (ed.) *The Rommel Papers* p. 16.

43   *The Guardian* Obituary 17 January 2005.

44   For all this see J. A. Gunsburg 'The Battle of the Belgian Plain, 12–14 May 1940' *Journal of Military*

History 56, April 1992 and 'The Battle of Gembloux 14–15 May 1940', *Journal of Military History 64*, January 2000.

45   Frieser *Blitzkrieg Legend* p. 246.

46   Quoted in Alexander chapter in Bond (ed.) *Fallen Stars* p. 124.

Chapter 8

1   Churchill *Finest Hour* p. 42.

2   Churchill *Finest Hour* pp. 42–43.

3   Quoted in Diamond p. 35.

4   Quoted in Diamond p. 37.

5   The Private War Journal of General Oberst Franz Halder Vol. IV The Campaign in France 10 May 1940 to 30 October 1940 (N-16845-D). Entry dated 16 May 1940. p. 13.

6   1 Pz. Div. Kriegstagebuch Nr. 3 9.5.1940 – 2.6.1940 p. 29.

7   Bowyer p. 27.

8   Quoted in Bowyer p. 27.

9   Bowyer p. 28.

10   Quoted in Frieser *Blitzkrieg Legend* p. 266.

11   B. H. Liddell Hart (ed.) *The Rommel Papers* p. 17.

12   B. H. Liddell Hart (ed.) *The Rommel Papers* p. 18.

13   B. H. Liddell Hart (ed.) *The Rommel Papers* p. 20.

14   Quoted in Frieser *Blitzkrieg Legend* p. 266.

15   Bloch pp. 47–48.

16   B. H. Liddell Hart (ed.) *The Rommel Papers* p. 22.

17   B. H. Liddell Hart (ed.) *The Rommel Papers* p. 26.

18   Fraser *Rommel* p. 178.

19   Quoted in Fraser p. 180.

20   The Private War Journal of General Oberst Franz Halder Vol. IV The Campaign in France 10 May 1940

47   Major General Sir Edward Spears *Assignment to Catastrophe, Vol. 1 Prelude to Dunkirk July 1939– May 1940* A. A. Wyn Inc., New York, 1954 p. 148.

48   Quoted in Horne p. 373.

to 30 October 1940 (N-16845-D). Entry dated 17 May 1940. p. 17.

21   See B. H. Liddell Hart *The German Generals Talk* New York, W. Morrow, 1948 p. 128.

22   The Private War Journal of General Oberst Franz Halder Vol. IV The Campaign in France 10 May 1940 to 30 October 1940 (N-16845-D). Entry dated 17 May 1940. p. 16.

23   The Private War Journal of General Oberst Franz Halder Vol. IV The Campaign in France 10 May 1940 to 30 October 1940 (N-16845-D). Entry dated 17 May 1940. p. 16.

24   Führer Directive No. 12 dated 18 May 1940 Author's Archive.

25   The Private War Journal of General Oberst Franz Halder Vol. IV The Campaign in France 10 May 1940 to 30 October 1940 (N-16845-D). Entry dated 18 May 1940. p. 18.

26   Quoted in Charles Messenger *The Last Prussian: A Biography of Field Marshal Gerd von Rundstedt 1875–1953* Pen and Sword, Barnsley, 2012 p. 110.

27   Maxime Dufour Interview 19 April 2013.

28   A. Danchev and D. Todman (eds.) *War Diaries of Field Marshal Lord Alanbrooke*. Entry dated 18 May 1940. pp. 64–65.

29   Quoted in Robert Kershaw *Tank Men* pp. 115–16.

30 Quoted in Robert Kershaw *Tank Men* p. 16.

31 *Courage* p. 34.

32 Quoted in Nigel Hamilton *Monty: The Making of a General 1887–1942* Hamish Hamilton, 1981 p. 347.

33 The Private War Journal of General Oberst Franz Halder Vol. IV The Campaign in France 10 May 1940 to 30 October 1940 (N-16845-D). Entry dated 19 May 1940. p. 19.

34 Quoted in Horne p. 472.

35 Gamelin *Servir* pp. 3–4.

36 See Alexander chapter in Bond (ed.) *Fallen Stars* p. 126.

37 *The Ironside Diaries, 1937–1940.* Entry dated 17 May. p. 317.

38 *The Ironside Diaries, 1937–1940.* Entry dated 17 May. p. 321.

39 Quoted in Frieser *Blitzkrieg Legend* p. 283.

40 Quoted in Robert Kershaw *Tank Men* p. 106.

41 Quoted in Stewart p. 67.

42 General Jodl's Diary (Armed Forces Operational Staff) from 1 February to 26 May 1940 Document 1809-PS. Entry dated 20 May 1940.

43 Gribble p. 27.

44 Churchill *Finest Hour* p. 52.

Chapter 9

1 Emmanuel Marcel Interview 20 May 2012.

2 Emmanuel Marcel Interview 20 May 2012.

3 Emmanuel Marcel Interview 20 May 2012.

4 Quoted in Robert Kershaw *Tank Men* p. 119.

5 B. H. Liddell Hart (ed.) *The Rommel Papers* p. 32.

6 B. H. Liddell Hart (ed.) *The Rommel Papers* p. 32.

7 B. H. Liddell Hart (ed.) *The Rommel Papers* p. 32.

8 Brigadier Peter Vaux *Arras, An Eye-Witness Account*. Author's Archive. Undated and upaginated.

9 Brigadier Peter Vaux *Arras, An Eye-Witness Account*. Author's Archive. Undated and unpaginated.

10 Brigadier Peter Vaux *Arras, An Eye-Witness Account*. Author's Archive. Undated and unpaginated.

11 B. H. Liddell Hart (ed.) *The Rommel Papers* p. 33.

12 Quoted B. H. Liddell Hart (ed.) *The Rommel Papers* p. 34.

13 Bowyer p. 69.

14 Bowyer p. 95.

15 Figures from Bowyer p. 97.

16 Peter Mansfield Interview 30 August 2014.

17 Douglas Manning Interview 12 November 2014.

18 Quoted by Robert Kershaw *Tank Men* p. 107.

19 Diamond p. 40.

20 Diane Lebeouf Interview 2 June 1996.

21 Julia Lapointe Diary. Entry dated 22 May 1940. Author's Archive.

22 Diamond p. 39.

23 Heeresgruppe A: RH 19I/37 Bundesarchiv-Militärarchiv Freiburg, Germany.

24 See The Private War Journal of General Oberst Franz Halder Vol. IV The Campaign in France 10 May 1940 to 30 October 1940 (N-16845-D). Entry dated 22 May 1940. p. 25.

25 Aris p. 37.

26 Quoted in Stewart p. 82.

27 Marc Leicht Letter 10 November 2014.

28 Gerd Reismann Interview 6 May 2011.

29 Gerd Reismann Interview 6 May 2011.

30 Heeresgruppe A: RH 19I/38 Bundesarchiv-Militärarchiv Freiburg, Germany.

31 6.PzDiv: RH 27-6/1D Bundesarchiv-Militärarchiv Freiburg, Germany.

32 Guderian *Panzer Leader* p. 117.

33 The Private War Journal of General Oberst Franz Halder Vol. IV The Campaign in France 10 May 1940 to 30 October 1940 (N-16845-D). Entry dated 23 May 1940. p. 33.

34 Figure quoted in Frieser *Blitzkrieg Legend* p. 310.

35 Von Bock *The War Diary 1939–1945*. Entry dated 24 May 1940. p. 152.

36 Ian Kershaw *Hitler: Nemisis* p. 295.

37 The Private War Journal of General Oberst Franz Halder Vol. IV The Campaign in France 10 May 1940 to 30 October 1940 (N-16845-D). Entry dated 25 May 1940. p. 35.

38 Heeresgruppe A: RH 19I/38 Bundesarchiv-Militärarchiv Freiburg, Germany.

39 A. Danchev and D. Todman (eds.) *War Diaries of Field Marshal Lord Alanbrooke*. Entry dated 23 May 1940. p. 68.

Chapter 10

1 David Schneider Interview 18 June 2011.

2 Quoted in Robert Kershaw *Tank Men* p. 128.

3 Andrew Hardcastle Interview 2 July 2013.

4 Von Bock *The War Diary 1939–1945*. Entry dated 26 May 1940. p. 158.

5 Quoted in Robert Kershaw *Tank Men* p. 126.

6 Gribble p. 47.

7 Quoted in Jon Cooksey *Calais: Fight to the Finish – May 1940* Pen and Sword, Barnsley, 1999 p. 115.

8 Quoted in Bowyer p. 99.

9 David McCullen Diary. Entry dated 25 May 1940. Author's Archive.

10 Jan Hoch Letter 13 January 2013.

11 Churchill *Finest Hour* p. 73.

12 David McCullen Diary. Entry dated 25 May. Author's Archive.

13 The Private War Journal of General Oberst Franz Halder Vol. IV The Campaign in France 10 May 1940 to 30 October 1940 (N-16845-D). Entry dated 26 May 1940. p. 37.

14 Quoted in Mike Rossiter *I Fought at Dunkirk* Random House, 2012 p. 147.

15 Figures quoted in Frieser *Blitzkrieg Legend* p. 308.

16 Gribble p. 44.

17 John Colville *Fringes of Power: Downing Street Diaries 1939–1955* Weidenfeld and Nicolson, 2004. Entry dated 27 May 1940. p. 113.

18 Alexander Wilkins Interview 12 August 2011.

19 Quoted in Sean Longden, *Dunkirk – The Men They Left Behind* Constable, 2008 p. 74.

20 Quoted in Longden p.75.

21 The Private War Journal of General Oberst Franz Halder Vol. IV The Campaign in France 10 May 1940 to 30 October 1940 (N-16845-D). Entry dated 27 May 1940 p. 38.

22   Quoted in Longden pp. 75–76.
23   Quoted in www.telegraph.co.uk/history/world-war-two/7753912/Wormhoudt/Every-day-I-thank-God-we-did-our-duty.html Accessed 12 December 2014.
24   For more on this atrocity, see Longden; Julian Thompson *Dunkirk – Retreat To Victory* Sidgwick & Jackson 2008 and Hugh Sebag-Montefiore, *Dunkirk – Fight To The Last Man* Viking, 2006.
25   Andrew Hardcastle Interview 2 July 2013.
26   David McCullen Diary. Entry dated 6 March to 20 August 1940. Author's Archive.
27   John Colville Diary. Entry dated 27 May 1940. p. 113.
28   Churchill *Finest Hour* p. 81.
29   See Brian Bond *France and Belgium 1939–1940* Davis-Poynter, 1975 p. 92.
30   B. H. Liddell Hart (ed.) *The Rommel Papers* p. 41.
31   *The Halder War Diary 1939–1942.* p. 63.
32   Von Bock *The War Diary 1939–1945.* Entry dated 31 May 1940. p. 163.
33   The Private War Journal of General Oberst Franz Halder Vol. IV The Campaign in France 10 May 1940 to 30 October 1940 (N-16845-D). Entry dated 31 May 1940. p. 172.
34   David Blundell Telephone Interview 1 May 2014.
35   Tom Reed Interview 12 May 2014.
36   Hans Liebler Interview June 2014.
37   The Private War Journal of General Oberst Franz Halder Vol. IV The Campaign in France 10 May 1940 to 30 October 1940 (N-16845-D). Entry dated 30 May 1940. p. 42.
38   Courage p. 41.
39   A. Danchev and D. Todman (eds.) *War Diaries of Field Marshal Lord Alanbrooke.* Entry dated 30 May 1940. p. 73.
40   A. Danchev and D. Todman (eds.) *War Diaries of Field Marshal Lord Alanbrooke.* Entry dated 26 May 1940. p. 70.
41   Figures quoted in Frieser *Blitzkrieg Legend* p. 301.
42   Barlone p. 58.
43   Courage pp. 42–43.
44   Mahlke pp. 99–100.
45   Cairns chapter in B. Bond and Michael D. Taylor (eds.) *Battle for France and Flanders Sixty Years On* Leo Cooper, Barnsley, 2001 p. 90.
46   Von Kluge Diary. Entry dated 25 May 1940 quoted in Messenger p. 118.
47   Figure quoted in Frieser *Blitzkrieg Legend* p. 299.
48   Rab Riley Interview 12 October 1991
49   Quoted in Stewart p. 117.
50   Mahlke p. 102.
51   Ernie Smith Telephone Interview 28 November 2014.
52   http://www.bbc.co.uk/history/ww2peopleswar/stories/40/a2447840.shtml Accessed 12 November 2014.
53   http://www.bbc.co.uk/history/ww2peopleswar/stories/40/a2447840.shtml Accessed 12 November 2014.
54   Quoted in Longden p.1.
55   Quoted in W. J. R. Gardner, *The Evacuation from Dunkirk: Operation Dynamo 26 May to 4 June 1940* Frank Cass, 2000 p. 108.
56   Figures from Julian Thompson *Dunkirk – Retreat To Victory* Sidgwick & Jackson 2008 p. 306.

57 Hansard 4 June 1940 http://
hansard.millbanksystems.com/
commons/1940/jun/04/war-
situation Accessed 10 December
2014.

58 5 June Order of the Day Quoted in
Patrick Wilson 'Dunkirk: Victory

or Defeat?' in *History Today* History
Review Issue 37 September 2000.

59 Führer Directive No.13 dated 24
May 1940. Author's Archive.

60 Quoted in Frieser *Blitzkrieg Legend*
p. 307.

Chapter 11

1 Quoted in Diamond p. 8.

2 Figures quoted in Werth p. 127.

3 The Private War Journal of General
Oberst Franz Halder Vol. IV The
Campaign in France 10 May 1940
to 30 October 1940 (N-16845-D).
Entry dated 2 June 1940. p. 46.

4 Michel Sigaut Interview 15 January
2013.

5 See Martin S. Alexander 'After
Dunkirk: The French Army's
Performance against "Case Red",
25 May to 25 June 1940' in *War
in History* Vol. 14 No. 2 April 2007
p. 225.

6 See Bruce I. Gudmundsson, *On
Armor* Greenwood Publishing,
Westport, Conn., 2004.

7 See Alexander *After Dunkirk* p. 230.

8 Quoted in Alexander *After Dunkirk*
p. 246.

9 See Alexander *After Dunkirk* p. 238.

10 Figures quoted in Kaufmann
and Kaufmann *Hitler's Blitzkrieg
Campaigns* p. 267.

11 Quoted in Alexander *After Dunkirk*
p. 235.

12 Quoted in Alexander *After Dunkirk*
p. 236.

13 Quoted in Melvin p. 162.

14 The Private War Journal of General
Oberst Franz Halder Vol. IV The
Campaign in France 10 May 1940
to 30 October 1940 (N-16845-D).
Entry dated 5 June 1940. p. 52.

15 Figures quoted in E. R. Hooton,
*Luftwaffe at War: Blitzkrieg in
the West 1939–1940* Ian Allan,
Hersham, Surrey, 2007 p. 84.

16 Daniel Le Roy Telephone Interview
28 March 2013.

17 Hauptmann Friedrich Treitler Diary.
Entry dated 16 May 1940.

18 The Private War Journal of General
Oberst Franz Halder Vol. IV The
Campaign in France 10 May 1940
to 30 October 1940 (N-16845-D). 4
June 1940. p. 49.

19 B. H. Liddell Hart (ed.) *The Rommel
Papers* p. 43.

20 See Williams *Ides of May* p. 274.

21 B. H. Liddell Hart (ed.) *The Rommel
Papers* p. 48.

22 See Telp chapter in Ian Beckett (ed.)
Rommel – A Reappraisal Pen and
Sword, Barnsley, 2013.

23 Von Bock *The War Diary 1939–
1945*. Entry dated 5 June 1940.
pp. 165–66.

24 B. H. Liddell Hart (ed.) *The Rommel
Papers* p. 52.

25 B. H. Liddell Hart (ed.) *The Rommel
Papers* p. 60

26 Quoted in Frieser *Blitzkrieg Legend*
p. 223.

27 B. H. Liddell Hart (ed.) *The Rommel
Papers* p.66.

28 Serge Winter Letter 4 May 2013.

29 See Alexander *After Dunkirk* p. 248.

30 Quoted in Alexander p. 248.

31 Quoted in Alexander *After Dunkirk* p. 248.

32 Dominic Lemaire Letter 1 May 1994.

Chapter 12

1 Serge Winter Letter 4 May 2013.

2 Serge Winter Letter 4 May 2013.

3 Serge Winter Letter 4 May 2013.

4 The Private War Journal of General Oberst Franz Halder Vol. IV The Campaign in France 10 May 1940 to 30 October 1940 (N-16845-D). 6 June 1940. p. 55.

5 Quoted in Stewart p. 122.

6 See Major General F. W. von Mellenthin *Panzer Battles: A Study of the Employment of Armor in the Second World War* Ballantine Books, New York 1971 p. 25.

7 The Private War Journal of General Oberst Franz Halder Vol. IV The Campaign in France 10 May 1940 to 30 October 1940 (N-16845-D). Entry dated 10 June 1940. p. 67.

8 11 June 1940 The Private War Journal of General Oberst Franz Halder Vol. IV The Campaign in France 10 May 1940 to 30 October 1940 (N-16845-D) p. 70.

9 The Private War Journal of General Oberst Franz Halder Vol. IV The Campaign in France 10 May 1940 to 30 October 1940 (N-16845-D). Entry dated 13 June 1940. p. 76.

10 Führer Directive No. 15 dated 14 June 1940. Author's Archive.

11 Quoted in Alexander *After Dunkirk* p. 256.

12 Werth p. 144.

13 Diamond p. 48.

14 Quoted in Rupert Butler *Hitler's Death's Head Division: SS Totenkopf Divisions* Pen and Sword, Barnsley, 2004 p. 76.

15 Quoted in Diamond p. 1.

16 Quoted in Diamond p. 43.

17 Quoted in Diamond p. 58.

18 Werth p. 160.

19 See Frieser *Blitzkrieg Legend* p. 326.

20 Quoted in Roy Jenkins *Churchill* Pan Macmillan 2012 p. 616.

21 Walter Reid *Churchill 1940-1945: Under Friendly Fire* Birlinn, Edinburgh, 2008 p.4.

22 Colville p. 124.

23 Quoted in Diamond p. 50.

24 Quoted in Diamond p. 199.

25 Quoted in Martin Gilbert *Churchill – A Life* Heinemann, 1991 p. 659.

26 Major General Sir Edward Spears *Assignment to Catastrophe, Vol. 2 The Fall of France June 1940* A. A. Wyn Inc., New York, 1954 p. 231.

27 Quoted in Diamond p. 96.

28 Quoted in Diamond p. 90.

29 Julianne Deros Letter 16 November 2012.

30 Julianne Deros Letter 16 November 2012.

31 Quoted in Diamond p. 4.

32 Quoted in Diamond p. 71.

33 See E. R. Hooton *Phoenix Triumphant: The Rise and Rise of the Luftwaffe* Arms and Armour Press, London, 1994 p. 266.

34 Georges Sadoul *Journal de Guerre* Paris, Les Editeurs Français Réunis 1977. Entry dated 13 June 1940. p. 314.

35 Von Bock Diary *The War Diary 1939–1945*. Entry dated 13 June 1940. p. 175.

36 Ralf Buckholtz Interview 16 April 2011.

37 Von Bock *The War Diary 1939–1945*. Entry dated 14 June 1940. p. 176.

38 The Private War Journal of General Oberst Franz Halder Vol. IV The Campaign in France 10 May 1940 to 30 October 1940 (N-16845-D). Entry dated 14 June 1940. p. 76.

39 Paul Henkelmann Letter 1 May 2013.

40 A. Danchev and D. Todman (eds.) *War Diaries of Field Marshal Lord Alanbrooke* later note to entry dated 30 May 1940. p. 74.

41 A. Danchev and D. Todman (eds.) *War Diaries of Field Marshal Lord Alanbrooke* later note to entry dated 14 June 1940. p. 81.

42 Figures quoted in L. F. Ellis *War in France and Flanders, 1939–1940* HMSO, 1954 p. 327.

43 For more on this see M. Romanych and M. Rupp *Maginot Line 1940: Battles on the French Frontier* Osprey, Oxford, 2010 pp. 36–45.

44 For more on the withdrawal plan and the subsequent German operations against the Maginot Line see M. Romanych, and M. Rupp pp. 52–91.

45 *Blitzkrieg In Their Own Words: First Hand Accounts from German Soldiers 1939–1940* Amber Books, 2011 p. 210.

46 *Blitzkrieg In Their Own Words* p. 211.

47 Malke p. 184.

48 Dominic Royer Letter 8 June 2012

49 See www.lignemaginot.com/accueil/indexen.htm Accessed on 15 December 2015.

50 Jean-Yves Mary, Alain Hohnadel and Jacques Sicard *Hommes et Ouvrages de la Ligne Maginot, Tome 3*. Paris, Histoire & Collections, 2003, p. 201.

51 See www.lignemaginot.com/accueil/indexen.htm Accessed on 15 December 2015.

52 See Romanych and Rupp pp. 90–91.

53 The Private War Journal of General Oberst Franz Halder Vol. IV The Campaign in France 10 May 1940 to 30 October 1940 (N-16845-D). Entry dated 19 June 1940. p. 84.

54 http://www.ibiblio.org/pha/policy/1940/1940-06-16d.html Accessed 3 November 2013.

55 Werth p. 192.

56 A. Danchev and D. Todman (eds.) *War Diaries of Field Marshal Lord Alanbrooke* later note to entry dated 14 June 1940 p. 80.

57 *Blitzkrieg In Their Own Words* p. 237.

58 Quoted in Julian Jackson *The Fall of France: The Nazi Invasion of 1940* Oxford University Press, Oxford, 2003 p. 143.

59 Daniel Le Roy Telephone Interview 28 March 2013.

60 Julianne Deros Letter 23 November 2012.

61 Sergeant John Rigson Email 2 December 2012. Rigson had not managed to be evacuated from Nantes and joined refugees heading south.

62 Sergeant John Rigson Email 2 December 2012.

63 Quoted in Max Hastings *All Hell Let Loose* HarperPress, 2012 p. 71.

64 For more on his action see Hastings pp. 71–73.

65 www.lehrmaninstitute.org/history/index.html Accessed 12 July 2013.

66 Quoted in Knox MacGregor *Mussolini Unleashed, 1939–1941: Politics and Strategy in Fascist Italy's Last War* Cambridge University Press, Cambridge, 1982 p.128.

67 Quoted in MacGregor p.129.

68 Quoted in Gerhard Schreiber, Bernd Stegemann and Detlef Vogel *Germany and the Second World War, Volume III: The Mediterranean, South-East Europe, and North Africa 1939–1942* Clarendon Press, Oxford, 1995 p. 246.

69 For more on the fighting in the Alps see Emanuelle Sica 'June 1940: The Italian Army and the Battle of the Alps' in *Canadian Journal of History*, [S.l.], v. 47, n. 2, May. 2014 p. 374, and Douglas Porch *The Path to Victory: The Mediterranean Theater in World War II* New York, Farrar, Straus and Giroux, New York, 2005.

70 Figures quoted in Sica p. 374 and Porch p. 43.

71 The Private War Journal of General Oberst Franz Halder Vol. IV The Campaign in France 10 May 1940 to 30 October 1940 (N-16845-D). Entry dated 21 June 1940. p. 89.

72 Von Bock *The War Diary 1939–1945*. Diary entry dated 25 June 1940. p. 181.

Epilogue

1 Robert Hughes *Of Gods and Monsters* in *The Guardian* 1 February 2003.

2 Robert Hughes *Of Gods and Monsters* in *The Guardian* 1 February 2003.

3 Albert Speer *Inside the Third Reich* New York, Simon and Schuster, 1997 p. 172.

Conclusion

1 Quoted in Gordon A. Craig *The Germans* Penguin, New York, 1991 p. 15.

2 *Dad's Army: The Movie* Screenplay by Jimmy Perry and David Croft. Norcon/Columbia, 1971.

3 See Doughty chapter in Millett and Murray Vol. 2 p. 66.

4 Quoted in Doughty PhD p. 294.

5 Doughty *Breaking Point* p. 26.

6 See Hew Strachan *The Direction of War* p. 40.

7 A. Beaufre *1940 The Fall of France* Cassell, 1967 p. 197.

8 See Douglas Porch's criticisms in *Military 'Culture' and the Fall of France in 1940: A Review Essay* in *International Security*, Vol. 24 No. 4 Spring 2000 p. 179.

9 See Faris Russell Kirkland *The French Officer Corps and the Fall of France 1920–1940* PhD Thesis, University of Pennsylvania, 1982 p. 242, also Robert Allan Doughty PhD, 1979. pp. 32–67.

10 See Doughty chapter in Millet and Murray Vol. 2 pp. 58–59.

11 Kirkland PhD p. 26. On the poor performance of French staffs and commanders see Beaufre, pp. 179–212 and also Jean Delmas, 'La manoeuvre general, surprise allemande, défense française' in Christine Levisse-Touzé (ed.) *La Campagne de 1940* Paris, Tallandier, 2001 pp. 117–25.

12 Melvin p. 160.

13 Gruppe von Kleist: RH 21-1/320 Bundesarchiv-Militärarchiv Freiburg, Germany.

14 See Martin Alexander *After Dunkirk*.

15 Alexander *After Dunkirk* p. 258.

16 See Frieser *Blitzkrieg Legend* p. 315.

17   E. A. Cohen and J. Gooch *Military Misfortunes. The Anatomy of Failure in War* New York, Free Press, 1990 p. 220.

18   Figures quoted in Horne p. 666.

19   Figures quoted in Frieser *Blitzkrieg Legend* pp. 318–19 and Horne p. 667.

20   Strachan p. 40.

Select Bibliography

This bibliography contains a variety of sources that have been used in the preparation of this book. Not all are quoted from, but those that are can be found in the endnotes.

Books

(Place of publication is London unless otherwise stated)

Blitzkrieg in the West After The Battle, Battle of Britain, 1990

Blitzkrieg In Their Own Words: First-Hand Accounts from German Soldiers 1939–1940 Amber Books, 2011

The Rise and Fall of the German Air Force (1933 to 1945) Air Ministry Pamphlet No. 248 Public Record Office, Kew, 2001

Allcorn, William *The Maginot Line 1928–45* Oxford, Osprey Publishing, 2003

Alexander, Martin S. *The Republic in Danger: Maurice Gamelin and the Politics of the French Defence 1933–1940* Cambridge University Press, Cambridge, 1992

Amersfoort, Herman and Kamphuis, Piet (eds.) *Mei 1940 – De Strijd op Nederlands grondgebied* Den Haag, Sdu Uitgevers, 2005

Aris, George *The British Fifth Division 1939 to 1945* The Fifth Division Benevolent Fund, 1959

Ashton, H. S. *The Netherlands At War* George Routledge & Sons Ltd, 1941

Atkin, R. *Pillar of Fire 1940* Sidgwick & Jackson, 1990

Bailey, Gavin J. *The Arsenal of Democracy: Aircraft Supply and the Evolution of the Anglo-American Alliance, 1938–1942* Edinburgh University Press, Edinburgh, 2013

Baldoli, Claudia and Knapp, Andrew *Forgotten Blitzes: France and Italy Under Air Attack 1940–1945* Continuum, 2012

Bankwitz, Philip Charles Farwell *Maxime Weygand and Civil-Military Relations in Modern France* Cambridge, Mass., 1971

Barnett, C. (ed.) *Hitler's Generals* Weidenfeld and Nicolson, 1989

Barnett, C. et al. *Old Battles and New Defenses: Can We Learn From Military History?* Brassey's Defence Publishers, 1986

Battistelli, Pierre Paolo *Panzer Divisions: The Blitzkrieg Years, 1939–40* Osprey, Oxford, 2007

Battistelli, Pierre Paolo *Heinz Guderian* Oxford, Osprey, 2010

Battistelli, Pierre Paolo *Erwin Rommel* Oxford, Osprey, 2010

Beaufre, A. *1940 The Fall of France* Cassell, 1967

Beckett, Ian (ed.) *Rommel – A Reappraisal* Pen and Sword, Barnsley, 2013

Belgium Ministry of Foreign Affairs *Belgium: The Official Account of What Happened 1939–40* Evans Brothers Ltd, 1941

Bell, P. M. H. *A Certain Eventuality … Britain and the Fall of France* Saxon House, 1974

Below, N. von, *At Hitler's Side: The Memoirs of Hitler's Luftwaffe Adjutant 1937–1945* Greenhill Books, 2001

Bidwell, Shelford and Graham, Dominick *Fire-Power – British Army Weapons and Theories of War 1904–1945* George Allen & Unwin, 1982

Blatt, Joel (ed.) *The French Defeat of 1940 – Reassessments* Berghan Books, New York, 2006

Bloch, Marc *Strange Defeat – A Statement of Evidence Written in 1940* W.W. Norton, New York, 1968

Bond, Brian *France and Belgium 1939–1940* Davis-Poynter, 1975

Bond, Brian *British Military Policy between the Two World Wars* Oxford University Press, Oxford, 1980

Bond, Brian (ed.) *Fallen Stars: Eleven Studies of Twentieth Century Military Disasters* Brassey's, 1991

Bond, B. and Taylor, Michael D. (eds.) *Battle for France and Flanders Sixty Years On* Leo Cooper, Barnsley, 2001

Bowyer, Michael J. F. *2 Group RAF – A Complete History 1936–1945* Faber and Faber, 1974

Brongers, Lieutenant Colonel E. H. *The Battle for the Hague – 1940: The First Great Airborne Operation in History* Aspekt, Amsterdam, 2006

Bruce, Colin John *War on the Ground* Constable and Company, 1995

Bruge, Roger *Faites Sauter la Ligne Maginot!* Fayard, Paris, 1973

Bruge, Roger *On a Livré la Ligne Maginot* Fayard, Paris, 1973

Bryant, Arthur *The Turn of the Tide 1939–1943* Collins, 1957

Buckley, John *Air Power in the Age of Total War* UCL Press, 1999

Burleigh, Michael *Moral Combat: A History of World War II* HarperCollins, 2010

Butler, Rupert *Hitler's Death's Head Division: SS Totenkopf Divisions* Pen and Sword, Barnsley, 2004

Caffery, K. *Combat Report – The RAF and the Fall of France* Crowood Press, Swindon, 1990

Cammaerts, Emile *The Prisoner at Laeken: King Leopold – Legend and Fact* Cresset Press, 1941

Chapman, Guy *Why France Collapsed* Cassell and Co., 1968

Cherry Niall *Doomed from the Start: The Allied Intervention in Norway 1940* Helion & Co., Solihull, 2016

Christofferson, Thomas R. with Christofferson, Michael S. *France During World War II: From Defeat to Liberation* Fordham University Press, New York, 2006

Churchill, Winston S. *The Second World War – Volume II: Their Finest Hour* Cassell, 1949

Citino, Robert M. *Quest for Decisive Victory – From Stalemate to Blitzkrieg in Europe, 1899–1940* University Press of Kansas, Lawrence, Kansas, 2002

Citino, Robert M. *Blitzkrieg to Desert Storm: The Evolution of Operational Warfare* University of Kansas, Lawrence, Kansas, 2004

Citino, Robert M. *The Path to Blitzkrieg: Doctrine and Training in the German Army, 1920–39* Stackpole Books, Mechanicsburg, PA, 2008

Clark, Lloyd *Arnhem – Jumping the Rhine 1944 and 1945 – The Greatest Airborne Battle in History* Headline, 2008

Clausewitz, Carl *On War* (Translated and edited by Michael Howard and Peter Paret) Princeton, NJ, Princeton University Press, 1976

Cohen-Portheim, Paul *The Spirit of Paris* Batsford, 1937

Cohen, E. A. and Gooch, J. *Military Misfortunes. The Anatomy of Failure in War* New York, Free Press, 1990

Cole, Alistair *Franco-German Relations* Longman, Harlow, Essex, 2001

Colville, John *Fringes of Power: Downing Street Diaries 1939–1955* Weidenfeld and Nicolson, 2004

Condell, Bruce and Zabecki, David T. (eds.) *On the Art of War Tuppenführung – German Army Manual for Unit Command in World War II* Stackpole Books, Mechanicsburg, PA, 2009

Cooksey, Jon *Calais: Fight to the Finish – May 1940* Pen and Sword, Barnsley, 1999

Cooper, Matthew *The German Air Force 1933–1945: An Anatomy of Failure* Jane's, 1981

Cooper, Matthew *The German Army 1933–1945: Its Political and Military Failure* Jane's, 1978

Corbett, Anne and Johnson, Douglas (eds.) *A Day in June: Essays to Commemorate the Sixtieth Anniversary of de Gaulle's appel de 18 juin 1940* Franco-British Council, 2000

Corum, James S. *The Roots of Blitzkrieg: Hans von Seeckt and German Military Reform* University of Kansas Press, Lawrence, Kansas, 1994

Corum, James S. *The Luftwaffe: Creating the Operational Air War 1918–1940* University of Kansas Press, Lawrence, Kansas, 1997

Courage, Major Guy *The History of the 15/19 The King's Royal Hussars 1939–1945* Gale & Polden Ltd, Aldershot, 1949

Crahay, Lieutenant General Albert *L'Armée belge entre les deux guerres* Louis Musin, Brussels, 1978

Craig, Gordon A. *The Germans* Penguin, New York, 1991

Crémieux-Brilhac, Jean Louis *Les Français de l'an 40, Tome I* Editions Gallimard, Paris, 1990

Crémieux-Brilhac, Jean Louis *La Guerre oui ou non? Tome II Ouvriers et soldats* Editions Gallimard, Paris, 1990

Crozier, Brian *De Gaulle: The Warrior* Eyre Methuen, 1973

Cull, B., Lande, B. and Weiss, H., *Twelve Days in May – The Air Battles for Northern France and the Low Countries, May 1940* Grub Street, 1995

D'Astier de la Vigerie, General François *Le ciel n'était pas vide 1940* René Julliard, Paris, 1952

Deighton, Len *Blitzkrieg – From the Rise of Hitler to the Fall of Dunkirk* Triad Grafton Books, 1981

Deist, Wilhelm (ed.) *The German Military in the Age of Total War* Berg, New York, 1985

De la Gorce, Paul-Marie *The French Army: A Political-Military History* Weidenfeld and Nicolson, 1963

De Jong, L. *Holland Fights The Nazis* The Right Book Club, 1941

Diamond, Hanna *Fleeing Hitler – France 1940* Oxford University Press, Oxford, 2007

Dildy, Douglas C. *Fall Gelb 1940 (1) Panzer Breakthrough in the West* Osprey, Oxford, 2014

Dildy, Douglas C. *Fall Gelb 1940 (2) Airborne Assault on the Low Countries* Osprey, Oxford, 2015

DiNardo, R. L. *Germany's Panzer Arm in WWII* Stackpole Books, Mechanicsburg, PA, 2006

Divine, David The *Nine Days of Dunkirk* Faber and Faber, 1959

Dix, Anthony *The Norway Campaign and the Rise of Churchill 1940* Pen and Sword, Barnsley, 2014

Doorman, P. L. G. *Military Operations of the Dutch Army 10–17th May 1940* Helion & Co., Solihull, 2005

Doughty, Robert Allan *The Breaking Point – Sedan and the Fall of France, 1940* Archon Books, Hampden, Connecticut, 1990

Dunstan, Simon *Fort Eben-Emael*, Osprey, Oxford, 2005

Duroselle, J-B. *Politique Etrangère de la France. L'Abîme, 1939–45* Imprimerie Nationale, Paris, 1982

Dutailly, Lieutenant Colonel Henry *Les problèmes de l'armée de terre française (1935–1939)* Imprimerie Nationale, Paris, 1980

Ellis, L. F. *War in France and Flanders, 1939–1940* HMSO, 1954

Evans, M. M. *Fall of France: Act of Daring* Osprey, Oxford, 2000

Evans, Richard J. *The Third Reich at War: How the Nazis Led Germany from Conquest to Disaster* Penguin Books, 2009

Falkenau, Rene Paul *Of Eagles and Falcons* Falcon Press, Newcastle upon Tyne, 2011

Fowler, Will *France, Holland, and Belgium 1940* Ian Allan, Hersham, Surrey, 2002

Fraser, David *And We Shall Shock Them: The British Army in the Second World War* Hodder and Stoughton, 1983

Fraser, David *Alanbrooke* HarperCollins, 1982

Fraser, David *Knight's Cross – A Life of Field Marshal Erwin Rommel* HarperCollins, 1993

French, David *Raising Churchill's Army – The British Army and the War against Germany 1919–1945* Oxford University Press, Oxford, 2000

Frieser, Karl-Heinz *The Blitzkrieg Legend – The 1940 Campaign in the West* Naval Institute Press, Annapolis, 2005

Galland, Adolf *The First and Last* Methuen and Co., 1955

Gamelin, General Maurice *Servir* 3 Vols Librairie Plon, Paris, 1946–7

Gardner, W. J. R. *The Evacuation from Dunkirk: Operation Dynamo 26 May to 4 June 1940* Frank Cass, 2000

Germond, G. and Türk, H. (eds.) *A History of Franco-German Relations in Europe: from 'Hereditary Enemies' to Partners* Palgrave Macmillan, New York, 2008

Gilbert, Adrian *PoW: Allied Prisoners of War 1939–1945* John Murray, 2006

Gilbert, Martin *Churchill – A Life* Heinemann, 1991

Gooch, John *Decisive Campaigns of the Second World War* Frank Cass, 1990

Goutard, A. *The Battle for France 1940* Washburn Inc., New York, 1959

Gribble, Philip *The Diary of a Staff Officer, Air Intelligence Liaison Officer, at Advanced Headquarters North B.A.F.F., 1940* Methuen & Co., 1941

Guderian, H. *Achtung – Panzer!* Cassel, 1992

Guderian, H. *Panzer Leader* Penguin, 2000

Guderian, H. (ed.) *Mit den Panzern in Ost und West* Volk und Reich Verlag, Berlin, Prague and Vienna, 1942

Gudmundsson, Bruce I. *On Armor* Greenwood Publishing, Westport, Conn., 2004

Gunsburg, Jeffrey A. *Divided and Conquered: The French High Command and the Defeat of the West, 1940* Greenwood Publishing, Westport, Conn., 1979

Hallion, Richard P. *The History of Battlefield Air Attack 1911–1945* Airlife, Shrewsbury, 1989

Hamilton, Nigel *Monty: The Making of a General 1887–1942* Hamish Hamilton, 1981

Harris, J. P. *Men, Ideas and Tanks – British Military Thought and Armoured Forces, 1903–1939* Manchester University Press, Manchester, 1995

Hart, Russell A. *Guderian: Panzer Pioneer or Myth Maker?* Pentagon Press, New Delhi, 2010

Haskew, Michael E. *De Gaulle: Lessons in Leadership from a Defiant General* Palgrave Macmillan, New York, 2011

Hastings, Max *All Hell Let Loose* HarperPress, 2012

Hauteclet, Georges *Rommel and Guderian against the Belgian Chasseurs Ardennais: The Combats at Chabrehez and Bodange, 10 May 1940* West Chester, Ohio, 2003

Hayward, J. *Myths and Legends of the Second World War* Sutton, Stroud, 2003

Hinsley, F. H. *British Intelligence in the Second World War Vol. I* HMSO, 1979

Historique de l'Armée (Official History) *Les Grandes Unités françaises: Historiques succincts* 5 Vols Imprimerie Nationale, Paris, 1967–1975

Hittle, J. D. *The Military Staff – Its History and Development* Stackpole, Harrisburg, Pennsylvania, 1961

Hooton, E. R. *Luftwaffe at War: Blitzkrieg in the West 1939–1940* Ian Allan, Hersham, Surrey 2007

Hooton, E. R. *Phoenix Triumphant: The Rise and Rise of the Luftwaffe* Arms and Armour Press, London, 1994

Horne, Alistair *To Lose a Battle – France 1940* Penguin Books, 1990

Horne, Alistair *The French Army and Politics, 1870–1970* Macmillan Press, 1984

House, Jonathan M. *Combined Arms Warfare in the Twentieth Century* University Press of Kansas, Lawrence, Kansas, 2001

Hughes, Judith M. *To The Maginot Line – The Politics of French Military Preparation in the 1920s* Harvard University Press, Cambridge, Massachusetts, 2006

Jackson, Julian *The Fall of France: The Nazi Invasion of 1940* Oxford University Press, Oxford, 2003

Jackson, Julian *Dunkirk: The British Evacuation, 1940* Arthur Barker, 1976

Jenkins, Roy *Churchill* Pan Macmillan, 2012

Joseph-Maginot, Marguerite *He Might Have Saved France: The Biography of*

André Maginot Doubleday, Doran and Co., New York, 1941

Kaufmann, J. E. and Kaufmann, H. W. et al *The Maginot Line – History and Guide* Pen and Sword Military, Barnsley, 2011

Kaufmann, J. E. and Kaufmann, H. W. *Fortress France: The Maginot Line and French Defenses in World War II* Stackpole Books, Mechanicsburg, PA, 2006

Kaufmann, J. E. and Kaufmann, H. W. *Hitler's Blitzkrieg Campaigns – The Invasion and Defense of Western Europe, 1939–1940* Da Capo Press, Cambridge, MA, 1993

Keegan, J. (ed.) *Churchill's Generals* Weidenfeld and Nicolson, 1991

Keegan, J. *Intelligence in War – Knowledge of the Enemy From Napoleon to Al-Qaeda* Hutchinson, 2003

Kershaw, I. *Hitler 1889–1936 Hubris* Allen Lane, 1998

Kershaw, I. *Hitler 1936–1945 Nemesis* Allen Lane, 2000

Kershaw, Robert *Tank Men – The Human Story of Tanks at War* Hodder and Stoughton, 2008

Kier, Elizabeth *Imagining War: French and British Military Doctrine between the Wars* Princeton University Press, Princeton, NJ, 1997

Kiesling, Eugenia C. *Arming Against Hitler – France and the Limits of Military Planning* University of Kansas, Lawrence, Kansas, 1996

King, Anthony *The Combat Soldier: Infantry Tactics and Cohesion in the Twentieth and Twenty-First Centuries,* Oxford University Press, Oxford, 2013

Knox, MacGregor *Mussolini Unleashed, 1939–1941: Politics and Strategy in Fascist Italy's Last War* Cambridge University Press, Cambridge, 1982

Kossmann, E. H. *The Low Countries 1780–1940* Oxford, Clarendon Press, 1978

Kurowski, Franz *Panzer Aces – German Tank Commanders of WWII* Stackpole Books, Mechanicsburg, PA, 2004

Levine, Joshua *Forgotten Voices – Dunkirk* Ebury, 2010

Levisse-Touzé, Christine (ed.) *La Campagne de 1940* Paris, Tallandier, 2001

Liddell Hart, B. H. *The Other Side of the Hill* Cassell, 1948

Liddell Hart, B. H. *The German Generals Talk* New York, W. Morrow, 1948

Liddell Hart, B. H. (ed.) *The Rommel Papers* Collins, 1953

Longden, Sean *Dunkirk – The Men They Left Behind* Constable, 2008

Luck, Hans von *Panzer Commander – The Memoirs of Colonel Hans von Luck* Cassell, 1989

Lukacs, John *Five Days in London May 1940* Yale, Nota Bene, 2001

Lyet, Commandant Pierre *La Bataille De France (Mai-Juin 1940)* Payot, Paris, 1947

Maass, Walter B. *The Netherlands at War: 1940–1945* Abelard–Schuman, Amsterdam, 1970

Mahlke, Helmut *Memoirs of a Stuka Pilot* Frontline Books, Barnsley, 2013

Mallinson, Vernon *Belgium* Ernest Benn, 1969

Martin, Benjamin F. *France and the Après Guerre, 1918–24: Illusions and Disillusionment* Louisiana State University Press, Baton Rouge, 1999

Mary, Jean-Yves, Hohnadel, Alain and Sicard, Jacques *Hommes et Ouvrages de la Ligne Maginot, Tome 3* Paris, Histoire & Collections, 2003

Maurois, André *The Battle of France* Bodley Head, 1940

May, Ernest R. *Strange Victory: Hitler's Conquest of France* Hill and Wang, New York, 2000

May, Ernest R. (ed.) *Knowing One's Enemies* Princeton University Press, Princeton, NJ, 2014

Mead, Richard *Churchill's Lion: A Biographical Guide to the Key British Generals of World War II* Spellmount, Stroud, Gloucestershire, 2007

Mearsheimer, John J. *Conventional Deterrence* University Press, Ithaca, New York and London: Cornell, 1983

Mellenthin, Major General F. W. von *Panzer Battles: A Study of the Employment of Armor in the Second World War* Ballantine Books, New York, 1971

Melvin, Mungo *Manstein – Hitler's Greatest General* Weidenfeld and Nicolson, 2010

Messenger, Charles *The Last Prussian: A Biography of Field Marshal Gerd von Rundstedt 1875–1953* Pen and Sword, Barnsley, 2012

Michel, Henri (ed.) *La Libération de la France* CNRS, Paris, 1976

Millett, Allan R. and Murray, Williamson *Military Effectiveness Volume 2: The Interwar Years* Cambridge University Press, New York, 2010

Millett, Allan R. and Murray, Williamson *Military Effectiveness Volume 3: The Second World War* Cambridge University Press, New York, 2010

Mitcham, Samuel W. Jnr *Hitler's Field Marshals and their Battles* Grafton Books, 1989

Mitcham, Samuel W. Jnr *Panzer Legions – A Guide to the German Army Tank Divisions and their Commanders* Stackpole Books, Mechanicsburg, PA, 2007

Moore, Mortimer William *Free France's Lion – The Life of Philippe Leclerc, de Gaulle's Greatest General* Casemate, Philadelphia US and Newbury UK, 2011

More, Charles *The Road to Dunkirk – The British Expeditionary Force and the Battle of the Ypres-Comines Canal, 1940* Frontline Books, Barnsley, 2013

Murray, Williamson, Knox, Macgregor and Bernstein, Alvin (eds.) *The Making of Strategy: Rulers, States and War* Cambridge University Press, Cambridge, 1994

Murray, Williamson *Luftwaffe: Strategy for Defeat* Quantum Publishing, 2000

Naveh, Shimon *In Pursuit of Military Excellence: The Evolution of Operational Theory* Frank Cass, Portland, Oregon, 1997

Neave, Airey *The Flames of Calais – A Soldier's Battle 1940* Leo Cooper, Hodder and Stoughton, 1972

Neitzel, Sönke and Wezer, Harald *Soldaten – On Fighting and Killing and Dying* Simon and Schuster, 2012

Newton, Gerald *The Netherlands: An Historical and Cultural Survey 1795– 1977* Ernest Benn, 1978

Nord, Philip *France 1940: Defending the Republic* Yale University Press, New Haven and London, 2015

Ousby, Ian *Occupation – The Ordeal of France 1940–1944* Pimlico, 1999

Overy, Richard *Why the Allies Won* W. W. Norton and Co., New York, 1996

Overy, Richard *The Origins of the Second World War* Routledge, 2008

Overy, Richard with Andrew Wheatcroft *The Road to War* Vintage, 2009

Peden, G. C. *British Rearmament and the Treasury, 1932–1939* Scottish Academic Press, Edinburgh, 1979

Pettibone, Charles D. *The Organization and Order of Battle of Militaries in World War II: Vol. I – Germany* (2006); *Vol. II – The British Commonwealth* (2006); *Vol. VI – Italy and France* (2010) and *Vol. X – The Overrun and Neutral Nations of Europe and Latin American Allies* (2014) Trafford Publishing, Victoria, Canada

Porch, Douglas *The Path to Victory: The Mediterranean Theater in World War II (1st ed.)* Farrar, Straus and Giroux, New York, 2005

Posen, Barry R. *The Sources of Military Doctrine: France, Britain and Germany Between the Wars* Cornell University Press, New York, 1984

Powaski, Ronald E. *Lightning War: Blitzkrieg in the West, 1940.* John Wiley, Hoboken, NJ, 2003

Preston, Adrian (ed.) *General Staffs and Diplomacy Before the Second World War* Croom Helm, 1978

Ramsden, John *Don't Mention the War: The British and the Germans Since 1890* Little, Brown, 2006

Reid, Walter *Churchill 1940–1945: Under Friendly Fire* Birlinn, Edinburgh, 2008

Resende-Santos, João *Neorealism, States, and the Modern Mass Army* Cambridge University Press, Cambridge, 2007

Reynaud, Paul *In the Thick of the Fighting 1930–1945* Cassell, 1955

Riboud, Jacques *Souvenirs D'Une Bataille Perdue (1939–40)* François-Xavier de Guibert, Paris, 2006

Richards, Denis *Royal Air Force Vol. I, The Fight At Odds* HMSO, 1953

Risser, Nicole Dombrowski *France Under Fire: German Invasion, Civilian Flight, and Family Survival during World War II* Cambridge University Press, Cambridge, 2012

Robb, Graham *The Discovery of France* Picador, 2007

Romanych, M. and Rupp, M. *Maginot Line 1940: Battles on the French Frontier* Osprey, Oxford, 2010

Rosbottom, Ronald *When Paris Went Dark: The City of Light Under German Occupation 1940–44* John Murray, 2014

Rossiter, Mike *I Fought at Dunkirk* Random House, 2012

Rothbrust, Florian K. *Guderian's XIXth Panzer Corps and The Battle of France – Breakthrough in the Ardennes, May 1940* Praeger, Westport, CT, 1990

Sadoul, Georges *Journal de Guerre* Les Editeurs Français Réunis, Paris 1977

Sartre, Jean-Paul *War Diaries: Notebooks from a Phoney War 1939–40* Verso Editions, 1984

Schneider, Wolfgang *Panzer Tactics – German Small Unit Armor Tactics in World War II* Stackpole Books, Mechanicsburg, PA, 2005

Schreiber, Gerhard, Stegemann, Bernd and Vogel, Detlef *Germany and the Second World War, Volume III: The Mediterranean, South-East Europe, and North Africa 1939–1942* Oxford, Clarendon Press, 1995

Schwarzschild, Leopold *World in Trance* Hamish Hamilton, 1943

Sebag-Montefiore, Hugh *Dunkirk – Fight To The Last Man* Viking, 2006

Shay, Robert Paul Jnr. *British Rearmament in the Thirties* Princeton University Press, Princeton, NJ, 1977

Shepley, Nick *Darkest Hour, Finest Hour: Norway, Dunkirk and the Battle of Britain – Britain at War: Part One* Andrews UK, Luton, 2013

Shirer, William L. *The Collapse of The Third Republic: An Inquiry into the Fall of France in 1940* New York, Simon and Schuster, 1960

Short, Neil *The Führer's Headquarters: Hitler's Command Bunkers 1939–45* Osprey, Oxford, 2010

Showalter, Dennis *Hitler's Panzers – The Lightning Attacks that Revolutionized Warfare* Penguin, New York, 2009

Smalley, Edward *The British Expeditionary Force, 1939–40* Palgrave Macmillan, 2015

Smith, M. A. *British Air Strategy Between the Wars* Oxford University Press, Oxford, 1984

Speer, Albert *Inside the Third Reich* Simon and Schuster, New York, 1997

Steiger, Rudolf *Panzertaktik im Spiegel deutscher Kriegstagerbücher 1939 bis 1941* Verlag Robach, Freiburg, 1973

Stewart, Geoffrey *Dunkirk and the Fall of France* Pen and Sword, Barnsley, 2008

Stone, David *Twilight of the Gods: The Decline and Fall of the German General Staff in World War II* Conway, 2011

Strachan, Hew *European Armies and the Conduct of War* Unwin Hyman, 1983

Strachan, Hew *The Direction of War: Contemporary Strategy in Historical Perspective* Cambridge University Press, Cambridge, 2013

Strohn, Matthias *The German Army and the Defence of the Reich: Military Doctrine and the Conduct of the Defensive Battle 1918–1939* Cambridge University Press, Cambridge, 2011

Thomas, Nigel *Foreign Volunteers of the Allied Forces, 1939–45* Osprey, 1991

Thompson, Julian *Dunkirk – Retreat To Victory* Sidgwick & Jackson 2008

Tombs, Robert and Tombs, Isabelle *That Sweet Enemy: Britain and France, The History of a Love-Hate Relationship* Heinemann, 2006

Tombs, Robert and Chabal, Emile (eds.) *Britain and France In Two World Wars – Truth, Myth and Memory* Bloomsbury, 2013

Tooze, Adam *Wages of Destruction* Allen Lane, 2006

Trevor-Roper, H. R. (ed.) *Hitler's War Directives* Sidgwick & Jackson, 1964

Tucker, Spencer (ed.) *Encyclopedia of World War II – A Political, Social and Military History* Santa Barbara, California, 2005

Turner, E. S. *The Phoney War on the Home Front* Michael Joseph, 1961

Villahermosa, Gilberto *Hitler's Paratrooper – The Life and Battles of Rudolf Witzig* Frontline Books, 2010

Warmbrunn, Werner *The Dutch under German Occupation* Stanford University Press, California, 1963

Warmbrunn, Werner *The German Occupation of Belgium* Peter Lange, New York, 1993

Warner, Philip *Battle for France, 1940* Simon and Schuster, 1990

Weber, Eugen *The Hollow Years – France in the 1930s* Sinclair-Stevenson, 1995

Weingartner, James J. *Hitler's Guard: The Story of the Leibstandarte SS Adolf Hitler 1933–1945* Southern Illinois University Press, Carbondale and Edwardsville, 1968

Werth, Alexander *The Last Days of Paris: A Journalist's Diary* Hamish Hamilton, 1940

Weygand, J. *The Role of General Weygand: Conversations with his Son* Eyre and Spottiswoode, 1948

Weygand, M. *Recalled to Service* Heinemann, 1952

Williams, John *The Ides of May: The Defeat of France May-June 1940* Constable, 1968

Williamson, Gordon *Loyalty is My Honour* BCA, 1995

Wiser, William *The Twilight Years –
Paris in the 1930s* Carroll and Graf
Publishers Inc., New York, 2000

Wright, Patrick *Tank – The Progress of a
Monstrous War Machine* Faber and
Faber, 2000

Young, R. J. *In Command of France:
French Foreign and Military Planning
1933–1940* Harvard University Press,
Cambridge, Mass., 1978

Young, Desmond *Rommel* Collins, 1950

Zaloga, Steven J. and Madej, Victor *The
Polish Campaign 1939* Hippocrene
Books Inc., New York, 1985

Chapters and Articles

Alexander, Don W. 'Repercussions of the
Breda Variant' in *French Historical
Studies* Vol. 8 No. 3 Spring 1974

Alexander, Martin S. 'After Dunkirk: The
French Army's Performance against
"Case Red", 25 May to 25 June 1940'
in *War in History* Vol. 14 No. 2 April
2007

Alexander, Martin S. 'The Fall of France'
in *Journal of Strategic Studies* Vol. 13
No. 1 1990

Ausems, André 'The Netherlands Military
Intelligence Summaries 1939–40 and
the Defeat in the Blitzkrieg of May
1940' in *Military Affairs*, Vol. 50 No.
4 October 1986

Brausch, Gerd 'Sedan 1940. Deuxième
Bureau and Strategische
Überraschung' *Militärgeschichtliche
Zeitschrift* Vol. 2. No. 2 1967

Cairns, J. C. 'Some Recent Historians
and the "Strange Defeat" of 1940' in
Journal of Modern History Vol. 46 No.
1 March 1974

Cinto, Robert 'The War Hitler Won:
The Battle for Europe, 1939–1941'
in *Journal of Military and Strategic
Studies* Vol. 14 Issue 1 Fall 2011

Doughty, Robert A. 'French Anti-tank
Doctrine, 1940 The Antidote that
Failed' in *Military Review* 56 May
1976

Doughty, Robert A. 'Myth of the
Blitzkrieg' in *Strategic Studies Institute
of the US Army War College* 1998

Fodor, M. W. 'The Blitzkrieg in the Low
Countries' in *Foreign Affairs* Vol. 19
No. 1 October 1940

French, David 'Doctrine and
Organization in the British Army,
1919–32' in *The Historical Journal*
Vol. 44 No. 52 June 2001

Frieser, Karl-Heinz 'Panzer Group Kleist
and the Breakthrough in France,
1940' in Krause, Michael D. and
Phillips, Cody R. (eds.), *Historical
Perspectives of the Operational
Art* Center for Military History,
Washington D.C. 2005

Gunsburg, J. A. 'The Battle of the Belgian
Plain, 12–14 May 1940' in *Journal of
Military History* 56 April 1992

Gunsburg, J. A. 'The Battle of Gembloux,
14–15 May 1940' *Journal of Military
History* 64 January 2000

Harvey, A. D. 'The French Armée de
l'Air in May-June 1940: A Failure
of Conception' in *Journal of
Contemporary History* Vol. 25 No. 4
October 1990

Howard, Michael 'The Use and Abuse
of Military History' in *Royal United
Services Institute Journal* No. 107
February 1962

Jackson, Peter 'Recent Journeys Along The Road Back to France, 1940' in *The Historical Journal* Vol. 39 No. 2 June 1996

Jackson, Peter 'French Intelligence and Hitler's Rise to Power' in *The Historical Journal* Vol. 41 No. 3 September 1998

Jacobson, Jon 'Strategies of French Foreign Policy after World War I' in *The Journal of Modern History* Vol. 55 No. 1 March 1983

Kirkland, Lieutenant Colonel Faris R. 'The French Air Force in 1940: Was It Defeated by the Luftwaffe or by Politics?' in *The Air University Review* September-October 1985

Lochner, Louis P. 'The Blitzkrieg in Belgium: A Newsman's Eyewitness Account' in *The Wisconsin Magazine of History* Vol. 50 No. 4 Summer 1967

M.B. 'The Strategic Position of Holland and Belgium' in *Bulletin of International News* Vol. 16 No. 24 December 1939

Marks, Sally 'The Myths of Reparations' in *Central European History*, Vol. 11 No. 3 September 1978

Mason, Henry L. 'War Comes to the Netherlands: September 1939 to May 1940' in *Political Science Quarterly* Vol. 78 No. 40 December 1963

Murray, Williamson 'The German Response to Victory in Poland: A Case Study in Professionalism' in *Armed Forces and Society* Vol. 7 1981

O'Connell, Colonel J. J. 'The Maginot Line: Dream or Reality?' in *Studies: An Irish Quarterly Review* Vol. 29 No. 116 December, 1940

Porch, D. 'French Intelligence and the Fall of France, 1930–40' in *Intelligence and National Security* Vol. 4 No. 1 January 1989

Porch, Douglas 'Military "Culture" and the Fall of France in 1940': A Review Essay in *International Security* Vol. 24 No. 4 Spring 2000

Porch, Douglas 'Why Did France Fall?' in *Quarterly Journal of Military History* Spring, 1990

Pugsley, Christopher 'We Have Been Here Before: The Evolution of Decentralized Command in the British Army 1905–1989' in *Sandhurst Occasional Papers* No. 9 Central Library Royal Military Academy Sandhurst, Camberley, Surrey 2001

Rajevs, Colonel Igors 'The French Army in the Interwar Period' in *Baltic Security & Defence Review* Vol. 11 Issue 2 2009

Sica, Emanuelle 'June 1940: The Italian Army and the Battle of the Alps' in *Canadian Journal of History*, [S.l.], v. 47, n. 2, May 2014

Strachan, Hew 'Operational Art and Britain, 1909–2009', in Olsen, John Andreas and van Creveld, Martin (eds.) *The Evolution of Operational Art: From Napoleon to the Present* Oxford University Press, Oxford 2011

Thomas, Martin 'French Economic Affairs and Rearmament: The First Crucial Months, June to September 1939' in *Journal of Contemporary History* Vol. 27 No. 4 October 1992

Wilson, Patrick 'Dunkirk: Victory or Defeat?' in *History Today* History Review Issue 37 September 2000

Young, Robert J. 'The Strategic Dream: French Air Doctrine in the Inter-War Period, 1919–1939' in *Journal of Contemporary History*, January 1974

Magazine Articles

France: Death & Crisis *Time* Monday, January 18, 1932

France: The Good Grey General *Time* Monday, August 14, 1939

'Blitzkriegen' *Time* Monday, September 25, 1939

Published Documents, Memoirs, Journals and Diaries

Alanbrooke, Lord *War Diaries of Field Marshal Lord Alanbrooke* Danchev, A. and Todman, D. (eds.), Weidenfeld and Nicolson, 2001

Balck, Hermann *Ordnung im Chaos. Erinnerungen 1893–1948* Osnabrück Biblio Verlag, 1980

Barlone, D. *A French Officer's Diary 23 August 1939 to 1 October 1940* Cambridge: At the University Press New York: The Macmillan Company, 1943

Bock, Generalfeldmarschall Fedor von *The War Diary 1939–1945* Schiffer Publishing Ltd, Atglen, PA, 1996

D'Astier de la Vigerie, General François *Le ciel n'était pas vide* Paris, René Julliard, 1952

De Gaulle, Charles *Mémoires de Guerre* (3 Vols) Plon, Paris, 1954

Detwiler, Donald S. (ed.) *World War II German Military Studies: A Collection of 213 Special Reports on the Second World War Prepared by Former Officers of the Wehrmacht for the United States Army Vol. 11 Part IV* Garland Publishing, New York and London, 1979

Grandsard, General C. *Le 10ème Corps d'Armée dans la Bataille, 1939–1940* Paris, Berger-Levrault, 1949

Halder, General Franz *The Halder War Diary 1939–1942* Burdick, Charles and Jacobsen, Hans-Alfred (eds.) Greenhill Books, 1988

Ironside, Sir Edmund *Time Unguarded: The Ironside Diaries, 1937–1940* Macleod, Colonel Roderick and Kelly, Denis (eds.) Constable, London, 1962

The Memoirs of Field Marshal Wilhelm Keitel Gorlitz, Walter (ed.) Cooper Square Press, New York, 2000

Manstein, General Erich von *Lost Victories* Chicago, Henry Regnery Co., 1958

Pownall, Lieutenant General Sir Henry, *Diaries of Lieutenant General Sir Henry Pownall, Vol. I 'Chief of Staff'* Bond, B. (ed.) Leo Cooper, 1972

Prüller, Wilhelm *Diary of a German Soldier* Faber and Faber, London, 1963

Spears, Major General Sir Edward *Assignment to Catastrophe, Vol. 1 Prelude to Dunkirk July 1939 to May 1940* A. A. Wyn Inc., New York, 1954

Spears, Major General Sir Edward *Assignment to Catastrophe, Vol. 2 The Fall of France June 1940* A. A. Wyn Inc, New York, 1954

Unpublished Sources

Doughty, Robert Allan *The Evolution of French Army Doctrine 1919–1939* PhD Thesis, University of Kansas, 1979

Kirkland, Lieutenant Colonel Faris R. *The French Officer Corps and the Fall of France 1920–1940* PhD Thesis, University of Pennsylvania, 1982

Parker, Robert *'Où est la Masse de Manoeuvre?': Maurice Gamelin and the Lessons of Blitzkrieg in Poland* MA Dissertation, Concordia University Montreal, Quebec, Canada, 2013

May, Ernest R. *The Intelligence Process: The Fall of France, 1940* Kennedy School of Government

Pierre Roussel diary 1939 and 1940. Roussel family archive.

Interviews and Correspondence

Germany

Ralf Buckholtz Interview 16 April 2011

Peter Gerber for information about his father, Karl Gerber 1 May 2014

Otto Gull Interview 18 and 19 July 2011

Paul Henkelmann Letter 1 May 2013

Jan Hoch Letter 13 January 2013

Marc Leicht Letter 10 November 2014

Hans Liebler Interview June 2014

Peter Meier Interview 21 April 2013

Gerd Reismann Interview 6 May 2011

Gerd Ritter Interview 16 April 2013

Albert Winkler Interview 16 March 2013 and Email 20 December 2014

The Netherlands

Lisa Hanson Email 8 April 2013

Conrad Houtkooper Letter 21 May 2013

Max Meers Email 20 June 2012

Peter Meier Interview 28 July 2013

Joop van Praag Email 1 August 2013

Belgium

Arnaud Bauwens Interview 21 November 2014

France

David Boyer Interview 18 February 2015

Bruno Cantel Letter 12 June 1995

Julianne Deros Letter 16 and 23 November 2012

Maxime Dufour Interview 19 April 2013

Diane Lebeouf Interview 2 June 1996

Dominic Lemaire Letter 1 May 1994

Charles-Michel Lépée Interview 16 November 2014

Daniel Le Roy Telephone Interview 28 March 2013

Emmanuel Marcel Interview 20 May 2012

Dominic Royer Letter 8 June 2012

David Schneider Interview 18 June 2011

Michel Sigaut Interview 15 January 2013

Serge Winter Letter 4 May 2013

Britain

David Blundell Telephone Interview 1 May 2014

Andrew Hardcastle Interview 2 July 2013

Douglas Manning Interview 12 November 2014

Peter Mansfield Interview 30 August 2014

Tom Reed Interview 12 May 2014

Rab Riley Interview 12 October 1991

John Rigson Email 2 December 2012

Ernie Smith Telephone Interview 28 November 2014

Peter Vaux Letter 20 February 1996

Alexander Wilkins Interview 12 August 2011

Author's Archive

The War Illustrated 21 October 1939 Vol.1 No. 6

The Guardian Obituary 17 January 2005

Brigadier Peter Vaux *Arras: An Eye-Witness Account*

Julia Lapointe Diary 1940

David McCullen Diary 6 March to 20 August 1940

Friedrich Treitler Diary Extracts (in a letter from Paul Treitler, his son, dated 16 May 2013)

Führer Directive 2: Hostilities in the West (September 3, 1939)

Führer Directive 6: Plans for Offensive in the West (October 9, 1939)

Führer Directive 7: Preparations for Attack in the West (October 18, 1939)

Führer Directive 8: Further Preparations for Attack in the West (November 20, 1939)

Führer Directive 10: Concentration of Forces for 'Undertaking Yellow' (January 19–February 18, 1940)

Führer Directive 11: The Offensive in the West (May 14, 1940)

Führer Directive 12: Prosecution of the Attack in the West (May 18, 1940)

Führer Directive 13: Next Object in the West (May 24, 1940)

Führer Directive 14: Continuation of the Offensive in France (June 8, 1940)

Führer Directive 15: Advance on the Loire (June 14, 1940)

'Die deutsche Mai offensive in den Tagen von 17. Bis 23. Mai 1940', in *Militär-Wochenblatt* 124, No. 48, May 31, 1940

Hans von Seeckt 'Grundsätzemoderner Landesverteidigung' in *Gedankeneines Soldaten* Leipzig K.F. Koehler, 1935

Translation of Taped Conversation with General Hermann Balck, 12 January 1979 Battelle Colombus Laboratories, Tactical Technology Center, 505 King Avenue, Columbus, Ohio 43201

Bundesarchiv-Militärarchiv, Freiburg, Germany

Wehrmachtführungsstab (Wehrmachtführungsamt) RW 4 Series

Allgemeines Wehrmachtamt: RW 6 Series

Wehrwirtschafts – und Rüstungsamt (Wehrwirtschaftsamt): RW 19 Series

Generalstab des Heeres: RH 1 Series

Heeresgruppe A; B and C: RH 19I; 19II and 19III Series

4. Armée; 12. Armée and 18. Armée: RH 20-4, 20-12 and 20-18 Series

Gruppe von Kleist; Panzerkorps Guderian; Gruppe Hoth; Panzerkorps Hoepner; Panzerkorps

Reinhardt: RH 21-1; 21-2; 21-3; 21-4 and 21-41 Series

1; 2; 3; 4; 5; 6; 7; 10.PzDivs: RH 27-1; 27-2; 27-3; 27-4; 27-5; 27-6; 27-7 and 27-10 Series

Infanterieregiment Grossdeutschland: RH 37 Series

VIII. Fliegerkorps: RL 8 Series

Central Library, The Royal Military Academy Sandhurst, Camberley, Surrey

The Belgian Tragedy: The Royal Question Report Drawn Up By Commission of Information Constituted By H.M.

King Leopold III on The 14th July 1946

Combined Arms Research Library, Digital Library, Fort Leavenworth, Kansas, USA

The Private War Journal of General Oberst Franz Halder – Chief of the General Staff of the Supreme Command of the German Army (OKH): 14 August 1939 to 10 September 1942 Vol. I: The Polish Campaign Part I (N-16845-A);

Vol. II The Polish Campaign Part II (N-16845-B); Vol. III The First Winter 7 December 1939 to 9 May 1940 (N-16845-C); Vol. IV The Campaign in France 10 May 1940 to 30 October 1940 (N-16845-D)

Liddell Hart Centre for Military Archives (LHCMA)

BRIDGEMAN 1/1 Lord Gort's Despatches

The National Archives, Kew, London

TNA, CAB 53/37, Memoranda Nos. 698 (Revise) CID, COS Sub-committee, *Military Implications of German Aggression against Czechoslovakia* 28 March 1938

TNA, CAB 85/16, MR (J) (40) (5) 2, Allied Military Committee, *The Major*

Strategy of the War. Note by the French Delegation, 11 April 1940

TNA, FO 371/22915, C 1503/30/17, COS 833, *The Strategic Position of France in a European War*

TNA, CAB 16/209 SAC/4th Meeting, CID, Strategic Appreciations Sub-Committee

TNA, CAB 53/37, COS 698 (revise), *Military Implications of German Aggression against Czechoslovakia*, 28 March 1938

TNA, FO 371/22922, C 1545/281/17 minute by Sir Robert Vansittart, on Cabinet Paper (CP) 40 (38), *Staff conversations with France and Belgium*, 10 February 1938

TNA, CAB 23/100, Cab 36 (39), Meeting of the Cabinet, 5 July 1939

TNA, CAB 21/903, Memorandum by the Air Staff, *Bomber Support for the Army*, 18 November 1939

TNA, CAB 66/4, WP (YO) 1, *Air Operations and Intelligence*, 1 January 1940

TNA FO 371/22917, C8681/130/17 and C9363/130/17 Colonel W. Fraser despatches, 16 June and 30 June 1939

WO 33/1305 1933 Notes on Certain Lessons of the Great War

WO 277/36 The Official History of Training 1939–1945

WO 231/161 MTP No.23, Operations Part 1: General Principles, Fighting Troops and Their Characteristics

WO 167/169 III Corps War Diary

WO 167/148 II Corps War Diary September 1939 to June 1940

WO 167/124 I Corps War Diary

WO 167/218 3rd Division War Diary, September 1939 to June 1940

WO 167/203 2nd Division War Diary, September 1939 to June 1940

WO 167/362 8th Infantry Brigade War Diary, September 1939 to June 1940

WO 167/459 4th Royal Tank Regiment War Diary, September 1939 to May 1940

WO 167/721 2nd Cameronians Regiment War Diary

WO 167/839 2nd Royal Warwickshire Regiment War Diary, September 1939 to June 1940

National Archives of the United States, Washington DC

T314/613-615 War Records of the XIXth Panzer Corps

T314/666-669 War Records of Panzer Group von Kleist

Service Historique de la Défense, Vincennes, Paris

29 N 27 2ème Armée Historique des operations

29 N 84 2ème Armée, Commandant des Chars

30 N 92 10ème Corps d' Armée, 3ème bureau

32 N 251 55ème Division d'Infanterie

32 N 318 71ème Division d'Infanterie

34 N 95 84ème Régiment de Fortresse

34 N 145 147ème Régiment d'Infanterie de Fortresse

34 N 174 295ème Régiment d'Infanterie

34 N 178 331ème Régiment d'Infanterie

1K 224, 9 Cabinet du Général Gamelin – Journal de Marche Fonds Gamelin

34 N 165 Rapport de l'Aspirant Penissou

34 N 165 Rapport de Lieutenant Colonel P. Labarthe

32 N 251 Rapport de Général Lafontaine

Instruction provisoire de 6 Octobre 1921 sur l'emploi tactique des grandes unités Charles-Lavauzelle et Cie, impr.-éditeurs, 1928

US Army Center of Military History, Fort McNair, Washington DC

Centre of Military History *Airborne*
   Operations – A German Appraisal
   CMH Pub 104-13, 1951

Yale Law School, Lillian Goldman Law Library, The Avalon Project, USA

General Jodl's Diary (Armed Forces
   Operational Staff) from 1 February
   to 26 May 1940 Document 1809-PS

Websites

www.bbc.co.uk/history/ww2peopleswar/
   stories/40/a2447840.shtml Accessed
   12 November 2014
www.hansard.millbanksystems.com/
   commons/1940/jun/04/war-
   situation Accessed 10 December
   2014
http://www.ibiblio.org/pha/
   policy/1940/1940-06-16d.html
   Accessed 3 November 2013
www.lehrmaninstitute.org/history/index.
   html Accessed 12 July 2013

www.lignemaginot.com/accueil/indexen.
   htm Accessed on 15 December 2015
www.telegraph.co.uk/history/world-war-
   two/7753912/Wormhoudt/Every-
   day-I-thank-God-we-did-our-duty.
   html Accessed 12 December 2014.
www.lightbobs.com/1940-
   1buckshazebrouck.html Accessed 13
   November 2014

Acknowledgements

Without the assistance and support of a large number of individuals and organizations, this book would never have been published and all deserve my very great thanks. At the Royal Military Academy: Sarina Davison, my colleagues in the Department of War Studies and the Director of Studies, Sean McKnight. At the University of Buckingham: the Research Fellows of the Humanities Research Institute together with Professors Martin Ricketts, John Drew, John Adamson and Saul David and also Claire Prendergast and Maria Floyd. I also owe a debt of gratitude to the post-graduates on the university's London-based MA Modern War Studies and Contemporary Military History course, as well as my MPhil and DPhil students. Many have listened patiently as I've discussed the 1940 campaign in the West with them, and on several occasions they made me rethink my arguments, or led me to useful source material. I am also grateful for enlightening conversations with and advice from General the Lord Richards, General the Lord Dannatt, Admiral the Lord West, General Sir Nick Carter, Lieutenant General Sir John Kiszely, Major General Mungo Melvin, Professor Sir Hew Strachan, Professor Sönke Neitzel, Dr Peter Leib and Sir Max Hastings.

I have been studying and teaching the Battle of France for more than a quarter of a century and over that period have always taken the opportunity to interview and correspond with its veterans and, latterly, those civilians that lived through the momentous events. As always, I felt honoured and humbled to learn from them: in Germany, Peter Gerber, Otto Gull, Peter Meier, Gerd Ritter, Albert Winkler, Marc Leicht, Gerd Reismann, Jan Hoch, Hans Liebler, Ralf Buckholtz and Paul Henkelmann; in the Netherlands, Lisa Hanson, Conrad Houtkooper, Max Meers, Peter Meier and Joop van Praag; in Belgium, Arnaud Bauwens; in France, the Roussel family, Charles-Michel Lépée, David Boyer, Bruno Cantel, Maxime Dufour, Emmanuel Marcel, Diane Lebeouf, Dominic Royer, David Schneider, Michel Sigaut, Daniel Le Ro, Serge Winter, Dominic Lemaire and Julianne Deros; and in the UK, Peter Vaux, Peter Mansfield, Douglas Manning, Andrew Hardcastle, Alexander Wilkins, David Blundell, Tom Reed, Rab Riley, Ernie Smith and John Rigson. I am also indebted to Toby Rees and Jenny Friend for tracking down many of these extraordinary people, and for their assistance with some interviewing, research and translation.

The following archives and libraries have also been unfailingly helpful in my researches, and often provided assistance that went beyond the call of duty: in Germany, the Bundesarchiv-Militärarchiv Freiburg; in France, the Service Historique de la Défense, Vincennes, Paris; in the US, the National Archives of the United States, Washington DC and the US Army Center of Military History, Fort McNair, Washington DC; and in the UK, the Liddell Hart Centre for Military Archives, London, the National Archives, London, the Central Library, Royal Military Academy Sandhurst, the British Library, London, the London Library, the RAF Club library, London, the Naval and Military Club library, London, the RUSI library, London and the Imperial War Museum, London. I should also like to thank the military historians Lieutenant Colonel Dr Karl-Heinz Frieser and Dr Robert A. Doughty along with all those that have conducted research and written about the fall of France and the Low Countries in 1940 for their endeavours have had a profound influence on this book. Their names and works can be found in the bibliography. Thanks are also due to Duncan Mason, Dr Paul Harding, Pierre Galliard and Dr Josef Leinberger for reading draft sections and chapters of this book as they spotted numerous slip-ups and offered immensely helpful constructive criticism. I should emphasize, however, that all the errors and omissions that remain in this book are mine and mine alone.

I also greatly appreciate the work done on my behalf by Charlie Viney, my magnificent agent, and at my publishers, Morgan Entrekin and Jamison Stolz at Grove Atlantic in the US, and James Nightingale at Atlantic in the UK. All have been remarkably patient and supportive. I would also like to offer my undying gratitude to my supremely talented editor, Angus MacKinnon. Without Angus's knowledge, good sense, eye for detail and literary skills, this book would have been very much the poorer. I would also like to thank Keith Chaffer for the maps that appear in this volume.

Finally, I should like to acknowledge the love, support and sacrifice provided to me by my family: Catriona, Freddie, Charlotte and Henry – thank you.

Wigginton Bottom and Camberley, February 2016

Index

A Note About the Author

Lloyd Clark is a senior academic in the Department of War Studies at the Royal Military Academy Sandhurst and Professorial Research Fellow in War Studies, Humanities Research Institute, University of Buckingham. He is the author of several books, including *Anzio: The Friction of War, Arnhem: The Greatest Airborne Battle in History* and *Kursk: The Greatest Battle*, has contributed to numerous others and lectures on military history all over the world. He lives in rural Hertfordshire with his wife and three children. For further information, please visit the author's website: lloydclarkauthor.com